RAOUL LUFBERY
AND
MARC POURPE

From the Birth of Aviation to the Lafayette Escadrille

1909–1918

JACQUES MORTANE
WITH DENNIS GORDON & RAOUL LUFBERY III

Raoul Lufbery and Marc Pourpe

From the Birth of Aviation to the Lafayette Escadrille, 1909–1918

by Jacques Mortane

Additional essays, articles, photographs, and notes contributed by
Dennis Gordon and Raoul Lufbery III

Translated by Anne Errelis
Image editing by Scott Gordon

Other Schiffer books by Dennis Gordon
The Lafayette Flying Corps: The American Volunteers in the French Air Service in World War I, ISBN 978-0-7643-1108-6

Other Schiffer books on related subjects
Zeppelin: The Story of the Zeppelin Airships, Hans G. Knäusel, ISBN 978-0-7643-4478-7
Wings of Honor: American Airmen in World War I, James J. Sloan, ISBN 978-0-88740-577-8

Copyright © 2023 by Jacques Mortane, Dennis Gordon, and Raoul Lufbery III

Library of Congress Control Number: 2022932788

All rights reserved. No part of this work may be reproduced or used in any form or by any means—graphic, electronic, or mechanical, including photocopying or information storage and retrieval systems—without written permission from the publisher.

The scanning, uploading, and distribution of this book or any part thereof via the Internet or any other means without the permission of the publisher is illegal and punishable by law. Please purchase only authorized editions and do not participate in or encourage the electronic piracy of copyrighted materials.

"Schiffer Military" and the arrow logo are trademarks of Schiffer Publishing, Ltd.

Cover design by Justin Watkinson
Type set in Bernhard Modern Std/Garamond Premier Pro

ISBN: 978-0-7643-6535-5
Printed in India

Published by Schiffer Publishing, Ltd.
4880 Lower Valley Road
Atglen, PA 19310
Phone: (610) 593-1777; Fax: (610) 593-2002
Email: Info@schifferbooks.com
Web: www.schifferbooks.com

For our complete selection of fine books on this and related subjects, please visit our website at www.schifferbooks.com. You may also write for a free catalog.

Schiffer Publishing's titles are available at special discounts for bulk purchases for sales promotions or premiums. Special editions, including personalized covers, corporate imprints, and excerpts, can be created in large quantities for special needs. For more information, contact the publisher.

We are always looking for people to write books on new and related subjects. If you have an idea for a book, please contact us at proposals@schifferbooks.com.

Contents

iv *Introduction to the English Translation*
vi *Foreword*

Part One: Two Great Knights of Adventure

3   *One:* The Childhood of a Volunteer
5   *Two:* The Distant Call of Wings
9   *Three:* A Difficult Start in Sidney
13   *Four:* Shattered Hopes
16   *Five:* Three Men in a Desert
19   *Six:* Confronting Bad Faith
23   *Seven:* A Cloud Lifts, a Critical Meeting
27   *Eight:* Back Home
33   *Nine:* A New Trip to Australia! But This Time …
40   *Ten:* A Wonderful Crusade in Indochina
47   *Eleven:* Lafberg Steps In
57   *Twelve:* Pourpe Comes to the Rescue of Our Colonial Prestige
66   *Thirteen:* The First Flight from Cairo to Khartoum
70   *Fourteen:* A Heroic Expedition above the Nile River
75   *Fifteen:* Back in His Childhood Country
79   *Sixteen:* And Then There Was War … and Death!
83   *Seventeen:* "I Will Avenge My Boss!"
87   *Eighteen:* The Bomber Becomes a Fighter
95   *Nineteen:* The Fighter Becomes an Ace
101 *Twenty:* The United States Comes to the Rescue of Our Rights and Liberties
105 *Twenty-One:* Lufbery's Method of Combat
108 *Twenty-Two:* "I Will Not Burn to Death"

Part Two: Essays and Articles

114 The Arrival of the Lufberys in France
120 Raoul Lufbery's Early Life and Adventures: March 1885 to July 1914
126 Raoul Lufbery's American Newspaper Articles
142 Raoul Becomes a Pilot
146 Raoul Lufbery Joins the Lafayette Escadrille
151 Lafayette Escadrille Squadron Locations
157 The Aircraft
160 The Enemy
163 The Front
167 The Patrol
175 The Bottle of Death
177 Paris
181 The Lafayette Escadrille Mascots
186 Raoul Lufbery's Medals
190 Raoul Lufbery's Winter of Discontent
194 The Death of Major Raoul Lufbery
200 A Real Soldier of Fortune
204 A Letter from Princess Ghika
205 Major Lufbery's Final Resting Place
212 Raoul Lufbery's Posthumous Honors and Legacy
217 Raoul Lufbery in Art and Print
222 Liane de Pougy: A Mother in Question
231 Escadrille Morane Saulnier 23
232 Raoul Lufbery Witnesses the Death of Marc Pourpe
234 Raoul Lufbery's 1917 Letter to His Father

236 *Acknowledgments*
237 *Bibliography*
238 *Index*

Introduction to the English Translation

Raoul Lufbery was twenty-seven years of age and Marc Pourpe was twenty-five when Jacques Mortane's Two Great Knights of Adventure first met in Calcutta, India, in early January 1913. Both men had been born in France; Pourpe to a young French naval officer and Lufbery to an American business man residing in France. Both their mothers had come from France's peasant class.

Both men hungered for adventure early on, and both had become world travelers while still in their teens. But the similarity in their lives preceded those days, reaching back to their infancy, when both were separated from their mothers and raised by their grandparents. Lufbery's mother died in France when he was fifteen months old, necessitating his father, Edward, to place him in the care of his maternal grandmother. Similarly, Pourpe's father was forced to turn his infant son over to the boy's paternal grandparents when Marc's mother abandoned the family.

When the two knights first met in January 1913, Marc was an exhibition aviator. Raoul, the jack of all trades, was soon to become Pourpe's aircraft assembler, public spokesman, and mechanic. The two men immediately placed their trust in one another so that Pourpe could continue to perform his long and dangerous flying-exhibition tour in exotic places in his primitive aircraft. Marc would later call his new assistant "a walking encyclopedia, always searching for practical information." He further noted that Lufbery was "a quick learner, had an adaptable good humor, and could speak in dozens of languages due to his world travels."

Raoul, as a child, had acquired only a rudimentary education. He was forced to abandon elementary school in order to help support his aged grandmother and his two brothers. In March 1905 the nineteen-year-old Lufbery departed France and set off to travel the world. He worked a variety of occupations while visiting Algers, Tunisia, Egypt, Turkey, the Balkans, and Germany.

In November 1908 he enlisted in the US Army in San Francisco and served in Manila, the Philippines, until discharged in July 1911. Then he resumed his globetrotting adventures. This time he headed east, to Japan, China, Sri Lanka, and finally to Bombay, India, where he took work as a ticket seller on the Great Indian Peninsular Railway in March 1912 under the name Gervais Lafberg. Lufbery was fired in early August for kicking the company's top stockholder out the door of the station after the man insulted him. When he first met Pourpe in Calcutta in January 1913, Raoul had had thirty different occupations during his nine-year globetrotting adventure. And he was twenty-seven years old, with no purpose and no calling in his life.

Marc, on the other hand, had been sent by his paternal grandparents to London's Harrow preparatory school, then to Paris's College Chaptal school for his secondary education. But his wanderlust had been too great for him to complete his schooling. "I would always start to get bored," he said, "when spending more than two weeks in the same place." Pourpe had found his purpose and calling at age twenty on a sea voyage to Australia, which culminated in his discovery of the new science of aviation. It soon became a passion he pursued until the end of his young life.

As we read Jacques Mortane's biographies of the two aviators, we might ask, What was it that created the strong bond between the two men? Both were near the same age, just two years apart, and both had become world travelers while teenagers in search of adventure. When they met on a racecourse in Calcutta in January 1913, Lufbery asked Pourpe for a job. The young pilot offered to let Raoul assemble his aircraft, then trusted him to do it. When Raoul accomplished the task, Marc gave him a position as lecturer to explain to the native population the functions of Pourpe's Blériot monoplane.

Three months later, when Pourpe's mechanic fell ill, Lufbery took over that position and accompanied Pourpe on his exhibition tour in Vietnam and Cambodia. Their next stop was Cairo, Egypt, where Pourpe made a nine-day record-setting flight to Khartoum. They then returned to Paris to plan an exhibition flight to eastern Asia. But war broke out in August 1914 between France and Germany before they could depart. Pourpe was called into France's Military Air Service as a reconnaissance pilot. Shortly thereafter, Lufbery enlisted in the French army and eventually joined Pourpe at his squadron in Toul, France, as an aviation mechanic.

The saddest and most eventful day in Raoul Lufbery's life was 12 December 1914. On that day, Pourpe was killed when his plane crashed into the ground while returning from a combat patrol. His friend's tragic death served as the catalyst that transformed Raoul and elevated this ordinary man with his youth behind him into an extraordinary pilot and human being.

Lufbery's desire to avenge Pourpe's death provided the impetus he needed to hone his already remarkable physical attributes and to transform himself into an aerial killing machine. Many war honors came his way during his two and one-half years at the front, which saw him destroy sixteen enemy aircraft and shoot down many more, which were never confirmed. He rose quickly in the ranks of acedom. As he shot down many planes, he received numerous citations and medals. He was promoted from French sergent to sous-lieutenant to a major in the US Air Service in January 1918, the date he officially became an officer and a gentleman.

His star burned brightly as the Western press followed his daring aerial victories. Then suddenly he was gone, shot down, not in an aerial duel with a skilled adversary, but by a German aerial gunner firing from the back seat of a reconnaissance plane.

Major Lufbery shouldn't have fallen the way he had. But it was fitting that he had gone out while the war was still raging. He thrived on the rush of aerial combat and fed off his lust for vengeance born from the death of his friend Pourpe. And he grew ill and despondent when he was temporarily deprived of those catalysts and put behind a desk and ordered to compose a pamphlet on how to kill Germans.

In his last letter home in April 1918 to his brother Charles in Wallingford, Connecticut, he was responding to Charles's request to come home to be his new nephew's godfather. Raoul wrote the following response.

> I wish to see Wallingford again, but it is not for me now. I like the game here, thank you—I prefer to perch among my clouds and shoot Boches even to passing a pleasant hour with all of you. I cannot come now. After the war, we shall see—but I shall not, I think, live so long.

There would have been no place in a postwar world for this thirty-three-year-old pilot with a rheumatic back whose résumé showed that the best thing he did was to shoot down German planes. His father, Edward Lufbery, recognized that fact when he spoke these words soon after learning of his son's death.

> It was the war that Raoul waited for as he wandered all over the world to find. He walked on the ground, lived on the ground, and worked on the ground. All the time it was the sky where he belonged! The war had been Raoul's mother, sweetheart, and wife to him.

But before Lufbery had left us, this Great Knight of Adventure had lived a full and action-filled life. In the process, he had proven his right to stand with the great aces in the aviation's hall of heroes. And the path he took to get there, and his love for his friend Marc Pourpe, make a fascinating tale.

Note: The images appearing in *Two Great Knights of Adventure* did not appear in the original book but were added by the contributors. —Dennis Gordon

Foreword

Two remarkable lives. A taste for adventure, a yearning for new horizons, and a passion for heroism. Two exceptional beings who would meet through a twist of fate in a distant land. I felt a brotherly fondness for Marc Pourpe and had a deep friendship with Raoul Lufbery. Talking to them was like traveling around the globe without ever having to get up from your armchair. They never bluffed. Their disposition was one of humility. They shared the same passions: living for progress, probing the unknown, dying for a great cause. Both gave their lives for France although one had already been honorably discharged from the military and the other was American. Marc Pourpe! Raoul Lufbery! The youth of today is not familiar with those names. Their elders remember them only vaguely.

In fact, a full and accurate retelling of these two lives was never published. I kept deferring the task of writing those beautiful and intriguing biographies. I was scared of this project. I feared that it would outmatch me. Would I ever be able to make the reader share my admiration for these men? Here I go. Years are going by. I have to finally bring myself to give Marc Pourpe and Raoul Lufbery the tribute they deserve. It is with all my heart, all my enthusiasm, that I start this endeavor. I hope I will not betray their legacy and will allow other people to love these two legendary heroes the way they deserve to be loved.

—Jacques Mortane
Paris, 1936

PART ONE

Two Great Knights of Adventure

ONE

The Childhood of a Volunteer

MARC POURPE'S LIFE is a testament to what someone can accomplish through nothing else than energy, bravery, and integrity. Discouraged, disillusioned, having started out his existence experiencing all of life's hardships and none of its joys, he decided at the age of fifteen that he would make a life for himself and tried his hand at various professions, defying obstacles and adversity and never losing hope. He was born in Lorient. His father, a lieutenant, died in Marseille at the age of thirty on September 12, 1892. He had previously divorced his wife. She had become an artist under the name of Liane de Pougy and later married Prince Georges Ghika. Marc Pourpe was raised by his paternal grandparents, who lived in Suez.

"From my youngest years," he told me, "I have had a taste for travel and the only reason I did not think of taking up flying as a child is that planes had not been invented yet. Depending on what the popular fictional heroes of the time were up to, or on what book I was reading, I would imagine myself roaming the seas on a ghost ship—with an empty box lying in my front yard as a stand-in for the ghost ship—or leading a caravan through the African desert. [That would have been between 1893 and 1898, when looting Dervishes were fighting British-Egyptian troops.] Incidentally, I empathized as much with the looters as I did with the soldiers, the defenders of innocent people; I would play either, depending on who the newspapers said won the latest battle. I can still see myself perched on a pepper tree's delicate branch, hidden in the foliage, watching out all afternoon for an armed faction that would never show up; or crawling on the burning sand of Suez, looking for an imaginary well to quench an imaginary three-day-long thirst. These perils that I pulled from my imagination and actually loved brought me joy on idle days and fed my nightmares at night."

Marc Pourpe

The education Pourpre received bolstered this natural inclination for adventure and travel. When he was eleven years old he went back to Europe to finish his schooling. He spent one year at Harrow, a preparatory school for the Universities of Oxford and Cambridge. There, he took up riding, soccer, cricket, rowing, and boxing. He then spent a year in Heidelberg, where he enjoyed skating and swimming. In Paris he enrolled at the Collège Chaptal. Over the 1903 winter break he spent a few days in Italy and wrote about his travels in English. I have, right in front of me, the notebook in which this studious pupil wrote down his experiences. No words are crossed out on these pages, and they all end with a summary of the child's expenses. Here he heads out with thirty-eight francs and ninety centimes and comes back with three. He is keeping an impeccable tally, and in the margin, still in English, you can read: "Left in my pocket out of the thirty-eight francs and ninety cents are three francs. Signed: Marc Pourpe, bank secretary."

It was too good to last. "To my great shame," he said to me later, "I have to admit that from my stay in Italy, during which I visited on average three museums a day, I brought back very few memories save for the strong impression the Roman athletes' and gladiators' muscular bodies made on me. That vexed my family, who thought me a philistine. By comparison, I always came back from my travels to Belgium, Germany, Switzerland, and Austria with a healthy look and a treasure chest of anecdotes. But I would always start to get bored when spending more than two weeks in the same place."

Soon Marc's personality developed a new trait; Marc Pourpe, always so independent, was craving more freedom. He wanted to live his own life. But how? That he did not know. He wanted more than anything to escape from any form of authority. His mother tried in vain to make him understand that he was not yet old enough to make decisions about his own life. However, through her divorce, she had lost all rights over her child, and parental authority was given to his father's family. She told him: "The only link that can exist between us comes from the heart. It relies on affection and on your behavior and feelings for me. You rebelled; you never listened to me or obeyed me. Now you will have to rely on yourself only, since all you want to do is follow your own whims."

Nothing could convince the child to go back home. Weary of these fruitless attempts, his mother finally wrote him using the formal *vous* instead of the informal *tu* in order to intimidate him.

"Be brave and consider your future with dignity. Fight; I wish everything would come easy for you. Having rejected all forms of authority, you will have to succeed by yourself. I wish thinking of me would inspire you and make you happy. It is my greatest desire and that is the only way I should affect you. My heart will rejoice at all the good things that shall happen to you. Build your life through order and moderation; count only on yourself and on what you have. All I ask you is to not hurt yourself, which will allow me to forgive you the ways in which you have hurt me."

Liane de Pougy

Later, Marc Pourpe would show me this letter and tell me: "This is what was hardest for me in this period of my life. Having my mother call me "vous" instead of "tu" almost killed my determination, but since she seemed to have some doubts regarding my desire to do things right and succeed honestly, through my own means, I accepted this challenge and continued fighting to live my life the way I wanted with even more eagerness."

It was not always a picnic. Especially considering that this teenager was now basically destitute. When he had decided to leave the collège and his mother's *hôtel particulier,* he had packed all of his belongings. He moved into a very modest furnished apartment. To his horror, two weeks after moving into his new home it was burgled. All that he had left was what he had on his person.

How nice his mother's princely home on rue Néva seemed to him now! How happy he would have been to play the prodigal son, but such a transaction would result in accepting his defeat and displaying weakness. He refused to go back. He would make sacrifices, he would suffer, but he would succeed without complaining or begging.

He picked up a multitude of jobs. He sold postcards, sewed lace, worked in a automobile plant, and assisted an insolvency trustee. Can you see the irony? Marc Pourpe, assistant to a licensed insolvency trustee! Fate has a sense of humor! But things started to work in his favor, and, though he was not rewarded per se for his efforts, this respite buoyed the obstinate young man who would not recognize any form of authority besides his own.

[A brief biography of Liane de Pougy appears on page 222]

TWO

The Distant Call of Wings

AVIATION HAD BEEN HAUNTING Marc Pourpe's thoughts for a while. When he had time—and he knew how to make time—he would go to Issy-les-Moulineaux, where Henry Farman, Léon Delagrange, and Louis Blériot were training. He would approach the machines. It was easy to do, partly because they would attract only a few devotees and because they rarely left the ground. The young man, with his handsome face, his distinguished demeanor, his polite manners, and his charm, soon became a regular with whom the mechanics and—on fortuitous days!—the pilots would strike up a conversation. He questioned them, he learned, and he thought. Soon he wanted to build planes too. But money was lacking.

He studied books on aeronautics, which were scarce and often unreliable. It was such a new science! Yet, Pourpe understood he must learn, compare, and keep looking. He was inspired by Louis Blériot's flight across the English Channel.

"I too will have wings," he would say over and over again. But how, he did not know. Purchasing a plane was out of the question. If he could have been sure that by becoming an aviation mechanic—he knew everything about engines—would allow him to eventually become a pilot, he would have risked this path. But he soon realized that, though pilots were few, there were still too many for him to try to join their ranks with no other asset than his gumption.

By happenstance, he met Mr. Defries,[1] a devotee of all kinds of sports. He knew nothing of aviation but had nevertheless bought a Wright biplane that he hoped would greatly impress people on his upcoming trip to Australia.

Australia! What a tempting trip! Marc was enthralled. He asked Mr. Defries to hire him as his engineer and mechanic. The conseil de révision had just deemed Pourpe unfit for military service. He was free. Nothing was holding him back. True, he was involved romantically and was engaged, but he could not get married anyway, considering his precarious financial situation. Australia, gold mines, aviation; he would leave Paris convinced he would return a millionaire.

Marc left Paris on 23 September 1909 with a heart full of hope. Tears were shed at the Gare de Lyon when he bid Jeannette farewell. But he was trying to secure their future together by leaving for a distant land.

Some family members were waiting for him in Marseille. His father was from Marseille. And Marc himself still talked with a southern accent. On Belsunce he met with his old friend Georges Verminck,[2] whom he had known during those trying times when money was scarce. Verminck had been a student, and Pourpe had been jobless.

"Hey, Marco! What are you doing here?" Verminck asked.

"I'm going to Australia for an aviation convention. I'm hoping to come back a pilot!"

"You lucky bugger! I'd like to go with you! I've been there already. I would love to go back!"

"Who's stopping you? You're a rich man. You're free. Pack your bags and come with me!"

"Don't tempt me! I would be only too happy!"

"Next time then," Pourpe said.

And right he was. Three years later he and Verminck would go to India and Indochina together, with their final destination Australia. Unfortunately poor Georges

---

1. Colin Defries (1884–1963) was a London pioneer racing driver who performed two short flights in Cannes, France, in early 1909 on a Wright Model A flyer. He crashed the aircraft on the second flight.

2. Georges Verminck (1886–1913) would be killed on a flight from Saigon, French Indochina, to Phnom Penh, Cambodia, in his Blériot monoplane *Raja* on 8 April 1913.

Verminck, who by that time had become a great pilot, never came back.

In Marseille, Marc paid visit after visit to a succession of uncles, aunts, and cousins. He felt little control over his own life. He would feel lonely in Australia, but in Marseille he to felt too sought after. He did not realize his family was so large. There were so many of them, and he had only so much time before his departure!

When the time came to leave, he was not sorry to part company and board the ship. He was pensive and melancholic when Georges Verminck walked him to the wharf. For years he had not heard from his friend. Now, fate brought them back together. It seemed unfair that he would now take off on his own.

"You should have let me know," Vermink said. "I would have found a way to come with you."

"How ludicrous!" Marc replied. "You talk about a voyage to Australia as if it were a mere day trip to Toulon!"

Marc Pourpe would eventually arrive in Sydney on October 29 after a "seemingly endless" thirty-six-day trek on the Orient-Line ship *Orontes*.

True to his childhood habit, Pourpe kept a diary. The day after their departure, after crossing paths with the ship *Orsova*, which was returning from Australia, they did a mock drowning drill. "We stopped for a half hour and waited for two lifeboats to rescue a buoy meant to represent a man who fell from the ship."

During each stopover, Pourpe used every minute to visit the local cities and monuments. In Naples, he turned down multiple offers from guides to take him to Pompeii. He had a plan. He is going to go marvel at the Duomo di Napoli, a fifteenth-century architectural masterpiece, then see paintings by Leonardo da Vinci, and Tintoretto's *Praying Virgin* at the National Museum. After a quick lunch—"Macaronis and Chianti, of course!"—he tried to see the interior of the San Martini church, but it was closed on Sundays. Disappointed, he went on.

"Except for a few main avenues," he wrote, "Naples is mainly made up of smaller side streets which, though they are quaint, are also dirty and smelly and filled with a disheveled and cacophonous crowd. As soon as a tourist appears he is surrounded by dreadful beggars: lame, one-eyed, deformed, and grimy. And this horde of people yells, begs, and whimpers until you give them the desired bit of change. Take another two steps and it's the same circus all over again."

While crossing the Strait of Messina, Pourpe was horrified to see the damage caused by the recent earthquake. The inhabitants were living in tents atop the ruins of the destroyed city.

Life was monotonous aboard ship. In the evenings, people danced, but without passion. There was an occasional concert. As it grew hotter at night, many passengers slept on deck. "I'll try it too, once we reach the Red Sea," Pourpe thought.

On October 1, they arrived in Port Said. What happiness he felt to be back in the country where he spent his childhood. "I grab my suitcase and jump in a small boat manned by a local who takes me to the wharf. I hail a ride to the station and jump on a train to Suez. I know this route well, and soon I notice that the vegetation seems to have grown since I left Egypt. I'm delighted to be back in this country after ten years abroad and see the locals with their Arabic features. Everything is coming back to me; everything is so familiar. I don't feel apprehensive like one does when he arrives in a place where the language and the mores are different. This Arabic language, which I knew a little by the time I left, is sounding familiar again. Understanding a few words here and there allows me to decipher the meaning of whole sentences. After a four-hour-long ride, we arrive at the Suez train station, where three of my uncles are waiting for me. I'm terribly happy but not the least bit emotional because I feel like I never actually left Suez."

He embraced his grandmother.

"I go visit her new apartment which used to be my poor deceased father's."

What a day full of memories! His whole childhood reappears before him. How happy are the oldsters when they reunite with the child they used to pamper and who is now a grown man, though still as tender and gentle as he used to be. The next day, at dawn, Pourpe heads out to board the *Orontes* when it arrives in Suez. The heat is getting oppressive. Trying to sleep in the cabins is hopeless and the bunks are veritable ovens. The temperature rises to 100°F and the air is stifling.

"At night, I take my blanket to the upper deck and make myself a bed there. I fall asleep only to be woken up in the middle of the night by a seaman dropping a windsock on my face to be used for ventilation. I fall back asleep but, at four in the morning, when the heat becomes more bearable, the passengers are asked to leave the deck so it can be cleaned. The horror! When I go back to my cabin and look at myself in the mirror, I see that I'm black from head to toe! What a strange and quick transformation happened on the deck! I have to thank the soot and the pieces of grit which blended with the morning dew to create an impressively stubborn coating."

On October the ship made a stop in Colombo. Pourpe and a few other passengers visit Mount Lavinia, 10 kilometers outside the city.

"Children up to about six or eight years old walk around in the nude no matter their sex. Most men only wear a pagne. The women aren't as beautiful as they are said to be. Some are pretty and graceful, but they are few and far between. They are, however, wearing more clothes than members of the stronger sex. You won't find any houses made out of stones in those villages. Homes are made of bamboo and covered with palms. The earth is brick-colored.

"Mount Lavinia isn't particularly interesting. The main perks of a visit lie in the quaint villages one crosses on the way there, and the view you get of the beautiful surrounding countryside. In between villages, you find villas where Europeans live, most of them British. Some look dreamy. It must be quite nice to live in them!

"After lunch, we board rickshaws pulled by Indians and go visit the Victoria Park, where we admire tree varieties that grow in the Indies. It is a beautiful layout. The color and size of the flowers there are a new sight for Europeans. The main artery evokes the Promenade des Anglais in Nice. A lot of people there are on horseback. Many are Hindus, who look imposing in their red turbans and their khaki uniforms."

That night, the *Orontes* left port. Two days later, they crossed the equator. All the passengers received an invitation signed "Neptune," which states: "Let it be known to all the sons of the sea on board of the *Orontes* which is currently sailing toward our Dominions under the command of our loyal and beloved brother, the captain P. N. Layton, that we, Neptune, King of the Ocean, will be aboard the aforementioned *Orontes* on Wednesday, 13 October 1909 to welcome and initiate the men wanting to join the Order of the Sons of the Sea."

Pourpe did not particularly enjoy the prospect of this Grecian masquerade. He let it be known that he had already paid his tribute to Neptune by getting soaked in seawater on more than one occasion. On October 20 he wrote down some impressions that denote his sentimental nature and his fear of isolation:

"Tomorrow, we will reach Fremantle. I will go visit the city. Walking on land, any land, is a good way to break the monotony of being at sea."

"It's always the same in life: you run into people and then you let them go. Still, you always grieve friends you lose out of sight, even the ones you had just barely met.

"This state of mind probably has to do with my loneliness through the countries I visit.

"Solitude feels awful to me. I will be happy to be in Sydney with the few friends I made on board. I'll have my work and my friends. I'm hoping that time will pass by quickly and that I will have no regrets.

"Enjoying everything and making others enjoy you is, I think, a good principle. When you're good to others you feel a deep satisfaction."

Fremantle is the first port on Australian territory. Pourpe is slightly concerned. "As I step foot on this land for the first time, I wonder what this country has in store for me."

His anxiety is mild, however. Even in the most serious circumstances this young Prince Charming approached every new situation with a sense of humor. His feelings were as intense—if not more so—than other people's, but he did not let them show. He was witty and found something funny in every situation. Still, the next minute he felt melancholic, but only briefly. What was remarkable was that his resourcefulness and energy fueled his actions. He was never fully happy but created an illusion of happiness for himself. He had to struggle from his early childhood. He never experienced the joys that come with being young. He was living for the future. He was always anticipating.

The question "What does this country have in store for me?" dogged him. He must provide the answer. "What is it to you?" he thought. "You'll see. You shouldn't worry."

They had almost made it to their destination. "The passengers are starting to pack up. Notebooks are circulating between friendly hands in which people are writing each other little farewell notes. I personally have to fill out about fifty of them. Sometimes I draw some verses by Baudelaire from memory, or I write down some original thoughts, but I always write down the date first. I have a little notebook too and ask some of my travel companions to write a few words in it. I dread leaving these people I barely know but have spent so many lovely hours with in countries so far away from our homes. These partings have a powerful impact on me and make me feel sad for hours on end."

It is hard to believe that such sentiments would come from an indefatigable globetrotter who seemed to be happy only when far away from his homeland. Before his arrival in Sydney, he wrote the following:

"Those last three days, October 27th, 28th, and 29th, went by very fast. We all enjoyed the last hours we spent together by resting comfortably in our 'deck chairs.' I think many of us would attempt this trip again, given the opportunity. True, it's not as comfortable as one's *chez soi* but at least you get to enjoy this form of intimacy, of familiarity which is so pleasant and evaporates so naturally as soon as one is on land again. I don't know why, but the impending end of this trip is a dreadful thought to me. I'd like to be three days older already and be done with it."

They finally arrived and Pourpe shifts his thoughts to the present and his future. He has almost forgotten about feeling blue.

"I visited numerous ports in Europe and other places, but nothing, in my opinion, compares to dreamlike, grandiose Sydney. The Australians aboard the ship had sung its praises to me, but I thought them biased. For the first time in my life I was not disappointed. On the contrary, I feel that all the good they told me about Sydney was an understatement compared to what I got to see.

"To enter the harbor, we pass through two massive rock formations separated from each other by a few kilometers. After that, all I see is creeks and bays formed by rocks and covered in trees. Further away, in the harbor itself, the rocks are peppered with beautiful, welcoming houses. The water is as blue as in Naples but I much prefer this port. Finally, we arrive in the heart of the city. Here I am. What awaits me tomorrow?"

THREE

A Difficult Start in Sidney

Marc Pourpe was elated when he arrived in Australia. He had found a job he loved. He did not foresee any difficulties lying ahead. You didn't ship a young Frenchman all the way to Australia when you didn't have a good, stable situation for him there.

Let's get to work! On the very next day after his arrival, he is expected to produce a detailed description of the Wright biplane. As soon as he is done with this exacting task, he goes back to being the social butterfly he has always been and gets invited to all kinds of balls and dinner parties thrown on English ships anchored in the harbor. While he is waiting on the aeroplane to arrive, he learns about the local mores. He visits the village of La Perouse, a colony of Indigenous people about an hour away from Sydney.

"The English do not let the few Blacks (70,000) who live in Australia reside in cities. Instead, they assign them vast expanses of land far away from any urban center. Every family gets its own plot. Indigenous people do not pay any direct taxes on their property.

"There is nothing 'savage' about them. On the contrary, they all speak proper English. Every village has a pastor and a school. Parents are not required to send their children to school, but if they do, they receive free food provisions, clothes, etc. Most people here live on what they catch from the sea. There is great fishing in this bay, which belongs to the indigenous people.

"I used this visit to try my hand at the national sport—throwing a boomerang. A Black grabbed his wooden weapon and threw it vigorously in the air. The boomerang took off spinning, drew a large circle followed by a smaller one, and then came back to land at the thrower's feet. The dexterity of indigenous people is astounding. I threw an apple in the air right ahead of me, and it took the Black only one try to split it in half with his boomerang, after which the device came back to land at his feet again. It seemed so easy that I felt I had to give it a try. I only managed to form a quarter of a circle with the boomerang, and vertically at that!

"I bought my Black's weapon and asked him to come give me lessons when I'll be at our Victoria Parks location. Still, I do not think I will ever match the skill of Australians who use their boomerangs to catch birds and even fish. They are so fast that they manage to slash a fish as soon at it gets near the surface. A long time ago, they used this innocuous-looking piece of wood to fight off their enemies."

Now back to work! Pourpe met with his agent, Mr. Tait, and the pilot, Mr. Defries. He put together a somewhat modest team: two carpenters and a mechanic.

On 13 November 1909, the *Orsova* arrived in Sydney with the Wright biplane. The boxes containing the plane were unloaded. They were sizable and heavy. The one that contained the plane's central part, including the engine, weighed over 2 tons. They had to pay a tax of 18.450 francs on it. The agent put giant stickers on the boxes.

This monumental cargo was transported to City Hall. Pourpe and Banks, the mechanic, start unpacking. The rudder was slightly damaged, but it was an easy fix. A more difficult task: taking the plane's central part out of its box and dismantling it in order to fit it through City Hall's exhibition room door, only to reassemble it once it was inside. It was a delicate and exhausting task that kept Pourpe and three other men—who know nothing about building planes—busy day and night until five in the morning on November 18.

At 1 p.m. on that same day, City Hall opened its doors to the public, who gasped at the aeroplane, a prodigious beast that will allow mankind to compete with birds.

However, this enticing display did not draw as many people as expected. Only a few friends and reporters showed up. The exhibition lasted until November 23.

"Our stint at City Hall did not meet our expectations," Pourpe wrote. "The public did not show much enthusiasm, and most people simply did not show.

"Several factors can explain this lack of interest. First of all, it seems that, for the last six months, there has been a new aeroplane (or pseudo-aeroplane) exhibition opening virtually every day. People probably assumed this was just another one of those inane demonstrations.

"Besides, Mr. Defries hasn't done anything here yet. He is still unknown to the public. Once he actually flies his plane, he'll actually have accomplished something, and the public who ignored him before will rave over him and consider him a hero. We have a long way to go!

"We should have had this exhibition after Mr. Defries actually flew. What a tactical error we made! On November 26, we take the plane apart, put it back into its boxes, and cross the city triumphantly (!), arousing the locals' curiosity—though a bit late—per all the eye-catching stickers hanging on the side of the boxes. Our little outdoor show felt like quite the circus parade."

Back at the training field, the tent had not been put up in time for the plane's arrival, even though Mr. Defries had wanted the Wright plane to be taken apart and put back together again within three days so he would be able to start practicing and try out a new suspension system developed by Marc Pourpe. Indeed, even though our young hero had not been able to build his dream aeroplane yet, he had come up with some very ingenious devices, like a very interesting suspension system. It proved very useful, but before its efficiency was demonstrated, Pourpe had to cope with a nerve-racking period of expectancy.

"I'm hoping for success," Pourpe confided in his diary. "Or else I shall lose people's trust. I know what it's like to fail. Everyone blames you, and the people who used to be your friends are the harshest in their criticism. Besides my work, I haven't been up to anything interesting recently. In the evening, I study mathematics, and I've been working on a draft of the plane I'm hoping to build here in Australia. Hence, formulas by Mousset, Mercier, Le Dantec, Canoretti, et al. are constantly on my mind."

On December 3, the plane is ready.

"The suspension system I came up with has been installed. I had two washers added near the axis to stop it from moving side to side. The trials have been satisfactory; however, the center of the axis seems weak to me. I'll reinforce it with a variable-tension tailrod. This should avert a sudden rupture. The front wheel works fine on a straight line, but since it's not adjustable it yields when ones try to go to the side. I have to find a way to make turns smoother.

"Tomorrow, the horizontal part I designed as an addition to the rudder will be ready. I'll have it installed immediately. I think that should stop the plane from see-sawing incessantly when it's in the air. Mr. Defries and I tested the plane's stability on a longitudinal axis. He's a bit abrupt in his command of the plane, but what's more is that the ailerons don't seem to be responding properly. That is a serious issue we need to address as soon as possible."

In those days, the equipment's quality was such that it had to to be worked on constantly to be usable. How many people died after routine repairs that proved deadly?

In spite of his youth, Pourpe was so experienced and ingenious that he did manage to perfect the plane he was put in charge of. On December 4, the trials became more interesting:

"We tied a rope to the front of the plane. Mr. Defries is piloting the plane, which is getting dragged at 15 km/hour. There is a tailwind to carry the plane. The suspension system is outstanding, but the front wheel still does not want to cooperate when it comes to taking turns.

"On his way back, the pilot tries working the rudder with the car still dragging it at the same speed. An air current picks up the plane and lifts it over a distance of about 5 to 6 meters. Then, the plane lands very abruptly. The pilot did not handle this maneuver particularly delicately (!!!), and I immediately worry about my wheels, but they look like they took it well.

"At four o'clock, we head to the hangar to try out the engine. The men handling the two propellers are inexperienced. The one working the right-side propeller is a sailor, while the one to the left is a carpenter. After doing some welding on the fuel pipe, we get the engine firing but alas! I notice a crack along the right-side propeller's axis. We install a new propeller and start over, with more success this time. The engine is working beautifully, and we let it run for about fifteen minutes, with a few intentional interruptions."

Everything went well except for the fact that the wind was too strong, which prevented more flight attempts. In those days, you had to wait days for the leaves to stop moving in the trees. Whatever the weather, though, Defries did not seem like the kind of aviator who would accomplish great feats.

Marc Pourpe seated in Lawrence Adamson's Wright Model A Flyer in Melbourne, Australia, December 1909. Grace's Guide to British Industrial History *and Wikipedia misidentified Pourpe as Colin Defries.*

"On Thursday, Mr. Defries flew twice, once over a distance of 100 meters and then over 150 meters. We broke a propeller when restarting the engine.

"Today is Saturday and we have a rather large audience, but it's windy. To satisfy our audience, I take the plane out of the hangar and start the engine. Mr. Defries has no intention to leave the ground; he'll just drive the plane around a little. I climb on the passenger seat and we start going. Suddenly, we hear a loud wood-cracking sound. The engine stops dead.

"What seems to have happened is that the wind pushed the rudder to the left, then a thread got caught into the propeller, which broke the support for the tailplane as well as the left propeller.

"I wouldn't call our audience hostile, but people sure like to tease us. So far, they just think of us as jokers. It's frustrating. But what can we do besides waiting for the right time to attempt a longer flight?"

A lot of patience was needed to persevere despite a myriad of small complications that kept interrupting flight attempts and damaging the equipment. One cannot help but admire the unflappable determination of these pioneers. Meanwhile, the wind kept making any flight attempt impossible.

"Time is passing by so slowly," Pourpe wrote. "After work, I spend my evenings toiling away on my own plane design. I hope it'll be ready soon. I'll try to get permission to build it in Melbourne. As for the business side of things, let's just say we could be doing better."

When the weather finally grew more favorable, the equipment refused to function properly. Finally, though, the engine started. It ran well, but Pourpe noticed that one of the propellers was spinning significantly faster than the other. After stalling the engine and taking out the propeller shaft, he noticed that the woodruff key helping stabilize the propeller broke, leaving it unhinged.

The next day the air was still. Mr. Defries finally got to make another attempt at flying. He flew over at a distance of 200 meters, but then his cap fell off his head and Mr. Defries, who probably worried about catching a cold, landed precipitously, damaging the engine again.

"Defries and Barns, Tait's associate, have a long discussion during which they call me as a witness several times. Barns claims that if neither the plane nor the pilot can handle flying when the wind is blowing faster than 10 or 15 kilometers per hour, then the whole endeavor is financially doomed. It is decided that we shall leave for Melbourne in two days. On December 21 at 2 P.M. I start packing up, and by 6 P.M. everything is ready."

In Melbourne, they will encounter more difficulties, even though Pourpe was hoping that this would be the place where he would learn to become the kind of pilot who can fly no matter what the wind is up to. Indeed, he had been promised a Blériot plane. It was to be shipped all the way from France. That way, they could organize double flight demonstrations, with Defries piloting his biplane, and Pourpe his monoplane.

As soon as he arrived in town, Pourpe headed to the Melbourne Motor Garage, the largest such establishment in the city, which belonged to Mr. Adamson[1] and was managed by none other than Mr. Defries. Mr. Barns took him to the field where the demonstrations would take place. It was smaller than the Victoria Parks location, but more convenient for landings.

"This is where I will try out my Blériot," Pourpe wrote. He is hopeful. But the next day he is bitter.

"Once more, I am spending Christmas around people who are unconcerned with me. It has been at least six years since I spent Christmas or New Year's Eve with my family. The pain is even greater with me being so far away from Paris. At least over there I would have been constantly around family and friends.

"This morning I took a pleasant bath with Defries. Then I had lunch with him and his wife and spent part of the afternoon in his sun house because the weather was so nice. This is the first time I have felt such a powerful solitude-induced form of ennui. A terribly oppressive feeling took over me. Defries noticed my sadness and guessed its cause. He suggested we go out, but I excused myself and left. I went home, where I was overcome by a bout of neurasthenia more intense than anything I have experienced before. I took a cold bath, which did not help in the least. I tried to read or write, but I could not focus on anything.

"At 7 P.M., I went out in search of a restaurant. Finding an open one would not be an easy task, it being Christmas Day. After searching for a long while, I found the 'Paris-Café.' This made me hopeful for a moment: who knows? Maybe I was going to feel like I was back home again, even if only by reading the items on the menu? What an awful disillusion. A horrible waiter made me repeat my order four times. The food was even less pleasant. I try to order a bottle of Saint-Julien, but it's nauseating. Country wine! I decide to go for some fruit and eat an entire pineapple! Then, I order some champagne: Moët & Chandon. I want to get drunk enough to roll under the table. I guess I am not quite the party animal type; after three glasses I feel queasy and stop drinking. I head home, feeling more and more helpless."

---

1. Lawrence Arthur Adamson, headmaster of Wesley College, Melbourne, Australia, was the true owner of the *Stella*, the Wright Model A aircraft powered with a four-cylinder engine.

FOUR

Shattered Hopes

FATE HAD ANOTHER SURPRISE in store for Pourpe. One day, Defries called for the young man and told him he had made a serious decision:

"My dear friend, either I wasn't made for aviation or it wasn't made for me. In any case, I have decided to quit flying," Defries said.

"What? After making such big investments you are giving into a mere mood swing?" Pourpe responded.

"No, my decision does not stem from a 'mood swing' like you say. I have been thinking. The recent deaths of your fellow countrymen Lefebvre and Ferber had already made me somewhat weary. The many difficulties we encountered lately did not help either. My wife is expecting, and it kills her to think of me flying through the air."

"If you have made up your mind, I shall not insist. But what is going to happen to me?"

"Tomorrow, we will go pay Mr. Adamson a visit, and I will ask him to hire you in my place. In fact, I think you are way better qualified than me. You'll get 10 percent of the money raised through flight demonstrations and better wages."

"Well then I can't thank you enough, and I applaud your decision, for my own sake."

Bursting with joy, Pourpe believed his dream of becoming a pilot was about to come true. His meeting with Adamson suggested as much, since the latter accepted Defries's resignation and agreed to hire the young Frenchman in his place. However, they still had to get Tait's approval.

Before his interview with Tait, Pourpe unpacked the Wright plane and put it together. The year 1909 was coming to an end. In lieu of celebrating the new year, Pourpe—the exile—wrote down a summary of the year he was leaving behind.

"The first five months were spent working for the insolvency trustee Lesage. What a surprising shift: going from being a mechanic to handling legal matters. And what twisted matters! Not only were they supremely intricate, but, more often than not, they were also quite shady."

"In June, I start taking steps toward finding a job related to aviation, a science I have been interested in for over two years and which I have been studying passionately. Fordyce gets me a job at Ariel, a company run by none other than Georges Clemenceau's son. I quickly find out about the Wright aeroplane.

"In August, Clemenceau introduces me to Defries and suggests that I go to Australia with him as his engineer. Defries learns the ropes of aviation under my tutelage, and, a month later, I sign the following contract":

1) This contract shall be valid for two years, after which both parties will have to observe a six months' notice. If the employer is the party interrupting the contract, he shall provide his employee with a return ticket to Europe. This dismissal may take place only if the employee neglects his duties, falls seriously ill, breaks a limb or, by his actions, ceases to serve his employer's best interests.

2) As soon as the employee leaves Marseille, all his food and travel expenses shall be covered by the employer.

3) The employee will collect 1% of the profit generated by the flight demonstrations and 5% of any cash prize won by the employer in flight competitions.

These sums will have to be awarded to the employee at the same time that the employer receives his own benefits.

For the first six months of the present contract, starting on September 15th, 1909, the employee's pay will be 20£ a month. After six months, this pay rate shall increase to 24£ a month, which will be allocated to the employee on the 15th of each month.

4) If the employee should voluntarily leave the service of the employer during his stay in Australia, he may not seek employment from another party under the same terms as the ones laid out in the present contract.

"A good job was waiting for me in Australia. Could I hesitate? No. In September, I leave Europe for Australia. All my impressions, from the day I left, are written down in this notebook. Here is my final assessment of this eventful year.

"On December 30 I was about to get Defries's job, but today I am practically without employment. A sudden reversal changed everything. Adamson had a meeting with Defries and Tait. Defries recommended me for the job again, but Tait ungently pressed Adamson to hire Banks, who has been in Adamson's service as a mechanic for two years. I learned this from Defries tonight at 6 P.M. What a pitiful way to end the year! I am facing injustice so far from all the people and things I love!"

The first letter Pourpe receives in 1910 is from Adamson:

"You are aware of the circumstances in which Mr. Defries relinquished his duties toward my Wright plane. I am bound to Mr. Tait by contract. I have to let him use the Wright for a 12-month period starting with its arrival in Australia. Mr. Defries's decision—which I will not question considering the reasons he put forward—put us in a very uncomfortable position.

"We have good reasons to seriously reconsider our ability to plan public flight demonstrations as we originally intended. In the meantime, we must attempt to reduce our expenses in every possible way.

"Consequently, I am unable to uphold the arrangement you had established with Mr. Defries since Mr. Tait and I have decided that the flights will be performed by Mr. Banks, who has been in my service for two and a half years. I sincerely regret seeing you penalized by Mr. Defries' resignation.

"I am currently negotiating the sale of the Blériot plane, which should arrive through the *Caudia* ship on January 24. I am willing to put you in touch with the buyer, who will probably need the help of an expert to set up the plane and learn how to fly it. In the meantime, I am willing —if you are interested—to hire you as a mechanic for the Wright, although I would only be able to pay you 5£ (125 francs) a week."

Pourpe's disappointment was intense, and he had to undertake lengthy negotiations in order to save his job and get out of this impasse. In the end, Adamson agreed to maintain his current allowance—8£ a week—until the Blériot's arrival, on the condition that he teach Banks how to fly the Wright. Pourpe agreed, of course, but felt quite dejected over having to put himself at the disposal of the man who poached his job. He made sure to negotiate a clause that would absolve him of all responsibility if anything happened to the plane or the pilot.

Taking his new responsibilities seriously, Pourpe soon visited the airfield to perform his duties. However, a surprise was waiting for him. When he entered the hangar, he found that the plane was undergoing repairs! A sheepish Banks was lying on the night watchman's bed and offered no explanation. The workmen seemed too embarrassed to talk to Pourpe. Finally, one employee agreed to answer the Frenchman's questions:

"You must know that Mr. Adamson entrusted the plane to Banks."

"Indeed, I knew that, but I didn't realize that it was for the purpose of destroying it, since Mr. Adamson asked me to teach Banks how to pilot the Wright."

Banks decides to tell Pourpe what happened.

"Last night, at four in the morning, I took the plane out of the hangar with some friends because I wanted to go for a flight, and there you have it."

Pourpe was shocked by the neophyte's audacity, but he made sure not to let that sentiment transpire. "And there you have . . . what?"

"I was taken aback by the plane's speed and couldn't dodge a fence. I tried to jump over it, but I failed. The tailplane and the right wing were damaged in the collision."

"I can see that. You acted recklessly. I had agreed to train you conscientiously, but under the condition that you would not try anything in my absence and without my approval. Since you decided to bypass my guidance, I cannot fulfill my assignment appropriately and I shall inform Mr. Adamson of what happened."

"He already knows," countered Banks. "and he did not make any remarks."

Pourpe found that he liked Banks, who was, in fact, a pleasant fellow, and he was too impartial to hold a grudge against someone who had simply been luckier than him. Hence, the young instructor decided to reason with Banks. "I am convinced that, if you follow my advice, you will become a good pilot. But know that it would be folly to try to learn to pilot a plane without the help of someone who knows how that plane works and can teach you how to use its controls."

"If you do not feel like teaching me," retaliated Banks, "then I will take it upon myself learn on my own."

Feeling that his situation was becoming increasingly delicate, Pourpe was just about to leave when Adamson and Tait arrived.

By then, the plane was fixed, but poorly. The tailplane was leaning 5 or 6 degrees to the right, which did not stop Banks from announcing that he was going to proceed to another flight attempt.

"What do you think?" Adamson asked Pourpe.

"It's madness. Not only is it too windy but the plane is in no condition to fly."

"It doesn't matter," proclaimed a reckless Banks.

"If that's so, if my opinion does not matter to you, I hereby abdicate any responsibility and shall not give you any more advice."

Soon after, the biplane was pulled from the hangar and the engine was started, although not without difficulty. A tire burst. It was replaced on the spot. Tired of waiting, Adamson took off, leaving Tait all alone.

The trial started a half hour later. After a 50-meter run, Banks tried to leave the ground, but he was not going fast enough. As Pourpe had foreseen, the plane was leaning dramatically to the right, and, suddenly, despite the aspiring pilot's efforts, the tail hit the ground and the rudder broke.

"It beats me," said Banks after his brutal landing. "What do you think, Pourpe?"

"It's quite simple. You tried to take off even though you weren't going fast enough. As soon as your wheels left the ground, you should have aimed for a horizontal trajectory to increase your speed before gaining more altitude. You did the exact opposite; you tried to gain more altitude first and thus squandered the little momentum you had left. That is when the plane scraped the ground. That's it. The only thing I'll add is that I'm quite happy to see that the suspension system I invented withstood the impact—and what an impact!—beautifully."

After this, Pourpe abstained from ever visiting the airfield again, although he stayed at Adamson's disposal and visited him every morning while awaiting the arrival of the Blériot, his last hope.

He wrote articles for Australian newspapers, took pictures, and went swimming to cope with the heat, which was excruciating in January in this part of the world.

"Here, you have to go to specific venues to swim in the ocean. You can't swim anywhere else because of sharks brazenly hunting right near the coast. These bathing establishments are spacious and very well set up. There are some for men and others for women. There are no co-ed baths. The male baths are fully nude. I wasn't aware of that fact and showed up for my first swim wearing a little pagne. People stared at me in bewilderment and hilarity ensued. I hurried back to my shack and came back in the same attire as everyone else, which was the only way to go unnoticed. Sometimes, I stay there from 8 A.M. to 1:30 P.M. and split my time between swims and sunbathing sessions.

"Here's what one does in those establishments: first, you take a freshwater shower, then you swim an hour or so. After that, you take another shower to clean the salt off your skin. After drying yourself thoroughly, you apply coconut oil to your skin and stretch down on some wooden planks lying in the sun.

"On the first day, I had not put on any coconut oil. After staying in the blazing sun for an hour, my skin turned scarlet. When I put my clothes on, my whole body started itching. Just wearing clothes was painful! At night, I couldn't lie down without experiencing unbearable pain. I didn't sleep all night.

"The next day a friend whom my misadventure amused recommended a softening lotion. I dearly needed it. I was braised from head to toe, front and back, and wearing clothes was a torture. I stayed in all day, breathing in the musty fumes of the ointment which promised to alleviate my pain. Finally, after two days, my skin was like new.

"Ever since that, when I go soak and lie in the sun for hours at a time with something to read, I never forget to coat myself meticulously in coconut oil. Another nice thing about it is that it gives one a handsome golden tan. I have seen northern Europeans with blue eyes and blond hair whose skin has turned a dark brown. I obtained the same result—which is the goal of all men who sunbathe—after about ten days.

"I guess the Australian trends of 1910 were the same as the ones you would have encountered in Juan-les-Pins and other French beaches. Nothing new here. Even sunbathing was subjected to the same rules on opposite corners of the world.

"After spending some time in the sun, the swimmers get back in the ocean for a little while before taking an ice-cold shower to eliminate the torpor resulting from the exposure to intense sunlight."

FIVE

Three Men in a Desert

Despite his commitment to work, Pourpe had some free time, so he decided to get together with two friends he met on the *Orontes* to do something they had wanted to do for a while but kept having to put off.

They had been wanting to go camping and hunt rabbits by the Yarra River for a few days. Their main goal, though, was to explore this part of the Australian desert they had heard so much about.

O'Neill, an Irishman, von Doozy, a Hungarian, and Pourpe, our Frenchman, divided up tasks ahead of their excursion. O'Neill was put in charge of renting three good horses, von Doozy volunteered to buy food ("Because he is an expert in this field since he is fond of everything that has to do with gastronomy"), and Pourpe was tasked with buying a tent and hammocks.

"O'Neill got the horses for the cheap price of eight shillings a piece per day. We also had to pay for their food and would be held liable if anything happened to them. O'Neill also gathered everything necessary to fish and hunt, including a Winchester for me since I do not own a rifle. I had to compliment him on his great prep work.

"Von Doozy did not mess around in the food department. We had enough to survive for a month. We split up the load between the three horses, but it was still quite a lot to carry for each of them. Von Doozy earned himself some praise too!

"As for me, I stuck to my rather humble ways and found, with Defries' help, a simple and practical tent that fit neatly on my saddle when folded up but turned out to be so spacious you would think it could fit an entire cavalry regiment, horses included. Even with all the tent posts (four large ones and twelve smaller ones) and the mallet fastened to my horse, I ended up being able to also carry part of von Doozy's food rations.

"So, at nine in the morning on January 25, we all headed to the train station. O'Neill stayed with the horses in the cattle wagon while von Doozy and I settled in the dining car. We were headed to Boort, a sheep-farming town three hours away from St. Kilda.

"Our convoy took off for the unknown, the mysterious desert. Or should I say the *maquis*, since I have to confess that the Australian desert or, at least this part of it, seems less like what we think of as a desert and more like dry shrubland.

"It seemed odd to have a Hungarian, an Irishman, and a Frenchman gathered in such a place. I wonder what our horses told each other about us!

"We had met in Marseille and spent the trip together. We never parted during the long crossing. We stayed in the same cabin and, although we differed in age, we immediately became excellent companions.

"Von Doozy is the eldest. He is forty years old but is neither the most serious nor the least lively of us three; O'Neill has no discerning characteristic, and I am the youngest, hence the most innocent one, although these two qualities do not always walk hand in hand.

"In this shrubland, there are no roads. Paths are rare and are interrupted for kilometers at a time by stretches of sand driven by the wind. We have to rely on our maps and compasses, which turns out to not be that difficult.

"This desert covers a surface of 800,000 hectares [approximately 300 square miles]. I mention this fact in passing in an attempt to appear erudite.

"We trot along until six in the evening. We covered about 45 kilometers in the last four hours, under the blazing sun. For the first day that's not bad at all! Von Doozy, who is a little bit chubby, is requesting that we take a break. His horse too!

"We set up the tent and prepare a delicious dinner but have to be satisfied with drinking undiluted whisky because we neglected to bring water since we thought we would spend our first night on the banks of the Yarra. Anyway, we dig into the old scotch, although it tastes somewhat like medicine to me. I say so to my travel companions, which earns me the ire of O'Neill, who calls me a 'frog eater' to avenge his wounded patriotic pride!

"The whisky put us in a good mood and made us forget how tired we were. We felt rather cheerful and von Doozy entertained us with some juicy anecdotes.

"We went to bed around 10:30 P.M., after checking on the horses and setting up our hammocks. I'm sorry to say that the hammocks I had picked up were not very comfortable. I would have preferred sleeping directly on the ground atop of my blanket, but my travel companions told me snakebite stories that would have scared even an Arab. So I had to tolerate the hammock's ropes digging into my back.

"Soon, all I could hear was the loud snoring of the Hungarian and the high-pitched whistle of the Irishman's breathing. I fell asleep to the sound of this harmonious ensemble. I did not wake up all night and have no idea what I might have sounded like in my sleep!

"I woke up at 5 A.M. I was the first one to leave the tent. What shock I had! There were only two horses instead of three!

"I told the news to my friends, who rushed outside thinking that the heat, which was already sweltering, had clouded my senses, but they soon had to admit we were indeed missing a horse. We were puzzled.

"We decided to have breakfast before taking any course of action. We had some canned food and cookies and drank whisky, again without any seltzer to dilute it. After that, we all had a smoke and came up with a plan of action.

"O'Neill would take one of the horses and head to the Yarra. We would follow him by foot or wait for him by the tent. He grabbed some food, his rifle, a compass and his pipe and headed out in a gallop. We estimated that the Yarra was about 30 kilometers away.

"By 8 A.M., I had been enduring poor von Doozy's whining for a while. To forget about his troubles, he was threatening to . . . Well, I want to be truthful in my account of the events and will hence print the very words he used: get wasted. I packed up the tent and put it on my horse's back with the rest of the food, after which we started heading northeast in O'Neill's footsteps, my rifle in hand.

"It was starting to get very hot. Von Doozy was already getting to regret embarking on this hunting trip in the first place. I, for my part, am more resilient and less plump and found our situation rather exciting. I was enjoying our adventure in the desert and whistling some tunes—including "La Matchiche" and "La Petite Tonkinoise"—which annoyed von Doozy to no end.

"At around 9 A.M., von Doozy killed two rabbits. The farther we went, the more rabbits we encountered. By the time we took our noon break, I had killed seven and missed several more. Von Doozy had killed eleven. We kept the ten biggest and left the other ones for the crows —which are legion here like everywhere else—to devour.

"We had not yet spotted O'Neill and were not planning on continuing to walk in this oven-like heat, so we decided to set up our tent and wait for our friend while smoking our pipes.

"I feel that my tale is getting more and more gripping; however, I swear I am not trying to gloat, and I did not meet any Eskimos like Cook or Perry did.

"Lunchtime: corned beef and roasted rabbit—I could even say charred rabbit. I cannot blame poor von Doozy, however. He is almost delirious with worry over O'Neill, whom he is convinced has been eaten by the cannibals living in this unsettled land.

"As a drink: White Horse whisky . . . and I'm starting to feel thirsty, very thirsty. But I am not the one to be most pitied. My poor horse is a sorry sight.

"I am starting to feel sleepy. It must be the drinking. But suddenly I am awakened by the sound of a horse approaching. Hooray! O'Neill, our liberator, appears in all his glory, as if in a ray of light (a little bit of enthusiasm can't hurt).

"I leave the tent and am in great awe of the fact that we have three horses again, although I have lost a dinner. This last fact deserves an explanation.

"That morning, after we realized that von Doozy's horse had disappeared, we had a crisis meeting, and I suggested that we head back. I was convinced that our disloyal nag chewed on his lead rope in order to head back to the last place where he had been able to eat some hay.

"O'Neill disagreed. In his opinion, the horse must have headed towards the Yarra to quench his thirst.

"Von Doozy was too affected by the horse's disappearance to form any opinion but decided to support O'Neill's hypothesis. The latter asked us to either wait for him where we were or follow him at a slow pace while he retrieved the escaped horse. We did not have anything to lose, so we followed his advice!

"The Yarra was not as far as we thought. It was 4:30 P.M. and we were about 6 or 7 kilometers away from it, so it must have been only 20 or 25 kilometers away from where we had camped the previous night.

"The horse had indeed broken his tether and, being thirsty, he let his instinct take him to where he could find fresh water. O'Neill found him peacefully grazing by the

Yarra and did not encounter any resistance when he recaptured him.

"This damned animal made me lose my bet: I now had to buy dinner for the three of us!

"At 5 p.m., we packed up and rode on happier than we had been that morning. A half hour later, we finally get to enjoy some tea, and I take a well-deserved bath.

"That was enough work for our first hunting day. I slept peacefully and uninterruptedly until four in the morning. Then I got up, took a bath and had breakfast. At 5 a.m., we're all packed up again: to the horses! We ride along the river until 10 a.m. The terrain is better, and our horses are rested.

"During our ride, O'Neill, who is a great shot, kills thirty-eight rabbits and two curlews. These are ibis-like birds, but instead of being pink and white, their plumage looks like the one of a quail. It was a couple. Nearby, we find a nest with three eggs. How thoughtful! That's one for each of us. They're the same size as the largest ostrich egg I have ever seen, and are white with brown and black spots.

"At 10 a.m. we have lunch and get some rest. We set up the tent in a charming spot. The water is deep and clear and the shrubland has given way to tall trees. We lounge about until 4 p.m. Then we have some tea and go for a swim. We take the load off our horses and have them take a bath as well.

"Von Doozy starts cooking. He is making us a Lucullus-worthy dinner. Judge for yourself: a stunning fish (I do not know the name of it), game, rabbit, canned foods, jam and jelly for dessert, and, for drinks, whisky and Benedictine. On top of that, we smoked excellent pipes.

"While we were waiting for our chef to prepare dinner, O'Neill and I raced our horses. I have to say that, as skilled as O'Neill is with a rifle, I quite surpassed him on horseback and inflicted him a defeat that even he, an Irishman, should remember for a while. I beat him by at least 600 meters in a 3-kilometer race.

"At 8 p.m. we sit down for dinner. I make sure we honor this meal, and we toast to the Hungarian monarchy, the impending Irish independence and the elegance of Mr. Armand Fallières. After that, we tell each other some stories. How nice it is to live like a savage. I am relishing this pleasant existence.

"My companions are most agreeable. O'Neill is used to this lifestyle. He has visited all of South Africa, as well as good part of South America and of Mexico. He loves nature and is a scholar on the subjects of botany and zoology. I think he regularly applies both sciences. The way he found our horse in this immense desert demonstrates how well he understands animal instinct. He is very interesting to listen to.

"Von Doozy loves nature too. He is an excellent explorer as well, and, better still, a very funny person. I love listening to these two discussing Darwin. O'Neill is a great admirer of his, while von Doozy's artistic mind refuses to wrap itself around his theories. He's an idealist when satiated and a materialist when he's thirsty.

"Tonight, he told us stories about all the places he's been. I laughed so hard I'm still feeling sore.

"When one is far away from home, from one's world, in a land inhabited by savages, you form bonds more easily. We feel a kinship and start caring for each other. That explains our need to confide in each other and tell each other personal stories that reflect our temperament.

"January 25, 10 a.m.: we pack up and head to Boort, which is 170 kilometers away. It's a good day for hunting, but we are starting to get tired of rabbits. There's too many of them and they are not worth the lead used to kill them. We let them live their lives.

"Besides, O'Neill, who, on day one, killed about fifty of them, was now absolutely opposed to the idea of me killing even just one more, saying—poor human heart!—that spreading death unnecessarily is cruel, even when it comes to the most expendable of animals.

"'It's a life,' declares yesterday's bloody killer, 'and you have to respect it. It is worth the same as ours, in its own way.'

"I admire his cynicism but do not tell him so. Some people only understand their cruel impulses once they gave into them.

"We set up camp at 5 p.m. We take our time because we easily covered two-thirds of the distance back to Boort.

"When we wake up, a surprise is waiting for us: instead of tea, von Doozy made us some coffee. We have enough drinking water, but we make sure not to waste too much of it to wash ourselves. One moistened towel is enough to clean up.

"The horses are thirsty, but we only give them a little water because we have a long way to go today.

"At 5 a.m. we take off. The day feels rather monotonous. Everything we enjoyed yesterday feels tiresome today. Alas! That is how men are. At noon, we have a quick snack. We arrive in Boort at 4 p.m.

"We are quite dirty. We had forgotten our razors and are in great need of a wash, but we decide to preserve this disheveled look until St. Kilda in order to appear more like explorers. How immature men can be, even at forty!

"We arrive in St. Kilda, where we join a crowd of strangers, a collection of so many different lives, and get back to our old daily activities, which, no matter what they are, will all end in the same way one day."

SIX

Confronting Bad Faith

Life goes on! Though it is not a very happy one for Pourpe, who nevertheless strives to make light of his own misfortunes so as not to let himself be overtaken by sorrow.

"I go to Melbourne to pick up my mail every Monday. Alas! There is never much for me!"

At that point in his life, Pourpe was in a lot of pain because of his almost complete solitude. He would see other people leaving the post office with many letters, and feel sad comparing them to the few that he had received. He did not show the same relentless energy in his emotional life as he did time and time again during his career as a pilot.

A ray of hope: the Blériot has arrived. But customs procedures will take about ten days because this item has never entered the country before, which means the authorities will need to calculate the import tax on it.

"Since he's very busy at the Melbourne Motor Garage, Mr. Defries asked me to pick up the Blériot. I'm having some difficulties and have to deal directly with the authorities, whose infuriating sluggishness reminds me of their French counterparts. In the last ten days, I have been able to observe how similar this country's government bureaucracy is to ours: French pen-pushers and Australian pen-pushers, how much you have in common!"

Finally, on 9 February 1910 the Blériot was taken to the Melbourne Garage's exhibition hall and, by the next morning, Pourpe started putting it together. By 1 P.M. the plane was ready. It had sustained almost no damage from the trip. The only part that seemed to have suffered a little was the rudder.

Our young pilot was delighted to finally have something interesting to do again. The following Saturday, he went to pick up his paycheck, but the accountant informed him that he was not on the past week's employees' list.

"Just put my name down twice for next week," suggested Pourpe.

"I'll do that," the accountant assured him.

During the next two weeks, Pourpe made a daily appearance at the Blériot exhibition. People paid one shilling to get in. All the money raised that way—minus the administrative costs—went to a fund helping the people affected by the sinking of the *Waratah*.[1]

Pourpe's job was to teach the public everything he could about the aeroplane and the way it worked. The audience seemed to be very interested and to understand everything Pourpe told them.

"I noticed that Australians seem to have better common sense than my compatriots. Not only have I attended every Paris Motor Show for the last three years, but I also went to the very first Aeronautical Salon and, every time, I was floored by other attendees' ignorance. It is true though that the people who make the effort to see the Blériot here in Australia are people who are particularly interested in new transportation devices and have read many articles on the subject. They generally seem to understand *plus lourd que l'air* [that which is heavier than air] very well."

But Pourpe's financial issues were not over. A week after not having been paid, he did not encounter better luck. The accountant grumpily answered his query:

"Looks like they left you out again."

"Well then I shall go see Mr. Defries."

"That's your problem."

The accountant's behavior made the pilot/engineer/mechanic/speaker weary, so he complained to Defries, who, flustered, could provide only vague explanations. They decided that a visit to Mr. Adamson—who happened to also be the headmaster of Wesley College—might clear things up.

---

1. The SS *Waratah* was a Blue Anchor Line passenger steamship that was scheduled to operate between Europe and Australia. In July 1909 it disappeared south of Durban, South Africa, with its 211 passengers and crew.

Harry Houdini, third from left, stands before his French Voisin biplane prior to making his historic flight at Digger's Rest, Melbourne, Australia, 18 March 1910. Marc Pourpe stands next to Houdini holding the camera he will use to record the flight.

Mr. Adamson seemed equally surprised by Pourpe's difficulties. He gave him a check for £10 and assured him that this would not happen again. After that, they discussed the Wright.

"Banks had a few more minor accidents at Digger's Rest," said Mr. Adamson. "But they were not very serious, and he is making encouraging progress. In a month from now, he should be able to give flight demonstrations."

"I ran into Banks two days ago," Pourpe said. "He himself confessed that he had only undertaken two trials lately, and they resulted in a broken wing and rudder. It seems like these recent flights were not better than the ones I witnessed. He said all he was able to accomplish was to make a few jumps in the air while driving on a straight line for about 150 to 200 meters. Do you still have the same plans we talked about regarding the Blériot? Can I count on . . ."

"I'm planning on selling it, but I will talk to its future buyer to make sure he hires you as a pilot."

"That would make me very happy because I haven't had anything to do over the last two months. I didn't come from such a faraway place for that!"

"Do not worry. But, in a few days, you will not be dealing with me anymore. I am going to hire a private company, Bailieu & Patterson, to handle this matter. I will write these gentlemen about you, and, from now on, you will work everything out with them."

"On February 23 Mr. Houdini came to see the Blériot. He's scheduled to give a show in Melbourne. His current act, which has already been a success in Paris, is interesting: He frees himself from a straitjacket and chains. It seems like nothing can stop him: confinement, boxes, chains, ropes, etc. People call him 'The Handcuff King.'

"He came to ask me about an airfield. He owns a Voisin aeroplane which he bought in France, from Mr. Sanchez-Besa. His plane is still in customs.

"I gave him all the useful information I could think of and introduced him to Banks, who happened to be there at the time. We agreed to let Houdini use Digger's Rest. He brought a mechanic from the Voisin company by the name of Brassac. He will be Houdini's instructor because he does not know how to fly a plane yet.

Two days later, Pourpe took the Blériot Model #29 apart and packed it up. At the garage he met Mr. Adamson's representative, Mr. Bailieu, who made Pourpe some vague promises regarding his future as a pilot and asked him to come see him in his office in two days.

During this visit, Pourpe learned that Houdini was negotiating the purchase of the Blériot.

"It's impossible!" Pourpe responded. "He has never flown before. He's going to kill himself with this plane!"

"Our idea is to use all three aeroplanes: the Voisin, the Wright and the Blériot for flight demonstrations on a racecourse."

"You are setting yourself up for failure! Every one of Banks' flight attempts has resulted in him damaging the plane somehow. Houdini doesn't know how to fly and, to top it all off, the local racecourses are too small for the Wright and the Voisin to even take off."

Harry Houdini's French Voisin Biplane at Digger's Rest, Melbourne, Australia, 18 March 1910

"Come back to see me in two or three days."

For the last three months, every single business meeting Pourpe had had ended with these words.

The young Frenchman was still seeing his friend von Doozy, who had his own problems: He was suing the person who had made him come over from England. It was a good cause, but paying for legal proceedings required money. True to the noble selflessness that drove all of his actions, Pourpe gave von Doozy all of his savings to help him pay for his legal fees.

"I am so happy to be able to help him. Who knows? Soon, I might be the one in need of help in this godforsaken country! His situation is rather alarming: He left his wife and baby in England and doesn't know how they are going to cope in his absence."

Meanwhile, accidents and other complications kept happening. On March 10, while trying to fly the Wright, Banks crashed again. He was incredibly lucky and got away with only a few scratches. The plane, however, was ruined.

Pourpe went to visit Mr. Baillieu again, but to no avail. He was always told, "Tomorrow." He was always given promises. But nothing was ever guaranteed.

"On March 9, I had an important, and possibly decisive, conversation with him. Like every time we talk, I reminded him that my success relies entirely on the time we are currently living in, the first two years after aviation was developed. Right now, one wasted week does as much damage as a whole year would in a few years from now. After I gave him my usual pitch, he answered that if nothing significant happened regarding the Blériot in the next two days, he might as well send me back to France. I told him that I would happily accept his decision and left.

"On March 11, I went back to see him. He gave me a bunch of excuses and asked that I keep waiting. That is when I started bringing up clauses from my contract.

"By January 24, I owed Mr. Adamson £24. We agreed that I would reimburse him by letting him take £3 from my weekly salary until March 5. I gave Mr. Bailieu those details and pointed out that, after March 5th, I should have started getting my full salary again. I also specified that, according to my contract, I should get a £4 raise on my monthly salary starting on March 15. So, starting next week, I should get £9 every Saturday."

"You have no right to make such demands," he answered. "You are not legally bound to Mr. Adamson, who is only paying you as a favor to Mr. Defries, who signed that contract with you. Mr. Adamson's generosity is the only reason you are still receiving a salary. If you think you have a case, then go talk to Mr. Defries."

"These words 'Mr. Adamson's generosity' exasperated me so much I warned Bailieu I was going to go see Defries and left without saying goodbye.

"Defries was indignant and immediately dictated a letter in which he said that I had been treated unfairly this whole time, and demanded that my salary be corrected. He added that he hoped I would obtain satisfaction because I was in the right.

"I was full of hope on the next day when I went to the garage to get my paycheck, but there was Defries, who told me: 'I had a talk with Mr. Bailieu. He asked me to pass on the following offer to you: He will pay for your ticket back to France and give you £10 for your travel expenses. If I were you, I would accept, because, if you refuse, they'll just stop paying you.'"

I did not let him go on. For the last two days, I had been in a constant state of anger.

"I understand exactly what's going on. If I don't agree to this ridiculous deal, I'll just be denied pay and left to starve. And you, the one person I thought I could trust, are the one telling me about this shameless arrangement! I'm starting to see what's happening here, and I firmly reject your offer.

"'I have nothing to do with it,' Defries pleaded. 'In fact, I am very sorry. You know you can always count on my friendship. Actually, I myself am about to abdicate my responsibilities at the garage because I am not getting along with Bailieu. Go see him; maybe it'll be easier to deal with him this time.'

"I did exactly that, but Bailieu repeated the offer Defries made me. I asked him if he was pulling my leg. He didn't seem shocked at all. 'I'm seeing Adamson this afternoon. We'll talk about your situation. Come back on Monday at 10 A.M.'

"That Monday I was given the same offer. I took notes and, after going over them carefully, showed then to Mr. Levinson, a neighbor of mine who happened to be a lawyer. He helped me write a letter in which I asked Mr. Adamson to give me what he owed me.

"No answer. Next, Mr. Levinson wrote Mr. Adamson directly and threatened him with legal action if he didn't honor my contract. Adamson essentially responded that he did not have any contract with me and gave us his own lawyer's address."

To clear his mind while awaiting the result of his legal pursuit, Pourpe spent a few days at Digger's Rest, where the Wright, Banks's perpetual victim, was undergoing painstaking repairs and where Houdini, "the Handcuffs King," was training daily.

On 21 March 1910 Houdini managed to conduct a flight with turns over a distance of 7 kilometers in seven minutes and forty-five seconds.[2] It was the first flight ever recorded in Australia. And to think that this feat would have been accomplished months earlier if Pourpe had been entrusted with the Wright or the Blériot! Instead, he had to be satisfied with taking pictures. He sold three of them to a Melbourne newspaper for ten shillings, which is 37.50 francs.

"This is a good opportunity to add to my meager savings," he wrote.

More days passed, as inauspicious as ever. Pourpe was in an alarming mental state. He wanted his problems to end, no matter what it would take.

"Sometimes, the worst thoughts go through my mind. However, when I manage to calm down and examine the situation more coolly, I tell myself that even though I am in a dire financial situation, I am in the right, and I am convinced that someone like Mr. Adamson, who is the headmaster of Australia's greatest university, will not let the press tarnish his name by making the details of this pathetic case public. My contract was established in France and did not get notarized here, but it is still binding morally, and Adamson is responsible for it. He cannot deny its authenticity. This country's justice system and public opinion will judge him, which will hurt him greatly since his social position does not allow him to endanger his reputation and make such risky gambles. Besides, I have letters that prove he has a responsibility in the matter. And he knows it.

"But how long the hours feel when you are awaiting a decision that will affect your whole career, your whole life! Indeed, when you think about it, if my trip to Australia ends in such a way, it will mean more difficulties for me in the future since I will lose some of my prestige and maybe even appear less trustworthy.

"Let's imagine I go back to France right now and return to my old company, Ariel. Will they believe me when I tell them the truth about what happened? I doubt it. It will hurt me. They'll think I'm an idiot or suspect there's foul play involved.

"Alas! I know exactly how French people think, or, to be more exact, how all men think when it comes to people attempting the sort of endeavor I did. If you succeed, you are—or at least you pass for—a hero. If you fail, they throw you to the dogs.

"Whose support can I count on here? No one's. So, if Adamson decides to keep antagonizing me legally, I will have to give up and will not only lose what I think he owes me, but also the offer he made me six weeks ago when he said he would pay for my trip back plus £10.

"My mind is always working. I'm thinking, thinking, thinking. When all I want is to forget for a few moments. Even in my sleep I am so restless that I have fallen out of bed several times over the past few nights."

Every time Pourpe told me about those days, my poor friend would admit that it had been the hardest period of his life because of how lonely he felt. Still, misfortune followed him until the end of his life.

---

2. Houdini's flight took place on 18 March 1910.

SEVEN

A Cloud Lifts, a Critical Meeting

While he was awaiting a solution, our expatriate was working. He was writing articles as well as translating English texts into French and generally did not go out much. He was corresponding with Houdini, who had a show in Sydney. He had some hope on that front. The performer was planning on buying the storied Blériot and let Pourpe pilot it. But that deal did not crystallize either. It was like all the others.

On April 10 Pourpe wrote: "Nothing. Nothing. Nothing seems to go my way. I haven't received any letters from France in three weeks, and God knows they would do me some good in such difficult times."

In an attempt to comfort himself, he wrote: "Anyway, I tell myself that everything has an end and that my present circumstances will have to change at some point."

On April 29 the court allowed a hearing to take place in Melbourne despite the fact that the contract at the heart of the case was French, not Australian.

"I hope Adamson is not going to let this case drag on any longer. In fact, that is my greatest hope. I am running out of money. I even owe the boarding house 200 francs. They are good people; they haven't been pressuring me, but it can't go on this way much longer. On top of that, my lawyer has asked me for 250 francs to carry forward legal proceedings. I don't have even a tenth of that sum. And the only friend I have here that I feel close enough to to dare ask for a loan probably doesn't have enough money to help me either. What to do? What to do?

"I told my lawyer a tall tale to buy more time. I told him I was expecting some money from France and that it should arrive in the mail any minute now. That leaves me three days. What a mess!

"It's even worse than in Paris. There is absolutely nobody here to whom I would even dare bring up the subject of money. Still, in spite of the terrible financial situation I'm grappling with, that is not what is upsetting me the most."

Here we see our hero's sentimental side come out. "What is causing me the most grief is that the letter I am waiting for never seems to arrive. The last one I received was quite blunt: She dashed all of my hopes; she was ending it all. She used her father, her mother, my youth, etc. as excuses while claiming that her 'tender affection' for me will always remain.

"I know my Jeannette well and often understand what's going on in her head. It never lasts more than a few hours; hence, though this letter made me sad, it did not trouble me any more than any of the letters I received from her when I was still in France. We have found ourselves in the same situation a hundred—actually probably more like a thousand—times over the last four years, but it never lasted more than two or three hours at most. And when it did last that long it was usually my fault. I'm the pigheaded one!

"Still, since I have left Paris, I have received at least one letter a week. I believe that she let her heart speak in these letters and that they are a testament to her genuine feelings for me. Thus, I am very sad at the thought that I might have been wrong, and every time I think about it I feel like I am on my own. I'm even more alone than I thought I was. Three weeks without a letter. What is happening? Why such obstinacy?"

Three days later Pourpe's mind was set at ease. "This week is off to a better start. I received two letters from Jeannette, and they confirmed my inkling. She was 'in a dark place' when she wrote me her mean letter. Now she's asking me to forgive her for her blunt behavior. We are in good terms again; I feel almost happy, though nothing else is going well.

"My lawyer has sent me another request for money and warned me that if I do not give it to him in four days, he will abandon my case."

Then . . . another offer! Another disappointment in the making? Mr. Watson, an American who owned the largest advertising company in Melbourne and, according to some, in Australia, called Pourpe in.

When Pourpe and Defries started their ambitious venture in Sydney, Tait, the agent, had published a brochure with a description of the Wright aeroplane written by Pourpe followed by a brief history of aviation, starting with the crossing of the English Channel, written by a man named Ambroise Pratt, and littered with inaccuracies.

Watson had overseen this project and widely publicized the brochures. He signed a 50,000-franc contract with some of the largest Australian companies. So when the plans for the Wright did not come through, Watson found himself in an impasse. People wanted their money back, and he could not ask Tait, his best customer, for it.

So how to make everybody—especially himself—happy? Watson had decided to allow Adamson to rent the Wright for three months. This way, the plane would be exhibited in Australia's main cities, and Watson would use this opportunity to sell the brochures. His customers wouldn't be able to complain anymore.

"I'm offering you to accompany me," he told Pourpe. "You'll give speeches on aviation and will show the public how the plane works, though it will stay on the ground. To spice the show up, I got my hands on some films showing notable flights, including an attempt by Latham to cross the English Channel, a performance by Louis Paulhan, footage from the *Semaine de Champagn*,[1] and a zeppelin flight. Do you accept?"

Pourpe considered the offer for a minute: What could go wrong? This tour would give him better name recognition. Maybe he would even find a buyer for the Blériot, and, more importantly, it would allow him to earn some quick money to pay off his debts and carry on his lawsuit.

"I'll do it," he answered.

"You'll receive £5 a week and 5 percent of admission ticket proceedings. Naturally, we will cover all of your expenses. During each exhibit, you will give a daily Q&A about the aeroplane from 3 p.m. to 5 p.m. and then a half-hour talk in the evening, sometime between 8 p.m. and 10 p.m. That's it."

A contract was signed. Pourpe agreed to work only for a month, so that he could attend the hearings for his trial against Adamson. He had four days to pack. He had to leave for his first show, in Adelaide, on May 9.

He immediately got to work. Within the next forty-eight hours, he had written a short history of aviation, using some documents he always kept with him. The posters promoting the tour were very large and bright, and the name "Marc Pourpe" was displayed prominently, in a dazzling font. Everything seemed to be going well, although the departure was delayed by two days because the plane was not ready to ship.

On May 10, Watson called for an emergency meeting with his young speaker. A new debacle on the horizon? Pourpe rushed to Watson's office, and Watson told him:

"I didn't think I had to let Mr. Adamson know that I had picked you as a speaker, but he found out through Mr. Tait, whom I had told about you because I did not think it would get you in any trouble. Mr. Adamson immediately asked to speak to me and informed me that he could not allow me to take you with me to do demonstrations involving 'his' aeroplane since you two are currently involved in a lawsuit. If you would like, I could serve as an intermediary between the two of you and try to turn this situation to your advantage, as long as you agree to drop your lawsuit again Adamson."

Fearing that, on the contrary, he was going to put himself in a more difficult position, Pourpe responded: "I should not be the one making an offer to Mr. Adamson. He should take the initiative and offer me a reasonable deal. Then I will not have any reason to turn it down."

Following that statement, Watson asked Pourpe many questions, but the Frenchman provided only limited explanations and stayed firm in his position.

"I intend to pursue legal action against Adamson until I get satisfaction."

"You should know you are going up against a multimillionaire. You will not be able to outlast him when it comes to legal fees. He's a clever man."

Suspecting a trap, Pourpe decided to bluff. "My trial's cost is the least of my concerns. I might not be a millionaire, but I put enough money aside to not only pay for this trial, but also to appeal its outcome in the unlikely case the judge's decision were not in my favor."

"How much money are you suing for?"

"The sum I am requesting is approximately £1680 (41,000 francs). If Adamson wants to send me that money, I'll consider this case closed within the next twenty-four hours."

"My poor friend," Watson replied, "you should know that even if you won, you would never get all the money you're asking for. You'll have to consider yourself lucky if you are granted even a quarter of this sum, and that will probably take four to five months, a considerable waste of your time. Think about it."

"I've thought it through. I'll wait for Adamson's offer. If it's reasonable, I'll probably accept."

"Very well. Come back to see me at 5 P.M. By then I will have talked to Adamson and will relay you his decision. I will try to be a good advocate for your cause."

Pourpe was rather moved by this gesture but tried not to show it. That same evening, he arrived at Watson's on time.

"Mr. Adamson gave me a hard time pleading your cause, but I persisted and convinced him to pay you £200 (5,000 francs)."

"I categorically refuse. There is nothing left for me to do now but to leave. I couldn't . . . "

Watson interrupted him. "Let me finish. Mr. Adamson agreed to lease me the Blériot on top of the Wright. And if you agree to take his £200, I'm ready to sign you as the Blériot's pilot for £8 a week and 15 percent of the profits."

He pulled a wad of money out of his pocket and put it on the table. "It's a quarter after five. I give you fifteen minutes to decide." This ploy made Pourpe's blood boil, although he was seeing his dream come true. What trap was getting set up for him?

"I am surprised by your conduct, Mr. Watson. You are American. Maybe this way of doing is common in your country. There might even be some who would have pulled a revolver on me and asked me to take the money or die. These intimidation tactics might work in the savanna, but not here, in civilization, especially when a Frenchman is involved. Put this money back in your pocket. There is no need to wait fifteen minutes. I reject your offer and bid you adieu."

He started toward the door, but Watson rushed to block his way and, laughing, told him: "I have to admit that your coldness surprises me, considering the situation."

What would he have thought had he known how desperate our wonderful young Frenchman was, and how he would have welcomed that money? Yet, even in the direst of financial situations, Pourpe would never compromise his pride.

Watson apologized. "I am sorry if I offended you. If I did, it is only because I did not express myself clearly. I work fast when it comes to business, and, on top of that, Adamson asked me for a receipt or his money back by tonight."

"I might look young, but I am not a child. Don't think you can intimidate me or make false promises to me. Ever since I arrived in Australia, that's exactly how people have treated me most of the time. As a consequence, I do not trust anyone anymore, including you."

"My dear Pourpe, you are absolutely wrong. Please do not let anger get the best of you. I am talking to you as a friend, and I advise you to take this offer. I'll sign the Blériot contract with you this instant. Here, to show you that I mean it, and that you can trust me, I'll give you an extra £50 (1,250 francs) myself, on top of Adamson's £200."

Pourpe managed to keep his cool—at least on the surface—despite the fact that the money he was offered seemed like a fortune to him and that this contract represented a chance at a brighter future.

"I will have to look into this with my lawyer," he said. I will give you an answer tomorrow morning."

"It will be too late."

"That's too bad."

Their conversation lasted a little longer, and suddenly Pourpe had an idea.

"Why don't you come with me to go see my lawyer?"

Watson agreed, and they headed to Levinson's together. Before he let Watson into Levinson's office, Pourpe briefed his lawyer. Levinson responded by saying: "The judge might award you £350, certainly no more than that. Let's try to get £300 out of them, and you'll have secured a good deal for yourself."

They brought Watson in, and Levinson started negotiating with him. "I can't go over the amount I already promised," Watson said. "Especially since you are asking for £300 when we are offering you £250 on top of the six-month contract I am ready to sign with you and which will guarantee you a £208 pay plus the 15 percent on profits, which could very well amount to £1000. If you take this deal, Pourpe, you will be able to consider yourself a very lucky man."

What Watson said did sound appealing to the young pilot, but after continuing to negotiate for about an hour, Levinson signaled to Pourpe to turn down the offer.

At that point, Pourpe felt very hesitant. He was tempted to say yes. A thousand thoughts were rushing through his mind. He could see himself broke and homeless if he said no, and wealthy if he said yes.

He stood up. "There is no point in keeping on talking. Mr. Watson doesn't want to raise his offer and Mr. Levinson thinks I will get less money than I am owed. As for me,

I'm fed up. I have been in Australia for eight months. Until now, I've encountered only difficulties and disappointments from all sides. I do not know if I should accept or not. So what I am about to do might seem somewhat naive to you, but it should put an end to my indecision. I am going to let fate decide for me once more. And I'm sure it will act in my best interests like it always does."

He pulled a coin from his pocket. "Tails for yes, heads for no."

When Watson saw this, he rushed to Pourpe and, grabbing his hand, said: "You are French, but, by God, you could just as well be American."

Despite how nerve-racking his situation was, Pourpe couldn't help but chuckle. In any other circumstance, such a remark would have angered him, but he understood what Watson had meant by it. It was the highest form of praise he could think of.

Pourpe was about to throw the coin in the air when Watson interrupted him again. "Listen, I'm impressed, and I'm ready to do better. On top of the £250 I have right here, I will give you an extra £50 on the day of your first public flight. There's no need for further hesitation now. Just say yes."

Pourpe glanced up at Levinson, who, until now, had been watching the events unfurl with remarkable detachment. The lawyer winked at him. What did that mean? The Frenchman didn't understand but wanted to continue appearing like he was in control, even if he was making a mistake. He threw the coin, and it landed on the table.

"Let's see," he said, "what fate, this great trickster, has decided for me."

Heads! It was a no!

A poignant moment of silence followed the verdict. Pourpe was already regretting his foolhardy gesture, but quickly pulled himself together and said, smiling: "As you see, it's a no." He turned to Watson. "All there is for you to do now is to make me another offer tomorrow after having seen Mr. Adamson. Then I'll think about it, without using a coin this time."

"Too late," replied Watson. "Good night."

After he left, Levinson declared that Pourpe would surely get a phone call the next day. "I strongly advise you to wait two or three days before going anywhere. I'm sure you will get your £350."

Pourpe felt dizzy leaving his lawyer's office after such a suspenseful day. He couldn't sleep all night. Seeing all these bills laid out in front of him and turning them down when he was almost penniless. He felt like Tantalus! Yes, but at least he had had his grand gesture.

The next morning, at dawn, he unwound by going for a swim in the ocean and then went on a long walk with his friend von Doozy. He arrived back at his boarding house at 11 A.M. only to be disappointed. Nobody had tried to call him.

Von Doozy advised him to wait until 2 P.M. "If by then you haven't heard from anyone, find some excuse to go see Watson and, this time, don't be a Don Quixote—take his offer."

At 2 P.M., Pourpe went to see Watson. "I would like to pick up the speech I had asked your secretary to type out for me. There's no more use for it now. That's unfortunate. I regret that we could not come to an agreement."

Watson let him into his office and told him: "I saw Bailieu and Adamson. They are not going to make any more concessions. However, if you agree to our £250 deal, I will personally give you £50 on the day of your first public flight. If you are ready to be more cooperative this time, I'm ready to sign you without delay."

After a short discussion, Pourpe, realizing that he could not hope for anything better, agreed and received the £250 on the spot, as well as a temporary letter of commitment, a receipt, and another letter regarding the £50 for the first flight.

The following month, he went to see Watson every day in the hope that he would have an update regarding his situation. Every day, new changes were made to the project. Realizing that Watson was not in a hurry to do anything anymore, Pourpe wrote him a letter asking him to give him a proper answer regarding their arrangement within the next two days or to start paying him the wage they had agreed on anyway. "If I do not have the Blériot by noon on Saturday, I will leave for France."

Nothing happened. Pourpe did not hesitate any longer and immediately headed to the Cook travel agency, where he paid for a cabin on the White Star Lines' *Afric*. He left for France on 16 June 1910.

His struggles were coming to an end, and his next great adventure was about to start.

EIGHT

Back Home

Pourpe was going to try to build the plane he had been dreaming about for a long time, since the dawn of aviation.

In June 1909 the following description was published in the sports newspapers:

> Marc Pourpe Aeroplane, 4 rue Fontaine, Paris. This machine is of the "monoplane" type. The propulsion system consists of a propeller located on the front of the plane and activated by an engine that does not appear very powerful but should allow the plane to go as fast as 70 or even 90 km an hour. The aerofoil allows for an adjustable angle of attack in order to increase or lower the plane's buoyancy. This aerofoil is both narrow and flexible.
>
> In the back, there is a cross-shaped balancing rudder. The angle of incidence and the balancing rudder's incline are calculated in a way to prevent the plane from flipping over.
>
> To steer and straighten the plane, one uses both the rudder and the adjustable aerofoil, which allow the machine to reach perfect stability on both a lateral and a longitudinal plane.
>
> The plane's frame always keeps a horizontal position, which facilitates carburation and allows the pilot to stay in an upright position.
>
> The plane's weight, once all the equipment is installed, should be barely 120 kilos.

So it seems that at a time when aeroplanes had just barely been invented, Pourpe had already developed an *avionette*. But buyers were rare in those early days, and Pourpe's prototype did not make it past the planning phase.

As soon as he arrived back in France, Pourpe resolved to pick up his old project again. This time Mr. Requillard showed interest, and the young flight engineer—probably the youngest in the world—built a monoplane entirely out of wood veneer. After some promising tryouts, Pourpe had an unpleasant surprise in Juvisy when his plane flipped over while he was flying 30 meters above the ground at a speed of 130 km per hour. He miraculously survived the brutal landing, but the plane was not as lucky. From here on out, Pourpe decided to settle for flying planes built by other people. It is true that he could have improved his creation, but he didn't have the money for it.

He was lucky enough to find a job as a head pilot in Nice, at the Brague airdrome, over the winter of 1910–1911. He achieved amazing results, training no fewer than a dozen students over a period of three months.

That is when I got the chance to reunite with the man I had first met several years prior, at his mother's, when he was still a high school student. I had gone to Nice as a special correspondent for two publications: *Excelsior* and *La Vie au Grand Air* (Life in the Open Air). I was to report on Lieutenant Bague's attempt to cross the Mediterranean and on the Nice-Ajaccio race. It turned out to be quite a relaxing assignment because none of the contenders ended up taking off on the day of the event. However, Bague ended up getting lost at sea in June 1911.

Pourpe was some kind of celebrity on the French Riviera, but he was not enjoying his situation and told me: "I have bills to pay. That is why I am teaching other people how to fly. I have other aspirations. I'm not planning on playing at being a teacher all my life. There is going to be a race from Paris to Madrid and another one from Paris to Rome, as well as the Circuit Européen. I want to compete in those. I'm doing my best to earn enough money to buy a plane. I can't risk flying the one I have right now in those competitions."

It was an aeroplane by the Cayre brothers. On 29 April 1911, he left the Brague airdrome and, after flying at an altitude of 60 meters, landed in Fontonne, on Mr. Alziary's property. He was "surrounded by an enthusiastic crowd. Bottles of champagne were cracked open to celebrate the aviation 'neophyte's' audacity."

Pourpe went back to Paris to try his luck among the greatest pilots of the day. He had been flying for a long time but, interestingly, had never obtained his pilot's license.

On 20 July 1911, he took off in a Blériot and rose so high in the air he got lost in the clouds. He flew over Paris at an altitude of more than 1,000 meters. He was surrounded by fog and did not know where he was. He was looking for the Eiffel Tower, but a thick cushion of clouds was obstructing his view. Finally, a clearing allowed him to spot the Sacré Coeur. He changed course, headed toward the Eiffel Tower, and came back to land in Juvisy after having flown for about an hour.

He still did not have his license!

Two days later, he finally resolved to go through all the administrative formalities. He passed with flying colors, and, rather than appearing in front of the auditors with the skills of a mere beginner, he impressed them with a performance worthy of a master.

With his precious certificate in hand,[1] he could finally enter official flight competitions. In August he went to Arras, where he impressed the crowd at the Hauts-Blancs-Monts racetracks with his stunts.

The audience's enthusiasm was indescribable. You could hear people yelling "Bravo!" from all sides. The crowd jumped over the barriers and invaded the centerfield to encircle the pilot, whom everybody wanted to shake hands with. Pourpe had a hard time cutting through the mass of people to get back to the bleachers.

He spent a half hour in the air, flew over the surrounding countryside, ended his performance with "graceful arabesques," and landed on the exact same spot he had taken off from after softly gliding through the air with his engine off.

The next day, at four in the morning, a crowd of onlookers gathered at the racetracks again to see Pourpe take off for Boulogne-sur-Mer. His fans were dedicated! At 5:47 A.M. the pilot took off on his Blériot, did a few stunts to entertain his audience, and headed toward Boulogne-sur-Mer. He arrived there at 6:50 a.m., covering a distance of 120 kilometers in one hour and thirteen minutes.

He was planning on continuing toward Folkestone. Since he did not have his monoplane yet when the last major flight competitions were staged, he wanted to show people what he could accomplish now. However, the organizers of the upcoming flight exhibition in Boulogne-sur-Mer asked him to postpone his trip to take part in their event. He agreed. His Blériot was transported to the casino and stored in a makeshift hangar "among the local bathing establishment's cars and tarpaulins, between the garage and the baths."

René Caudron, Darioli, and de Laët were all scheduled to attend the event. Now Pourpe was going to join their ranks. In front of fifteen thousand people, on a very windy day, Pourpe performed three flights. During the two first ones, he flew over the city and, for his last performance, executed some stunts that gave the crowd a thrill.

As not to be charged with aggrandizement and bias, I shall quote the *Télégramme du Pas-de-Calais* on the events of 21 August 1911. It is so easy to get caught up in untruths when one looks back on things that happened such a long time ago!

"The first thunderclaps resonate. Lightning bolts crisscross the sky and rain starts to fall. René Caudron has put his plane back in the hangar, and Darioli and de Laët soon do the same.

"Marc Pourpe is the only one left on the beach. Suddenly, he jumps in his monoplane, starts the engine, and takes off. Where to? Nobody knows.

"We can see him wavering above the sea, like a mere dragonfly. We try not to lose him out of sight, but he soon disappears into the storm. We wait anxiously. We stare at the horizon with marine binoculars. He is nowhere to be seen. After ten minutes, a little dot appears on the horizon.

"The crowd erupts: 'There he is! There he is!'

"He gets close enough that one can see him clearly without binoculars again. He lands and breaks the propeller he had installed this very morning and had been so happy with.

"We rush to interview him. Not seeming the least upset, he tells us: 'It's the first time I damaged this plane. It's too bad.'

"We ask him where he has been to: 'I spotted the Folkestone ferry on its way to Boulogne, so I decided to go up to it to greet its passengers. I traveled only over seven nautical miles.'

"While the plane is put back in the hangar, we cheer the young pilot on for his performance, although he himself does not seem to think that he accomplished anything out of the ordinary."

Carrying out such a flight in the middle of a storm in 1911 was proof of our outstanding pilot's audacity and skill.

---

1. Pourpe received his civil pilot certificate, number 560, on 25 July 1911.

Marc Pourpe seated in his Blériot monoplane following his return from his two-day flight across the English channel to Folkestone, England, 27–28 August 1911

The Boulogne-sur-Mer flight demonstrations lasted for three days, during which Pourpe continued to distinguish himself by flying over the city and the surrounding beaches and taking nosedives above the sea.

"Pourpe is challenging Garros," wrote the *Télégramme*. That was the best compliment one could make an aviator.

"At 5:32 A.M. Marc Pourpe decides to try one last flight. He takes off, goes around in circles above the sea for a bit, and then comes back toward the cliff. He flies past the audience, staying only about 50 meters away from it, kills his engine, and takes a nosedive from the cliff. He passes the audience again, this time getting as close as 30 or 40 meters. People who are not familiar with the mysteries of aviation do not realize that his dive is intentional and fear an accident. When he is about 4 meters away from the ground, Marc Pourpe straightens his plane, starts his engine again, and flies back out to the sea before returning to the beach and landing. The audience applauds his bold performance."

Here is an account published in the *Aéro*, probably the most influential publication on the subject of aviation at the time:

"I already knew what Caudron, Laët, and Darioli were capable of, and I have often admired their performances, but when I first heard the heretofore obscure name of Marc Pourpe, I did not expect him to be the prodigy he proved himself to be when he took off from the cliffs of Boulogne to go fly above the blue sea. I think that this man who was, until now, unknown to the public, will soon be amongst the most famous of our country's aviators."

The third and last day of the event involved landings on neighboring beaches: Wimereux and Ambleteuse. *La France du Nord* chronicled Pourpe's return flight:

"Marc Pourpe comes into sight at the Boulogne beach. He flies 200 meters over the cliff, kills his engine, and, in the style of Garros, takes a nosedive and plunges toward the crowd at incredible speed. The onlookers who gathered on the seawall soon start to panic, although there is nothing to fear because the pilot has perfect control of his plane. After almost touching ground on the beach, he straightens his plane to go circling a liner anchored just off the coast, and then comes back to land."

Again, the young pilot earned a comparison to the illustrious Garros.

After the end of the Boulogne flight demonstrations, Pourpe started thinking about his crossing of the English Channel again. He wanted to do it his own way. People had done it before, at times taking off from the Cap Gris-Nez, and at others leaving from the outskirts of Calais. In other words, everyone always tried to take the shortest possible route.

"I will go from Boulogne to Folkestone and come back by my own means, without the help of a conveyor," Pourpe declared. He wanted to cross the Channel where it was as its widest.

On 27 August 1911 he left Boulogne-sur-Mer at 6:25 A.M. and took with him the first England-bound letter that would ever be shipped by plane. It had been written in Esperanto by the chief engineer of Boulogne's harbor and was addressed to the French consul in Folkestone. The wind made Pourpe's plane drift east, and his compass started malfunctioning, so he found himself unable to correct his course. At 6:55 he flew above Dover, which he identified by its castle. He described a wide circle above the city before landing in a location that seemed convenient to him.

It turned out to be inside the citadel. People took him for a German pilot, and diplomatic relations between Germany and the United Kingdom happened to be tense at that time. A hostile group of soldiers marched toward the pilot. Pourpe, however, was perfectly fluent in English and was quick to explain the situation to an officer whom he showed his pilot license to. The formerly adverse soldiers broke into cheers and helped him store his plane, assigning six men to guard it all night.

The next morning at 5:30 Pourpe took off again and, six minutes later, arrived in Folkestone, where he delivered the letter.

At 9:38 A.M. he left for France. Since he couldn't count on his compass, he used the Folkestone-Boulogne ferry as a point of reference. He gave it a half-hour head start, caught up with it, and then continued toward the Continent. He landed in Boulogne-sur-Mer at 10:10 A.M. after covering a distance of 45 kilometers in thirty-two minutes.

It was the first time someone crossed the Channel both ways at its widest point. Newspapers pointed out the fact that Pourpe had accomplished this feat "for his own enjoyment, with no intention of profiting financially from his endeavor."

At that time, planes participating in flight demonstrations were usually shipped by train. Out of whimsy, defiance, and, truth be told, lack of money, Pourpe, on the contrary, would always get from one location to the next by plane.

He left Boulogne for Roubaix, where he was going to take part in a flight exhibition on August 29. On his way out, he made a point of giving the people of Boulogne a great show above the harbor to thank them for having showed him so much support.

A little bit later, Pourpe noticed that a torsion spring had broken, so he landed near Béthune, in Verquigneul, where he waited for his mechanic. After taking off again, he got lost in the mist. He landed again, this time in the swamp of Arques, near Saint-Omer. During the landing the plane flipped over, and Pourpe injured his face and hands slightly. Still, that incident delayed his arrival in Roubaix by only one day.

A series of mishaps began shortly after. On Thursday, September 7, after giving a flight demonstration at the exposition's airfield and flying over Roubaix, Tourcoing, and the surrounding countryside, Pourpe crash-landed his plane and ruined it. He emerged unharmed from the pile of wood, canvas, and string. Fortunately, the gas that was leaking from the engine did not catch on fire.

"We will work night and day," declared the brave pilot, "to be ready to fly next Sunday. To succeed, I will need discipline, and I will have it."

Indeed, after an accident that could have proven catastrophic, Pourpe's first impulse was to make sure he would not disappoint his audience. Day and night, he would help his mechanic—a man named Paris—fix his plane. They entirely reconstructed the monoplane with material they found on site and without any outside help. It was a tour de force that only a pilot and engineer of Pourpe's caliber could have accomplished.

He was able to start flying again. Over the next month, he became the biggest feature at the Roubaix flight exhibition. One day, he flew over the city and threw loads of half-priced tickets for another event he was organizing to raise funds for the victims of the explosion of the *Liberté* battleship. A bag tore, and a sea of paper plugged the cloche[2] at the base of his control wheel. Holding to the wheel with only one hand, Pourpe leaned over and began an emergency cleanup. A few weeks later, Brindejonc des Moulinais

---

2. The cloche is a bell-shaped dome located at the base of the Blériot control stick. Wind-warping and elevator cables are connected to it, which allow the pilot to manipulate his flying aircraft.

encountered a similar issue but wasn't as quick to react and couldn't avert a fall. He crashed into a house. His plane was damaged, but he got away with only a few scratches.

Pourpe was a real Prince Charming. Everywhere he went, he tried to please the locals with some kind of thoughtful gesture. During the Fêtes de l'Entente Cordiale that took place in Roubaix on 23 September 1911, just as the British delegation was arriving, he flew over the city and released thousands of flyers proclaiming "Long live the Entente Cordiale!," which elicited a unanimous cheerful reaction.

"One cannot hear a single word be uttered," wrote the *Journal de Roubaix* on 24 September 1911.

"Everyone's attention is centered on the great human bird. The pilot arrives in front of the spire of the City Hall and continues his majestic trajectory. The Grande Harmonie starts playing the *Marseillaise* while all the onlookers wave their hands as a show of support. It is a moment of inexpressible emotion for the spectators of this grandiose display. It would be pointless to even attempt to describe the feelings that awoke in people's hearts as everyone experienced the same quiver of patriotism, achieved through Pourpe's evocation of French valor and fearlessness in the presence of our loyal friends."

To thank him for his flights, the authorities insisted on granting Pourpe a silver medal from the city of Roubaix. The mayor, Mr. Eugène Motte, declared: "You can be certain that the people of Roubaix will always keep fond memories of the incredible feats you accomplished during your stay here. You proved yourself to be both a daring and judicious pilot. Hence the name of Marc Pourpe shall remain in our city's annals as a synonym for bravery and courage."

From Roubaix, the champion headed to Châtellerault, where he stayed for a week. There, he famously climbed to an altitude of 2,700 meters. He landed after gliding so gracefully that the crowd—which had followed him to the airfield in defiance of a strict security personnel—carried him in triumph.

At City Hall, a toast was given in Pourpe's honor, and the mayor gave a speech that reflects the dominant state of mind at a time that is so often erroneously said to have been a peaceful and happy one. "Marc Pourpe, a young man whose audacity has no bounds, gave us the most comforting spectacle our nation could hope for.

"Indeed, gentlemen, one shall not forget that beyond the border, we are being watched, and that the skilled demonstration our guest just gave us in his new machine probably gave pause to those who, since 1870, have been taken aback by our recovery and the new superiority we established through our recent great maneuvers.

"Men like Pourpe are few and far between.

"Indeed, to achieve such greatness, one has to have qualities that are found most commonly in our race, and that the German man envies in us, as he is unable to acquire them.

"Did you not shudder when you saw that young man dropping 2,700 meters? Did you not fear that he was going to crash to the ground?

"Yes, you surely did. And, undoubtedly, you went from fearing for his life to rejoicing when you saw how skillfully he landed on the exact same spot he had taken off from."

After this new triumph, Pourpe headed to Saint-Omer, where he exchanged his tired Blériot monoplane for a Tellier with a Chenu engine. He ended up staying awhile in this city where he became famous both thanks to his masterful daily flights and his friendly interactions with the locals.

The Tellier workshops were located in Saint-Omer. They were overseen by Mr. Schreck. Pourpe was the brand's best pilot and thus would test every plane it produced.

On 11 April 1912, he had an accident that could have been considerably more devastating if not for his ability to keep a cool head. He was flying at an altitude of about 60 to 70 meters when his plane suddenly started falling diagonally toward the ground. After a substantial effort, he managed to straighten his plane's course but only for a short time. The Tellier started to fall again and plunged to the ground at full speed.

Seeing that no matter how hard he was trying, he could not regain control of his plane, Pourpe left his seat and spread himself across one of the wings, which absorbed the shock. His presence of mind unquestionably saved his life.

The newspapers soon reported that he had lost an eye and broken his legs in the crash. Pourpe made it a point to reassure his many friends. He wrote me a letter from the hospital. "My accident was considerably less serious than the newspapers implied. In short, I have a dislocated kneecap and a broken ankle. And as for my eye, it is perfectly intact. The left side of my face is slightly scratched, almost as if I got into a fight rather than a plane crash. My right leg is in a cast, and I will have to rest for maybe as long as a month. That is what bothers me most.

"I am not the least resentful toward my plane, and I will start flying again as soon as possible."

As soon as he had recovered, Pourpe started his flight demonstrations again, but he also wanted to complete longer trips. He discarded the Tellier and went back to the Blériot.

On 15 August 1912 he left Etampes in the hope of flying all the way to Berlin. This trip had never been done before, and, in fact, the first person to achieve this performance would be Edmond Audemars—a prewar natural.

Sadly, the weather did not work in Pourpe's favor, although it did not stop him from accomplishing a very impressive deed by making it all the way to Liège despite flying in stormy weather. The storm had started in Saint-Quentin and forced the pilot to make a stop in Breuilly, near Hirson, where he waited for the weather to get better. It finally did the next day, but barely. It was raining, and the wind was blowing, but less violently than the day before. Pourpe decided to leave Breuilly at 5 A.M. He used his compass to try to find his way despite a thick fog. He followed the Meuse valley and at 6:30 A.M. landed in Liège, near the cemetery.

"It was the most difficult part of my flight," he said. "The noise was deafening, but I still managed to maintain course.

"I was planning on flying over Liège without stopping because I do not trust the terrain that surrounds it, as it is generally not convenient to land on, but since I was caught in that storm, I decided to touch ground at the Ans airfield. In fact, I was happy to stop in Liège, where the locals are so welcoming, particularly when it comes to pilots, whom they always keep their doors open to.

"A violent gust of wind forced me to land faster than I would have liked. I touched ground on Robertmont, by the woods of Breux. I was unlucky and, as I was getting tossed around by the wind, I landed on plowed earth, and the front of my plane hit the ground a little abruptly, which resulted in some minor damage.

"During this section of my trip, I traveled at a speed of up to 180 kilometers per hour.

"This excursion was not the most pleasant. I would probably have postponed it if the crowd that came to see me take off in Etampes had been more patient."

Pourpe would have liked to continue on toward Berlin, but the weather continued not to cooperate. It was to be the last European performance of the "young French aviator, a good-looking boy with a smooth face, soft features, and an honest look, and whose gleaming eyes betrayed an implacable will," as he was described by a writer from the Meuse who interviewed him.

Pourpe was to become the great champion of colonial aviation.

NINE

A New Trip to Australia! But This Time...

Ever since he had come back from Australia, all Pourpe could think about was going back to that country where he had suffered so many setbacks. What he really wanted was to complete a well-coordinated plane trip. Such a performance would undoubtedly be lauded in places where people did not often have a chance to see men fly aeroplanes so competently.

Pourpe had learned a lot from his first journey to Australia. He had taken in all the pitfalls to avoid. This time, he knew what to expect.

"Such an expedition," he often told me, "has to be, above all, well constructed. Not only do you need good personnel, like pilots and mechanics, but you also need to bring all kind of supplies to make sure to never find yourself in an impasse because you are missing a paltry bolt, or a rubber hose, or some essential custom-made wooden component."

Pourpe had to wait until mid-July 1912 to start preparing for his trip. Two old friends who had also traveled to Australia and knew how auspicious this time of year was in that part of the world decided to join Pourpe as he resolved to leave as soon as possible and make a stop in the East Indies.

While his two teammates were learning to pilot a plane in Étampes, Pourpe was steadily working on his expedition.

His two friends were very wealthy men from Marseille: Georges and Charles Verminck. Georges was the very friend Pourpe had run into in Marseille on the day he left for Australia.

The three planes were of the Gnome-Blériot brand. The first one was delivered on 4 August 1912. It was intended for Pourpe and was dubbed *La Curieuse*. The boxes were quickly built on the Étampes airfield. They were designed specifically for this kind of trip. Pourpe made sure the boxes could hold both the planes and all the necessary spare parts.

Little by little, all four boxes were filled. The fourth one was made into a workshop, with a fold-up workbench, tool shelves, etc. Our adventurers had everything their hearts could wish for. A tent big enough to cover three monoplanes was set up near the boxes.

In the end, here is a nonexhaustive list of items that left Étampes for distant lands on October 24: three airplanes (as well as enough wood to make at least five more), a fourth Gnome engine, a great number of spare parts, wheels, tires, enamel, linen (to fix the wings), bolts, sheet metal, steel, aluminum, tubes, tools, and 2,500 kilos of castor oil.

This cargo took off from Antwerp and was to be picked up in Colombo, Ceylon. The team that would be responsible for it comprised three pilots (Pourpe, Georges Verminck, and his brother Charles Verminck), as well as a secretary by the name of Maurice Gleiser and a mechanic called Sébastiani. They were supposed to be joined by an extra mechanic in Colombo and, in Calcutta, by a coolie who would be responsible for putting together the tent. Georges Verminck and Pourpe boarded the *Orontes*. For personal reasons Charles Verminck was going to join them later.

They met their first difficulties in Colombo when they had to deal with police and government authorities to obtain the necessary permits to hold their flight demonstrations.

The previous year, a German pilot by the name of Oster greatly disappointed his audience when he failed to fly his Taube on the day he was scheduled to do so, although he pocketed the proceeds from the ticket sales. After that, he made more attempts that were equally unsuccessful and made a deal with another pilot by the name of Brown, who had come over with a Blériot but was only planning on "showing it around" and had no actual intention to fly it.

Oster had actually tried to fly, which resulted in him crashing, breaking his shoulder and leaving a pile of debris on the airfield; the Blériot had met a bitter end before it even had gotten a chance to start. That is how the people of Colombo got introduced to aviation.

Consequently, could one really blame the local authorities for their intransigence?

That accident, which could have had very serious consequences for the audience, compelled them to submit the Frenchmen to very strict rules. Pourpe and Verminck were asked to perform a trial flight in private, comply with every demand from the police, pay a 1,500-rupee (2,250 franc) deposit in spite of the fact that they were already insured, and not leave the airfield, as not to endanger anyone.

Pourpe and Verminck wanted above all to be able to hold their flight demonstrations, so as to prove that they could be trusted and that they were not like Oster. They agreed to those severe terms, and on 7 December 1912 they were allowed to perform in front of a bevy of local public figures. Sir McCallum, the governor, did not attend but sent his aide-de-camp, the captain Theobald. Also present were the general Sir Ian Hamilton, the colonial secretary L. W. Booth, the mayor of Colombo, K. W. B. McLeod, members of the press, and some attractive socialites.

Pourpe and Verminck—who had quickly become an accomplished pilot—both completed ten-minute flights at an altitude of about 200 meters and ended their performances by gliding down to land exactly on top of two small markers that had been outlined on the ground with whitewash. The audience was a good one and cheered for the pilots. As for the authorities, they had to admit that these two Frenchmen were skilled, and agreed to relax their restrictions on how far away from the airfield they would be allowed to fly.

The airfield was also used as a racetrack and was spacious enough for planes to take off and land, but its surroundings were very dangerous because of the abundance of coconut palms and the marshy quality of the terrain.

The press was enthusiastic, as evidenced by the glowing reviews they published.

Now was the perfect time to announce their next flight demonstration. When it took place, it drew a large crowd of Europeans (the locals settled for watching the event from outside the venue). Both pilots completed two flights each: the first lasted about fifteen minutes, and the second twenty minutes. They performed stunts for their audience—spirals, glides, etc. It was a terrific success.

The local police department had deployed 380 men to help with road congestion, on the pilots' dime, of course!

The next day, they put on another show. After the success they had met the day before, Pourpe and Verminck expected an even bigger crowd. Quite to the contrary. The public showed little interest. Only five hundred people were sitting in the bleachers and about a thousand in the cheaper section. What a disappointment! Hence, it was decided that there would be only one flight. As per Pourpe's old habit, the pilots flipped a coin to decide who would perform it. Pourpe won.

La Curieus was pulled from its tent and, almost immediately, the pilot took off, quickly climbing to 300 meters. He did a few stunts above the airfield and then decided to go fly over the city, which was located about 5 kilometers away. He headed toward the harbor and in a wink was giving the people of Colombo an aerial show. For a moment, everything came to a standstill in the city. Everyone froze and raised their eyes to the sky so as not to miss even a second of the remarkable—and free!—show they were given.

The pilot made it to the harbor, described a circle above it, and then turned left, back toward the water and the airfield. He was being pushed by a strong backwind and made the return trip very quickly. He landed right in the center of the circle that had been drawn in the middle of the field.

The audience cheered enthusiastically for Pourpe, but one person who wasn't thrilled was Mr. Dowbiggin, the chief of police. He came up to Pourpe looking angry. Taken aback by such an icy welcome, Pourpe asked what was wrong.

"You broke your promise by flying over Colombo," said the chief of police. "That is a very serious offense. We shall keep your 1,500-rupee deposit, and I forbid you to fly in Colombo again."

The Frenchman protested loudly. "What did I do wrong? Yes, I did fly over the harbor and the fort. In France, pilots are not forced to stick to such a tiny area, one that is, to top it off, surrounded by trees. If you want us dead, just say so. Let me tell you that Paris has fortifications too and that our chief of police never harassed any of your fellow countrymen for flying above them."

Meanwhile, the audience was hoping to see another flight demonstration and openly showed its discontent when it got wind of the chief of police's ban.

In the end, Pourpe got tired of arguing and left the airfield with Verminck. They headed to the Princess Club to have tea with some friends. They were discussing the incident when a policeman sent by the chief of police came to fetch Pourpe.

Pourpe immediately complied and was joined by Verminck and a friend, a British army captain named Valentin Webster.

The chief of police was going to conduct a search in the tent where the planes were kept. He asked the pilots to follow. Captain Webster insisted on joining them to serve as a witness. However, the chief of police was becoming increasingly rude and rebuffed him. He went as far as to assign four men to prevent this officer—who also happened to be one of Ceylon's wealthiest plantation owners—from behaving like the gentleman he was.

By the tent's entrance, Pourpe spotted a civilian and asked him what he was doing there.

"I am an artillery officer and was sent here by my superiors to inspect your planes."

"Nothing proves to me that you are an officer," answered Pourpe. "In France, officers wear a uniform when they are on duty."

After a heated discussion during which he tried to force this newcomer to prove his identity, Pourpe gave up. He and Verminck even joined the policemen in the tent and helped them carry out their task, although Pourpe did so while maintaining his signature dignified brand of insolence. He had a knack for making people look foolish without ever coming off as rude.

The "henchmen" were starting to regret their venture. They were feeling deflated. They searched the tent carefully but, of course, could not find anything incriminating. In the end, they triumphantly seized two cameras, probably in the hope that they would be able to expose the two Frenchmen as spies.

They had even mentioned searching Pourpe himself, but he firmly resisted such an invasion of privacy and made sure to let them know exactly how he felt about their lack of manners. They did not dare insist and resolved to take the pilot at his word. They were likely starting to fear that they would trigger a diplomatic incident if they were too insistent.

The authorities developed the film inside the cameras. All they got were photos of the planes, the boxes they had been packed into, and a garden party that had been thrown by Mrs. Webster. The chief of police became the laughingstock of Colombo.

On the night after the search, Pourpe received a letter from the artillery officer he had had a run-in with. He apologized for what he had done when following orders, and extended his sympathy to Pourpe. He added that the incident would not have any consequences and that the planes and the cameras would be returned the next day. He kept his promise.

Still, the press picked up the story. Long articles that were very critical of the chief of police and supportive of the Frenchmen were published. Concern was expressed regarding what diplomatic consequences such treatment of the pilots could have.

The next morning, Pourpe, Verminck, and a lawyer named Van den Straten headed to the office of the colonial secretary, who greeted them warmly and, being a sports person himself, did not make a secret of how much he admired Pourpe and made a point of extending him his respect as a government official. After a friendly conversation, he promised Pourpe that he would get the 1,500 rupees back and that he and Verminck would be allowed to fly again.

The only restriction the pilots had to agree to was not to fly over the battery. Indeed, concerns for its safety were at the root of the recent strife between the pilots and the local authorities.

"Mr. Secretary," said Pourpe, "all these troubles could have easily been prevented if the chief of police had told me about this restriction from the beginning instead of telling me that the drastic security measures he put in place were meant solely to protect the audience."

This episode did a lot for the pilots' popularity and was great publicity for them in the East Indies. The flight demonstrations that followed drew impressive crowds.

The *Times* of Ceylon said it would award a silver cup to the first pilot that would reach an altitude of 1,000 feet (300 meters). The two friends decided that Verminck would be the one to pursue that prize. He easily won it during a flight to Mount Lavinia.

The sportsmen who witnessed the performances of those two pilots—who were both equally humble and well mannered—were impressed by how quickly they would get ready to fly, how easily they would take off, and how gracefully they would land. Even when the tropical heat became barely tolerable and the wind reached a speed of 10 to 12 meters per second, as long as the public had come out to see them, Pourpe and Verminck would fly. Never was there anything cocksure about their performances. Never did their words betray any arrogance.

Still, flight demonstrations were not easy in such a place. Here is something Pourpe wrote in his notebook regarding the difficulties posed by the quality of the terrain there:

"I do not think that it will ever be convenient to use aeroplanes in Colombo. The island is too forested and, what's even worse, very mountainous, especially in the center. Seaplanes would be more effective to guard the coast in case of an insurrection, but the English do not seem to trust these machines.

"The warm climate hasn't stopped us from flying, and the notoriously dangerous air pockets we were warned about so often did not turn out to be an issue. But will flying be as easy year-round?

"In any case, when flying our birds, we have been able to enjoy the most-beautiful views one could ever dream of. We will keep wonderful memories of our flights in Colombo, which were our first ones in the tropics.

"How sweet it is to feel like a bird, even when the local police and government keep antagonizing you."

After that, Pourpe and Verminck decided to head directly from Colombo to Calcutta in order to take part in the city's Christmas and New Year celebrations, which were known to draw big crowds. Many races and competitions were to be held during that time, and the Anglo-Indians, who were big gamblers, would probably be very interested in watching the two pilots' impressive performances.

"On December 18 we boarded the Messageries Maritime's ship *Dupleix* with all of our equipment. Our boxes were stored on the second-class section's deck, so that the poor second-class passengers had to sacrifice their comfort for the sake of aviation and make do with just a few meters in the back.

"We made a stop in Pondicherry, and I left the ship to see if I could find a landing spot for a later date, but, to my disappointment, it turned out that the city is completely surrounded with coconut palms, which would make flying in the area virtually impossible.

"When we arrived in Calcutta two days later, we had the hardest time finding a place to stay. We had to settle for probably the foulest rooms in all of the Grand Hotel. The city's population had grown threefold for the festivities.

"Our accommodations weren't comfortable by any stretch of the imagination, but how heartened we were by the turnout!

"The only place where we could fly was the racetracks near Fort Williams, a huge space that could hold the entirety of Calcutta's European population in case of a riot or a revolt of the indigenous.

"The racetracks are owned by an organization called the Turf Club, which is helmed by a secretary by the name of Hutchinson, a Scottish man who has been embittered by twenty years spent in the colonies. He made us jump over a number of hurdles before allowing us to use the space. He claimed that the last time they hosted a flight demonstration, the crowd swarmed over the turf and damaged it greatly.

"The name of Jullerot was mentioned. Apparently, the pilot had made the audience wait three hours because of bad weather. In the end, people got so impatient that they broke the fences and trampled the field.

"Finally, after long negotiations with the Stewards, and thanks to the support of Sir Apcar, we were allowed to use the coveted racetracks. On the same day we got the go-ahead from the people in charge, our boxes were taken to the tracks, our tent was installed, and the two planes, *La Curieuse* and *Rajah*, were assembled.

"We also had to gain permission to fly from the military authorities. The general, Brian Mahon, also a Scotsman, had no objection to us doing so. He even allowed us to fly over the city's fortifications. Sir Frederick Halliday, the chief of police, gave us full freedom of movement and promised to help us on the day of the event. How differently we were treated than when we went to Colombo!

"Nothing was left to chance. For five days newspapers published full-page advertisements, flyers written in the indigenous language were distributed in low-income neighborhoods, posters by Poulbot were put up all over town, and men wearing sandwich boards were sent to walk up and down the streets. In short, we launched quite a sweeping ad campaign.

"We had a screen made of palm leaves built around the tent and the boxes and allowed the public to come see the planes for the price of one rupee (1.70 francs).

"On Sunday, January 6, at 9:00 in the morning, the police started herding the people who had gathered outside the racetracks. At 10:30 A.M. the European troops arrived—850 Scotsmen from the Black Watch who were stationed at Fort Williams. They were followed by two flying camp battalions of indigenous soldiers totaling about 1,000 men, an artillery contingent, military engineers, and 140 horsemen from the Jacob's Horse. They were the most magnificent riders we had ever seen and were coming straight from Tibet.

Marc Pourpe standing before La Curieuse, *his Gnome-powered Blériot monoplane, following his flight above the Calcutta, India, racetrack on 6 January 1913.*

"Counting the police forces, we had a total of 2,700 men to protect us.

"General Bryan Mahon had made the trip to see the event in person and brought the governor: Sir Carmichael. Those two men were the ones who provided the necessary troops to maintain order.

"As was announced, the first flight started at exactly 3 P.M. I dashed through the air above the racetracks on *La Curieuse*, making the occasional turn left or right. Verminck followed me closely. We ended this first demonstration by performing several glides.

"When we landed, we were genially congratulated by the authorities while cheers erupted from the crowd, which could barely be contained by the security personnel.

"Next, Verminck took off. As we had planned, he circled the field a few times and then headed toward the city. A few seconds later, I took off after him and followed him, first above Calcutta, then the Hooghly district, and later the Ganges River, on which hundreds of large ships were resting idly.

"Watching Verminck flying his big white bird from the seat of my *Curieuse* was both intriguing and awe inspiring, especially as we were hovering above a city that was teeming with indigenous people of all races. The sun shone on us, and the sky was a beautiful blue hue.

"Soon, I saw Verminck take a left turn after having passed the Howrah reservoirs. Following his lead, I veered a little to the left as well. I was planning on getting close to him and waving at him, but when he saw me approaching, he moved away to maintain a distance between us. *Rajah* is quite shy whereas *La Curieuse* is a beautiful flirt. Maybe he's right to be cautious.

"Our first day in Calcutta ended on an enthusiastic note, which surprised me coming from the English. We received loads of compliments and shook many hands. In the end, Frederick Halliday had to intervene to rescue us from the crowd's exuberant show of devotion.

"Still, we did not make a huge profit. We didn't even recoup our considerable costs even though the event was otherwise a complete success.

"We immediately decided to organize another demonstration, on the cheap this time. After this first success, we had to try to convince the public to pay to see us despite the fact that we had no real way of shielding our performance from outside spectators.

"On Wednesday, January 9, at 3 P.M., Verminck took off. His performance was remarkably bold and skillful. His turns demonstrated how confident a pilot he was. He brought to mind those elite riders at dressage shows. Around me, I could hear people gasp in surprise. Never had they imagined that a man could be so in control of his winged horse and of the natural elements. Georges's graceful performance was met with the tremendous success it deserved.

"Twenty minutes later, I took off as well. I mostly flew over the Hindus. I made them nervous by diving toward them and then straightening my plane barely 1 meter above their heads a few times, but after a while they realized I was just having fun and they relaxed. I ended my first flight by landing right in front of the tent.

"Later, I flew over an open-air charity event. From my plane, I was able to see the people who were milling about various booths raise their eyes to look at me. I headed back to the racetracks and was, again, warmly greeted by the crowd.

"Thus ended our second flight exhibition in India. We demonstrated what our country's industry could accomplish, and we did so without running into any difficulties. Hence, although it had not allowed us to make any money, our endeavor wasn't for naught. That was enough to make us happy.

"We decided that I would leave for our next destination—Rangoon or Singapore—first to prepare our next event and not waste any time like we did in the previous cities we had visited.

"So I headed for Rangoon on the British India shipping lines' *Angora*. Three days later, I was in Burma's capital."

During that trip, on 11 January 1913, Pourpe wrote me the following letter:

"I left Calcutta this morning. I'm trying to get us a good head start in Rangoon by making all the necessary arrangements before Georges arrives with all the equipment. We were very successful in Calcutta. On the first day, we had over 150,000 spectators (although most of them were Black, of course). We had 2,000 Scotsmen (Wearing those little skirts! Can you believe that, old friend?), 200 indigenous horsemen, and 500 policemen to contain the crowd. I heard that even the King of England's visit didn't generate as much excitement. There were zero incidents. We performed two flights each. During our second one, we both flew over Calcutta. The roofs were covered in Negroes. We followed the Hooghly to Howrah, halfway to Chandannagar. I couldn't even start to describe the locals' enthusiasm.

"From a financial point of view, we're not doing great: we can't find airfields that are fenced off. So people just come in and pay whenever they feel like it.

"Lipton Tea offered us a 1,000-rupee (1,700 franc) cash prize to fly over its building. I won that prize. That is the only incentive we received since we never stay long anywhere.

"Our second flight demonstration was very successful too. Georges is becoming great. What surprises people the most is the fact that we never make any trial flights. As soon as the planes are pulled from their boxes, we're ready to perform. De Caters came here two and a half years ago, but almost every time people made the trip to see him fly he would flake. Jullerot came here last year but did not do much with his Bristol plane. We had people requesting to buy planes and asking to be taught how to fly.

"You know what, old pal? Nobody has ever flown in Rangoon, where I'm headed. I hope it's going to work out for us. Next, I'll head to Singapore, Saigon, and Shanghai.

"We are all in good health and, except for our mediocre financial situation, we are pretty satisfied. We're having fun."

In Rangoon, Pourpe received a very warm welcome both from the local personalities and the press. However, as soon as he mentioned business the room got cold. Everybody told the Frenchman to move on because Rangoon was too poor, and its few wealthy citizens would likely not care to support any endeavor that was unrelated to the cultivation of rubber and coconut trees.

Besides, there wasn't any field big enough to host a flight exhibition, and there wasn't any fencing. Any attempt to organize a flight demonstration would surely be a financial disaster.

So Pourpe decided to send a telegram to Verminck, who was still in Calcutta, to tell him to meet him in Singapore.

He left Rangoon after merely two days and headed to Singapore via Penang.

During his short stop in Penang he realized that there wasn't any chance he could organize a flight demonstration there either. Flying would have been very difficult. As in every English country, there were airfields, but they were poorly maintained, not well enclosed, and surrounded by hills people could very easily go perch on to enjoy the air show for free.

"Penang is located in a jungle. It's covered in coconut and other palm trees," wrote Pourpe.

"There are no flat areas. I wonder if we would ever be seen alive again if we crash-landed in this thicket.

"I wasn't very enthusiastic when I first arrived in Singapore. The layout of the city did not seem very favorable, and on top of that, I had already been made weary by some things I had been told. Apparently, an American pilot had come here about two weeks ago with a Curtiss hydroaeroplane. He raised 12,000 francs but never took off because of a broken float. The audience complained but was not reimbursed.

"Two years ago, Christiaens came over with a Bristol and made some good money, but his performances were pretty basic: he would fly in a straight line for about 300 meters and then land neatly. The audience wasn't impressed. At the very least, people would have liked to see him circle the field a few times.

"Christiaens claimed that his plane could not fly any higher because the air wasn't carrying well. I think that the coconut palms around the field had something to do with his tame performance.

"Yet, in spite of an overall lack of enthusiasm, I insisted on starting the necessary administrative procedures for our demonstration. I headed to the Sporting Club, which had sponsored Hotwatter, the American pilot, and Christiaens. I have to admit that I did not receive a warm welcome—they kicked me out. No matter, I went back the next day and acted so indignant that the club's secretary, Mr. Owen, agreed to see me.

"I chatted with him for a bit and told him that we needed his racetracks. At first, he refused, but after he took a look at the newspaper clippings I brought, he agreed to deliberate with the club's administrators. In the end, he agreed to let me use the tracks on one condition: before we would be allowed to sell admission tickets, we would have to perform a trial flight in front of some members of the Sporting Club.

"I agreed to those terms, although I told them I would have to talk to Georges and asked to be given 12,000 francs after we performed a successful flight.

"Georges's arrival, with all of our equipment, made quite the impression. The press wrote that we seemed absolutely trustworthy. Finally, we decided to complete our trial flight. We had only one of the planes, *Rajah*, and the tent taken to the racetracks.

"It was no easy task. The ground was soaked from the torrential rain that had been falling for the last ten days. Our truck's wheels would sink so far in the ground that we could not even drive a whole kilometer in a day.

"On Tuesday, February 3, at 6:00 in the morning, an audience that had been summoned specially for the event and was made up of members of the government, military personnel, people working for the consulate, and members of the press was gathered at the racetracks.

"*Rajah* was pulled from the tent and taken to the point it would take off from. A random draw had decided that Verminck would be flying first. My friend sat down in his plane and took off, to the audience's great surprise: people had expected longer preparations.

"The plane gained altitude, circled the field several times, and suddenly left the racetracks area to go fly over the indigenous city and a section of the harbor—which we had been allowed to do! After fifteen minutes, we saw a black spot steadily growing bigger on the horizon. Georges was back above our heads. He seemed to be enjoying himself in his bird. He took a few turns during which he tilted his plane in a way that made the audience shiver. He landed to a thunderous applause.

"When my turn came, I circled the field a few times as well in order to get used to the plane again. I landed fifteen minutes later. The audience was delighted."

The next day Verminck left for Saigon on the ship *Paul Lecat* while Pourpe stayed in Singapore to give more flight demonstrations at the insistence of the local personalities and the people of the city. For his own enjoyment, and to prove that he wasn't solely motivated by money, he completed an extra flight on the day of his planned demonstration. He went all the way to Johore, stayed in the air for thirty-eight minutes, and reached an altitude of 500 meters.

That aerial performance was a tremendous success. Not only were the locals excited by the performance itself, there was also an element of pride involved. Previous pilots had claimed that it was impossible to fly in Singapore. In those times, everybody always believed pilots. Aviation was still a mysterious discipline. After what had happened with the American Hotwatter and the Belgian Christiaens, people were convinced that Singapore was cursed for pilots! Verminck first and then Pourpe had masterfully disproved this assumption. Thus, not only did people think of them as virtuosos but also as saviors.

TEN

A Wonderful Crusade in Indochina

Pourpe went to join his friend Verminck in Saigon. With him, he took a young assistant whom he had hired in Calcutta, who became his traveling companion on many adventures.

The assistant went by Raoul Lafberg, though, in fact, that was not his real name. His actual name was Lufbery, and he was American. But let's leave it at that for now. We will come back to him as his role, which seems modest for the moment, becomes central to our story.

Pourpe and Verminck's arrival in Saigon was triumphant. The only pilot that had ever given a real performance in that immense colony so far was Lieutenant de Laborde, who completed two flights taking off from Saigon, one to Bien Hoa and one to Thu Dau Mot. After that, he broke his plane. His flights hadn't happened in front of an audience, so the locals had not been given the chance to acquaint themselves to the mysteries of aviation. Later, the famous Belgian ex-cyclist Van den Born and the Russian Kouzminski gave a few demonstrations as well.

Hence, Pourpe and Verminck were considered to be the real pioneers of aviation in Indochina because they were planning to go on excursions across the entire country.

Right after they arrived they carefully studied maps, contacted the local authorities. and told themselves: "We will start with a flight from Saigon to Phnom Penh. Then, we'll go from Saigon to Cap Saint-Jacques without making any stops, and fly back." Such an explicit plan was a big departure from the previous flight demonstrations that had been given in our colony!

The pilots settled near the racetracks. As soon as their planes were ready, Pourpe and Verminck showed off their skills by flying over the surroundings for a half hour despite strong winds.

On Sunday, 16 February 1913, Pourpe and Verminck surprised people by landing at the tracks during a race. They were welcomed with frenzied cheers from all sides while the orchestra played *La Marseillaise* in their honor. The pilots went up to the official gallery, where Mr. Gourbeil, the governor of Cochinchina, congratulated not only the two Frenchmen but also their passenger—a three-month-old tiger Verminck was carrying under his arm.

Their demonstration had been as elegant as can be. Our pilots, serving as ambassadors of French aviation, won over the colony through their dexterity, their selflessness, and their refinement. As the press wrote: "They caused our national prestige to shine brighter."

The next day, Pourpe wrote me the following letter: "We will stay in Saigon for at least a month. We are happy to have reached a French country after visiting so many English ones. On Sunday, we landed at the tracks during a race. Our performance was a roaring success. We are receiving offers for longer trips, including one from Saigon to Phnom Penh through My Tho. That's 280 kilometers. We don't know who will do it yet. Géo or me? We'll let chance decide. There's also the Cap Saint-Jacques trip, which is 120 kilometers. We are hoping to raise 10,000 francs. Fingers crossed!

"We work a lot. We take care of all the planning, which is quite demanding. Georges is starting to get the hang of it and is helping me a lot, but I'm tired. I would like to succeed at this and be done with it.

"You will have to take care of us when we're in France again. When I come back, I will seriously have to settle down. I have wanted to accomplish a lot, but I have had no luck. I don't even know how I managed to accomplish the little I did. Anyway . . . It'll get better!

"My old friend, I'm feeling a little blue, and I don't know how to react. This letter is stupid; you have to forgive me. If I'm feeling more cheerful tomorrow, I'll send you some colorful descriptions of the local mores.

"Mr. Garros Senior has been very friendly and is a great help when it comes to dealing with the local authorities."

Indeed, the father of the immortal Roland Garros[1] was a lawyer in Indochina. He took the young pilots under his wing and tried to make sure that they would be compensated fairly.

He even wrote a column in the Saigon newspaper *L'Opinion* after Pourpe took off for his trip from Saigon to Cap Saint-Jacques on 20 February 1913:

"Today, at daybreak, as the world was still covered in an opalescent morning dew and as a large audience cheered on, Pourpe swiftly took off on his Blériot with the intent of flying from Saigon to the bay of Cap Saint-Jacques. Soon, he came back and landed gracefully at our airdrome, where he was congratulated by the authorities of Cochinchina and by the same audience that had applauded him two hours earlier.

"This excursion truly constitutes a remarkable athletic achievement, less because of the distance the pilot had to cover and more because of the very limited number of spots one can land a plane on in that area.

"After Pourpe's success, the next performance shall come from his friend Verminck, who will attempt to fly from Saigon to Phnom Penh. This trip will be not only longer but also more treacherous because Verminck will have to fly through some dangerous areas above our mighty rivers.

"Will our Cochinchina, which is known for its exquisite and sumptuous sense of hospitality, elect to let those two gentle and bold young Frenchmen whose character radiates heroic valor generously perform deeply engaging flight demonstrations for the benefit of both our European and Indigenous population without offering them anything in return? With Georges Verminck and Marc Pourpe, Cochinchina gained two authentic champions of aviation: an eminently French science. That is, for this country, a great fortune. Our two young heroes, whose

---

1. Roland Garros was a prewar exhibition pilot who set early aircraft and distance records. On 2 August 1914 he was assigned to Escadrille M.S. 23 with Marc Pourpe. On 18 April 1915 his plane was shot down over German territory, and he was made a prisoner of war. On 14 February 1918 he escaped captivity and eventually returned to the battlefront. He was killed in aerial combat while flying with Escadrille SPA 26 on 5 October 1918. France's Roland Garros tennis stadium was named in his honor in 1928. The stadium serves as the site for the French Open tennis tournament.

Raoul Lufbery, 28, standing before La Curieuse *at the Saigon Racetrack, 20 February 1913*

athletic notoriety had already crossed the seas of Europe long ago, did not want their glorious series of awe-inspiring excursions throughout the cities and the towering peaks of ancient Asia to end without them making a stop in the sunny capital of our Indochina. Paying us such a visit is not only a lovely gesture, it is an excellent one when you think—one has to risk a guess because they will not tell you anything on the subject—of the financial burden their generous fancy must have imposed on their expedition's already considerable budget. As someone who knows firsthand how costly such endeavors can be, I will venture to say that our young friends' monthly expenses cannot be far from thirty thousand francs. Thirty thousand francs a month until the French birds regain their first home, the nest they were born in: when they return to Issy-les-Moulineaux, or maybe another place in France! The people who enjoy those demonstrations of French aeronautics and who are comforted and given a self-confidence boost by them when our race is facing such a perilous future generally do not realize what costs touring pilots face. For Géo Verminck and Marc Pourpe, those expenses are multiplied by two!

"Are we going to let them carry that burden on their own?

"Will we let their enthusiasm nurture our souls for a whole week without compensating—I do not think that the word 'paying' really applies in this case—our young virtuosos for the sacrifices that they are making through such a patriotic—and French—gesture?

"Are we planning on continuing to benefit from the generosity that comes to them so naturally but which we should feel ashamed to encourage?

"We know that our honorable governor, Mr. Gourbeil, is ready to make a reasonable contribution, although that would apparently require the approval of the governor-general. A telegram was sent to ask for it.

"We are waiting impatiently for a response....

"Why don't the Aéro-Club (since there is one in Cochinchina), the municipality, the Comité d'Initiative of Southern Indochina, the Cercle Sportif, and any other potentially interested parties unite to petition the local government?

"And what shall we do with the eight thousand dollars that were raised to purchase an aeroplane either for Indochina or France, although neither the military nor the civil authorities seem to actually be interested in it? Could we not use part or all of that money to help Mr. Verminck and Pourpe recoup their costs? We would simply have to give notice to the citizens who contributed to that sum and, in the unlikely case any of them complained about having their money used for that purpose, reimburse them.

"The people who helped raise that money are asking the same questions. Far from opposing the solution we are offering, they are—how could they not be?—ready to support it unconditionally.

"As a conclusion, it is our duty to help fund the greatness of these sons of France who are coming to us already having acquired a glorious reputation. We should show them our admiration and gratitude without reservation. Alas! When you waste an opportunity to reward the courage of a pilot—what a hard and perilous profession!—you put yourself at risk of being able to do it only when it is too late . . . after the inevitable event which leaves only bleeding flesh and defeated heroism.

"Let's celebrate those children now that they are close to us; let's open our arms to them and cover them in flowers devoutly and fervently, because those children are heroes, pure and simple!"

La Curieuse *inside the Saigon Aerodrome hangar on 20 February 1913 surrounded by Saigon's public figures, including the governor of Cochina and French admiral Henri Colloc'h de Kerillis*

This beautiful homage by the father of the man who is one of the most perfect heroes of not only France but humanity proves what enthusiasm followed the trip from Saigon to Cap Saint-Jacques and back: the first aerial excursion by one of our two audacious pilots in Indochina.

Pourpe and Verminck had decided that they would not charge people to see the former take off for that trip and then land back in Saigon. At 6:49 A.M., in front of a huge crowd and all the major personalities of Saigon, Pourpe took off. He circled the field twice before heading east. He arrived in Cap Saint-Jacques at 7:52, flew around the lighthouse hill, and headed back for Saigon.

It was the first time a plane flew over Cap Saint-Jacques, so Pourpe made quite an impression on the natives, who wondered what this otherworldly machine was.

At 8:25 Pourpe landed in front of the airdrome's hangar and was congratulated by all of Saigon's public figures, including the governor of Cochinchina and Admiral Henri Calloc'h de Kérillis, who was the commander in chief of the Far East squadron.

Pourpe completed the 160-kilometer trip despite violent winds and did not land at Cap Saint-Jacques for fear of not having enough gas to fly back.

During his flight, Pourpe had suddenly realized that his engine's rpm, which should have been around 1,200, had abruptly dropped to zero. For a second, he thought he was going to have to make a sea landing, but his engine was still going. It had been, fortunately, a false alert. The engine was fine; the culprit was the rpm indicator.

The press of Cochinchina was enthusiastic and showed its admiration for the grit and class of the two young men who "offered tremendous shows for free, as opposed to previous foreign aviators."

On February 28, Georges Verminck took off for his trip from Saigon to Phnom Penh through My Tho, a 380-kilometer trek! He had to make a stop in Tan Chau because he was out of gas, but then he went on and became the first pilot to ever fly to Cambodia!

In Phnom Penh, Verminck joined Pourpe, who was giving flight demonstrations there and getting ready to undertake their next long trip. On March 4, he flew from Phnom Penh to Banam Prey Veng in one hour and forty minutes. His Majesty Sisowath of Cambodia had given him a message to pass on to the people living in the provinces of Prey Veng and Soai Rieng.

To thank him, Sisowath granted him the Royal Order of Cambodia, which meant that Pourpe could now request protection from the guard of honor at any time, in any Cambodian city. He never used the privilege!

Here is the content of the message—written in Cambodian—that was transmitted via airmail:

"Royal message from HM Preah Bat Samdech Preah Sisowath Chamchakrapong Hariréach Barminthor Phouvanay Kraykéofa Soulalay Preah Chau Krong Kampuchea Thippadey, King of Cambodia, to all the Kromokars and the people of the Prey Veng district.

"We are very happy to announce the arrival, through the air, of the French aviator Marc Pourpe. This magnificent performance allows the entire world to witness the power of French innovation. Hence, we feel it more and more necessary to state how proud we are to be under France's generous and efficient protection.

"I am also very happy to be the first ruler of Cambodia to be able to send such a message by plane. I would like to tell you how pleased I am about this year's good harvest from our paddy fields. I urge you to sustain and even double your efforts when working your land in order to increase your well-being and guarantee our country's prosperous future. By doing this, you will demonstrate that your patriotism is genuine and show your gratitude to both the great government that protects us and provides us with more and more benefits and your king, who, together with the résident supérieur, loves and supports all good people.

"Signed: Sisowath, at the Royal Palace, on the 9th day of the waning moon of the 3rd month Meacthom of the year Rat Chut Chatavasrak of the 1274 Cholasakrach era, which corresponds to March 2, 1913, of the Christian era."

This message was delivered to the Résident of Prey Veng, who read it to an exhilarated crowd and congratulated Pourpe on behalf of Sisowath and the résident supérieur.

The résident added that this event "impressed the people in a way that undoubtedly helped increase France's prestige. More people keep flocking into town to see tonight's flight demonstration, which will surely generate even more enthusiasm."

Here is a telegram that Pourpe sent to the Résident of Prey Veng:

"Am very happy and proud to have fulfilled the mission His Majesty honored me with. The content of the royal message which fell from the sky greatly impressed the natives. I would like to personally thank you for your kindness. I will never forget how graciously you welcomed me and how attentive you were. Please also extend my gratitude to Mrs. Outrey and assure her of my deepest respect."

After enchanting Europeans and natives alike with another flight demonstration, Pourpe took off from Prey Veng on March 4 at 6:33 A.M., flew over Ba Nam at 6:50, and landed in Soai Rieng at 7:34. He had accomplished a very difficult trip. He gave a demonstration in Soai Rieng before heading back to Saigon exactly on time, on March 5, at 6:45 A.M. He followed the Vaïco to reach Tan An, where he was forced to land because of the fog. He took off again shortly after and reached Saigon at 9:15 A.M.

That is how Pourpe and Verminck flew from Saigon to Phnom Penh and back, thus managing to do something that had been considered impossible so far. The people living in the provinces of Prey Veng and Soai Rieng got to see flight demonstrations, something they had never dreamt of. Cambodians were amazed by what they perceived as a testament to French prowess.

Pourpe described in his own words the trip from Phnom Penh to Saigon: "On Monday afternoon, I gave a flight demonstration in the presence of HM Sisowath, King of Cambodia, Mr. Outrey, the résident supérieur, the entirety of Phnom Penh's administrative staff, and a crowd of 30,000 natives, who came from all corners of the kingdom because they had been so impressed by Verminck's amazing performance.

"During that event, I flew several times over the king's palace: the Silver Pagoda, the Four Arms. The king did not hold back when it came to congratulate me. He and his entourage were very enthusiastic. He insisted on granting me the Royal Order of Cambodia in person. Mr. Outrey was as emotional as me and embraced me. It was decided that I would leave for Saigon (with stops in Prey Veng and Soai Reng) the next morning at six, so a mechanic took a look at La Curieuse and filled the gas tank.

"The next morning, at dawn, a huge crowd that included Mr. Outrey and all of the Europeans of Phnom Penh gathered at the racetracks. His Majesty, surrounded by his entourage, was at the Four Arms on *the Comet,* his royal yacht, waiting to see me fly by. After one last farewell, I climbed in *La Curieuse*. At 6:30 A.M., I took off, circled the field, and headed to the Four Arms. The sun was starting to rise. A light mist was covering Phortzon. I started following the Mekong, which looked like a giant silver ribbon. I sighted a few black spots on it, which must have been junks and sampans. I flew over a few islands and soon caught sight of the Banam church. I started to get a little worried about getting lost, so I decided to fly at a lower altitude (about 150 meters) and headed toward Prey Veng.

"In the distance, I spotted the five fires I had asked people to start in order to demarcate the makeshift landing strip that had been arranged for me. Soon, I could clearly see the two whitewashed lines that showed exactly where I should land. I stopped the engine and, a few seconds later, I was surrounded by all of the Europeans of Prey Veng (including a few French people) and a crowd of natives. It was 7:29. Mr. Bellan, the Résident of Prey Veng, welcomed me warmly. He introduced me to the local authorities. We immediately headed to a makeshift platform. Along the path that led to it were maybe fifty Cambodian dancers who were moving to the rhythm of flutes and tom toms.

"I gave Mr. Bellan the message the king had given me. He promptly read it—in its original Cambodian—to the people that had gathered around us. Judging by the natives' shouts, the king's dispatch made quite the impression.

"That afternoon, at 5:00, I headed back to the field, again in the company of the Cambodian dancers moving to the same flutes and tom toms. When I took off for my forty-five-minute demonstration, I threw down about a hundred piastres in ten-cent coins. That caused fights to erupt: some people were boxing, while others favored a strange technique that entailed striking their assailant with the palm of their hands. A few people even jumped into the lagoon bordering the field. My demonstration included some steep ascents as well as some dives toward the ground, which completely failed to startle the crowd. I ended my performance with a few spirals.

"That night, there was a big party at the house of the Résident of Prey Veng. Many speeches were given. I think I even answered in Cambodian!

"The next morning at 6:38 I left Prey Veng and headed back to Banam, doing the exact same trip I did the day before but in the opposite direction. When I reached Banam, I spotted the peaks of Ba Phnum in the distance. I went over and flew around them for a bit before heading to the Kampong Trabaek River, which would lead me east to the village of the same name. I was flying at an altitude of about 300 meters. When I reached the village, I descended to about 50 meters in order to find the stone road that should lead me to Soai Rieng. As soon as I felt confident that I was heading in the right direction, I climbed back to 250 meters and headed straight to the landing strip in Soai Rieng, which was also outlined by five fires.

"Mr. Morel, the acting résident in Soai Rieng, gave an enthusiastic speech and introduced me to the authorities the same way other résidents did in previous cities I visited. He also provided Cambodian dancers.

"That afternoon, I gave a fifteen-minute flight demonstration, repeating the stunts I had done the day before to the amazement of the natives, who marveled at the sight of the 'magnificent white bird.'

"After the flight, the natives threw a party for me. Same as before: people fighting using the palm of their hands, dancing, music, etc.

"In the end, though, it became time to think about the trip to Saigon. I checked the map the governor of Cochinchina was nice enough to give me. I had prepared the following itinerary: I would go from Soai Rieng to the Vaïco, then cross it near Soc-noc, where I would take the colonial road to Saigon. That road can be found between the great Vaïco and the river of Saigon.

"At 6:33, I left Soai Rieng and followed the road that was going to lead me to Soc-noc. That road was white and very easy to see against a backdrop of dry blackened grass. I reached the great Vaïco very easily. I was flying at 200 meters when I saw thick fog ahead of me. I wondered if I should stay on course or if I should instead follow the great Vaïco until I reached the railroad tracks between My Tho and Saigon.

"In the end, I decided to take the shortest route, which would mean I would continue flying over the road, and headed straight for the fog. Soon, as I was flying at only 100 meters, I could not see the ground anymore and was shaken around by strong turbulences. I had three options:

I could go back, change course to head toward the great Vaïco, or keep going and use my compass to find my way. I chose the last option, knowing that if I continued heading east there was no way I could miss the Saigon River.

"I think I must have been around Trang Bang by then.

"I was still going at a fast clip when I reached the Saigon River, just like I thought I would. I started heading southeast and followed the river, which, according to my map, should lead me to Saigon. I could hardly see anything because of the fog, which reduced visibility but did not stop the sunlight from blinding me.

"I reached a place where the river was curving in such a way that it was almost describing a full loop. It seemed to match a spot on my map, which would mean that I was only a few kilometers away from Saigon. I kept going. However, after ten minutes, I could still not see Saigon. I was convinced I had gotten lost, though I could not have deviated from my course too much. I started heading south. My plan was to keep going for about fifteen minutes. If, by then, I had not spotted Saigon—where I should have landed long ago—I would land in the first city I saw. Soon after, I sighted some railroad tracks, a river, a bridge, and a few houses. I did not hesitate. I killed the engine and landed in a paddy field 200 meters away from a train station, just as a train heading toward My Tho was leaving it. As soon as I arrived, I asked a European where I was. He gave me all the information I wanted.

"Meanwhile, a mass of people gathered in the paddy field. It came to a point where they made it impossible for me to leave. I took a rickshaw to the post and telegraph office. I sent Mr. Grégori a message to let him know that I was going to take off again. Then, I went back to my paddy field. More than five thousand natives had gathered there. There were also three or four Europeans who gladly helped me out. We commandeered five or six militiamen to help us push my plane to the back of the paddy field, facing the wind. The most difficult task was getting people to leave the field. It took at least a half hour. After that, I had the French stand behind the plane while I gave them instructions for the takeoff. I fed my trusty Gnome engine a little bit of gas and climbed aboard. It took only one rotation of the propeller for the engine to start going. I repositioned myself, put on my hat and goggles, adjusted the carburetor, and started heading toward the south end of the field.

"My plane had a few jolts, but that was to be expected. It continued accelerating, and, after about 50 meters, it took off as easily as if I had been driving it on nice firm ground instead of a paddy field. I flew over Tan An for a bit, passed the bridge, and followed the railroad tracks until I reached Saigon, which I spotted very late because of the fog. Soon, I saw the artillery district and the racetracks. I took a left turn and landed.

"I will always remember this trip fondly because, anywhere I went in Cambodia, I was welcomed warmly. Also, it only reinforced the trust I already had in my Blériot. There is no trip, no matter how long, I would be too scared to make in it, and there is no part of the world I would avoid flying it in.

"I'm happy about the small incidents we encountered during our journey because we always managed to solve them ourselves. That should be enough to silence people who are still casting doubt over the viability of aviation in Southeast Asia."

After this series of flights, Pourpe wrote me from Saigon on 13 March 1913. "Yesterday, I finished the series of flights we had planned to make in this region. We are planning to leave for Tonkin within a week. We will probably be kept quite busy there as well. Oh well . . . that's for the best!

"You probably heard of our accomplishments through 'Havas,' so I will not dwell upon them. I'll save my most detailed account for when I see you back in France.

"Here are some press clippings from local newspapers that contain all the information you could want regarding our flights, which we accomplished 'without any special preparations' in a country we were not familiar with despite unfavorable circumstances. We flew over paddy fields, swamps, and forest. The sights were nothing to speak of.

"According to all the old settlers, be they civilians or in the military, we did more for the prestige of France in two weeks than others did in ten years of colonization. People there have never been more enthusiastic. It is not my place to stress the impact of our flights, but all of the people in charge agree on the patriotic influence of our tour there. It was very effective in showing what could be accomplished in the field of transportation in countries where people waste days, if not weeks, to complete trips that could be made in three hours or less by plane.

"The sun and the heat are merciless here. Let's hope they do not get the best of us!

"I don't know when I'll hear from you, old friend. As you see, we changed our itinerary. We will not be in Australia any time before May. After we go to Tonkin and

Annam, we will come back here for a fifteen-province tour. People are already setting up locations for us to give demonstrations and raising money."

A few days later, on March 29, Pourpe wrote me to tell me that the Australia tour was compromised by the amount of work they still had to do in Indochina. Charles Verminck, Georges Verminck's brother, had been stuck in France because of an accident. Now, he was going to join his brother and Pourpe.

"We are waiting for Charles. When he arrives, we will decide if we want to go to Australia or head back to France. Our trip to the Far East has completely modified our tour. We might find ourselves in Australia during a season that is not ideal for flying. Maybe we'll go next year instead.

"We still have six commitments here: in My Tho, Sa Dec, Vinh Long, Soc Trang, Long Xuyen, and Bachéen. We will be done in about two weeks. It's very hot here. About 37° Celsius in the tent. We sometimes have trouble staying at an altitude of 300 meters, especially with planes that were not made for hot countries. Still, our Gnome engines are just as good as when we first got them, despite the long treks we have put them through.

"I'm starting to feel a little tired. Such an expedition is exhausting, especially considering that I have to take care of everything. I handle all the planning, I fly, I tend to the equipment. I feel like this is going to be the end of me. Oh well . . ."

Alas! The tour was going to be struck by a gruesome accident. Georges Verminck, after proving himself a veritable hero thanks to his flight from Saigon to Phnom Penh, crashed in My Tho on April 8 as he was giving a flight demonstration.

I received the following telegram: "My poor companion Géo Verminck died in a brutal crash. We don't know exactly what caused it. He died during the second flight of a demonstration he was giving. The previous day, he had followed the Mekong from Saigon to My Tho. He had accomplished that trip with ease, as always.

"Yesterday (April 9), we gave him our last farewell. Everybody was stunned. A huge crowd had gathered. Even on the natives' faces, you could read pain and sympathy.

"His brother's sorrow is heartbreaking. Poor Charles was just arriving from France and so happy to be reunited with his brother, to join us in our adventures, to share our efforts and our accomplishments. All he got to do was collect his brother's dead body. And in what state!

"I am still under the spell of these deeply sad days. We will soon come back home. Géo's last flight will also be the last of our Asian tour. We canceled all of our upcoming engagements.

"I might head back before Charles, who is making arrangements to repatriate his brother's body."

ELEVEN

Lafberg Steps In

Soon after poor Georges Verminck's death, shared grief, as it too often happens, gave way to financial concerns.

His brother Charles wasn't cut from the same cloth. He had been hit by a tragic event as soon as he had arrived. He did not feel like persevering and gave up on the tour. What was to become of Pourpe, the star of the bunch? He managed to keep the plane he made famous, although not without great difficulties. Now he was all alone with *La Curieuse*. Charles Verminck had fired all of the tour's employees.

We mentioned that an assistant mechanic who was put in charge of setting up the tent had been hired in Calcutta. Here is how it happened: The man was strolling along the Ganges River when he heard about the French pilots. He immediately headed to the racetracks where the flight demonstrations were scheduled. He had wanted to see an aeroplane up close for a long time.

He went up to Georges Verminck. "Do you need an assistant?"

"Don't need anybody," answered Verminck, quite curtly. He must have been preoccupied with something, because he was usually a friendly fellow.

The aspiring assistant was a good judge of character. He did not insist. The other pilot seemed more approachable. He waited for Pourpe to be alone to go introduce himself.

"Are you a mechanic?" asked the great Frenchman, who knew how painful it is to want to work without being able to.

"No, but I have had so many different jobs that I'm sure I'll learn this one just the same. Meanwhile, I can make myself helpful in many ways. For instance, I could serve as your spokesperson. I have a decent command of all the local dialects."

"That's actually a good idea. Nothing bores me more than explaining our aeroplanes to visitors. You're hired. You'll be our speaker. When we exhibit our planes, you'll be the one telling visitors how they work. Don't worry. I'll teach you. I had the same job during a difficult period in my life. What is your name?

"Raoul Lafberg."

"Are you French?"

"Yes, I was born in Auvergne."

This is how a man with a glorious future was hired. Pourpe and Verminck were very satisfied with the way he fulfilled his duties. However, when the latter died and his brother fired all the employees, Pourpe found himself without anyone to help him out. Everyone had abandoned him. Lafberg approached him:

"Mr. Pourpe, you do not need a speaker anymore, but you could use a mechanic. Would you let me work for you?"

"My poor friend, you do not know anything about how this plane's engine works. You were busy being our speaker, and I neglected your mechanical training."

"I don't see a problem here. Teach me. I'll learn quickly. You're in a tough spot. Everybody is leaving you. You were good to me. I will not let you down. If you decide to teach me, I guarantee you that in a week from now I will know as much as you."

And so, our two heroes came to an agreement that quickly led to them striking up a friendship.

Where did this strange but honest boy come from? His real name was Raoul Lufbery, but, after having been rebuffed by Verminck, the young man became a little apprehensive. When he approached Pourpe for the first time, he was a little worried about being turned down because he was a foreigner. "Lufbery" sounded American, whereas "Lafberg" could pass for French.

This is why, until the moment he enlisted in August 1914, Pourpe and I earnestly thought his name was Lafberg.

This French American man's life was even more intriguing and colorful than Pourpe's. He was born on 14 March 1885 in Chamalières, Puy-de-Dôme. Records show that his full name was Gervais Raoul Victor Lufbery.

How did he manage, in those circumstances, to become the most notorious ace of the Lafayette squadron, whose members were American volunteers? It's a long and wonderful story.

His father, Edward Lufbery, was born in New York on 30 July 1854. His grandfather, Charles-Samson Lufbery, who died on 11 September 1874, and his grandmother (née Ann-Weaner Phebe), who died in 1880, were both American citizens. Their descendants were English and had migrated in the late 1600s. One could hardly be more American.

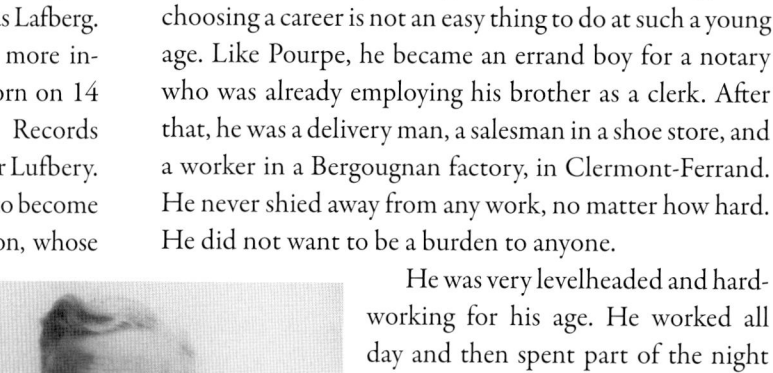

Raoul's father had been sent to Europe when he was fifteen years old. He did the last leg of his schooling in Germany. Then, in 1873, he moved to France. For a few years, he worked for his older brother, Georges, who manufactured chemicals in Chauny, Aisne. He became a respected chemist and specialized in the production of rubber, which was a fledgling industry in France. He became the director of the Torrilhon factory in Chamalières in 1876. That is where he met and married Raoul's mother, Anne Vessière, whose family had been in Auvergne for generations.

Raoul had barely turned two when his mother died in June 1887. His father put him in the care of a family in Montrodeix, a hamlet located in the foothills of the Puy-de-Dôme. Growing up, the child was coddled by his foster parents while enjoying the mountains' pure and invigorating air.

For six years, as he lived in the wild countryside, he acquired excellent observation skills and developed a strong fondness for animals and the great outdoors. He felt a deep love for our inferior brothers and often preferred spending time with them rather than with humans.

When his father remarried and started a new family, Raoul and his two brothers were sent to live with their maternal grandmother. He went to elementary school in Chamalières, but a stroke of bad luck put his grandmother in a dire financial situation, and, at twelve, he had to leave school to make a living.

Edward Lufbery, the American father of Raoul Lufbery.

He was already courageous and full of energy, but choosing a career is not an easy thing to do at such a young age. Like Pourpe, he became an errand boy for a notary who was already employing his brother as a clerk. After that, he was a delivery man, a salesman in a shoe store, and a worker in a Bergougnan factory, in Clermont-Ferrand. He never shied away from any work, no matter how hard. He did not want to be a burden to anyone.

He was very levelheaded and hardworking for his age. He worked all day and then spent part of the night studying schoolbooks that belonged to his brothers, who would try to help him when they had time.

Raoul had a passion for reading. He devoured books and particularly enjoyed adventure tales, especially when they were about great hunts, or told of people exploring uncharted territories, colonizing distant countries, etc. He learned everything about the travels of great pioneers like Marco Polo and Bougainville. By his bedside, he had novels by Jules Verne, Thomas Mayne-Reid, Gustave Aimard, and Pierre Loti.

He fantasized about leaving his humdrum life behind. He wanted to exert himself physically and mentally. He enjoyed exercise. It made him feel truly alive. His hobbies included gymnastics, weightlifting, wrestling, boxing, and shooting. He even won a local Greco-Roman wrestling competition in the middleweight category.

Until he turned eighteen, he lived in Clermont-Ferrand, which he left only a few times to visit Paris or go to Blois to see his father, who was working at the Poulain chocolate factory.

During the spring of 1905, without telling anyone, not even his brother Julien, in whose house he had been living for the past three years and whom he cared for deeply, Raoul put the plan he had in mind for years into action: he took off to conquer the world!

Raoul had a curious mind, but he was thorough and prudent nonetheless. He aspired to start learning through experience instead of solely by reading books. He wanted to undertake a long trip around the entire world, on his own, and with only about 300 or 400 francs to his name. The little money he had he had managed to put aside by making big sacrifices and depriving himself of many things. Little by little, he had saved enough to sustain himself for a bit.

He had established guidelines for himself: he would pull money from his modest funds only if he was forced to do so by some extreme reversal of fortune. He was convinced that a brave young man who was willing to use his strong arms for any honest work he would be offered would be able to make it anywhere and under any circumstances. He proved that nothing was more feasible.

Later, he told me that he had never been without a job for more than a week, even when he did not know the language of the country he was in. He believed that if you're really trying to survive, you'll always find a way to make yourself understood.

So he left Clermont-Ferrand in late March 1905. He headed to Marseille, where he spent a week in order to familiarize himself with the fast-paced life of a big seaside town. One morning, in April 1905, he arrived in Algiers, the first stop on his worldwide tour.

His first concern was to find a job. As soon as he arrived, he got hired as a docker. He worked twelve to fifteen hours a day (there was no talk of a forty-hour work week in those days). At this rate, it did not take long for him to start suffering from a hernia. He had to go to the Mustapha civilian hospital.

At the hospital, this tall, loyal, and smart boy told his story to the nuns, who worked as nurses. They took a liking to him and had him hired as a nurse. He kept the job until March 4, 1906. During the ten months he spent in Algiers, he used his free time to visit every nook and cranny of the city and socialize with colonists and natives alike. When he felt he knew everything there was to know about life in Algeria, he decided to take off.

He went to Tunisia and stayed in Tunis until late April. There, he found work, first as a kitchen assistant for the Société Française de Bienfaisance and then as a road builder. He found himself in the Tunisian backcountry, installing railway tracks.

In Alexandria, he worked as a warehouse clerk for the gas company. In Port-Saïd (where Pourpe spent part of his childhood), Raoul became a piece worker for the Universal Maritime Suez Canal Company. He stayed there from May 9 to June 13. Later, he worked as a cook on a sailboat that carried merchandise between Egypt, Turkey, and Greece. That way, he was able to visit Cairo, Constantinople, and Athens.

He was getting older. Soon, he would qualify for conscription. He wondered if he should go back to France to do his military service. Spending three years in the same barracks? Not really an exciting prospect for such an avid traveler. It was time to make a choice: France or the United States? He felt that France did not need him for the moment. When time would come to defend it, he would rush to its aid, but, in the meantime, he chose to prioritize his American nationality. He headed to the French consulate in Cairo to make his decision official.

This is how Raoul Lufbery, from Auvergne, made it possible for himself to become the greatest American ace there ever was, although that would happen nine years later.

Once he had settled everything with the authorities, there was nothing left to stop him from traveling to more and more distant places.

When he was in Constantinople, in August 1906, Lufbery felt like starting a business. He decided to make and sell fruitières—fruit baskets that were made out of wire and used to carry fruits and cakes. They weren't difficult to make and sold very well. There were fruitières stores in Cairo and Athens. He headed to the latter and found a business partner, who ended up disappearing with all the money they had made. All Lufbery was left with was some small change.

Following this misadventure, Lufbery became wary of business ventures in general and Greek business partners in particular.

Still, no stroke of bad luck could diminish the young man's drive. He immediately went back to work. To recover financially, he returned to Constantinople, where he took on a job as a *garçon d'hôtel* and waiter.

Concurrently, he managed to acquire a small collection of exotic novelty items and decided to visit the Balkans. It had been a long time since he had seen any mountains, and he missed them. He crossed Bulgaria in no time, stopped briefly in Bucharest, passed through Budapest and Vienna, crossed Tyrol, and arrived in Bavaria—more specifically in a town called Fulda—in September 1906.

He stayed there seven months, having been hired by a brewer, Mr. Seipel, who took a liking to this hardworking boy whose personal history seemed a testament to his exemplary behavior and his integrity. Raoul befriended his employer's son, a student who was the same age as him and taught him German. He was thrilled. He already knew a little bit of Arabic, Turkish, and Greek. He was excited at the prospect of mastering a language that could prove useful during his travels.

He also learned to appreciate different types of people. He liked talking about his impressions of Germany.

"In the hotel where I lived, I met an old man from Alsace who, in order to get away from the authorities and the people of German descent who constantly got in his hair there, had moved to Fulda. His sons had crossed the border in order to avoid serving in the German military. Life in his hometown had become execrable ever since. He decided not to follow his sons, so as not to lose the assets he had inherited, which guaranteed him a small income. So he had decided to live in this isolated part of the Hesse region.

"At night, after I was done with work, I was happy to chat in French with my friend. Our conversations were most interesting. They often revolved around German people.

"My boy," he would say, "You do not understand German people, and that is too bad. In France, people are too trusting and welcoming. French people do not know of, do not see, the menace that has been lurking for thirty years. They do not realize what influence the people in power here have over the population. In fact, the Germans do not realize it either, for one very simple reason: They do not suffer from it. They actually enjoy this situation.

"Would you like to know what method they use? Well, it's simple. It starts with school. Going to school is mandatory in every country, but here, 'mandatory' is not an empty word. As soon as he is able to walk, a child is sent to school and goes there until he turns fourteen.

"You might think kids there only learn to read, write, do math, and understand geography and history, which would be all well and good. Yes, they learn all that, but they also learn how to think, which is an entirely different matter. Here, school shapes a kid's brain so that he is convinced that he, a German, is privileged, is of a superior essence, thanks to the hard work of the ruling class and the effectiveness of his government. In short, he has become a full-grown Pan-Germanist.

"Once he leaves school, a German boy does not regain his free will. He has no chance of breaking free. Everything is still planned, taken care of. The hold over him remains. The child, now a young man, stays in close touch with his masters. He goes to night school; he is a member of all sorts of organizations, clubs, and associations where the same ideas are being repeated. His schoolteacher is still his friend, his confidant, and his supervisor. This grotesque pseudo-intellectual, whose government guarantees him access to an unending supply of young minds, is devoted to the tyrant that treats him so favorably. School, in Germany, is in the hands of the government, and the government is one single man: the emperor. The emperor is involved in all areas of human activity—the army, the navy, the merchant marine, finance, the media, public works, industry, commerce, farming, and even religion. He has a say in everything. He is in charge—either openly or secretly—of all important things. And the German people are convinced that this state of affairs is fine.

"How could it be any other way? A German youth leaves his teachers only to find new masters—his military instructors. He leaves school for the military, which immediately eradicates any taste for independence that might have been left in him. They terrorize him; they throw him into a panic. There is no other place in the world where military discipline is as severe and brutal.

"When he leaves the force, he stays under the spell of Germany's power. He is convinced that all of its institutions, especially its military, are the strongest there are. '*Deutschland über alles*!' are the words he lives by. Gradually, cunningly, he was shown, was imparted with, what he could gain from this strength. People use brochures, books, newspapers, conferences, etc. to demonstrate the superiority of German people over their neighbors, especially the ones in the West and in the East. They are given statistics which are partly accurate but mostly erroneous to expose their neighbors' weaknesses—diminishing birth rates, ignorance, carelessness, decadence, etc. Still, these countries abound in natural riches which he, '*Der Deutsche Michel*,' does not get to enjoy.

"Where are his rich lands, his green pastures, his prosperous colonies? Doesn't he belong to a populous, that is to say, a powerful nation? Little by little, his greed, his hunger are awakened, aroused, and stimulated. We should all fear the day when the pack will be unleashed. They are capable of anything. You're young. You'll see it happen soon."

"This is how my friend talked. I listened to him because he was an elder and I respected him, but I thought he was probably exaggerating a bit. I felt that his resentment, as an oppressed Alsatian, made him fixate on remarks I might not even have made if he hadn't pointed out so many things about Germans in the first place.

"Every time he went on like that, I would think of fat old Seipel, and I could not picture this honest fellow, who always had a smile on his face, going on the warpath and brandishing a tomahawk. Neither could I picture his son, a pale student who was always very kind to me, doing the same. In fact, all everyone in Hesse seemed to be passionate about was a big plate of sauerkraut and sausages flanked by tall steins of good beer.

"It is true, however, that everything that had to do with the military there seemed to have a prestigious aura. Be it on the street, in a café, or at a show, woe betide him who does not step aside for an officer. There were barracks and arsenals everywhere. There were parades and all kinds of demonstrations aimed at allowing the military to show off their weapons happening constantly. The people of Fulda would inevitably ooh and aah at those displays. Subofficers and *feldwebels* were always regarded with the utmost respect and admiration. Nothing seemed as prestigious as wearing a military cap and tunic with shiny boots and carrying a sabre! How enraptured by uniforms people were! It's crazy what you could get away with when wearing one.

"Here's a story that actually happened and proves my point: One day, a cobbler from Berlin put on a colonel's uniform and headed to Köpenick. There, he rounded up some men from the local barracks, headed to City Hall, grabbed all the money he could find, and had the mayor and his wife arrested. Such a plan could succeed only in Germany. Nobody suspected a thing. The uniform! It's always the uniform!"

Every time he visited a country, Lufbery came back with fascinating memories and impressions. Everywhere he went, he did his best to live like the locals. He would try their food and study their mores, using his outstanding observation skills. No detail was small enough to evade him. On one trip, he even got a tattoo. He, the American, got a beautiful Gallic rooster on his left forearm.

He stayed in Fulda until April 1907. In the spring, he followed the swallows north and went to Hamburg. There, he started working as a docker again until he found a job as a kitchen assistant aboard the *Ascan-Ubermann* liner. This way, he could travel for free. He left for America, where he was planning to join his brother Charles, who lived in Wallingford, Connecticut. He was also hoping to reunite with his father, who had left his job as a chemist to get into the stamp business. Lufbery arrived in New York in May and immediately went to see his brother, who did not expect him, especially in such circumstances.

"Where did you put your luggage?"

"Here it is," said Lufbery, laughing.

All his belongings were contained in a seaman's handkerchief, whose corners he had tied together. All he had were some spare clothes, toiletries, a small French-English dictionary (why, an American citizen should speak English, shouldn't he?), and a prized collection of postcards from all the places he had visited. On their backs, he had carefully written down information regarding the climate, the weather, the mores, and the customs of these places. Later, when Pourpe prepared his flight excursions, Lufbery was able to give him precious information regarding the places that he was going to travel through.

From the moment he left Clermont-Ferrand until he became Pourpe's partner, Lufbery only ever traveled with his handkerchief in place of a suitcase. When he started working for Pourpe, he finally traded it in for a small brown canvas bag that "looked a little bit more elegant" but wasn't any bigger than the seaman's handkerchief.

Lufbery stayed ten months in the United States. He visited its main cities, always while working, of course. He tried his hand at goldsmithery in New Haven, operated a lift in a New York hotel, and worked in a cotton mill in New Orleans. He went all the way to Mexico, visited Quebec, crossed the United States from east to west, and arrived in San Francisco.

He learned English and could read and write as well as a native. But the skills he picked up were of no use to him in "Frisco," which was overrun by adventurers from all countries. Let's make one thing clear: Lufbery was not a seeker of adventures; what he was seeking in his travels was knowledge. His capital did not increase in the country of millionaires. To continue his trip around the globe, Lufbery had to cross the Pacific, but he did not know how. What to do?

His time in San Francisco seems to have been one of the most difficult in his life. He couldn't find a job he enjoyed. He didn't like the city's heterogeneous population. He wanted to leave at all costs. He was aimlessly wandering the streets, stopping every once in a while to read a poster, when a man approached him to tell him about the perks of being a soldier. Lufbery was in the habit of letting people talk uninterrupted. It's the polite thing to do and the best way to find out what the person speaking to you wants from you. Plus, if you're keeping quiet, you can't give away anything that could put you in a disadvantageous situation.

The man went on and on with his propaganda and took Lufbery to an office where he asked him his age and name before handing him a paper to sign.

"What for?" asked Lufbery, who was a little worried.

"Well, to join the military!"

The man was a mere army recruiter. What he told Lufbery sounded interesting: he would join the 20th Colonial Regiment,[1] which was about to go to Hawaii and the Philippines. It was a godsend. Here was his ticket to cross the Pacific! The enlistment bonus was appealing and the pay would be more than generous. And on top of that, Lufbery would spend eighteen months living in an idyllic place: Hawaii, the "Pearl of the Pacific," before going to the Philippines. Serving in the colonial army did not

---

1. This was the US 20th Infantry Regiment.

Raoul Lufbery's 1908 US Army enlistment documents

U. S. W. INFANTRY

DESCRIPTIVE AND ASSIGNMENT CARD OF

Gervais Lufbery

Residence: **Sacramento, California**
(Town or city.) (State.)

Name and address (street and house number, if any) of person to be notified in case of emergency, giving degree of relationship; if friend, so state:

(Friend) Joseph Cook 22 Chapel St. New Haven, Connecticut.

Accepted for enlistment in **Infantry**
(Arm of service or organization.)

on the **18th.** day of **November 1908.**, 190__, at **Sacramento, Cal.** and forwarded this date to **Depot of R. & C. Angel Island, Cal.**

Charles Smart
1ST LIEUTENANT, 1ST FIELD ARTILLERY
Recruiting Officer.

Sacramento, Cal.
(Station.)
November 19th. 1908., 190__

Received at **FORT McDOWELL, CAL.**, **Nov 19**, 190**8**
(Depot.) (Date.)

Born in *Paris* *France*
(Town or city.) (State or country.)

Age *22¼* years; occupation *Laborer*;
Eyes *Blue #10*; hair *Dk Bro*;
Complexion *Ruddy*; height *5* feet *5¼* inches.
Married or single: *Single*

Indelible or permanent marks as shown on enlistment paper: *Front: FSM below r nipple ¼" d, l nipple 3rd r leg ½" d, Back 3 l arm ½" d, r up arm ½" d*

Identification Record *Made*
(See G. O. 68, War Department, 1906.)

Enlisted **NOV 20 1908**, 190__, at **FORT McDOWELL, CAL**
by *Capt Juenemann Med Corps* for *3* years.

Last discharged _____, 190__, from _____
_____ with character _____; continuous service at that date ____ years, ____ months, ____ days.

Qualified as _____, 190__
(Gunner, expert rifleman, sharpshooter, or marksman, with date.)

Vaccinated **Nov. 18th. 1908.**, 190__; result _____

STATEMENT OF ACCOUNTS.

Money value of clothing drawn since enlistment: $ *31.80*

Due United States: Laundry work $ _____

Last paid by *Pay due from enlistment.* to _____, 190__

Form No. 25, A. G. O.
Ed. Apr. 27—08—200,000.   (OVER.)
3—1292

sound bad at all. Without hesitation, Lufbery signed. He was an American soldier! Things were looking up!

The detachment he joined was made up of one captain, two lieutenants, five sergeants, five corporals, two buglers, two cooks, one munition specialist, and fifty soldiers. He arrived in Honolulu on 4 December 1908.

Life was easy there. He enjoyed the climate, which reminded him of Egypt. He had an easy time fulfilling his duties. He had a lot of free time, which he used to hunt, fish, go climbing, and study the local flora and fauna. In short, he lived a fully happy life during the eighteen months he spent in Hawaii.

In March 1910 his detachment took off for the Philippines, where he was stationed in Manila. There, he lived a life of luxury again. He traveled around the whole archipelago, climbed volcanoes, and befriended the locals as well as the many Chinese and Japanese people who lived there.

He was discharged in July 1911. His time in the service allowed him to join the police or become a railroad worker, but he had saved a lot of money in the past thirty-six months. He was going to be able to travel more easily. He finalized his crossing of the Pacific and went to Yokohama. This time, he paid for his own ticket! Then, he visited Tokyo and some seaside towns.

In August 1911 he found a job in Hong Kong, working for customs. But it was too hot for him in China. He stayed there only three months before taking off for Colombo. There, he applied for a plot of land to start a rubber plantation. While awaiting a response from the authorities, he visited Madras, Calcutta, and Singapore. However, upon his return to Ceylon, he learned that it would take months for him to be given a plot of land.

So he left for Bombay. There, he met a famous tiger hunter with whom he killed a few big cats. Then, he became a manager at the Exposition du Vieux Bombay, a kind of public garden with American-inspired tourist attractions.

He was put in charge of the "joe-wheel," an elevated wooden platform shaped like a circle that was connected to an engine by an axle. The engine allowed for the platform to spin very fast. Around the circular platform,

Raoul Lufbery (standing far right) *with his 4-person tiger-hunting party in Bombay, India, October 1911. A renowned tiger hunter is seated far left. A wealthy Belgian globe-trotter sits next to him. The hunting party's photographer stands between them. Their hound awaits the tiger hunt.*

there were two padded walls: one that people could rest on and a second one that formed a small space for people to walk around the platform.

Four to six daredevils would climb onto the platform, which would then be put in motion. The rotation would start slowly but accelerate gradually so that the passengers would be pushed against the padded walls. Meanwhile, people who were awaiting their turn could watch.

"My job was to maintain order on the joe-wheel. It was a difficult task in a country where people were divided in competing castes. I had four English Indian men to assist me, but they had no authority, so I was always forced to get involved.

"One day, a group of Indians overstayed their welcome on the ride. It seemed like they were determined not to let anyone else use it.

"I asked them to leave the ride three times, but they didn't listen. Finally, I was at the end of my tether. I grabbed one of them by the back of his pants, lifted him out of the ride and dropped him on the other side of the wall. I did the same for two others that were light enough. Seeing this, the rest of the group stepped out, although they did not do so without complaining audibly. I could not have cared less.

"The incident would probably have ended right there if a European hadn't started criticizing me for handling the situation in such an uncivil fashion.

"Seeing that a white man was taking their side, the Indians did something they surely would not have dared doing if not for this regrettable intercession. They surrounded me, insulted me like only they can, and threatened me. My assistants, who did not feel like getting a beating, had bravely run away.

"I was going to have to defend myself on my own. I decided to try my luck. I jumped onto the platform—which was now at a standstill—and faced my assailants. I was going to fight all of them, one after the other, in single combat. This dampened the rioters' enthusiasm a little. I thought I had the situation under control when one of them, undoubtedly a practical and thrifty man (although not a very honest one), asked for a refund. The others followed, and soon they were surrounding me again, shouting, 'My three annas! I want my three annas back!'

"They were starting to threaten me again. They raised their fists. I was now in a dire situation. There was going to be a fight for sure, and I knew I would not have the upper hand on this pack of troublemakers.

"Fortunately, at that exact moment, a group of English soldiers appeared out of nowhere, switches in hand. They came down on the howling bunch harshly and firmly. After a few moments, they had all run away and we were victorious.

"I thanked those good Tommies warmly for their fortuitous and efficient intervention. Without them, chances are I would have been lynched. And the saddest part is, it would all have been because of a white man's gaffe.

"I have held English soldiers in high esteem ever since. They are not as indifferent as people say!"

On 5 March 1912 Lufbery started selling tickets for the Great Indian British Railway. He worked there until August 14. On that day, he had an unfortunate run-in.

A tall and solemn Hindu came up to the counter. "Where are you headed?" Lufbery asked him.

"I will ask you to call me 'Sir,'" the man replied.

We already know that Lufbery was not a very patient man. He came around from behind the counter, grabbed the traveler, made him turn around, and kicked him out of the station. Relieved, he went back to his seat.

A few minutes later, his boss called for him. "How dreadful! You behaved in an awfully discourteous way. You disrespected and even used violence toward a maharaja who happens to be our company's largest stockholder. I cannot keep you with us for one more second. He wants to see you fired this instant."

"I have only one regret," Lufbery replied.

"What is it?" asked the manager, probably hoping to hear Lufbery express remorse.

"That I did not hurt that walking jar of shoe polish more!"

Bombay wasn't working out for Lufbery, so he went back to Calcutta, where he was hired by Pourpe. He kept that job till the war, which does not mean that he stopped traveling.

Not only did he bring back unique memories from his distant journeys, but he also learned a lot. He had a philosophy of life and had collected nuggets of wisdom all around the world.

"When you're traveling the globe," he liked to say, "you have to show restraint and show the utmost respect for the locals and the customs of the countries you are visiting. If you fail to do so, you are exposing yourself to dire consequences."

"Here's an example: I was walking around a Bombay suburb. (Bombay, again!) The heat was sweltering that day. I was thirsty and could not find any place to quench that thirst. So I went up to a young Indian woman who was standing in her doorway. I explained my situation to her.

"She understood and kindly fetched me some water. While she was filling a bowl for me, I mindlessly lifted a plank that was lying near me. It was covering some kind of jar.

"The young woman saw this and started yelling. In an instant, she had roused the whole neighborhood.

"When people heard what had caused her to be so angry, they got enraged too and started insulting and threatening me.

"All I could think of was to run away, pursued by a vengeful crowd.

"I ran until I encountered a policeman. He was able to explain what had happened. When I lifted the plank, I exposed a batch of preserved cucumbers, which, apparently, was a very serious offense. Now the cucumbers had to be thrown away. Nobody would want to eat them because they had been defiled by a *roumi*'s indiscretion.

"I made up for my mistake by compensating the poor Indian woman for her spoiled cucumbers. But the lesson I learned was priceless. I swore that from now on, I would always be careful."

Raoul Lufbery's "letter of recommendation" given to him following his dismissal for physically ejecting an unruly customer from the "joe-wheel" in Bombay, India

Lufbery's certificate of service from the Great Indian Peninsula Railway of Bombay, which was given to him following his dismissal by the company for kicking the firm's largest stockholder out of the Bombay station

TWELVE

Pourpe Comes to the Rescue of Our Colonial Prestige

Pourpe and his diligent collaborator Lufbery eagerly went back to work. Weren't those two young men, whose lives had been so parallel so far, made for each other? They had the same taste for adventure, the same desire to learn. Both were loyal and intelligent. Only death could separate them.

Thanks to the intervention of Maître Garros—the great hero's father—Pourpe was able to continue his series of flight demonstrations and trips throughout Indochina. His plane, *La Curieuse,* was getting older but still fulfilled its duties excellently.

On April 30 Pourpe went on a long and dangerous journey. The route he was going to take offered very few landing spots because that region was mostly wetland. His trip took him to Chau Doc, Cam An, Sa Dec, and Saigon. He flew every morning and covered a distance of about 60 to 100 kilometers. In the afternoon, he gave light demonstrations in front of crowds of native people who came from every corner of the province to see the May Bay.

First, he flew from Chau Doc to Long Xuyen. He spotted his designated landing spot very easily thanks to the whitewashed lines that delimited it. Lufbery joined him that evening. The next day, after giving a breathtaking flight demonstration, Pourpe left for Can Tho. The trip took him forty minutes. Europeans and natives did not hesitate to wade in the water—which was up to their knees—to greet him enthusiastically. The plane was parked close to the bleachers, and a straw hut was built for it in case of rain. However, Pourpe quickly realized that the field was too small and marshy for the plane to take off again. So, as soon as Lufbery had joined him, Pourpe enlisted him to help him take apart *La Curieuse*'s wings and move it to a paddy field that would be a better place to attempt taking off from, although it was quite bumpy.

The next stop would take Pourpe to Soc Trang. There was a strong wind and low-hanging clouds that seemed to indicate a storm was brewing, but Pourpe knew people were expecting him. He wanted to stick to his schedule as closely as possible. Every time he passed a village, he would descend to only a few meters above the ground and perform some stunts to show off his French wings. As he was nearing Soc Trang, he had to change course because of the wind, which was blowing harder and harder. Finally, he landed in a big paddy field close to the city. Strangely, though, nobody was there. After a bit, the city administrator arrived by car and apologetically informed Pourpe that the racetracks, which had been converted into an airfield for the occasion, were located 2 kilometers away. A huge crowd had gathered there. Pourpe did not hesitate. He restarted his plane and went to land where he was supposed to, on a lawn that had been carefully prepared and turned out to be the best landing spot of his whole trip.

The next morning it was raining. That did not stop Pourpe from performing his daily flight demonstration. The spectators were very impressed by his temerity and cried out: "Enough! Enough!" But Pourpe did not let the bad weather deter him and headed toward Bac Lieu, where he landed thirty minutes later.

The next day, after giving a fifteen-minute flight demonstration, Pourpe took off for Cam An. The trip from Bac Lieu to Cam An was to be the most difficult and the longest stage of his journey. He would have to fly over paddy fields and grasslands that were completely submerged.

"I saw some sampans on the canal. I was flying against a headwind. It took all of forty minutes before I finally spotted Cam An in the distance. It was disappearing under mangrove trees and tall grass. In vain I looked for the marks I had asked for to indicate where I should land. I circled the city several times but could not see them or find any place that looked like a safe place to land. So, after ten minutes, I decided to return to Bac Lieu. Now I had a tailwind to push me. I reached a dizzying speed. I encountered the same landscapes as before, which brought to mind the Chaos, a distant time when Earth was just starting to take shape. I was very surprised to spot Bac Lieu after a remarkably short flight. I landed in the same welcoming paddy field I had taken off from earlier. The locals were very surprised. It had taken me one hour and ten minutes to fly 146 kilometers. Add to that the ten minutes I spent flying above Cam An, and I probably flew for a total of about 170 to 175 kilometers at a nice speed of 150 km/hour. It was to be the last stretch of my Chau Doc-Cam An trip."

And so ended Pourpe's series of flights in Cochinchina. He had flown over places that few Europeans or even natives had ever dared venture.

Pourpe's performance made quite an impact. In fact, some people could literally not believe what feats aviation could accomplish. They claimed that the aeroplane was nothing but a big kite that Pourpe and Lufbery were dragging around, thanks to invisible cables while hiding on the ground.

"But you can see that the pilot is inside the plane when it takes off!" some would tell the incredulous natives.

"Yes," they would answer. "It looks like he is, but before the machine starts, he leaves through a trapdoor."

They wanted so much to prove that they were right that they tried to replicate what they thought Pourpe had done. They used bamboos, paper, and string to build a device that vaguely resembled the Blériot.

How to simulate the sound of an engine? Easy—they put a bees' nest inside the contraption. The angry insects made such a racket that one could have confused them for an actual Gnome engine. But the plane refused to fly or even to budge. The ingenious builders came to the conclusion that a spirit was inhabiting *La Curieuse* and willed it to move. They decided that such a powerful machine should be destroyed.

As a consequence, the plane had to be guarded day and night. Lufbery volunteered for that task. There was nothing more to fear.

One day, Lufbery did some scouting in a city where good landing spots were rare. He chose a place that did not seem too bad, and painted some whitewashed marks on the ground to guide Pourpe. Some soldiers were called up to secure the grounds.

When the pilot arrived in sight of the city, he started performing some stunts for his audience before landing. The Indigenous soldiers rushed to the whitewashed marks. Lufbery ran up to them, yelled, and vociferated, but to no avail. The soldiers were obeying orders they had been given and did not want to move from the spot where Pourpe was supposed to land. They did not realize how much space the plane needed upon landing. In their mind, it would gently touch ground, like a bird.

To avoid a disaster, Pourpe had to land a little bit farther away. The soldiers were a bit offended by what they perceived to be the pilot's ingratitude. They had so carefully stood guard around the white stripes!

Pourpe was getting ready to go back to France. He had even announced he would return on June 21, but then he was invited to continue his publicity campaign in Tonkin. Until then, the governor-general, Mr. Albert Sarraut, had paid little attention to our hero's flights in other provinces. Life had been hard for the pilot after the administrators had decided not to subsidize his flights, despite the fact that these did so much to advance France's prestige.

The situation there was not brilliant. The natives weren't very trusting, which was not good for business. French prestige was in dire need of a boost, as it had been tarnished by the authorities' failure to subdue the Annamite bandits that were terrorizing the region.

"It seems like the best method," advised the local press, "is the one that was used highly successfully in Morocco on the initiative of the distinguished colonial leader General Lyautey. Every time a dissident group was identified, a pilot would fly over the troubled region. As he did so, he would drop manifestos that did not quote Anatole France, like the new Annamite newspaper in Tonkin has been doing, but demonstrated French people's moral, intellectual, and physical superiority and made clear that any rebellion would be severely repressed.

"The *résidence supérieure* is looking for ways to appease people who are currently afraid and disoriented. This is a unique opportunity for it to take measures that will be more effective than speeches and articles.

"We strongly believe that appealing to Mr. Pourpe's patriotism would not be in vain, and that if we can make him understand what favor he would do France by accepting this mission, we could surely get him to agree to terms that would be particularly favorable to us. Our French pilots have always demonstrated great abnegation and selflessness whenever their patriotism was stirred. Mr. Pourpe is too well informed not to share these feelings. Besides, the government might reward the esteemed pilot with an honorary distinction, which would make up for his troubles."

Mr. Sarraut agreed to this plan and had the young pilot come to Hanoi to work out details. Pourpe did not want to make too many promises because his plane was getting worn out. Over the last eleven months, the Blériot had flown for about 160 hours, more than 16,000 kilometers. It had done so in a tropical region while not being cared for very well.

After several meetings with Mr. Sarraut, Pourpe agreed to the following schedule:

- Hai Phong to Hanoi: 104 kilometers. Flight over the delta of Tonkin.
- Hanoi to Lang Son: 150 kilometers, including 70 above the mountainous region of Cai Kin.
- Lang Son to Porte de Chine: 40 kilometers
- Hanoi to Nam Dinh: 90 kilometers. Flight over the delta.
- Flight demonstrations in every city on the itinerary

The aviator agreed, although he did not know anything about the region where he was going to fly. He trusted his plane, he trusted his Gnome engine, which had proven itself reliable time and time again, and, most of all, he trusted Providence.

He arrived in Tonkin in the summer, the hottest time of the year. It would get as hot as 36°C in the shade and 48°C in the sun. Everything was going against him, but he wanted to carry forward with his study of aviation in the colonies and keep making adventurous and dangerous trips through the heart of Indochina.

The plane, which had to be transported from Saigon, arrived in Hai Phong on 10 June 1913. Lufbery immediately started putting it together, with Pourpe's help. Mr. Sarraut came from Hanoi to visit the young hero. The start of the tour was delayed.

"This delay," a local newspaper wrote, "will allow the authorities to notify the natives living in the regions the pilot will fly over. Indeed, what is at stake here is our nation's welfare. Therefore, it is necessary for the locals to be warned in advance so that they can congregate to the areas the pilot will fly over. Judging by the impact Mr. Pourpe's flights had in Cochinchina (Entire villages came to see him fly. Many people climbed onto crowded rowboats, and some rich Annamites even showed up in automobiles.), it would be ill advised not to properly advertise such an expression of the genius of our race."

The day of the Hai Phong flight demonstrations was treated like a holiday. The Blériot monoplane was kept in a straw-and-bamboo hangar that had been built on the racetracks and looked after day and night by a group of Indigenous guards.

The entire population—Europeans, Chinese, and native—gathered at the racetracks. So, when Pourpe showed off his skills, he did so in front of an immense and incredibly enthusiastic crowd. When Kouzminski the Russian had come here, all he had managed to do was flit around for a bit. Finally, a real aviator was flying, and how expertly!

A journalist from *Le Courrier d'Haïphong* was curious enough to attend the event to see how it would impact the natives. "They had quite the reaction! Every time the pilot would glide down to only about a couple of meters above their heads, they were literally stunned and compelled to pray to Buddha. Marc Pourpe's exploits gave them a very high opinion of French pilots, and there is little doubt that this demonstration will enhance our national prestige.

"Here is an anecdote that will convey how passionate the Annamites are about all this: This morning, two coolies were discussing Marc Pourpe's chances to make it to Hanoi. One was certain the pilot would have no difficulties completing that trip, while the other claimed the Frenchman was bluffing and would never attempt such a risky adventure. The conversation was turning sour. Soon, the man advocating for Pourpe told the other man that his negativity might bring bad luck upon the pilot, and ordered him to stop talking. That resulted in a full-blown fight, which, luckily, did not have too-serious consequences.

"Though we shall not read too much into this incident, let us say it again: Marc Pourpe's achievements have had a salutary moral effect on the local population."

On June 14 at 6:11 A.M., Pourpe left Hai Phong for Hanoi: "This magnificent spectacle," the newspaper gushed. "A French aeroplane piloted by one of our countrymen flying over the Dong Trien mountains, which used to shelter pirates, shall never be forgotten."

Halfway through Pourpe's trip, in the city of Hai Duong, the streets were packed with people. "Magnificent! Heroic! How amazed the Annamites were!" Finally, upon his triumphant arrival in Hanoi at 7:21, the pilot was welcomed at the racetracks like a hero.

Pourpe did not like spending too much time at any of his stops. He left Hanoi for Lang Son on June 17, at 6:05 A.M., but engine trouble forced him to land in a flooded paddy field, where he ended up capsizing. Luckily, he did not get injured and his plane only suffered minor damage, including a broken wheel.

As he was waiting for Lufbery, who was riding in the car of Mr. Gueyffier, the head of the Aviation Tonkinoise, Pourpe asked some locals for help, but they were terrified of the aeroplane, this extraordinary beast they were seeing up close only for the first time, and they refused to touch it.

Not only were the natives afraid, but the local mandarin was openly reluctant to help the pilot. After having been called to the crash scene, he took over an hour and a half to show up. When he was asked to provide coolies to cut bamboo to lift the plane out of the water and move it to a dry place, he left and did not come back. This behavior led to the mandarin being subjected to disciplinary action. As for the village that had not cared to help the pilot, it was issued a 300-piastre fine.

Fortunately, about twenty French soldiers arrived on horseback, on mules, and on bicycles. They were joined by railway workers who had been following the plane. They did not hesitate to jump into the mud and pull *La Curieuse* out from this quagmire.

Pourpe had been blinded by the sun. Since he could not see anything, he had decided to turn around. That is when he was betrayed by his engine.

The monoplane was transported to Hanoi, where Pourpe and Lufbery quickly repaired it. When it was functional again, it went on another trip with Pourpe, by train this time. To avoid facing the sun again, the pilot had decided that he would complete the dangerous flight above the mountains in the opposite direction—Lang Song to Hanoi. He was accompanied by Lieutenant Salel and Lufbery. On June 26 he did a flight demonstration, followed by a trip from Lang Son to Dong Dang, Ai Nam Quan, and Porte de Chine and back.

On June 28 he left Lang Son at 6:25 A.M. The French hero soon flew over the cloud-capped Cai Kin mountains and landed in Hanoi at 8:30. "The difficulties people imagined when they thought of what it takes to travel through these supposedly impenetrable regions evaporated in the face of Marc Pourpe's successful flight," wrote the local press. "We owe this achievement to Marc Pourpe's courage and dexterity. He won the honor of being the first man to fly above the wild region of Cai Kin."

Here is what *L'Avenir du Tonkin* had to say about Pourpe's feat: "Now that Pourpe has accomplished his exploit, we can admit to how worried and scared we were about his daring plan to fly over the mountain range that separates Lang Son from the delta all the way to Kep, especially at this time of year when heavy fog obstructs the view almost every day.

"We feared that the fog or the chaos of the mountains would cause him to lose his way and land in one of those remote places from which it is hard to come back and which might not be reached by a rescue party in time.

"Surely, Pourpe was aware of these difficulties and these dangers, but his audacity, his perfect command over his plane, and his absolute trust in it prevented him from backing down. He bravely faced the formidable dangers that were lying in his way. He overcame them. Now, we can breathe again. He was beaten by the blinding sun once, but this time he triumphed over it simply by turning his back to it."

When he arrived, Pourpe was greeted and congratulated by Mr. Sarraut, the governor-general. He was asked how he felt about his flight.

"The best part," he said smiling, "is finding myself here, among you, after what I saw from up there."

The next few days were spent in celebrations and receptions. After that, Pourpe went on with his schedule. On July 7 he gave a very successful flight demonstration in Hanoi. The next morning, at 5:45, he headed for Nam Dinh. He landed there at 6:44. Many Asians had flocked to the city by train to see the flight demonstrations that were going to take place there the next day.

The natives were amazed by what they saw: "It's like a spirit descending from the sky," they said, with devout admiration in their voices.

The pilot headed back to Hanoi by train and insisted on taking part in the Bastille Day celebrations. He flew over the military parade, trailing a French flag behind *La Curieuse*. The crowd was rapturous. People were clapping from all sides for the French bird.

As he was returning to the racetracks, Pourpe got caught in the rain. He could not see the field at all and improvised a blind landing, which damaged his landing gear and broke his propeller. Luckily, he did not injure himself.

After the plane was fixed, Pourpe headed to Annam because young Emperor Duy Tân wanted to see him fly.

A little bit before that, on July 22, Pourpe had sent me a letter from Hanoi in which he drew some conclusions from the amazing tour he had completed. These remarks, written by a pioneer, are interesting to read now that colonial aviation has made so much progress, although flying is still difficult and dangerous in Indochina.

"Cochinchina is essentially made out of paddy fields, grassland, cattail-covered plains, immense rivers (as well as countless smaller streams), and mangrove-tree-covered swamps.

"Tonkin, on the other hand, is very mountainous. The delta occupies only a small surface of the country, which mainly consists of mountains, thick forests, and rounded hills. The mountains are rocky and dry. The hills are curvier and covered in tall grass, which makes them almost as dangerous as the mountains themselves.

"Where should we establish Indochina's aeronautical military center?

"Cochinchina wants it. They claim that aviation will do the most good there because of the favorable terrain: wide waterways, flat plains, etc.

"In Tonkin, one can only really fly in the delta. The mountainous regions are just too dangerous and inaccessible for our planes.

"The two countries have been fighting over this for the last two years. A bunch of inquiries have been conducted; numerous reports have been published. A group of administrators prepared a project that has been unofficially vetted by the Ministry of the Colonies. This project calls for the main aviation hub in the colonies to be established in Saigon.

"Though I had not formed a professional opinion yet when I first arrived in Tonkin and talked to the governor-general, now that I am done with my tour, or, more exactly, with my ordeal—because, indeed, it was an ordeal—now that I have successfully flown over the delta (with my flights from Hai Phong to Hanoi and Hanoi to Nam Dinh) as well as over the mountains (with my flights from Lang Son to the Chinese border and Lang Son to Hanoi), I have proven that flying is achievable in Tonkin the same way it is in Cochinchina. And aeroplanes, as well as hydroplanes, might be even more useful here.

"Now that the trickiest issue has been solved and that even the most skeptical people have been shown that one can regularly fly in Indochina without fearing mysterious tropical eddies, treacherous winds, typhoons, etc., all we have to figure out is where it would be most logical and advantageous to establish the aeronautical center.

"Cochinchina has the advantage of having streams that can not only carry rowboats but allow for all kinds of fluvial modes of transportation. It also has roads that have nothing to envy our best highways back in France and facilitate car traffic, which is not yet very substantial but will surely increase like it has in other places. There are also some railways. Hence, it is relatively easy to reach separate points of the colony.

"All those means of transportation are slow, for sure. Aeroplanes and hydroplanes will certainly be advantageous, especially if used for military purposes. But it is important to note that Tonkin possesses very few of the advantages that make Cochinchina so productive.

"Indeed, Tonkin's uneven terrain does not facilitate regular and year-round fluvial travel. As for roads, they are rare, and you should see what state the ones that do exist are in! Sure, more can be built in the delta. Considerable construction projects have been undertaken there. But, after the delta, one runs into arid rock formations whose peaks cannot be smoothened. How costly would it be to attempt to build roads and rails on this labyrinthine terrain that abruptly goes up and down and that only the Annamite horse seems to be able to travel through, albeit slowly and painstakingly?

"How can one travel through and watch over this mountainous region that constitutes four-fifths of the country?

"How will you keep them clear of packs of Chinese bandits that still abound in the mountains where they go into hiding after terrorizing the peaceful farmers down in the delta?

"Just think of De Tham. This blackhearted bandit was able to foil the authorities for twenty years by hiding in the Cai Kin mountains, which I recently flew over. Think of all the energy, all the lives that were wasted for so many years because a gang of forty pirates was able to elude a contingent of 600 soldiers, wounding or killing fifty-seven of them. Nobody could ever follow them and find their hideaway. A plane will come in handy in such a situation and spare us that kind of trouble.

"Tonkin is bordered by China in the north and the northeast. This border is almost 1,000 kilometers long and is being guarded by only a handful of men. Wouldn't a few planes prove extremely useful in that area? Not only would they fulfill a military purpose, but they would also have a moral influence. At the very least, wouldn't they accomplish much more on the border with China than they would in Cochinchina, which has no borders to defend, and whose coasts are being guarded by torpedo boats and destroyers, which are still more efficient than hydroplanes for this purpose?

"The governor-general of Indochina is ready to support the expansion of our planes in the interest of our national prestige and for the good of our colony and of our new industry. But, faced with all these administrative and financial difficulties, and all those inessential discussions, he's hesitating, and, in the end, nobody takes the initiative even though a path has already been drawn and all there is to do now is to follow it.

"I will end this dissertation by talking a little bit about my most recent flights, which were not always very pleasant. Everything is difficult here when it comes to sports. The tropical, humid climate is putting my plane's best qualities to the test. Climbing to 950 meters here is as difficult as climbing to 2,500 meters in France. During my flight from Lang Son to Saigon, it took me thirty-five minutes to climb up to 950 meters, and, when I did so, I did not manage to maintain that altitude although I pushed my engine as far as it would go.

"Ah! What a trip! It procured my most emotional flight this far!

"It is true that I have been flying the same plane for a year now. We have visited Ceylon, the British Isles, Burma, the Malay Archipelago, the Sultanate of Johor, Cochinchina, and Cambodia. I was planning on going back to France so that my Blériot and I could get some rest when I was asked to do these flights in Tonkin. Could I refuse?

"The distance between Hanoi and Langson is inconsequential (150 kilometers), but there are many complications. For the first half of the way, one flies exclusively over immersed paddy fields. The other half is mountainous. The mountain range one has to fly over is steep and desolate, and a relentless sun shines on it. For 150 kilometers there is not one adequate place to land, and if you do land somewhere within the last 70 kilometers, you can be sure that no one will be able to find you except for the wild beasts that live there undisturbed.

"I took off from Hanoi one morning in July in the middle of the Tonkinese summer. The temperature was up to 40°C in the shade and up to 60°C in the sun.

"I left Hanoi and its small, suburban, bamboo-made houses behind. I saw the Red River, a gigantic silver ribbon peppered with sampans. It was already threatening to flood its fertile banks. There was almost no wind. A light mist was rising from the water-soaked paddy fields. I was facing the sun. It was burning my eyes and forcing me to blink constantly.

"When I reached Thuong Kep, the clouds were as low as 150 meters, but I could not fly above them. Besides, flying over these inhospitable mountains was very dangerous. My eyes were crying so much that, after an hour, the pain became intolerable. So, above Pho Vi, a little bit over halfway through my trip, I decided to go back to Hanoi and try this flight again on a less cloudy day.

"It turned out that I had made a very wise decision. I had barely flown for about 15 more kilometers and had just left the mountains behind when my engine suddenly stopped. I was flying over small, waterlogged paddy fields. I started heading down as slowly as possible, on an almost horizontal trajectory. Once I landed in a paddy field, I capsized. I did so 'adequately' though; that is to say that the plane was completely overturned. As a result, I did not hit anything too sensitive and there was very little damage.

"My plane was brought back to Hanoi, and people asked me if I was going to take off again. How many times have I been asked that haunting question? I was also asked what my plans were etc. I was very indecisive. I did not feel as confident anymore. My engine had summarily let me down. I suspected the magneto was to blame, but the same thing had happened three times in the last ten days. It felt like a sign. It was not prudent to attempt such an adventure with an exhausted engine. I was going to let people know I was ready to give up. I was discouraged.

"For the last three months, I haven't had a true mechanic. I do have a young assistant by the name of Raoul Lafberg. He's extremely loyal and resourceful, but he had never touched an aeroplane before starting to work with me. One cannot become an expert in such a short time.

"I had a hard time honoring my commitments. I felt incompetent.

"When my friends saw me in that state, they tried to cheer me up. They made me see that I could not give up, that I had to succeed, that the Europeans had made it this far, and that throwing the towel in now would have a disastrous effect on the natives. And, as Mr. Henri Lemônier said, isn't the road to Lang Son sort of our very own Appian Way, since it has been soaked in human blood? The road to Lang Son is the one that was taken by the heroic troops of Briére de l'Isle and General de Négrier. The names that adorn so many of the buildings in this area of the world resonate like strokes of the gong. They bring to mind bloody battles and victories. They also bring back the grueling and ferocious fight against the followers of the bandit De Tham, who attacked posts and convoys and abandoned our countrymen's corpses in remote grasslands before running to hide in the Cai Kin mountains.

"Under the influence of these feelings that were being stirred up within me, I decided to try again. I promised to do so, but I had a nagging feeling I was going to fail.

"To avoid the sun that had burned my eyes, I left from Lang Son for Hanoi, turning Phoebus into an ally without asking him for his permission. That is quite something in Tonkin!

"On June 28, one day after having flown over the Great Wall of China in Ai Nam Quan, I left Lang Son for Hanoi.

"That is when I started my laborious thirty-five-minute-long climb to 950 meters. I was feeling like a piece of paper, even at this low altitude. In a few moments, I was flying over a rocky and barren land.

"Immediately, my *Curieuse* started doing brutal head-first dives. After a bit, she became docile again, until, suddenly, a depression started the whole thing up again. It went on like that for a bit. I was going up and down in a way that was quite worrisome, and trying not to lose altitude as I was approaching the arid peaks of Cai Kin. I felt like I wasn't making any progress, though the wind was almost completely nonexistent. It almost seemed like my propeller wasn't doing anything. And in front of me—those immense, intimidating rocks! I was so certain that I wasn't going to be able to pass them that I stopped fighting. I waited passively for my engine to stop like I was convinced it would. I didn't even try to look for a place to land, since I had been told over and over again that I wouldn't find any here.

"I fell into an awful torpor, almost as if I was under the influence of a drug. The only thing keeping me awake was the way my plane was being violently shaken. Some jolts would practically send me sprawling down on the wings in outlandish positions.

"I did not feel any fear. I wasn't thinking of anything—neither of the past or of the present, not even of the future. All I could feel was an acutely painful burn on my head, neck, and back. My awfully white wings were reflecting the light so that the sun was attacking me from behind and I was blinded in spite of my sunglasses. I had to keep my eyes closed. I was being carried like a mere coconut flowing down a stream above the gloomy and wild territory of De Tham.

"I could barely figure out where I was heading using my compass, whose needle was going crazy. I went through the pass of Than Moi. I didn't fly above it; I actually went through it, through some sort of passageway punctuated by ridges. Every time I went by a ridge, I was hit by a gust of wind that felt like a slap. I was waiting for the end.

"My arms were barely holding the steering wheel, which seemed to be steering itself. Two or three times I actually felt like I wasn't even flying anymore.

"Finally, in the distance, I saw a bright and soft light. It looked boundless. I was used to the same monotonous landscape—paddy fields as far as the eye can see. But as they were reflecting the light of the merciless sun, these fields now looked like a golden sea. I came back to my senses and started feeling hopeful again. I straightened up. I wanted to live. I wanted to make it to my destination. I looked down at the path I should follow with eyes that were almost lifeless. I started to maneuver again and felt my *Curieuse* obediently following my lead.

"I flew 500 meters above Pho Vi, the place I had turned around at last time. Anguish had left me. I felt wild with joy. I was singing and yelling. I waved at all those good Naiqhé working the paddy fields and looking up at me in astonishment as I was flying above their heads. I was told that after they saw me, they lamented: 'Now no more way be pirates.'

"I arrived in Bac Ninh, which was close to the paddy field where I had capsized. I dove toward it and, when I had dropped to 20 meters above the ground, I went back up and continued toward my goal, which I was getting very close to.

"Soon, I spotted the Paul Doumer bridge, which crosses over the Red River in Hanoi. It was covered with people. I did a few stunts above Gia Lam and landed in front of the Hanoi racetracks' bleachers three or four minutes later.

"At that moment, I felt incredibly happy. Still, this joy was not enough to make me forget how despondent I had felt a little bit earlier.

"I am but a simple pilot, but I think that what I accomplished during Indochina's first aerial crusade will have a positive impact. I had started this trip with my poor friend Geo Verminck to do some flight demonstrations from India all the way to Oceania. But the natives' enthusiasm in the French colonies and the way the authorities encouraged us made us change our plans.

"Now that my friend is gone, I will continue what we started together. It is true that I am not making any money, but I feel in my heart that I am working to further France's interests. Isn't that more commendable than just chasing big paychecks? I know the way I see the world comes with some disadvantages. But oh well! I just have to think of home and of my friends to immediately feel better. Every once in a while, I feel discouraged. But I get over it easily. I just tell myself I need to fly to show the natives that the French do not fear anything and that they will never hesitate to fight those who betray them, no matter the circumstances.

"One can hardly conceive how much of an impact our planes have on the populations of the colonies. They think we have been sent there by some superior being. They have complete trust in us. They don't see us as men, but as demigods. Alas! Our sky is full of difficulties and problems. This is what makes me realize how far the natives' perception is from reality. But you have to make do with what you have! I'm fulfilling a mission, and I will go all the way, no matter what happens!

"I hope that my trusty Blériot-Gnome will serve me well until the end of my tour in spite of everything I have put it through. Then, I shall return to Paris and be happy and proud of the work I accomplished."

This long letter perfectly reflects Pourpe's personality: humble, heroic, selfless, and ready to achieve extraordinary feats not just to boost his own ego but to make himself useful to his homeland.

Despite his bravery, which he put at the service of France, despite the way his triumph contributed to our prestige—which, in those days, so dearly needed to be increased in Tonkin—Pourpe received only colonial distinctions and was never awarded the Legion of Honour. Official recognition will always be an empty phrase!

The daring pilot did not want to turn down the Emperor of Annam's invitation. His plane was getting in worse and worse shape. The fall he had taken after his Bastille Day performance did not help the poor *Curieuse*. Repairs took two weeks.

Pourpe, Lufbery, and the plane arrived in Hue on August 2. The champion of colonial aviation was welcomed enthusiastically by the local public figures as well as the general population. They came to congratulate him and see what he looked like.

The Blériot was immediately put together, and two days later Pourpe gave a flight demonstration at the Cavalier du Roi, with the beautiful citadel, the royal palace, and the Annamite mountains in the backdrop. Trains meant to carry mainly tourists were bringing Europeans and natives from all sides. The latter were still incredulous.

At 5 p.m. a salvo of nine cannons announced Pourpe's first flight. The Annamites were immediately won over. They were amazed by Pourpe's audacity and bravery. The pilot completed two flights (the first one was twenty minutes long; the second lasted fifteen minutes) during which he showed the extent of his skills. Thoughtful as always, he decided to do something very kind and flew toward the hospital to entertain the people there with some aerial stunts.

In the official gallery the Emperor Duy Tân, sitting next to the résident supérieur and surrounded by princes and dignitaries wearing ceremonial garb, was the one to give the signal to clap, which he did often. He insisted on granting Pourpe the first-class Kim Kahn award and Lufbery the second-class one.

Two days later Pourpe gave an equally successful flight demonstration. The newspapers called it "splendid and enchanting." That night, there were fireworks, a boat fair, and a grandiose banquet to mark the end of the festivities and honor the pilot. Pourpe gave a short and gracious speech in order to thank not only his hosts for the way they welcomed him but also the 600,000 natives who came to see his flight demonstrations.

"The European population," he said, "has warmly cheered for me and made all kinds of nice gestures toward me, so much so that I spent all my time thanking people."

"On Saturday, I will leave Hue for Tourane," he added. "I will give my last Indochinese flight demonstrations for this year there, on August 11. I say 'for this year' because I intend to come back and accomplish great things here. Still, despite my plan to return to Indochina soon, I feel sad thinking about all the people I will have to part with, all these French people I will leave behind. The way they welcomed me is evidence of the famed 'kindness of colonists.'"

The Tourane flight demonstrations were a great success as well and brought a close to Pourpe's tour. He returned to France in September 1913 after having flown more than 17,000 kilometers over our colonial empire.

People there were sorry to see him go and would remember him dearly.

Here is an article that was published in the local press at that time: "Marc Pourpe is not only a dexterous pilot who, through his outstanding flights, gave the people of Indochina the opportunity—and what a great and marvelous opportunity!—to witness France's genius. He is also, above all, a charming and humble young man whom people here not only admire because of his courage, his discernment, and his dauntlessness but genuinely like for his rare personal qualities.

"We wish him all the best and hope that his upcoming projects will come to fruition so that he can come back to us soon." What project were the newspapers talking about? Pourpe had alluded to them when he bid Indochina farewell (it was a true farewell, because—alas!—he would never come back).

The daring pilot was planning a flight from Paris to Saigon for the next year. With the help of Lufbery, who was very familiar with all the places Pourpe would fly over and could teach him about their climate and the obstacles he would meet in each one of them, he had carefully prepared an itinerary. He was ready! But Germany decided otherwise.

The first flight from Paris to Saigon ended up happening years later, in 1924. It was completed by Georges Pelletier d'Oisy, who decided to undertake this trip after I told him about the dream poor Pourpe could not fulfill.

"I will try to succeed at the task he wasn't able to take on," he told me. "And I will dedicate him this flight."

Marc Pourpe at the Hanoi racetrack, June 17, 1913, about to begin his 150 kilometer flight northeast over the Cai Kin mountains to Lang Son City. Albert Sarraut, governor general of French Indochina, is to his right. M. Gueyffier, head of Aviation Tonkinoise, is to his left.

THIRTEEN

The First Flight from Cairo to Khartoum

Pourpe was not the type of man to take time off. Neither was Lufbery. In a letter he wrote me on 7 September 1913, while on the *Amazone*—the ship that was taking him from Hue back to Marseille—the great pilot told me: "I am coming back with the intention of immediately starting to work hard again."

He soon had a new project: he wanted to fly from Cairo to Khartoum and back. It was a 4,000-kilomete trek. Nobody had thought of attempting such an audacious trip before. At that time, people did not vacation in the desert yet, and the only landmark one could use to find their way through it was the Nile River. What plane would Pourpe fly?

He had made Blériot's planes famous with his flights in the colonies. His outstanding achievements did a lot to boost the brand's image. So, he asked me to intercede in his favor and ask Louis Blériot and Alfred Leblanc—the brand's director—to give him a deal on a new plane.

"That's very interesting," said Alfred Leblanc. "I am fully on board with this idea. Go ahead and tell Blériot about it."

I thought it was a done deal.

"Great idea," Louis Blériot answered. "I'm very interested. Please go speak to Leblanc about it."

"But . . . he's the one who told me to speak to you."

"He did? Well if he already knows, he has to make a decision. I cannot do anything more."

It was the tennis gambit: They were going to continue striking the ball at the other player's court until it landed out of bounds. How clever!

Consequently, I advised Pourpe to do what Roland Garros did and give up on such an ungrateful brand. We paid the now sadly deceased Léon Morane a visit. He outfitted Pourpe with a glorious plane, a plane that made history—the Morane-Saulnier. Garros had just crossed the Mediterranean Sea on one of these.

This monoplane was not easy to maneuver for someone who was used to flying a Blériot. So, our loyal friends Roland Garros, Léon Morane, and Edmond Audemars came together to advise Pourpe on how to land properly and avoid troubles that Garros himself had encountered when he first started flying this remarkable plane.

Pourpe and Lufbery left Paris for Cairo at the end of October. Everything had been planned and organized. The pilot was already a master. He had prepared his itinerary most thoroughly.

The equipment arrived in early December. Pourpe wrote me: "After a few days spent taking care of formalities—an experience which ended up being quite pleasant because I was always so warmly welcomed in the various Egyptian agencies I visited—I managed to send out all the supplies I will need for my trip. They will be kept along the route I will take. On my way to Khartoum from Cairo I will stop in Minieh, Assiut, Nag Hammadi, Luxor, Shellal, Wadi Halfa, Station Number 6, Abu Hamad, and Atbara.

"Here are all the main flights I will perform if everything goes well:

- Cairo to Luxor (510 kilometers)
- Luxor to Wadi Halfa (540 kilometers)
- Wadi Halfa to Abu Hamad (410 kilometers)
- Abu Hamad to Khartoum (520 kilometers)

"Contrary to what has been announced, I will not go any farther than that."

Mr. Defrance, our plenipotentiary minister in Cairo, introduced me to Lord Kitchener, who oversees Khartoum. This remarkable and famous officer was very kind to me and spent over an hour giving me advice regarding my itinerary. He told me he was very interested in my trip.

"Lord Kitchener is the current record-holder for the fastest Khartoum–Cairo liaison. He has completed it

Marc Pourpe seated in his Morane-Saulnier monoplane in Cairo, Egypt, 17 December 1913. Raoul Lufbery, his mechanic, stands second from right.

many times, using the quickest modes of transportation available, especially when he is being called to England for some important matter. The fastest trip he's made was only seventy-two hours. Of course, express trains would be put at his disposal. Other trains would move aside to let him pass. In Wadi Halfa, a specially appointed boat would take him to Shellal in no time. There, he would catch another express train that would have only one car and take him to Cairo.

"I'm hoping to complete this trip by flying for only twenty-five hours, although those hours will be spread over four days. If one could guarantee access to supplies, mechanics, landing spots, and spare parts, I think this trip could be made in less than twenty hours in the same day, with only a few hours spent flying in the dark since it can be light for up to sixteen hours around here in some seasons.

"Before I leave, I would like to fly over the Pyramids, which has never been done before even during the 1910 Heliopolis flight exhibition."

He was the first man to ever rise above the forty-one-century-old monuments. But before that, a small setback occurred.

He was going to go on a test flight, helped by some Arabs, whom he had taught how to hold his monoplane before the takeoff. The natives seemed to have understood. But one of the men holding the fuselage must have been so impressed at the sight of the plane that he did not let go, and just stood there mesmerized until he was hit by the empennage. Fortunately, the man was not hurt, but the empennage was damaged.

Though it was not a serious incident, it infuriated Pourpe, who was counting on flying that day. The big crowd that had gathered around the field was not able to see the plane fly. "I hate not keeping my promises," Pourpe said to me. "It had never happened before then, and I hope it will be the last time I have to deal with such a ridiculous stroke of bad luck."

Pourpe's flight above the Pyramids took place on December 17, to the amazement of the Cairenes who saw a plane fly over their city for the first time. Pourpe took off from the Heliopolis airfield at 11 A.M., despite strong winds. He flew 1,100 meters above Cairo, crossed over the Nile, descended to 800 meters to fly over the plain of Giza, and circled above the pharaohs' tombs. His trip there took him twenty-five minutes, but he made it back in only seven thanks to the wind that was pushing him and allowed him to reach a "dizzying"—as Pourpe put it—speed of 180 km/h.

"It would be pointless to try to convey the joy the Cairenes expressed when someone flew over their city for the first time," wrote the *Journal du Caire*. "The impromptu quality of Pourpe's daring excursion certainly caused some potential spectators to miss it. Still, many people saw him fly above the metropolis and cheered for him. Everyone greatly admires the young and brave French pilot."

Lord Kitchener insisted on seeing Pourpe again before he took off for his great adventure. What happened during this meeting? Here's what Pourpe says about it: "He told me he knew about my flights in the East Indies and quoted some facts about them. He also kept track of my flights in Indochina. He knew about every single one of them. He asked me questions regarding details that seemed inconsequential to me but later turned out to be of great importance. After a while, he went back to my dear project and abstained from asking me those same disappointing questions I heard so many times before in similar situations: 'Did you do a lot of research to build your itinerary? You are tackling an impossible task. Be careful!'

"He did not list a whole collection of responsibilities like the ones our colonial administrators keep using as excuses in order to avoid ever taking any initiatives.

"He simply asked: 'Do you have your itinerary with you? I have been thinking. Show it to me.'

"He took it, read it, turned to a 1:250,000-scale map of the region, traced my itinerary with his finger, and suddenly turned to me and said: 'Do not stop in Korosko. There will be no police force there to protect you. Instead, stop in Derr, 60 kilometers to the south.'

"After examining the itinerary all the way to Khartoum, he added: 'Everything else is perfect. You have made up your mind, haven't you?'

"When I answered in the affirmative, he called in his aide-de-camp, Commandant Fitzgerald, and gave him my itinerary, saying: 'Mr. Pourpe, whom we know well from the newspapers, will leave for Khartoum by plane. Give orders for people to guarantee he will have access to the fields he is planning on landing in and taking off from and be able to receive all the necessary supplies. I am hoping Mr. Pourpe will be successful and am counting on you.'

"I was going to thank him, but he interrupted me, countering: 'I should be the one thanking you and encouraging you. I am wishing for your success with all my heart, and I am counting on you to brighten the festivities that will happen in Khartoum on January 17 to celebrate the second anniversary of King George V's visit there.'

"You can understand how much I want to succeed and keep the promise I made this esteemed statesman."

Pourpe was full of enthusiasm and felt honored by such a prestigious patronage. He wanted to leave as soon as possible. But fate was not on his side.

When he flew over the Pyramids, his 60-horsepower Gnome engine had worked wonderfully. The Morane-Saulnier plane had withstood the violent wind. Pourpe trusted his equipment and sent Lufbery to Wadi Halfa.

Everything was ready. He decided to leave on December 22. The day before, it had rained all day and night. A southern wind had blown hard. But the young hero was impatient and did not want to postpone his trip. He thought he could make it.

He took off with 150 liters of gas in his tank. It was enough to reach Luxor without making any stops. Unfortunately, after 20 kilometers, he realized that the part that was allowing for the gas to circulate between the tank located in the back and the one in the front was loose. So, instead of going where it was supposed to, the fuel was leaking out of the plane. Pourpe had to head back to Heliopolis.

When he landed, the plane's wheels sank into the wet sand and caused it to capsize. As a result, the cabin and part of one wing were damaged while the rudder, the propeller, the front of the engine, and a wheel broke.

Pourpe immediately sent for Lufbery, but it took five days for him to make it back from Wadi Halfa.

In the letter he wrote me on December 24 and in which he wished me a happy new year, he told me how saddened he was by that incident.

"I have been incredibly unlucky over the past two weeks. I am completely discouraged. Christmas celebrations are going to delay me since most workshops will close for two or three days.

"Everything will be fixed little by little. I work from 6 A.M. to 8 P.M. Autogenous welding is not an option here. I knew it! I will have to get pieces for the cabin that need to be specially jointed, riveted, and brazed. I will not be ready before January 4 at the earliest."

I had arranged for Pourpe to get the exclusive story of his Egyptian journey published in two papers, *Excelsior* and *La Vie au Grand Air*. For this reason, my thoughtful friend was worrying, although unnecessarily. A detail from our correspondence shows how scrupulous he was in all of his actions. "How are you going to be able to arrange that now, my poor Jacquot? It's for you that I worry. You're the one who was able to put everything in motion here while being over there. That is the reason I am so displeased with myself! Of course, 1913 had to end so poorly! Well, say what you want, but be assured that I'm not wasting time. I'm working as fast as I can and I'm very concerned about your situation.

"If I had had a Blériot, the repairs would already be over. But the need for autogenous welding is complicating everything! They don't know how to do it here. The only welding equipment available is the one used to solder or cut rails. If the plane didn't need welding, I could fix it myself. I have learned enough to handle all kinds of basic repairs."

In the end, the plane ended up being fixed faster than expected because Pourpe and Lufbery spent entire sleepless nights working on it. The Morane-Saulnier was ready on 31 December 1913. Yet, Pourpe was still enraged to receive a letter from the Ligue Nationale Aérienne in Paris, which was sponsoring Pourpe's endeavor, although they had not offered him any funding.

"I received a letter from the Ligue on December 31," Pourpe wrote me. "They are telling me that I need to leave as soon as possible. They seem to be implying that I'm being hesitant and am putting off the trip on purpose. I am not even going to answer them, because they do not know me and are misjudging me. When I have a trip in mind, I intend to complete it. I never give up on my projects.

"I encountered two major issues I never would have had if I still had a plane like *La Curieuse*. The resources necessary to repair the Morane-Saulnier are not available here. That is why it took me ten days to get ready again. I realize this will not be the last time I damage the plane. It was a mistake on my part to pick such an unstable plane, especially with how sandy the ground often is around here. Everything sinks in it. But don't worry: I will make it as far as possible.

"But I will not have the Ligue and its administrators try to pressure me with nonsense like 'prestige.' Let them try to fly a plane over here. Maybe then I'll listen to what they have to say. In the meantime, instead of lecturing me, they could send me some money. I'm up to 15,000 francs in expenses and I haven't even left yet. I do not see how I'm going to be able to recover that sum.

"I can't charge people to see flight demonstrations now that the Ligue has put a patriotic stamp on the whole thing and turned it into some kind of official mission. And I can't just go begging for money. Talk about putting our prestige in jeopardy!

"I don't know what the Ligue is thinking, but they have some nerve! I had a run of bad luck, had to spend a bunch of money, risk everything, put myself on the line, and now I'm getting scolded by them! You know what, old friend? Blast it all!

"Anyway, don't worry yourself. Let me take care of it. I'm going to work hard, but I miss my Blériot dearly. I would already be back by now if I still had it. Oh well!"

Once this remarkable pilot got a better command of the Morane-Saulnier, he changed his mind. It was a champion's plane and, as such, wasn't necessarily easy to handle at first.

At the end of 1913 great pilots flocked to Cairo. Jules Védrines flew there all the way from France and arrived on December 29. He was enthusiastically welcomed by everyone there. He was the first person to fly that route. "That is without a doubt," Pourpe wrote, "his best performance to this day as far as bravery, endurance, and stamina go. And that is not saying nothing, considering he has flown 127,000 kilometers, not counting the distance he covered performing above airdromes."

Sadly, the popular champion's behavior cast a shadow over his success. Indeed, he attacked a fellow countryman, a man named Roux, who was working with Pierre Daucourt, a pilot who had attempted the same trip as Védrines but who had had to give up after the passage of the Taurus. Daucourt had had no trouble refueling during his whole trip, whereas Védrines had an Indigenous worker deny him access to fuel during one of his pit stops. It might have had something to do with him asking for it rather curtly, but, instead, Védrines speculated that Roux must have given orders to prevent him from refueling. So, when Roux congratulated him and presented him with the tricolored ribbon in Cairo in front of a crowd of officials, Védrines, to the audience's dismay, insulted and slapped him. All the celebrations and feasts that had been planned in the French hero's honor were canceled.

This incident saddened Pourpe, who was always so well mannered. "I was so upset that I confronted Védrines to make him understand the consequences of his gesture. But, although I tried to be as diplomatic as possible and develop a genuine friendship with him, it was all in vain. The colony does not want to have anything to do with him anymore. Still, I have not given up on him, and I'm trying to sort things out. Now that Bonnier has arrived, I think we can try to arrange it so that Védrines will be honored the way he should have been but wasn't because of the vulgar way he has behaved, seemingly without even realizing it.

"Bonnier and his passenger just arrived from France. I decided to try out my plane after all those repairs and go meet him about 50 kilometers out of Cairo. I could not tell you how fast my heart was beating during this whole trip at the thought of getting close to the end of it.

"I am fully ready. The day after tomorrow, or maybe Sunday, at the latest, I will take off for my trip. Believe me, old friend, I will do everything in my power for my dear Jacquot to be proud of his old pal Marco.

"1914 is off to a good start and will surely be a good year since the first new year's wishes I received were from you."

Alas! As well as that year started off for my poor dear friend, he would not see the end of it.

FOURTEEN

A Heroic Expedition above the Nile River

Pourpe took off from the Heliopolis polo field on Sunday, 4 January 1914, at 9:07 a.m. After circling the field twice to thank the crowd for having come to see him take off, he headed directly south.

Despite a thick fog covering the Nile valley, Pourpe was able to follow the river to Beni Suef. There, the clouds were as low as 350 meters. He decided to fly over them and use his compass to find his way.

He flew for about thirty-five minutes without really knowing where he was. He remembered Lord Kitchener's words: "Do not lose the Nile! If you have an emergency landing too far from the river, nobody will ever find you!" One has to be quite brave to just follow one's intuition when flying. That was especially true in those days, considering the kind of equipment available at the time. When Pourpe dipped below the clouds, he realized he was flying above the craggy mountains that flank the Nile, but he could not see the river itself anywhere. Where could it be?

"I have to admit; I was seriously worried. After thinking for a while, I guessed I must have gone too far east and started heading west. I was right. To my great relief I reached the Nile again ten minutes later.

"That was all well and good, but where was I actually? I had no clue. All the river bends looked the same. I kept flying until a quarter to twelve, in the hope I would reach a landmark that would help me figure out where I was. Finally, I spotted the Aswan Dam. That meant I was 225 kilometers from Luxor. I was full of hope and kept on going. A half hour later, a minor malfunction forced me to land.

"I gently touched ground on an island in front of Menshah. Although it was a very unfavorable terrain, the landing went well enough."

This impromptu stop was warranted by a broken intake valve.

It took Pourpe 3 hours and 15 minutes to cover the distance from Cairo to Menshah. The two cities are 450 kilometers apart, but, considering the detours the pilot took, he must have actually flown for more than 500 kilometers.

Pourpe promptly called for Lufbery, who was staying in Luxor and arrived that evening. He immediately went to work with his usual acumen and conscientiousness. He took apart the whole engine, which was filled with sand, and then put it back together. When that was done, they waited for supplies to be brought via felucca (small wooden sail boats that ply the Nile).

On January 6 Pourpe arrived in Luxor after a 250-kilometer trip that took him two hours to complete. He was delayed by the wind that was blowing from the southwest and violently shook him for the whole duration of his flight.

"The distances on the itinerary I prepared are wrong. I cannot, under any circumstances, get too far away from the Nile. When you get even just 20 kilometers away from it, you find yourself above desolate mountains made out of rock and sand. If I were to crash there it would be the end of me. To find out how many kilometers I traveled, we can just use the railway as a point of reference."

He left Luxor on January 7 at 10:15 a.m. and arrived in Wadi Halfa at 2:15 p.m. He covered 590 kilometers without making any stops.

"All I will say about today's trip is that it wasn't exactly leisurely. This country isn't particularly attractive, especially when you're looking down at it while flying at 600 meters' altitude. Everything looks awfully flat and dreary.

"Before Aswan, which is the point tourists will not go past, the land is still a bit cultivated, but, after it, all you have is jagged mountains that reminded me of the Cai Kin ones, although they are shorter and less abrupt. However, the Cai Kin mountains went on for only 80 kilometers.

These spread for over 350 kilometers without offering any landing spot.

"Of course, the weather was gloomy as per usual, which made this outing even more bleak. After a while, I left the mountains behind to fly over the desert, which is not much more to look at. Even though I am used to the sun by now, the way this yellow sand reflected the sun really hurt my eyes.

"I will fly again tomorrow and am planning on making it to Abu Hamad. When I do so, I will have covered three-quarters of my trip.

"For 500 miles all I could see was some railroad tracks cutting through the desert, which was mostly flat, although there were a few random mounds peeking out here and there.

"There isn't really anything enjoyable about this trip. I am following the Sudanese government's advice by sticking to the railroad tracks. I came to realize that it is imperative for me to do so if I don't want to break my bones! I am too used to traveling through desolate lands to be tempted to take any unnecessary risks.

"I have flown 1,290 kilometers between Cairo and here. It's a good stretch. If the wind continues to cooperate, I will finish this trip within the next twenty hours.

"Let it be known that the English authorities, including their maritime and rail services, have been very helpful and are doing everything in their power to make sure I reach Khartoum. Thanks to Lord Kitchener, who, as you know, has been taking really good care of me, everyone is interested in my expedition.

"When I arrived in Luxor, everyone was very enthusiastic. M. C. Legrain gave me his speech in writing because he was too emotional to read it. Here are a few excerpts I found particularly moving:

'Today, the ancient pharaohs and the modern Egyptians alike saw, flying in the beautiful sky above them, a tayir: a bird that scared away eagles, vultures, and kites. The old pharaohs might have believed that the devastation that Daniel predicted would strike their country was finally upon them, had they not heard their descendants cheering *What a sweet and beautiful bird that has been sent to us by European civilization!*

'The era of Leviathan and other apocalyptic beasts is behind us. Scientists have replaced the loud prophets of the past. Instead of frightening us with eschatological tales, they are building a new world bathed in light and beauty.

'Everything gets better with time. In a bygone era, God Almighty only ever spoke to announce catastrophes.

Marc Pourpe in the Morane-Saulnier monoplane he flew on his historic round trip flight from Cairo, Egypt, to Kartoum, Sudan, and return, 4 January to 3 February 1914.

'You, Sir, have spread the Good Word like an angel or a cherubim on your white-winged bird and have given us confirmation that no country can evade civilization. That is why I would like to thank you, Sir, in the name of everyone here, Europeans and Egyptians alike. Thank you for the bravery you have demonstrated by so adeptly completing this wonderful mission. What makes me even prouder is that you are French, which means that our country can now claim one more peaceful victory.

'When one grows older, one starts wondering if the next generations will be driven by the same enthusiasm that has guided us in the past. I have had some doubts over the past few years, but now I feel that we can grow old in peace. Our successors are not only worthy of us, their forefathers, but may even be superior to us. You have proven as much today, my dear compatriot.'"

Pourpe continued his trip with great consistency and skill. He stopped following the Nile for a while because the part of the river he reached formed an immense curve, and instead took a shortcut through the desert. It took the pilot two hours and thirty-five minutes to fly 400 kilometers and reach Abu Hamad on January 9. This "very young man's frail and elegant demeanor is deceptive. He actually has remarkable stamina and has gained international acclaim." Pourpe regularly accomplished miracles. He wrote me from Abu Hamad on 10 January 1914.

"I have finally completed the second-to-last stretch of my trip and did so without making a stop like for the previous one. It was a 385-kilometer trek through the Sudanese desert. I won't claim I enjoyed it. Far from it! There is not much pleasure to be had in seeing only sand for three hours (especially when it reflects the sun that is already shining in your eyes), flying over the occasional arid mountain (people here call them 'gebels') around which the air is very unstable, and, every 40 kilometers or so, spotting a lonely shack that sometimes has a well near it. None of this was particularly entertaining, but that is all I got to see on my trip from Wadi Halfa to Abu Hamad. So you can imagine how happy I was to reach my destination.

"I was constantly bothered by wind blowing from the northwest. It was lifting clouds of sand that sometimes completely obstructed my view. And that's not even that bad! Yesterday, the wind was blowing only 7 km/s. Today, its speed has reached 14 to maybe 16 km/s. Even as low as 10 meters from the ground one cannot see a thing. It is impossible to travel during those storms, so I'm very happy to have completed this part of my trip yesterday. Because, otherwise, I would have been delayed by at least three or four days.

"I wouldn't call it atmospheric disturbance per se, but I have observed a very strange phenomenon. Every once in a while, as I'm flying above a flat and dry area, I'll be shaken around as if I were caught in a storm. That could go on for as long at 150 kilometers! Formidable gusts of wind would batter me about as easily as if I were a feather. When I come back—as a tourist next time—I will study this intriguing phenomenon.

"My eyes are very tired. I can't go out without wearing thick sunglasses and am not allowed to expose myself to artificial light. Such are the consequences of my exposure to the sun's glare reflected by the sand.

"I'm waiting for Lafberg because my engine needs a thorough checkup. Then I'll do Abu Hamad–Khartoum. It'll be a 555-kilometer trip. If possible, I won't make any pit stops. You know, old pal, it might not be my most nerve-racking trip, but it will be the longest and toughest one. In the Far East, my enemies were paddy fields and the heat. Here, it's the sun and the sand. I don't know what's worse.

"Since Luxor, I haven't been able to take any pictures because I keep leaving with only six hours' worth of fuel and the weather never wants to cooperate. I removed everything that was not absolutely indispensable from my plane. Lafberg says it will take him three days to travel from Luxor to Wadi Halfa, a trip I completed in only four hours. That—and the mechanical trouble I encountered on the first day—is the reason why, in the end, my trip will last nine days instead of five.

"Like many people, the Ligue Internationale does not know that there are no trains between Shelah and Wadi Halfa because of the 350-kilometer stretch along the Nile.

"I'm happy, but this trip is eating up all the money I brought back from Indochina. I thought I could earn about 20,000 francs in Egypt, but there are two other pilots trying to make good in Cairo. I can't blame them, but it doesn't make things easy for me.

"In any case, I would like to say that I stuck 'almost perfectly to the 2,500-kilometer itinerary' (I hadn't planned to make a stop in Menshah). That is the same distance as between Paris and Constantinople. I did it in 'nine days,' which is a 'record.' All in all, I have flown 1,592 kilometers in twelve hours and five minutes."

Finally, I received a triumphant letter sent on January 1 from Khartoum. "I arrived here in Khartoum yesterday, and today I received the letter in which you wished me a happy new year and, more importantly, gave me some encouragement. See, I didn't give up, my dear Jacques! Instead, it's misfortune that gave up on me finally!

"Thank you for what you wrote me. You know how dearly I care for you and our friendship. I would like to be even more successful and achieve even greater feats, so I can make you proud of your pupil and thank you for your trust in me!

"Here's another telegram I received: 'Mission beautifully accomplished. Thank you for prestige increased. Can you do Bagdad? Signed: Quinton.'

"Can you believe these folks at the Ligue? Let them reimburse me the 20,000 francs I just spent on the Khartoum expedition and then we'll see. The nerve!

"The last part of my trip was particularly trying. My face is all red. The sun cooked me like an apple! When I left Abu Hamad the wind was blowing at 17 km/s. I had enough gas and oil for a seven-hour trip and had to cover 580 kilometers. I made it without having to take a single break and reached Khartoum as planned.

"The Nile is interspersed with islands and tributaries, and the current is very fast in this stretch. As a consequence, I was shaken a lot. It is a normal phenomenon, but not a pleasant one. So I decided to follow the tracks a bit to the east. The sun was so relentless that the temperature in my plane reached 27°C. I had to fight the toughest atmospheric disturbance I have ever encountered. It was brutal and constant, not very attractive qualities. The disturbance did not stop for even one second. My wrists are sore, and the gas tank I was resting against did a number on my back.

"Until Atbara, I didn't know my speed, but by the looks of it I was going pretty fast. I left the Nile and was soon flying over a sandy desert. This parched landscape was peppered with thin, thorny bushes that looked like they had been burnt by the sun. For a couple of hours, I gazed upon this barren land, which always looked the same save for a random gebel here and there. I flew over a few hundred wadis, which caused some disturbance that put me into some uncomfortable positions. Wadis are dry gullies formed by the rain when it flows down from gebels into the Nile.

"I was flying at a 400-meter altitude and could not get any higher, even with my Morane-Saulnier, which was designed for fast ascents, and in spite of my 60-horsepower Gnome engine. A couple of times, I turned around to face the wind and gain a hundred meters or so. But even that did not go without great difficulties. Then, I would change course again to head south. My throat was dry and my eyes were almost completely closed because of the brightness of the sun, but being close to my goal gave me courage. I kept picturing Khartoum appearing on the horizon.

"I finally reached the gebels that border the Nile. They are about 1,700 meters high and not much to look at. I passed them on the left. Soon, I spotted a white line that was parallel to the line formed by the horizon, and then another one that was a little wider and perpendicular to the first one. Those lines turned out to be the Blue Nile, on the banks of which lies Khartoum, and the White Nile, which was the line pointing south. I could see the battlefields of Omdurman and Khartoum more and more distinctly. I spotted a light white smoke, which I guessed must have been emitted by the fires I asked for to indicate where I could land. I headed right toward it. I was flying at about 300 meters. My heart was beating hard and I was so emotional that tears started swelling in my eyes. I thought, 'Please let my plane not encounter any trouble before I fly over the bridge I see over there that crosses over the Nile with its white arches like a big caterpillar.'

"My plane experienced a little jolt when I flew over the Blue Nile. I turned slightly to the right and flew over the palace of the sirdar and governor-general of the Sudan: Sir Reginald Wingate. I drew an eight above the landing field and then touched ground in the middle of the white circle that had been drawn for me.

"Something extraordinary and thrilling happened then; a crowd of more than 20,000 European and Sudanese people rushed toward me.

"Sir Reginald Wingate welcomed me and told me how happy he was that I made it safely to the capital of Sudan, which was seeing an aeroplane for the first time in its history. He introduced me to his wife, Lady Wingate, who also had kind words for me. He then introduced me to Colonel Smith, who was going to host me during my stay in Khartoum, and to the other officers of the garrison.

"I delivered the mail I had brought from Cairo, which caused people to cheer again. Even English people, who tend to be so even-tempered, were rushing me and shouting gaily. I kept shaking hands and being introduced to persons of note by the sirdar. That night, he invited me to dinner. All the military and civil officials attended in their formal dress. The whole time I was there I was treated like a king. Or at least that it was it seemed like! I have never seen anything as beautiful, as enchanting, as the sirdar's palace (not even in the Indies, Cochinchina, or Annam).

"I had barely just arrived when I received a telegram from Field Marshal Slatin Pasha. He was just repeating a message that Lord Kitchener had given him for me. Lord Kitchener will arrive here tonight, and I am supposed to go see him tomorrow. Friday and Saturday I will give flight demonstrations and will probably leave on Monday, after the celebrations. I am intending to make more stops because Lord Kitchener has politely asked me for some more detailed notes.

"Let me finish this letter with a rundown of my trip and some updated statistics, like the actual distance between each stop:

- January 4th: Cairo to Menshah; 467 kilometers in 3 hours and 15 minutes
- January 6th: Menshah to Luxor; 200 kilometers in 1 hour and 55 minutes
- January 7th: Luxor to Wadi Halfa; 570 kilometers in 4 hours
- January 9th: Wadi Halfa to Abu Hamad; 385 kilometers in 2 hours and 55 minutes
- January 12th: Abu Hamad to Khartoum; 580 kilometers in 4 hours and 13 minutes

"In the end, I flew 2,202 kilometers in 16 hours and 18 minutes; the previous record for this trip—which had been achieved by traveling by land—being 72 hours."

During the whole week that followed the hero's arrival, there were official receptions. The sirdar had a banquet and a ball to celebrate the pilot's successful excursion and even invited him to a private lunch.

On January 17 Pourpe kept the promise he had made to Lord Kitchener and flew over Khartoum and its surroundings for a long while. An enormous crowd had gathered in the city to see the grandiose celebrations organized to commemorate the King of England's visit to Sudan.

First, the French hero started by flying in every possible direction at a low altitude. After a little while, however, he surprised his audience with a very considerate gesture: he flew over the battlefield of Omdurman, where the English troops, under the command of Lord Kitchener, won their last battle against the Khalifa. A mixed army of 50,000 English and Egyptian soldiers had faced off against 75,000 Dervishes. Pourpe flew his plane above this part of the desert where over 20,000 men had died within a few hours.

This flight was very emotional for the people of Khartoum and Omdurman. That afternoon, in the speech he gave at Gordon College, the sirdar praised the French people's acumen and ardor and applauded Pourpe's chivalrous gesture and his valor.

During his stay, the young pilot had several meetings with Lord Kitchener. Here is what he wrote me on that subject: "You could very clearly see how happy he was. He asked me to do three things: first, write a report on my expedition; then, try to figure out how to set up regular flights between Cairo, Khartoum, El-Obeid, the Nile valley, and the various oases; and, finally, to do some research on building an aviation center. He would like to have it either in Egypt or Sudan to train aspiring military and civil pilots who want to serve in Britain's Asian and African colonies.

"He wants to get to work on these projects as soon as 1915 comes around. Knowing the man, I do not doubt that he will go through with his plans, although these might seem a little unrealistic to less daring people.

"Every time we speak, Lord Kitchener shows great interest in the stories I told him about the impact I have had on the natives. Some anecdotes are particularly colorful and testify to the acute sense of observation some natives possess.

"A nice Sudanese soldier did not want to believe that I had just come out of the 'belly' of my plane or that I had used it to cross the desert he knew so well. He claimed that the big bird that had made such a loud noise when it had flown above his dirt hut and his palm trees had come here of his own volition. I pointed out that the 'bird' was not a living being and could not move on its own. He turned things over in his head for a while and then said: 'Well! If you're not worried about it flying away, why do you tie it to the ground like we do our camels?'

"He was referring to the two stakes I used to fasten my wheels so that the wind wouldn't shake the plane around too much.

"The sirdar approached an old servant of General Gordon's and asked him some questions about my 'bird.' 'What I find most surprising and admirable,' the man answered, 'is that he thought of putting a fan in front of him because he must be very hot when getting so close to the sun.'

"But the most extraordinary reaction to my flying came from a man who had seen me fly above the sirdar's palace and Omdurman. I had performed aerial stunts, had glided through the air, etc. 'May he be blessed by Allah and safely find his way back to him with all the earthly treasures he can carry.'

"The sirdar asked him what he meant. 'His father, who, like him, is a birdman, must have gone on a trip and gotten lost. Now his dutiful son is looking for him everywhere. That is why he came to the desert and is searching in every direction without ever stopping. He will find him. Inshallah!'

"Monday, I will leave Khartoum for Cairo. I must admit that I am very sad about it. I was treated like a king here. I delighted in my hosts' friendliness and sense of hospitality, lovely traits that are shared by all English people.

"On my way back, I will make all the pit stops that had originally been planned. I have no right to be rude to the natives who had expected a visit from me and have gone through the trouble of preparing landing spots for me, although all they ended up seeing was a dark spot quickly traveling through the sky."

Another nice gesture! Pourpe had a thought for the people living in the desert. He did not hesitate to prolong his stay and live uncomfortably to thank the people who had been ready to do him a favor. Having such a good heart is a rare thing.

FIFTEEN

Back in His Childhood Country

Pourpe left Khartoum on 19 January 1914 at 6:45 a.m. Lord Kitchener, Sir Reginald Wingate, and all of the city's persons of note insisted on bidding him farewell. As he took off, he was cheered on by an ebullient crowd. They all admired him, but they also all feared for him because he was exposing himself to the desert's many dangers.

His first stop was Atbara. It took him three hours and fifty-five minutes to travel 330 kilometers because he was slowed down by a strong northern wind.

His second stretch, between Atabara and Abu Hamad, was 220 kilometers. He took off at 6:35 a.m. on January 20 and landed at 8:50. He flew against the wind. In the air it was 32°C. Abu Hamad was a small town with a train station. Only one European lived there, an Englishman named More. Pourpe landed by his house. That afternoon, he gave a flight demonstration for the natives.

The next morning, he left at 10 a.m. and landed at Station Number 6, by the railway that crosses the desert to link Wadi Halfa to Abu Hamad. He flew 220 kilometers in two hours.

"I keep getting welcomed warmly everywhere I go. Kitchener sent instructions to every train station manager between Khartoum and Wadi Halfa to help me if need be. All the stations are supposed to volunteer all trolleys they have, including the motorized ones, so that engineers can come help me if I have an accident. The governors of Wadi Halfa and Berber also received orders to give me anything I might need for my trip and to publicize my visit so that the natives will be ready to help if I encounter some plane trouble.

"Everything has been planned for. One could not ask for better hospitality than that provided by the British government."

On January 22 Pourpe flew another 200 kilometers, this time between Station Number 6 and Wadi Halfa. It took him three hours.

"I finished my crossing of the desert and have finally reached the Nile again. I hadn't seen it since Abu Hamad. I was happy to fly over this great landmark. I didn't even mind the fog and the atmospheric disturbances that go with it, because flying above the sand is the most monotonous, the most rotten ordeal one can imagine."

The next day, he flew from Wadi Halfa to Derr: "I keep flying about 200 to 300 kilometers every day. Today, I had to deal not only with a severe northern wind that occasionally culminated in devastating gusts, but also with fog. Fortunately, I wasn't forced to land, which I am very happy about because I do not want to make any more stops than were planned for my 4,500-kilometer round trip between Cairo and Khartoum. If I manage to make as few stops as possible, I'll be very proud of myself."

On January 24 he arrived in Aswan after a 220-kilometer flight. "This last flight went quite smoothly. The wind has finally decided not to bother me too much. Or maybe it is not blowing less hard. Maybe I actually just got used to it. I cannot tell for sure; all I know is that he and I are finally getting along. Every once in a while, though, I encounter an annoying air pocket. Still, my plane is doing well in spite of the treacherous elements. Ha! The people who avoid flying because of atmospheric disturbances should come here to practice for a few months. After dealing with the kind of weather we have here, they'll stop worrying so much about which climate is more or less favorable to planes and which places are appropriate or not to fly in. They'll realize that you can fly anywhere with a good plane and a solid engine.

"I know what I'm talking about! I flew in Australia, the Indies, Indochina, Egypt, and Sudan. The atmosphere in these places is not that different from the one in Europe.

"I'm having my engine checked out, as a matter of precaution. So I will spend a day in Aswan, although I wish I was done with this trip already.

"All the Egyptian and Black people living in the places I have stopped in are exceedingly interested in me. Especially the people who live in the cities I skipped on my way to Khartoum. Thousands of them came to admire the great bird, which 'in the immense desert, surpasses even the trusty camel.'"

On January 26 it took Pourpe three hours to cover the 250 kilometers lying between Aswan and Luxor, because of a very strong wind. "I enjoyed the ride anyway," Pourpe wrote, "because it was taking me closer to Cairo." Pourpe spent three days in Luxor to do some research pertaining to the assignment Lord Kitchener had given him regarding the achievability of air travel in the desert.

He took off again on January 30, this time for Nag Hammadi. He flew 150 kilometers in 1 hour and 15 minutes.

"I have performed a veritable aerial pilgrimage above the most extraordinary and moving region I have ever been in during any of my trips to faraway lands.

"I flew over the temples of Karnak and Luxor. I crossed over the Valley of Kings in Thebes, which contains the tombs of Taharqa; Ramesses I, II, and III; Amenhotep; Thutmose I and II; Sesostris I and II; Seti; and Hatshepsut. I marveled at the temples dedicated to Amun and Hathor. I sound like a treatise on Egyptian history, but I acquired this knowledge only very recently. I had been warned!

"I couldn't even start to express how beautiful, how majestic, the view was from my plane. It is wonderful! On my way to Khartoum I did not even get to appreciate this beauty because it was cloudy, but once the sky cleared, the landscape turned out to be absolutely breathtaking. It fills me with joy to think that I am the only person to have been able to enjoy this enchanting view so far."

The next day, he flew from Nag Hammadi to Assiut. He covered the 230-kilometer stretch in only two hours despite flying against the wind. Around that time, Pourpe was happy to find out that the Aéro-Club had awarded him one of the three silver medals they give out every year as an acknowledgment of the great feats he had accomplished in Indochina in 1913. The two other laureates were none other than famous pilots Eugène Gilbert and Adolphe Célestin Pégoud.

Some engine concerns slowed Pourpe down in the last leg of his trip, so he finished his wonderful journey only on February 3.

"I landed on the Heliopolis polo field at 10:30 A.M. The last part of my otherwise rather monotonous trip actually went very well. I enjoyed this last stretch. I managed to complete it without making any stop, like I did for all the previous ones. I flew 350 kilometers without encountering a single incident.

"The crowd's enthusiasm when it saw me arrive was comforting. All my fellow pilots who were staying in Cairo came to congratulate me. I was moved and felt that their compliments were sincere, because they must have some idea of how difficult what I accomplished is. Yet, in spite of the receptions and the parties, I don't want to stay too long. I am looking forward to going back to Paris. I am going to stop briefly in Port Said and Suez. Then I'll go home. I'll do so knowing that I did a good job, which makes me happy. When I'm back, I'll start preparing for another expedition in Indochina."

In addition to this rather sober report, this much-admired hero wrote me a more personal note. I would like to share it here despite its intimate nature, because I think that there is no better testament to my friend's purity of heart and compassion:

"My dear Jacquot, I have received your nice (and eagerly awaited) letter yesterday. I don't know how to thank you for your kindness and sincerity. I am very happy to hear your mother is feeling a bit better. See? You should not get discouraged, my dear Jacquot. I hope that when I get back home—which will I hope happen soon—she will have completely recovered and you will be happy. In the meantime, don't forget to remind her and your entire family how dear I hold them. I just received a very affectionate telegram from my mother. I can't tell you how good that makes me feel after an entire month spent working so hard in these distant lands."

This is how one of the most memorable chapters of prewar aviation ended.

Pourpe insisted on concluding his trip with a flight that was, let's say, of sentimental value. He had spent ten years—his whole childhood—in Suez. He still had family and friends there. He was going to go see an aunt who had cared lovingly for him when he was a child. She was ecstatic to have him pay her a visit, although the thought of "Marco" flying on his illustrious plane terrified her.

He left on February 12. One hour later, he had crossed the Eastern Desert. It was smaller but just as unpleasant as the Nubian and the Bayuda Deserts, which he had flown over on his way to Khartoum. He landed among an ebullient crowd. The spectators weren't just showing their admiration for the pilot. They were reminded of the past, and many were brought to tears by the prodigal son's return. Pourpe spent two days giving flight demonstrations.

On February 17, he ended his Egyptian visit by following the Suez Canal from the Mediterranean to the Red Sea. He left Suez at 9:17 A.M. and landed in Port Said at 10:43. At that time, it took boats sixteen hours and express trains 4 hours and 15 minutes to complete the same trip.

Pourpe's notes about seeing the land of his childhood again are very moving. "My resilient plane and engine have just undergone a full checkup. However, it turned out to be an unnecessary precaution. There was nothing to fix, not even a pin or a bolt to tighten. Think about it! This plane has traveled over 7,580 kilometers if you take into account the 2,500 kilometers my friend Roland Garros covered when he traveled from Paris to Marseille, crossed the Mediterranean, and gave flight demonstrations.

"On Thursday, February 12, at 9:40 A.M., I took off from the Mataria airfield and quickly climbed to 500 meters despite the heat.

"Instead of following the railroad tracks, which make a huge detour to go through Ismailia and then follow the Suez Canal, I decided to cross the desert to follow the ancient pharaohs' road, which has been abandoned for centuries. Also, I knew that towers had been constructed every 10 kilometers or so during Napoleon's time, although I wasn't sure what state I would find them in. Besides, I had to travel only 140 kilometers. So, as soon as I spotted one of these towers, I started heading east. Below, I could see this road that has been linking Suez to Cairo since the days of pharaohs and could still be used if it wasn't interrupted every 3 or 4 kilometers by giant gullies that were formed over time by torrential rainfalls.

"From time to time, the road, this faint ribbon, would disappear out of sight, and I would use my trusty compass to stay on track.

"I was going fast. The farther east I traveled on this trip (which seemed incidental after my expedition to Khartoum), the better I could see the enormous shape of the gebels of Attaka which were extending over the horizon. The closer I got, the faster my heart was beating. Yes, it was beating fast, faster than it ever has throughout my entire career as a pilot, which has now spanned over six years and started in the heroic times of the likes of Delagrange and Lefebvre.

"I was getting closer to Attaka. Underneath me, the ground was changing. Instead of sand and wadis, I was now flying over arid, black rock. The air was changing too. I could tell I was going more slowly and felt almost cold. I climbed from 500 meters all the way to 1,200 meters to

Marc Pourpe in Paris, France, 12 March 1913, having just been awarded the Aero Club of France's Great Ruby Medal in recognition of his round-trip flight from Cairo to Kartoum

go through the pass between the gebels of Oweibed and Attaka. I was significantly slowed down because I was facing the wind, which was rushing between the two mountains. On top of that, I was sometimes furiously shaken around. But I did not care. I knew that over there, between the wild mountains and the Red Sea, everyone was thinking of me and waiting for me with beating hearts.

"Suddenly, my eyes, which were trained on the horizon, located a dark spot surrounded by some sort of mist along a straight silver ribbon. Then, for a second, I could not see anything besides a distant light, and everything became blurry. I was crying. My heart was beating so fast I thought it was going to break. I could tell that what I had spotted was Suez, which I had left fourteen years earlier after spending my whole childhood there. It was there that my kind grandmother raised me and where she now rests forever; it was there also that I saw my poor father for the last time when he came back from the war in China.

"My wild and nomadic childhood came back to me in the blink of an eye. I could see my old friends again: my partners in crime from back in the day. I knew they were in Suez and were thinking of the same things I was.

"After a while, I spotted the field I was going to land on. It belonged to a full airdrome with an official gallery, fenced-off bleachers for the harem, a cafeteria, and a beautiful hangar. The whole complex is encircled by a neat enclosure. There are not many people in Suez, and they are not very rich, but they all gathered and did their best to properly welcome "Lil' Marco" back.

"I kill the engine and start diving. I quickly drop from 1,200 meters to 100 meters. Then, I turn the engine back on again and go fly over the city and its thrilled Indigenous inhabitants.

"Then, I circle back and land.

"At first, I cannot hear a sound or see anyone move. The scene is quite extraordinary. Then, suddenly, the crowd rushes to the plane and to me. They grab me and kiss me. They are all crying. My good friends, my loving aunt, and my uncle are laughing through their tears. My little cousin, who was supposed to give me a bouquet of flowers, hands me the wrapper. He lost the flowers somewhere along the way. The frère directeur who had me as a student for eight years is there too and crying like everyone else. He embraces me, which leaves me dumbfounded.

"The French consul, Mr. Altemer, is very moved as well and says a few words to me in a trembling voice, which is making this moment even more emotional.

"To conclude this memorable welcome, an orchestra plays *La Marseillaise*. We respectfully listen to our national anthem under an unforgiving sun. People have honored me many times by playing this glorious hymn, but I have never felt more proud hearing it.

"I gave flight demonstrations on February 13 and 15. I flew over the harbor, the mouth of the Suez Canal in Port Tewfik, and all of the city's most important buildings. It was my way to say hello to some old friends.

"I spent the next three days attending various receptions, first with my old professors, the brothers of the Christian schools, and, after that, at the Cercle Français, at the Cercle Egyptien, at the Comité, etc. Everybody applauded me. I felt people were genuinely happy to have me, and that they were not hosting me just because that is what is expected of them when a French pilot is in town. I felt like I was part of a family, which put my mind and heart at peace in spite of how exhausting the last two months were."

On March 4 Pourpe boarded a Marseille-bound ship in Port Said. One week later, he arrived in Paris. I was waiting for him at the train station, alone. Arrangements were made for him to stay at the Excelsior hotel. The president of the Ligue Nationale Aérienne, Dr. René Quinton, announced that he was going to petition the Ministry of War to have the young hero be awarded the Legion of Honour. Although Pourpe amply deserved this distinction, he never actually received it. And they say people in high places aren't good at recognizing merit!

For lack of a red ribbon, Pourpe received the Aéro-Club's Great Ruby Medal during a feast that was given in his honor.

SIXTEEN

And Then There Was War... and Death!

Every day, Pourpe and Lufbery shut themselves away for hours at a time in the pilot's elegant apartment on Gustave Courbet Street to plan his trip from Paris to Saigon the same way Costes would sometime later, when he prepared for his crossing of the Atlantic first in the south and then in the north. He left nothing to chance. Lufbery expertly advised Pourpe on the best times of the year to travel. They were making quick progress.

In the meantime, the ace wanted another chance to show the European public what he was capable of, but he was foiled by the ungratefulness of the plane manufacturers, for whom he had done so much. He wanted to take part in the Monte Carlo rally (which would be won by Roland Garros, with Brindejonc des Moulinais coming in second place), but no one was willing to lend him a plane.

Although no pilot deserved to be respected and honored as much as Pourpe, the manufacturers and the government turned their backs on him. He didn't let it affect him. He kept working without ever complaining. He was being treated unfairly, but he had lived enough to have learned that people care about others only when it is in their own interest to do so.

Roland Garros and I founded an organization together, the Groupe des Aviateurs, whose members, including Pourpe, were all accomplished pilots. I was honored with the title of general secretary. On 14 June 1914 I organized a party in Juvisy. Its goal was to get the general public excited about aviation again, build up a new audience, and collect funds. Our organization's primary concerns were France's prestige and national defense. The festivities were dazzling. Although all the pilots performed pro bono, they gave their all and flew with great skill. Their names were Edmond Audemars, Baudry, Bill, Brindejonc des Moulinais, Maurice Chevillard, Dr. Espanet, Roland Garros, Gaubert, Eugène Gilbert, Molla, Péquet, Pourpe, Maurice Prévost, and Rose. Until then, flying exhibitions usually had only two pilots at most. This time, there were fourteen of them. They all came, although they were not going to financially profit from the event.

Colonel Estienne, a major figure of military aviation, was there. "I have never seen anything like this before," he said. "I never thought I would admire as many great performances on the same day."

"There is nothing that can be done on a plane that hasn't been achieved today," added Henri Farman. "The only way to top today's performances would be by detaching a wing midflight and catch it again before landing."

Indeed, the performances the pilots gave on that day were so beautiful, moving, and impeccable, one could justifiably wonder how they could ever improve upon them. Pourpe was flying his Deperdussin-Gnome for the first time. As soon as he took off, he showed complete mastery of his plane by flying in a graceful loop. It looked like he was breaking down the move in several steps. As soon as he got his plane upside down, he stayed in that position for a while as if he was glued to the sky.

It was a memorable celebration, but it was to be the last of its kind. And for good reason! The pilots had united to protect their interests since people seemed to have forgotten about them. Alas! People had not actually lost sight of them. Many of these pilots would perish on the field of honor!

Before he was to embark on his expedition from Paris to Saigon—which would by far have been the most ambitious flying exploit to date—Pourpe made another thoughtful gesture. He invited all the colonists who were in Paris at the time to attend a flight demonstration on 4 July 1914. All the persons of note who were invited attended the event, including Mr. Albert Sarraut, the governor-general of Indochina; Mr. Guesde, the résident supérieur of the colonies; Mr. Merlin, the governor of Equatorial Africa; Mr. Mahé, the résident supérieur of Laos; et al.

Marc Pourpe (standing at left) visiting the French lines during a lull in the 1914 Battle of the Somme

First, Pourpe took off on his Deperdussin monoplane, which had a 50-horsepower engine. He immediately demonstrated that he had become a master at flying. Then, he flew the Morane he had used for his round trip between Cairo and Khartoum. He let some distinguished passengers fly with him, including Mr. Sarraut.

Here is what *L'Echo des Sports* had to say about Pourpe in the event's aftermath:

> Marc Pourpe, who gave such a beautiful flying demonstration in Juvisy last Saturday, is going to leave for the Far East again. Considering the great job he did in Indochina and Egypt, it feels like this kindly young man has been somewhat neglected. Might it be because his modesty exceeds even his prowess?
>
> At the very least, you cannot accuse him of being a tabarin, which likely works in his favor."

Sadly, his humility—although he was praised for it—did not make it easier for him to gain recognition and earn money.

Just as Pourpe was going to take off on his next colonial adventure, the war broke out. Two days earlier, some members of the Groupe des Aviateurs had dinner together, like we did every week. The situation was already so tense by then that I was tasked with writing the following letter for the minister of war: "Dear Sir, the pilots of the Groupe des Aviateurs have the honor to inform you that they and their planes will be at your service in case of war. They believe that they might, by virtue of their experience, be able to make themselves useful in the defense of France and would be happy to sacrifice their lives for it if necessary. They would like you to allow them the privilege of putting together squadrons so that they can serve our country's glory and greatness in war like they already have in peacetime."

The letter was signed by all the pilots who attended the dinner: Garros, Pourpe, Chevillard, Espanet, Gilbert, and Gaubert.

When the fighting started, nobody knew what to do with these admirable recruits. They were sent to Saint-Cyr, where they had nothing to do, although they were eager to fight. It took several days to outfit them properly. As for the squadrons, they were adjourned indefinitely. Aviation was sorely neglected by military superiors, these creatures of habit!

After a seemingly interminable month of August, Pourpe joined me in Longvic, near Dijon.[1] I was studying there, although it was a bit late for that. We spent a few days together. We stayed in a barn and slept in the hay. The cows that were sleeping below us kept us warm.

---

1. Pourpe received his military pilot license, no. 432, on 24 March 1914.

Then we finally had to say farewell. He left for Nancy. He had been assigned to the M. S. 23 Squadron along with Garros, Gilbert, and Pinsard, whereas I was to join the M. F. 5 in Belfort.

He wrote me on 16 September 1914. "My old Jacquot, I arrived in Nancy last morning. The entire squadron left Toul for good. Tomorrow, we will be sent to Verdun. We are not sure about anything, but we will see what happens.

"I was delayed by dreadful weather in Neufchâtel—and by the flu I caught in your barn—but, as soon as I arrived, I reunited with Garros and Gilbert. I told them about your adventures and your desire to join us.

"My glin-glin is working fine. It hadn't been tuned well. Lufbery fixed it. We're going to do some good work; I assure you of that."

On 29 October 1914 I received the second-to-last letter from my friend, who was to die soon. He was trying to comfort me after the death of my older brother, who had been a councilor at the Court of Appeal in Guyana. He had voluntarily enrolled and soon died on the field of honor after being mortally wounded in Vic-Sur-Aisne.

"I found out about your poor brother's death today. I can only imagine how devastated you and your family must be. I know how close all of you were to each other. You know how dearly, how completely, I care for you and your family, so I know you will believe me when I tell you that I share your heartbreak.

"I wish I were with you, my old Jacquot, although I feel that, in the present situation, mere words can hardly give you any comfort.

"Quite a lot has happened since I left Dijon. I have been on thirty or so reconnaissance trips. I was mentioned in dispatches for being hit by shrapnel (which I didn't even realized had happened) but successfully completed my mission anyway (I realized I was missing a chunk of my propeller only after landing). No stripe so far. I heard only the *deuxièmes réserves* get that kind of accolades. Dumas is a corporal: he's covered in red all the way up to his shoulders!

"Garros is on a trip to Paris. Gilbert is here. He's thinking of you and would like to offer you his condolences.

"As for me, old friend, I have been depressed over the past few days. It's freezing here. I'm not used to this; I feel wretched. Also, our reconnaissance flights are rarely under three hours.

Pilot and observer standing with their two mechanics beside their Morane Saulnier aircraft following a reconnaissance mission

"I'm fed up with this war. Alas! I'm not the only one! Poor old Jacquot, don't be scared. Be careful! Don't do anything too risky."

The next letter, which he sent on December 1, was the last one he would ever write.

How did he die? He had gone on a reconnaissance mission with Lieutenant Vauglin.[2] On the way back, they were caught in a sea of clouds. You could hear the plane, but you could not see it. Suddenly, it appeared. It was spinning. The adept pilot was not reacting. The Morane continued to spin until it hit the ground. What had happened? This very capable pilot could not have made a mistake. Remember what he wrote me in the letter I received on October 29: "It's freezing here. I'm not used to this; I feel wretched. " He probably fell victim to the cold weather and wasn't able to straighten his plane up.

---

2. Lt. Eugene Vauglin was Pourpe's observer.

He was mentioned in dispatches again. "Pourpe (Marc), a pilot from the M. S. 23 Squadron, and Vauglin, an artillery lieutenant, undertook a reconnaissance mission at a particularly dangerous time: the weather was cloudy, windy, and extremely cold. On their way back, they were caught in a cloud bank that was over 700 meters thick. They lost control and died in the ensuing crash."

My best friend was gone! He had closely followed my big brother in death. Such is war!

Pourpe posthumously received a military medal long after this. In the months preceding his death, he had proven he deserved no less than the Legion of Honour. Instead, he died, and as a simple soldier. There is no justice in this world!

Marc Pourpe's crashed Morane Saulnier Parasol aircraft near the Villars-Bretonneaux airfield, Somme, 2 December 1914. Pourpe and his observer, Lt. Eugene Vauglin, were both killed following their 28th reconnaissance mission while attempting to land in bad weather.

Here is the last letter the glorious hero wrote me: "We have left Amiens for the second time yesterday. Our tents—which had been destroyed by the wind—have been fixed, so we camped near a little village called Treux (210 inhabitants). I heard that we are essentially going to have to hibernate unless our infantrymen want to move forward, but I doubt it.

"My poor Jacquot, I am in quite the impasse. Because of some improbable circumstances, I am still only a second-class private. Lacrouze had barely spent two weeks with us when he was made corporal, and now he's going to become a sergeant. Our captain, de Vergnette, was apologetic. He told me that my lack of promotion had been an oversight. He also told me that, after having been wounded in September and been mentioned in dispatches, I should have been awarded a medal. The officer who was on my plane the day I was hit by shrapnel received the Legion of Honour! I am furious, and my companions are very surprised.

"What's worse, I have lost my cool and told off our superiors several times, so now I'm really not in their good graces. I am so unlucky. I was supposed to get the Legion of Honour and now I won't because of the war! Since the beginning of the war, I have been on twenty-seven reconnaissance flights (that's seventy-eight hours spent flying above enemy territory), but I have not been awarded a single stripe. I am the only one in my squadron to have been injured, to have been hit by the Boche. G-------it! I'm fed up and I feel I might start playing tricks. I'm sick of this, old pal. I'm telling you all this to feel a little better, because I'm down in the dumps.

"Do you think this clique I have to deal with right now is going to leave us the hell alone anytime soon? I'm ready to part way whenever! I was not born to be in the military. Don't get me wrong, I'm enjoying taking out those Teutons and fighting this war, but everything else is always so unfair! So often, it's the mouthiest ones that get what they want. I'm sick and tired of it!"

Pourpe shared his resentment with me. He expressed his bitter feelings with his habitual candor. He hated injustice, and there he was, face to face with it again. How unacceptable was this? He was still a common soldier after fighting for five months, getting wounded, and getting mentioned in dispatches! Wouldn't you think his superiors were to blame? Why would they do this?

Still, the poor kid who had never truly been happy and would die the next day added a PS: "I'm being crazy. Do not pay attention to this foolish letter."

He felt guilty for complaining. This letter was found on his lifeless body. It shows that, until his very death, he had to endure men's petty-mindedness and cowardliness. That is how my wonderful companion died. Although he had occasionally fallen victim to melancholic episodes, he had always been disarmingly considerate, elegant, distinguished, modest, and heroic.

[A description of Morane Saulnier 23 appears on page 231. A description of Raoul Lufbery witnessing the death of Marc Pourpe appears on page 232.]

SEVENTEEN

"I Will Avenge My Boss!"

Raoul Lufbery felt a deep sorrow when the man he had cared for so purely and nobly fell to his death. When he lost Pourpe he lost a brother; a brother who had shared his adventurous life around the world!

"I will avenge him!" he immediately cried out.

The magnitude of his pain gave him the will to make the enemy pay for Pourpe's death.

How did this American manage to join the M.S. 23 Squadron as Pourpe's mechanic?

This situation calls for an explanation because it is not a common one. When Pourpe joined the army, he encouraged "Lafberg" do the same. That is when the truth came out: Lafberg's name was actually Lufbery and he had been an American citizen ever since he had come of age.

What to do? Pourpe asked for his loyal assistant to be able to continue working with him. He approached understanding military officers who made it possible for Lufbery to stay with Pourpe without having to jump over too many hurdles: Lufbery was to go to the Permanence de l'Aéronautique. He would officially sign to join the 1st Foreign Regiment but would instead be assigned to the aviation division. Lufbery started this process on August 14. By August 31, he was able to come meet me and Pourpe in Longvic. Now that the team was back together, they could join their squadron.

Lufbery did not waste any time. On 2 December 1914, he sent in a request to start training to become a pilot. However, he had to wait until 17 May 1915 to be sent to the aviation school in Chartres. He was certified on July 29 on the Maurice Farman[1] and was assigned to the V.B.1 02 Squadron on 7 October 1915. His first assignment was to drop bombs from a Voisin plane.

Here is what he wrote about his baptism by fire: "11 October 1915. I'm not too terribly bad off for the moment here. I managed to find a bed. Yesterday afternoon, I started doing some useful work behind enemy lines. I had the honor of being greeted by the Boche. They stayed with me almost the whole time I was there. But their shells did not stop me. The funny thing is that I felt some kind of strange pride to see all the trouble they went to just because of me."

After that, Lufbery went on one expedition after the other. He would have preferred to be like Pourpe and be able to avenge him on a fighter plane, but he kept flying his bomber with the same conscientiousness and energy he put in everything during his whole life. Here is his account of a bombing he carried out on 6 November 1915: "I just came back from a rather long trip. There were some tense moments, but I made it safely. I was congratulated by my captain and my commandant. Of the twenty planes that took off, only four managed to fulfill their mission. I was one of them."

During a bombing in Metz, he was targeted by two enemy planes. "I was attacked twice by Aviatik planes. The first one rushed toward me shortly before I reached my objective. I let him get as close as 150 meters and then I fired at him with my machine gun. He must have found that greeting a little bit too warm because he did not stick around. He changed course and left. Since he was faster I didn't even try to follow him. Besides, my cabin was full of shells, and I had a mission to complete.

"The second skirmish was another story. I was taken by surprise. My assailant approached me from behind so I couldn't see him. I realized I was getting attacked only when I heard the bullets. I took a sharp turn to try to face him, but then I saw that one of our planes was firing at him, and he ran away. Unfortunately, I had been hit twice. One bullet was lodged in the empennage and the other in an aileron."

---

1. Lufbery's Aeronautique Militaire pilot brevet number was 1286.

Lufbery's squadron's primary task was bombing, but that did not stop him from engaging in one-on-one combat as well. He sent me the account of his first confrontation with a German fighter for *La Guerre Aérienne*: "In January 1916 I was flying a Voisin with a 140-horsepower engine. I was part of the bombing squadron number 102.

"On one beautiful afternoon, around 1:15 P.M. we were told to get ready for a new mission. As usual, we were not immediately told what our target was. However, considering the amount of fuel we were given and the direction the wind was blowing, we guessed we were probably supposed to hit the Metz-Sablons train station.

"All the available planes were expected to take part in this raid. There were forty or so of them. About half of them belonged to my squadron, while the others were part of the 101 group, which was under the command of the fearless Commandant Roisin.

"The planes are arranged on a single line at the end of the field, facing the wind. The mechanics check the engines one last time. The machine gunners check their guns and lay the bombs in their compartments. These shells weigh 10 kilos and apparently do as much damage as 155 regular bombs. I'm taking six of them with me. Some pilots take eight, nine, or even ten. It all depends on how performant your engine is, how fine-tuned your plane is, etc.

"We're ready. We're just waiting for the final instructions. We finally receive them. We are given maps with the itinerary we are supposed to follow. All the pilots set their watches to match the mission's leader's. Fifty minutes after taking off, we will have to all be flying at least 2,000 meters above Saint-Nicolas-de-Port. Then, depending on the commandant's signals, we will keep going until we reach enemy lines, or we will turn back. The latter may happen if the weather is bad (wind, clouds, etc.) or if all the planes haven't successfully assembled.

"You can hear a rumble coming from the left side of the line of planes. A plane starts moving forward; it goes on for a few seconds before taking off. A second and then third plane follow. I'm number seven. Soon, it's my turn to take off. I turn to my observer, Maréchal des logis Allard, and ask

Raoul Lufbery seated in the cockpit of a Voisin bombing aircraft studying his roller map prior to a flight with Escadrille V.B. 102.

him if he's ready. When he tells me he is, I turn on my engine and push it as hard as it will go. Like my companions before me, I drive for a few seconds before leaving the ground.

"Before our departure, my travel companion told me that he was going to try to sleep for a little while as we gain altitude, so that he will be well rested when it comes time to read the map after we cross over enemy lines. I have no objection to that, especially considering that there isn't really anything for him to do while I'm trying to reach the perfect altitude. I turn around several times while we're climbing: Allard has his eyes closed, but I'm wondering if he is actually sleeping. He is right to get some rest though. Soon, he will need all his self-control and energy.

"2:20 P.M.—I'm right on time and so are most of my fellow pilots. Suddenly, I see flares being launched from the lead plane, which is easily recognizable thanks to its red pennants. It's the signal we were waiting for. All there is for me to do now is follow the group.

"As we are crossing enemy lines, the fastest planes flip around a couple of times to give the ones in the back a chance to catch up. Now that all the planes have converged, we keep moving forward, although we get the occasional shrapnel fired at us. No one is particularly worried because those strikes don't do anything most of the time. It's a matter of making a 'lucky shot.' For a shell to actually do real damage, it would have to hit the pilot himself or an essential part of the plane. You can have several holes in your wings and still be fine.

"I'm watching the landscape we are flying over. To our right is the Seille River. You can barely make it out right now because the water has risen so much that the banks are flooded. It looks like a string of swamps and ponds. To our left, the Moselle River and its adjoining canal form two beautiful silver strings that seem to disappear in banks of mist to the north. I then realize that what I thought was mist is actually smoke coming from the factories in Metz.

"As we get closer, I can make out some things through this curtain of smog: clusters of houses and churches as well as long red-brick buildings that I'm guessing are barracks.

Nieuport training planes collide on the airfield at Pau.

The city is surrounded by little green geometrical shapes—the famous forts! They look so harmless from up here!

"Only a few more minutes before I fly over my target, the city's massive train station. The planes in the lead do another round of loops to let the stragglers catch up. My engine has 10 less horsepower than theirs, which means that I'm not so fast that I need to let people catch up with me. So, instead, I continue toward our objective and am the first one to get there.

"It looks like they were expecting us. Several enemy planes are there, flying in all directions. They are ready for us. One of them is coming toward me, probably to exchange greetings. I quickly turn to my passenger to make sure he's on his guard and has his finger on the trigger. He is. Perfect! Let's wait . . . When he's a mere 150 meters away from us, the Boche biplane changes course abruptly so that his right side—the one with the machine gun—is facing us. This maneuver has become outdated because most two-person planes are outfitted with two machine guns now—a stationary one toward the front of the plane, and one in the back, on a turret.

"I don't lose the enemy plane out of sight. I can distinctly see the black crosses on its fuselage and rudder. The fight starts. Both machine guns are firing. After a while, the enemy plane gives up and takes a dive to get away from me. I decide not to chase him. The coast is clear, and I have an important mission to fulfill.

"Through the triplex in the cabin I can see railroad tracks, warehouses, and some trains, a few of which are parked while others are taking off from the station.

"My passenger taps me on the shoulder and gestures for me to continue forward. He taps me on the shoulder again to let me know he launched the bombs. We're done. Time to turn around and try to make it back as quickly as possible. There are more and more Boche. We are on high alert but are taken by surprise by a Fokker monoplane anyway. After one quick burst of gunfire, he disappears. We don't even have enough time to try to face him. A couple of distinctly sharp sounds make it clear that our assailant aimed well and that we have been hit. However, the engine is still going, and my companion thinks that the gas tank is unscathed.

"The wind is blowing from the north, which favors our trip back. Soon, we're out of enemy territory. For some reason, I start laughing. I turn and see that my passenger is laughing too. We're relieved and jubilant! Now that we are safe, we would like to share our impressions about what just happened, 'examine the attack' as pilots say, but the engine is too loud. We wouldn't be able to hear a word. So we have to be patient and wait until we land.

Nieuport aviation de chasse school, Pau, France. A Nieuport II fighter plane and a Caudron G.4 bomber sit on the airfield.

"I slow down as we start our descent and slowly glide above the Meurthe valley. We are gently drifting back. My companion lights up a cigarette and is nice enough to hand it to me for a few puffs. I enjoy them thoroughly.

"Little by little, the landscape becomes more tangible. You can see that those lovely green moss carpets are in fact forests, that those black ribbons are railways, and that those white lines are roads and country lanes. The structure I thought was a big factory when I saw it from afar, partly hidden by a black smoke curtain, is looking more and more imposing. It turns out to be the beautiful city of Nancy. I'm now flying 200 meters above the airdrome. One last spiral and I land. The first thing I do after touching ground is check my plane. My wings' canvas has several bullet holes in it.

"Several of my comrades have not come back yet. Some say we will probably be missing men. Several people claim they have seen Voisin planes go down. Every so often, a white shape appears on the horizon, which prompts people to speculate about who that might be. 'That must be the one I saw flying far behind me.' And 'No, I think that's the one I saw on my way back,' etc.

"Now we have all made it back. Our captain, who was visibly gloomy and concerned, lights up. He can't hide his relief seeing that his whole squadron is safe.

"Alas! The same can't be said for the other parties. Although it is still too early to know for sure, it looks like some of our companions will be eating K.K. bread tonight."[2]

These pages testify to the "American" hero's high spirits. Lufbery never saw any situation in a difficult or tragic light. He was forthright and not susceptible to fall victim to this particular brand of melancholy that soldiers dubbed "the blues." He was waging war in the same way people play sports. His amazing self-control made a great impression on the people who got to see him in action.

Still, being part of a bombing squadron did not satisfy his spirit of adventure or his desire to avenge Pourpe.

He asked to become a fighter pilot so that he could join the Lafayette Squadron, a new unit that was made up of American volunteers and whose creation had been an arduous process. He went to train in Nieuport from April 10 to May 22 and joined his new unit on 24 May 1916.

---

2. German bread that was served to French prisoners of war.

EIGHTEEN

The Bomber Becomes a Fighter

In those days, the Lafayette Squadron had only six American pilots: Norman Prince, William Thaw, Kiffin Rockwell, Victor Chapman, and James McConnell.[1] Capt. Thénault was the group's leader, and Lieutenant de Laage de Meux was second in command. All were brave men whom I will talk about more in future books on war volunteers.

Lufbery joined this group of heroes. He was soon going to prove himself to be an indisputably talented pilot whose ability to always keep his cool was stunning. He was also a remarkable shot. During his service in the Philippines, he had been awarded a gold badge in a shooting competition, although some of the contenders had worked on ranches. These men's love of rifles, Colts, and six-shooters was in a way their philosophy of life.

On 1 June 1916 Lufbery carried out two two-hour-long barrage flights above our lines. He found himself flying above the Verdun area, where the battle that had started on February 21 was still raging. It had been going on for one hundred days without a single break. He was able to witness the enemy's work of destruction firsthand.

"It is heartbreaking to see what state the wooded hills surrounding Verdun in the north, the west, and the east are in. From above, they look like an enormous sponge because of how they have been dug over, smashed open, shredded, pounded and crushed by the German artillery."

Three days later, on June 4, Lufbery engaged in his first fight. He had spotted two enemy planes while on patrol. One seemed to be taking pictures. The other, a small Fokker fighter plane that was flying a few hundred meters above the first one, was in all likelihood escorting it. As soon as they were done, they started heading back, but the French American pilot did not hesitate for a second and attacked the Fokker. However, it turned out that the German pilot had been anticipating such a move and shot at Lufbery. One of the bullets dug a hole through Lufbery's interplane strut. As he was emptying his fifteenth cartridge, his machine gun got jammed. Luckily, the enemy fighter did not seize this opportunity to get the best of him. A vexed and sheepish Lufbery headed back to his base. As he was doing so, he thought: "I reflected on what I had learned from this run-in that could have ended really badly for me."

---

1. At this time, the squadron had seven American pilots. Mortane doesn't mention Bert Hall and Elliot Cowdin.

The Escadrille Americaine at Bar-le-Duc, July 1916. Left to right: *Lt. DeLaage, Charles Johnson, Laurence Rumsey, James McConnell, William Thaw, Raoul Lufbery, Kiffin Rockwell, Didier Masson, Norman Prince, and Bert Hall.*

On June 16 he completed three flights and spent a total of five hours and fifteen minutes in the air. He chased two enemies, including a two-seater Aviatik plane. He attacked it, but his adversary fought back and shattered Lufbery's mirror. Once again, Lufbery was lucky to make it back alive!

His third fight happened the next day. The luckless enemy pilot seemed to take a dive, but he did so too far past German lines for Lufbery to be absolutely sure that he indeed took him out.

June 23 was a bad day. Just north of Douaumont, the Lafayette Squadron ran into a group of five skilled and courageous adversaries that carried out their attack with astonishing discipline. Lufbery took on an Aviatik whose pilot seemed as talented and fearless as he was. The ensuing duel was heart-stopping. After flying from one adversary to the other with stunning dexterity, Chapman took out an enemy plane and was able to go lend Lufbery and Norman Prince a hand. Together, they chased the remaining German planes away.

The squadron headed back to its base except for Chapman, who wanted to bring oranges to a hospitalized friend of his named Clyde Balsley. When he took off for his friendly mission, though, he was attacked by two enemy planes and crashed behind German lines with his wings folded together. In less than a month, he had two officially recognized victories.[2]

Lufbery led fight after fight. He often forced his adversary into a difficult position, but, for the longest time, he did not manage to fully take out any enemy plane. His companions were regularly victorious in combat, but he

---

2. Chapman had no confirmed victories with the squadron.

Raoul Lufbery, June 1916, standing before his Nieuport 11 fighter, No.1256, at Behonne. He scored his first four victories in this aircraft.

Nieuport 16, no. 1390, assigned to Didier Masson. Lufbery wrecked this fighter while landing at Behonne on 25 July 1916.

kept flying for hours at a time without obtaining any official results. He vowed he would get a victory under his belt before the end of July. On July 29 he had his fourteenth and fifteenth confrontations with enemy planes, but still no victory.

Was he going to fall short of his objective? Here's what he wrote me on 30 July 1916: "I've been having really bad luck lately. I hope it's going to get better. I took a brutal fall the other day. Now my plane is nothing but a pile of wood, canvas, and wire. Luckily, I made it out of there without a scratch, which is almost a miracle because I was flying 160 km/h when I flipped over. It happened when I had to dodge another plane, a Farman, because it was going to land on the wrong side of the field. I took a turn in a vertical position, but I was too close to the ground and the wing hit it.

"I've had several clashes with the Boches lately, but they haven't been very lucky during them. I got close to an enemy and attacked him, but even though I shot forty-seven bullets at him, I still didn't take him out."

Soon, though, Lufbery's luck got better, and he won a fight before the end of the month (on July 31) like he vowed he would. "As I was patrolling the area this morning, I ran into a Fokker. I quickly rushed to him without giving him time to even realize what was going on. It all happened very fast: after one round of bullets he spun down and crashed just before the woods of Macé, in German-controlled territory. I checked to make sure I had finished the job and headed back to write my report. The lookouts that were positioned on the ground had already confirmed the outcome of the confrontation, and my victory was officially recognized the same day. I finally did it!

You can see how happy I am! It took me two months and sixteen fights to get there! I was counting on my streak of bad luck to finally end and I knew that hunting the Boches is like everything: the first step is the most difficult one."

This feat debuted a long line of victories for Lufbery. On August 4, he had two successful fights in a row. At 8:10 a.m. he shot down an Albatros plane just east of Vaux. Then, at 9 a.m., with the help of a plane from another squadron, he took down a second Albatros, which crashed not too far from the first one.

Lufbery didn't have to wait long for a fourth triumph. It happened on August 8. "In every fighter pilot's life, there are some victories that are particularly memorable. The clash I remember best is the one that gave me my fourth victory.

"It was about 11 A.M. on August 8. McConnell and I were on patrol northeast of Verdun, between Douaumont and Vaux. The weather was beautiful. The air was so clear we could distinctly see shell craters, landmine gaps, and even some trenches underneath us. I had gotten to know the area quite well in the two months I had spent flying over it. I needed to check the map only every once in a while, just for peace of mind. I could confidently name every single mass of whitish rubble popping up here and there amid the chaos. For example, here is one that used to be the charming village of Douaumont. A little bit farther north, at the very tip of the plateau not far from the fort whose geometric lines are barely visible, is a small pile of ashes; that's what's left of Bezonvaux. That one over there on the right is Dieppe. And here are Damloup, Eix, Abaucourt, Hautecourt, and Fromezy. What's left of these villages lies on either side of a brown line that used to be the railroad tracks running parallel to highway number 18, which links Verdun to Etain. So many ruins! I got somewhat distracted contemplating this vast battlefield where so many ill-fated men are resting. In lieu of a proper grave, they lie at the bottom of shell craters that have been partly reopened after more rounds of fire. I lost my companion out of sight. McConnell too must have been somewhat inattentive because he had stopped following me.

"Being alone, I decided to focus on the task at hand. It was important that I do not let the enemy surprise me. So I started flying left and right, changing direction constantly like sailboats do. That way I was able to see in every direction. According to my altimeter, I was flying at 36,000 meters. I slowed my engine because this height was perfect for the Nieuport *Bébé*.

Nieuport 16, no. 1390, after it was wrecked by Lufbery in a collision with a Maurice Farman bomber on 25 July 1916

"Suddenly I noticed a camouflaged plane that was flying about a thousand meters below me and heading toward French territory. From a distance, it was difficult to tell what nationality it was, but its shape looked suspect to me. It was way too big for a Nieuport, the only French plane that could possibly be confused for a German one.

"It was a great opportunity, but I had to act quickly. I carefully looked around to make sure that my coveted prey did not have an escort. I did not want to fall into a trap. I was starting to become familiar with the enemy's favorite trick: they would send out a slow and heavy plane to fly at a medium altitude while one or two fast fighter planes followed it higher up in the sky, ready to take out any pilot foolish enough to go for the bait. I had fallen for that ruse a few times and had become wary.

"Considering how fast the Boche was going, I could safely assume that he had not seen me and that I should act now while I had the upper hand. I promptly shut off my engine and dove toward him. I was right—it was an enemy. Despite his camouflage, I could very distinctly see the two black crosses painted on the supporting plane. I made a few abrupt turns to stay out of his line of fire and positioned myself about 30 meters behind his fuselage and just a little bit underneath him so that his vertical stabilizer would shield me. That is when he saw me, but it was too late. In vain, he tried to tilt his plane so that his gunner could shoot me. I fired all forty-seven bullets in my machine gun.

"I was so close that I had to lean toward the left a little to prevent the planes from colliding. Then, I straightened up and looked for my victim. The enemy plane was right there below me, but I was amazed to see that it had somehow turned white. I had not a clue about what was going on, and removed my goggles to try to see better. That's when I realized that the plane was upturned; its chassis and wheels were facing up. The pilot did not manage to recover, and his plane plunged. I made big circles in the sky while watching the fall. Black smoke and then flames started coming out of the aircraft. The fire grew as the plane plummeted toward the ground.

"Finally, this ball of fire crashed in the *Ravin de la Couleuvre*, a few meters away from our trenches.

"I was happy and proud of myself as I started heading back toward our airfield. I was thinking of our good poilus, who, from down below, had assuredly witnessed this aerial battle, cheered me on, and applauded the triumph of the plane with the tricolored cockades."

McConnell, a talented fighter pilot and writer, recounted this duel—which he had personally witnessed—in one of his books.

"Lufbery evidently discovered a secret formula: according to official statistics, he shot down four planes since his arrival in Verdun. He collected four palms on the ribbon of his Croix de Guerre. He holds the record in our squadron!

"A pilot rarely gets the satisfaction to see what happens after he fires a round at an enemy. It is very easy to lose a falling plane out of sight as it's whirling and spiraling. Therefore, one rarely gets to see the defeated plane actually crash.

"Lufbery's recent victory is an exception because he was able to see everything that was unfolding as if he were watching from a front-row seat. Meanwhile, I was sitting in the upper balcony, so I was able to see just as well. It was August. We had left together around noon, and, for the first time in such a situation, we got lost behind enemy lines. Since I did not see any Germans, I just wandered around high above the reconnaissance planes. Lufbery, on the other hand, spotted an enemy and took him out in an instant. Just at that moment, I turned south and laid eyes on a German plane that was falling from the sky above German territory.

"As he turned over, the plane exposed its white belly for a moment and then zigzagged wildly toward the ground. The pilot must have been holding the wheel tightly even after his death, because the way his plane fell was quite odd. He crossed my line of sight briefly and then disappeared into some woods.

"As I went down a bit to see where it had crashed, I saw it again. It was skimming a field and heading toward a brown strip of land. You could see its outline against the ground that was riddled with shell impacts. It looked like a tiny insect. Then, it crashed on the battlefield just northeast of the Douaumont fort. Flames and smoke engulfed the wreck. I watched it burn for a little while and then headed back to the reconnaissance planes.

"I thought that Lufbery would show up and go take a look at the place where his victim had fallen, but he was taking awhile. I started worrying that the plane I had seen crash to the ground was his and not an enemy's. I spent an hour anxiously waiting for him before heading back to the squadron. When I landed among my comrades, I finally found out that Lufbery was safe. He had hurried back to camp to report on his successful fight, so nobody else would claim this victory as their own, like it so often happens. The lookout posts, however, had already confirmed his account, and Lufbery was as happy as can be. Yet, during lunch, I heard him muttering, 'Poor chaps!' to himself.

"The German machine gunner had probably survived the fight, so he must have been terrified as the plane plummeted to the ground. Lufbery says he watched the whole thing unfurl circling the sky above the crashing German plane. From the way the pilot was flying, he felt he must have been a novice. In my mind, I pictured an eager young man carrying out his first flight above enemy lines and dreaming about the brilliant career ahead of him. Maybe as he was trying his luck at flying he was dreaming of the Iron Cross, or of his Gretchen. Instead, he got a quick death and the artillery-blasted ground near Douaumont as his tomb."

The men who had been in that plane were Lieutenant Schneider and Vizefeldwebel Stanschus.

Sergeant Lufbery was rewarded with a military medal. A dispatch noted the following:

"This man of exemplary dexterity, self-control, and bravery deserves credit for his numerous long-range bombings and daily fights against enemy planes. On July 31 he did not hesitate to engage in short-range combat with four enemy planes. He took one of them out not far from our own territory. He managed to defeat another one on 4 August 1916."

Soon after that, he was mentioned in dispatches again. This time, he was a sergeant major: "A remarkably driven pilot. He attacked and fell an enemy plane on 4 August 1916. It crashed on its own territory. He repeated that exploit on August 8. The enemy plane crashed and burned near Douaumont."

Whiskey, the squadron's lion cub mascot. The pilots purchased him in Paris in September 1916. Lufbery just caught the cub chewing on a hat. This ongoing habit would later cost the lion his right eye.

At the end of August, only three months after he joined the Lafayette Squadron, Lufbery had flown for 129 hours and thirty-five minutes, had been involved in twenty-nine fights, and had accrued four official victories. He was allowed to take a leave to get some rest. He was even granted two additional days as a reward for his medal and palms. "There you go," he said. "The system actually works!"

During his trip, he again proved how kind, generous, and altruistic he was. He was in a second-class car when a peasant woman who was going to visit her severely injured husband sat down next to him. She was so agitated that she did not realize she actually had a third-class ticket. When the ticket inspector noticed, he asked her to leave or pay the difference.

Lufbery, who until then hadn't seemed to want to get involved in the dispute, asked in a cocky voice:

"How much?"

"How much what?" asked the inspector.

"I asked, 'How much?' Am I not speaking French? How much does this lady owe you?"

He paid the inspector and went back into his corner, where he had been trying to take a nap until he had been interrupted by the intransigent employee.

He was headed to Nonette, a small Auvergne village lying at the top of a hill in the heart of Limagne, surrounding the ruins of a medieval castle. He loved this place that was perched high up like a bird's nest, offering a beautiful view on the surrounding countryside.

It was a tender affection that took him there. The Allier River flows at the foot of the hill. To cross it, people have to get on a boat. Lufbery paid close attention to the poor ferryman straining to keep the boat moving along the cable that crossed the river. He could not understand how people were still using such a rudimentary mode of transport. He quickly thought up an alternative: a pulley-based mechanism that would use the current from the side. This way, the boat wouldn't require steering; it would automatically cross the river. After a while, the ferryman understood Lufbery's explanations, but routine was more appealing than the perks of progress.

When he went back to his squadron on 7 September 1916, the other pilots seemed very agitated. There had been talk of leaving the Verdun area to go back to Alsace. Four days later, they received instructions to leave for Luxeuil, a charming and renowned spa town where the aviators would be very comfortable. Indeed, one can wage war and still enjoy a pleasant lifestyle.

While the equipment was getting directly transported to Luxeuil by road, the pilots made a detour through Paris. There, William Thaw and Kiffin Rockwell started looking for a mascot for the squadron. It was the latest trend. They picked a gorgeous four-month-old lion cub whom they named Whisky. *Noblesse oblige!*

Whisky befriended Lufbery, who adored animals and always formed special bonds with them. Although he was quite sober and temperate, he loved Whisky!

"He was intelligent and sweet, graceful and agile. His playfulness was entertaining, and he never displayed any kind of wild instincts. He had a weak spot for kepis though [French army caps]. There was nothing he loved better than playing with them. Every time he got a hold of one, he would tear it to pieces.

"This quirk almost cost him his life. One day, he stole one of our mechanics' kepi. That stunt did not go over well, and the man made Whisky let go of his hat by beating the poor animal so violently that he lost an eye.

"I tended to him as best as I could but, from there on, he would have only one eye. After that, we became thick as thieves. He would follow me like a little dog, zigzagging on his big paws. We often spent hours fooling around. I would tell him: 'Whisky, you are the most beautiful of lions. In fact, you are better and worse than a lion: you are a person. Whisky-man is your name. Come give me a kiss.'

"He was very receptive to that kind of praise. You should have seen him looking at me attentively, sitting on his tail, staring at me with his one eye. He looked like he was actively listening to me and could understand what I was saying.

"Whisky, Fram (Captain Thénault's German shepherd), and Mimiss (Lieutenant de Laage de Meux's little fox terrier) were an entertaining trio. We would gather around them to watch them play."

On September 19, the squadron acquired two more Nieuport planes. They were brand-new models. One was given to Lufbery and the other to Rockwell.

Four days later, during a trial flight, Lufbery shot down a plane but was immediately attacked from behind by two Fokkers that riddled him with bullets. Three bullets went through his supporting strut. Lufbery fought back, but he ran out of ammunition and fuel and had to land close by, on the Fontaine airfield, 5 kilometers from Luxeuil. When he got there, he found out that his squadron mate, Kiffin Rockwell, had died after being shot in the throat with an expanding bullet.

Thus, Pourpe's avenger also became Rockwell's. Lufbery filled up his gas tank, stocked up on ammunition, and took off in search of an adversary. He couldn't find one, though, so he went to challenge the enemy face to face by flying at a low altitude above the Habsheim airfield. Still, no one accepted his challenge.

Life went on. It was dull.

"The weather is terrible here, so we don't fly much. To kill time, we go fishing, hunting, and gathering mushrooms. When the rain is too heavy, we stay inside and mess around with the phonograph. I have been in combat a few times and have received a couple of bullets since I arrived here, but I still miss Verdun, where the Boches were abundant."

Lufbery enjoyed hare hunting, but he was more partial to mushroom gathering.

One day, he went for a walk to look for something to upgrade their meals for the day. The two friends who were accompanying him went to look for a bridge, while

Lufbery in his flying gear, September 1916, following a patrol in Nieuport 17, no. 1485. This plane may have had Lufbery's name painted on the fuselage.

Lufbery kept walking straight ahead, as was his habit. He found a fallen tree that was crossing over the river. He decided to use it to get to the other side, but, just as he reached the middle of the tree, he slipped and fell in the water. He was a good swimmer and soon climbed out of the water on the other side of the river, but, to his companions' delight, he was soaked to the bone.

He would shortly have his revenge though. As the three friends were looking for a foot soldier willing to lend Lufbery his coat so he could dry his clothes, a dreadful storm started and, soon, rain was pouring down, drenching Lufbery's two heretofore dry companions. Now they needed three coats!

On October 4 and 9 Lufbery encountered two major predicaments. The first one occurred above Mulhouse. True to the vows he had taken after Rockwell's death, Lufbery had gone out to provoke some enemy pilots above the Habsheim airfield.

That day, however, four or five of them came out to meet him. He gained altitude to be in a more advantageous position and then attacked one of his adversaries. As soon as he did, his machine gun jammed. He gave it a hard blow to try to make it work again, but all he managed to accomplish was to loosen a piece enough that it fell into the propeller and got crushed.

"Fortunately, while I was trying to fix my machine gun, I managed to get away. I shut off the engine and, although I was flying at 4,500 meters' altitude, I managed to glide back to the Fontaine airfield. It felt like it took forever. I had been flying for three hours and my gas tank was empty."

And here is what happened on October 9: "I had taken off for a solo expedition. I don't remember why I did, but I had likely forgotten about hunting the Boches. In fact, when my altimeter reached 2,000 meters, I looked below and what I saw was so beautiful that all I could do was to admire the view. How pretty was the countryside in the Vosges, with its pleasant vales and its green pastures! To enjoy this beautiful landscape even more, I made a detour to fly over the Ballon d'Alsace. On its northern side, at the bottom of a narrow valley, I saw a tiny silver mirror—Lake Gerardmer. I got closer. The temptation was too strong. I forgot about everything: the war, the Huns . . . I casually circled above the lake, trying in vain to see my Nieuport's reflection on its peaceful surface.

"This could have lasted for a few more minutes if my engine hadn't started making incongruous noises. At least, that is what it sounded like to me at first. After listening for a little while longer, I determined that the engine seemed to be running fitfully. That is all I needed to start seriously worrying. I got back on track, hoping to gain speed and having only one thing in mind, to leave this place whose untamed beauty I had just admired but that did not offer a single good landing spot and would be difficult for a rescue squad to reach. So I headed toward an area that was less rough. As I was nearing the plain, though, I noticed that my engine seemed to be doing fine. In fact, it sounded like it was working perfectly. I came to wonder if I had fallen victim to an illusion—I dare not say a slight fit of anxiety.

"I felt a little bit ashamed of my weakness and resolved to keep an eye on such an unfortunate proclivity for nervousness. In the meantime, I had reached 4,600 meters. Where was I? I looked beneath me and saw the city of Mulhouse. A few kilometers to the right, in a clearing I knew very well, was the Habsheim airfield. Good! I had crossed enemy lines without even noticing. I started heading toward a mountain whose peak caught my attention because of its reddish color, which made it stand out. It was the Hartmannswillerkopf, made famous by our Chasseurs Alpins' heroic defense of it. The ancient crown of Vieil Armand withstood enemy fire without turning a hair. The enemy troops failed to break through here the same way they did in Verdun.

"At that moment, I was fired at, but the shots lacked precision, so I felt like I did not need to make a detour and lower my altitude like I usually do when I'm under fire. I partly turned to the right and then to the left to check every direction around me. Here we go: a little bit below and behind me was a small one-seater biplane that looked like a Fokker or a Halberstadt. He was alone, which was surprising. It was the first time I saw that type of plane in a position that is so unfavorable to combat. He surely saw me. What is it? A ruse or simply a lack of experience? I was about to see. The wind was blowing to the west and pushing me farther into enemy territory. I decided to not let the enemy have the upper hand and strike without delay.

"After a U-turn and two more quick shifts, I was just a little bit behind him. I charged at him, but he caught on and slipped away from my firing range with remarkable skill. This first interaction proved that I was dealing with a master. No more messing around! I swayed my plane back and forth and spotted him a mere 40 meters or so below me. He reared up and, maintaining this rather awkward position, fired a round at me. I tilted a little to the right to dodge his bullets. I attacked him again, but still unsuccessfully.

"The wind took us north of Mulhouse. Was I playing into my adversary's hands by lingering here with him? Suddenly, near Belfort, I spotted flakes[3] that seemed to indicate there were enemies nearby. It was the perfect opportunity for me to withdraw from this fight in an honorable fashion. Still, before I let go, I wanted to show my adversary why I was running away. So, I extended my left arm, and, after pointing it toward the explosions, I waved goodbye. The German understood what I was getting at and waved back.

"I rushed toward Belfort looking for the culprit and soon found him. It was a big white two-seater, a real beauty! I went closer. I was delighted at the thought of fighting above French territory for once. This prospect caused me to act recklessly, but I shouldn't have been counting my chickens . . .

"It was time to act. I got in line with the enemy, about 50 meters behind him. I fired just as my plane—which was the faster of the two—was about to collide with him. I abruptly changed course, jumped over the obstacle, and started a gliding maneuver to the right in an effort to pick up speed again to try my luck a second time. Alas! I was

---

3. Lufbery is probably referring to white puffs of smoke and shrapnel from French antiaircraft explosions fired up by Allied crews to warn pilots of approaching enemy aircraft. This was a common practice throughout the war.

out of luck! My engine had received a fatal shot and was breathing its last.

"As I had passed my rival, his rear gunner had had enough time to fire a round of bullets that did quite some damage. I looked back—my stabilizer was ruined. My enemy did not take advantage of the situation though. He headed back toward his own territory. Maybe I hit him as well. His flight meant I was now in control of the battlefield; it was a small comfort.

"I was falling faster and faster. I finally landed on the Fontaine airfield, although it was not an easy task! I was all you could see. Everybody ran to me and asked me questions. They saw the clash. They wanted to know the details. All I could tell them was that I ran into a Boche joke.

"He proved as much: I had three bullets in my engine, a punctured gas tank, a broken mount in my fuselage, and several holes in my hood, and the stabilizer's left side was shredded to bits. My poor Bébé number 1,830 was beyond repair and unusable.

"As for me, I made it with one bullet lodged in my suit and another one in my shoe. I came to the conclusion that my skin was too thick to be pierced by bullets. That brought to mind the following thought: Over the last forty-one months I have spent on the battlefield, I ran into a multitude of snags. I have had rough landings. I have capsized trying to make it back to the airfield. I have been riddled with bullets (so much so that my plane was sometimes barely able to stay in the air). I even spent a whole day hanging from a tree that I hadn't seen because of the fog. In spite of all this, I always made it without a scratch or a bruise."

NINETEEN

The Fighter Becomes an Ace

ON 13 OCTOBER 1916 LUFBERY scored his fifth victory and officially became an ace. The bulletin mentioned his name for the first time that day. It happened during the war's second great air battle. The first one had happened that same year, on March 18, when Habsheim was bombed.

The goal this time was to attack the Mauser military factory in Oberndorf, Wurtemberg, about one-hundred-twenty kilometers from the French border. All the bombers from every French and English squadron stationed in that area took part in the expedition under the command of Captain Happe, the "air pirate." There were about forty pilots.

Fighter planes were tasked with escorting them during part of their trip there and back. Four pilots from the Lafayette Squadron took part in that convoy: Lieutenant de Laage de Meux, Lufbery, Norman Prince, and Didier Masson. Since Lufbery's plane had been decommissioned after his most recent misadventure, he borrowed Captain Thénault's.

The planes started taking off at 1 P.M., with a squadron taking off every ten minutes. The English were the first to leave. As they were flying over Alsace, they had to endure the enemy's heavy antiaircraft artillery. Between Colmar and Neu-Brisach the barrage rose to a terrifying intensity. The enemy lines the pilots had to cross were as high as 1,200 meters, but since they were carrying up to 300 kilos of munitions, the Farman and Breguet planes couldn't fly any higher than 600 meters and sometimes even struggled to get past 400 meters. They were easy prey for gunners!

Sergeant Major Baron—an expert nocturnal bomber who had earned his stripes as an ace among the Spahis and had been mentioned several times already in the bulletin—was taken out by a shell that hit him with full force and broke his Farman in two. "He was one of my good French companions," Lufbery said.

Adjudant Norman Prince seated in his Nieuport 17c.1 fighter on the Luxeuil airfield days before his 12 October 1916 flying accident, which took his life

"I had met him in Champagne when I was still a bomber myself and serving in the V.B.1 06 squadron. We all already admired his exploits then. We had been decorated at the same time. During the ceremony, Captain Happe granted the Legion of Honour to Baron, and the military medal as well as the Croix de Guerre to me. I still have a picture from that day. For the occasion, Baron had traded in his legendary *spahi chechia* for a gorgeous kepi that obscured his manly, energetic features."

The Oberndorf raid was not as successful as one could have hoped. The damage caused was not particularly impressive considering the size of the contingent. After the antiaircraft guns, our Allied forces were attacked by several fighter plane squadrons. We lost ten planes. Nine men were killed and eight were taken prisoner. The French report claimed that six German planes had been shot down. That is incorrect. Only one enemy victim was listed for that day—Subofficer Drewes, who was gunned down by Lufbery.

The battle reached its peak as the pilots were on their way back. Lufbery and Prince distinguished themselves through their bravery.

"We flew together," recalled Lufbery. "We attacked a group of four enemy planes. Prince took one out with only a few bullets. I rushed the three others and forced one of them to cower below his two accomplices. I fired at another one and he started falling. The third one must have thought I was going to follow his companion, which would allow him to shoot me in the back.

"I quickly showed him how wrong he was. I abruptly changed course so that I was facing him (to be more exact, I was perpendicular to him). He was taken by surprise by my unexpected maneuver. I took him out with one round of fire. His plane went into a tailspin and crashed on Schlettstadt.

"Although it gets dark early in October, we stayed until all the bombers came back. I followed the last ones and landed on the small airfield in Corcieux, not very far from our lines and about 60 kilometers from our own airfield. Although I had never landed there before, I did so without difficulty.

"Alas! I can't say the same for my good friend Norman Prince. He was following far behind me and arrived a full fifteen minutes after me. It was completely dark by then, but I still managed to make out his plane describing large circles above the field. He was flying at a very low altitude, trying to find a way to land normally. However, in such darkness he could not see an electrical cable that ran along some trees planted at the edge of the field. His landing gear slammed into it and the plane stood up, fell back down, and flipped over two or three times. In a stroke of bad luck, Prince's seatbelt broke and he was thrown far out of his plane. We rushed to help him. Although the impact was brutal, Prince had not lost consciousness. Both his legs were broken, and he felt a lot of pain inside.

"Extraordinarily, though, he kept a clear head—a testimony to his unshakeable courage—and told us exactly how to carry him. I will always remember the amazing thing he said next, when he heard another plane approach: 'Turn on the damn lights so that nobody else does what I just did!'

"My poor dear friend. He seemed so composed in spite of his pain. Little did I know his wounds would be fatal. I boarded the ambulance that had rushed to the airfield from the hospital in Gerardmer. During the whole trip, Prince kept chatting and joking around as per his usual good mood, which was one of his most engrossing qualities. He talked to me about everything that had happened that day, and told me about his desire to get better quickly so he could come back to fight with us. He must have been in a tremendous amount of pain, though, because sometimes his face would get all contorted. His hand, which I was squeezing in mine, was damp with sweat. However, he had so much stamina that every time the pain got too strong he would start singing to avoid fainting. It was heartbreaking to see him fight back like this.

"At the hospital, I waited until his wounds were bandaged to leave him alone and let him get some rest. I promised him I would come check on him the next day, along with our squadron mates. He held out his hand again, to say goodbye: 'So long, my dear Luf! Good luck, and see you soon!'

"It didn't take him long to fall asleep, but he would not wake up. The next morning, he was in a coma. A blood clot had formed in his brain. He died two days later without having regained consciousness.

"The deaths of Marc Pourpe and Norman Prince were the two most painful events of my life. Pourpe was my friend and mentor. Prince was my best, my most intimate friend and confidant."

This is how the founding member of the Lafayette Squadron died, the glorious unit that did so much to help the Allied powers.

Lufbery had the satisfaction of being an ace, but this courageous man who should be a role model to the younger generation because of his energy, his bravery, and his self-control was also a very simple and good-natured man. A fighter who is honored the way he was would probably be filled with pride. Instead, here is what Lufbery wrote on the subject sometime later:

"Ace . . . I was an ace! From this point onward, I belonged to this special class of fighter pilots who get to see their names printed in the official bulletin every time they are successful.

"In those days, five recognized victories were enough. Later, it would take ten victories to be mentioned in the official bulletin. That makes much more sense in my opinion. I'll add that I have always thought so, even though I did benefit from the more generous rules early on.

"Being on the honor roll doesn't mean that one has become an exceptional fighter or is better than one's companions. A little bit of luck is often enough to achieve a fifth victory. You need to have fortuitous encounters close enough to our lines for people to witness the confrontation and record its outcome. When it comes to official recognition, people are not too strict here in France.

"The bulletin has the same shortcomings as every other type of reward aimed at honoring someone's bravery and determination to win the war. It can't always praise the person who deserves it the most, or at least you could have reasonably made that argument when shooting down five planes was enough to be mentioned in the bulletin. Unless one is singularly talented—which is rare—it would be extremely conceited to claim to be an ace after a mere five official victories.

"That being said, I have to admit that I was very happy to be put on this celebrated list. One couldn't be blamed for thinking that I didn't even need to say so. A little bit of prestige is always nice, and I know people will believe me when I say I'm not indifferent to it."

Listen to Lufbery's confession: "My friends tell me I'm humble. But I'm not! Not really. I'm not that high-minded, you know! Take this definition of modesty by a great thinker from the seventeenth century: *Modesty is a virtue that prevents us from being arrogant in our thoughts and in our words.* I'm far from conforming to the first of those two requirements, because I have to admit that I am very satisfied with my little self—See! How presumptuous!—and I believe, in my heart of hearts, that the awards I have received are proof that I'm not doing bad work. As for the second requirement, it is quite easy for me to conform to it since I am not very talkative by nature."

Lufbery follows this up with a memory: "I'm going to make another confession. I feel like it today; you should take advantage of that! Being popular has its drawbacks, although they are not that bad. Here's one of them: in the October 15 bulletin the newspapers didn't just publish my name. A good number of them included a short biography that wasn't always very accurate, especially regarding my roots. I can't blame them though. It's my fault. Sometime ago, when I had no idea that I would end up gaining some notoriety one day, I told people some fibs on the matter. It really wasn't that important, and it actually got rectified later on. But I laughed at the first biographies that were published about me. A press agency made sure to send them to me in three thick envelopes, which is more than I needed to know how lucky I was."

Raoul Lufbery on the Cachy airfield in Nieuport 17c.1 fighter no. 1844, 29 October 1916. Didier Masson holds the lion cub Whiskey on the plane's fuselage. Robert Soubiran stands behind Masson.

He was mentioned again in the bulletin.

"A brave and skillful pilot, he downed his fifth enemy plane on October 12, during a decisive mission."

The squadron was going to leave Luxeuil for Cachy. On 18 October 1916, they were instructed to leave for their new post just as the first stage of the Battle of the Somme was ending. "I left Luxeuil by plane on 22 October 1916. My trip was not very pleasant. The rainy and foggy weather forced us to fly at a very low altitude. It was cold, and I was looking forward to making it to our destination. I was hoping to stop in Rosnay-en-Champagne, where there is a beautiful airfield, but I wasn't able to. It would have given me a chance to pay my brother Julian a visit. He lives in that area. Julien is six years older than me. He started the war in the trenches but was poisoned by gas on two occasions, so in January 1916 he was assigned as general staff, becoming the sergeant-secretary of an army corps. I promised him I would come see him on my way to Somme. He had been waiting for me since the eighteenth, but the bad weather that delayed our trip for several days stopped me from seeing him like I had wanted.

"I have another brother, Charles. He was serving in the infantry and had just been injured in Soyécourt, Somme."

Cachy left a bad impression on the new ace. The field was covered in thick, greasy mud and was far away from everything. Until then, the Lafayette Squadron volunteers had been stationed in cities that were somewhat distant from the battlefront, and had lived very comfortably. Times were about to change, but you have to make the most of what you have.

The cold weather and constant fog made it so that the pilots could seldom fly, and only for short flights. Every time they flew they seemed to have engine trouble. However, on November 6, Lufbery did have a run-in with an enemy—a Halberstadt, a redoubtable fighter plane. Its pilot was using the clouds to hide. The ace decided to put an end to that little game. He waited for his adversary outside his hiding places, in which he could not stay for too long. He counted on "the feeling one gets when one flies through a particularly thick cloud, as if one was just hit with a burst of cold mist." His tactic worked. Lufbery dove and planted himself in the axis of the enemy plane's fuselage, slightly below it. He fired sixty bullets from behind his enemy and hit the pilot hard. It was as if the plane was a rabbit that had been shot by a hunter. It fell from the sky at dizzying speed. Lufbery's victory wasn't officially recognized because he was too far within enemy territory. That did not stop Lieutenant Gürtler from getting killed!

At the end of November, Lufbery headed to Le Bourget to pick up a 140-horsepower Hispano biplane produced by the SPAD.[1] That plane opened a new era in the history of fighter planes.

"I was very happy with my new 'bird' and hurried back to the squadron. I guess my plane was less satisfied with me than I was with it though. Indeed, I had been flying for only about 12 kilometers when a gas tank came off and tore a portion of the interplane's canvas apart. As it was floating in the wind, the loose flap of canvas pulled on the interplane and broke several of its ribs. Fortunately, I was flying at only about 200 meters and managed to land without encountering any more issues. This little incident didn't give me a very good opinion of the SPAD's craftsmanship."

The cold, humid weather awoke the rheumatism Lufbery had been suffering from since he had been fifteen years old. In spite of his pain, he did not let himself be assigned somewhere else and took part in seven expeditions in December. The last one of these tours gave him his sixth victim: an Aviatik that caught on fire and fell southeast of Chaulnes after a fight that lasted only a few seconds. The defeated pilot had fought back wholeheartedly and lodged four bullets in the victor's plane. In fact, he had been a great ace himself. His name was Lieutenant Leffers.[2] He had nine victories to his credit and had been awarded a Pour le Mérite.

Adjudant Raoul Lufbery standing before his new Spad SVII fighter aircraft at Cachy, November 1916

The ace of the Lafayette Squadron finally received the Legion of Honour, although he did not get promoted, remaining at the rank of sergeant major.

> Chose to serve under the French flag for the duration of the war. Proved himself to be a remarkably daring fighter pilot and took out six enemy planes to this day (27 December 1916). Has already received two Citations à l'Ordre de l'Armée and a military medal.

---

1. SPAD are the initials of the Paris company that manufactured the Spad fighter plane that came out in the autumn of 1916. They stand for Société Pour Aviation et ses Derives.

2. Gustav Leffers, a nine-victory ace piloting a Jasta 1, was not downed by Lufbery. He was shot down on 27 December 1916 while piloting a captured French Nieuport fighter over Wancourt. He was shot down by Captain J. B. Quested and his observer, No. 11 Squadron, Royal Flying Corps. Quested was piloting an FE2b pusher aircraft at the time.

In Somme, life was monotonous, especially for Lufbery. His companions had turned the central room of the barracks into a sort of parlor with a bar that could be used for holding meetings, playing games, reading, or writing letters.

"I very much enjoy the company of our mechanics. Almost all of them are from Paris. They are good men and very witty. They use a special kind of jargon. You have to be an insider to understand them. They're nice lads, although they can be a little defiant. They are easily entertained and easily offended. They always find a way to say something that will make the whole room double over with laughter. They always do what they are told, even if they object to it at first. They are devoted to their 'boss,' especially if he's an ace. Just ask my own two mechanics, Renaud and Michaux, two swell grease monkeys who do everything I ask of them—as long as I do so nicely, because they have a temper! The thing is that their pilot's prestige spills over onto them. They take their share of it, and believe me, they are quite proud! It is true that a pilot wouldn't be able to do much without the help of conscientious, competent, and faithful mechanics."

This praise is well deserved and comes from a peer, as Lufbery had himself been an outstanding assistant to Pourpe. Here's Lufbery talking about a strong belief of his: "A pilot's life is in the hands of his mechanic. Too many young pilots don't understand this quickly enough or at all. They tend to think of them as servants when, in fact, they are precious, dedicated, loyal, and modest teammates.

"Not only do you need to enjoy working with machinery to be a good mechanic, but you also need a lot of goodwill because, sometimes, you need to do a considerable amount of work to become good at your job. I know what I'm talking about. Every pilot should start by being a mechanic. All the great aces did. That is how Guynemer started out. It helped him be so extraordinarily successful."

Soon, though, Lufbery's rheumatism worsened. On 9 January 1917 he had to be hospitalized. He stayed there a week and then went to Auvergne for a bit to recover some more.

He returned to the battlefront on January 22. Although he was still feeling stiff, he was in good enough shape to continue accumulating victories.

Walter Lovell, left, and Edmond Genet on the Ravenal airfield discussing a March 1917 combat patrol with Raoul Lufbery and James McConnell. McConnell would be killed in an aerial engagement on 19 March 1917. Genet was killed in aerial combat on 16 April 1917.

Indeed, three days after his return he had two triumphs. The first one happened at 10:05 a.m. He took out an Aviatik with a burst of sixty bullets. It caught on fire and crashed near Chaulnes. The pilot had been Lieutenant Erdmann. He was flying with Lieutenant Kallenbach. The second victory happened forty-five minutes later, northeast of Chaulnes. Only the first victory was officially recognized, because the second one was claimed by another pilot from a French squadron who insisted that he had been the one to deliver the coup de grâce. That sort of thing happened often!

The next day the Lafayette Squadron left for Ravenel, a small village in Oise. The weather alternated between rain and snow. Strong northern winds were blowing on the plateau, which did not help Lufbery's rheumatism. He had another bad bout and had to go back to the hospital. After leaving the hospital, he went to Nice to recuperate, and stayed there until the end of February.

On March 15 Lufbery's engine stopped working just as he was attacking several enemy two-seaters somewhere between Roye and Lassigny. His adversaries did not take advantage of the situation, and he was able to glide back to the base.

On April 7 his squadron was sent to Ham, 40 kilometers from Ravenel in an area that had been taken back by the French. Lufbery was able to witness firsthand the work of destruction of the retreating German troops.

"About fifty years ago, my uncle left New York for France and built a chemical plant in Chauny that quickly flourished. About thirty years later, my uncle passed the factory ont o one of his sons and left for Florida, where he bought orange groves. During our stay in Ham, I took advantage of our proximity to Chauny to go see how my cousin's plant was doing. I had hoped that Chauny, an industrial city, would have been at least partly spared the same way Roye, Nesle, and Noyon were. Because these cities were so close to the front, they hadn't been damaged too much. Later, I realized that the reason these three cities hadn't been completely ravaged was that destroying them would have tipped off the Allied forces to the German troops' impending retreat. The same didn't go for Chauny. The poor city had been looted, set on fire, and devastated with cheddite. I asked someone to show me the way to my cousin's plant. All that was left of it was a pile of rubble. The private house had been emptied of all of its furniture. The park that surrounds the building had been laid to waste. Some trees had been chopped down or torn out, while others, the larger ones, had been gutted with dynamite.

"But the worst part was the cemeteries that had been defaced."

On April 6, Lufbery downed a defensive enemy plane. It crashed on Saint-Quentin, in a fire that had been started by the Germans. This victory happened too far from French lookout posts, so it was not officially recognized.

Two days later the ace successively attacked three two-seaters. He was flying at 5,000 meters when he spotted them. He charged at the first one, turning his back to the sun. One round of fire and the helpless enemy plane fell from the sky. The two others had already fled. He caught up to the closest one, but the other one fell back and attacked Lufbery to allow his companion to flee. Lufbery wanted to get back at the interloper, but this time it was the first plane that came to his mate's aid. The French American fighter decided not to chase the two planes farther into enemy territory.

The first plane's demise was witnessed by French lookouts, but since nobody saw any smoke coming from the ground, Lufbery was not granted an official victory. It is almost certain that Lufbery's victims were Lieutenant Nauck and the pilot, Glindkamp. Lufbery had another likely triumph on April 12.

His eighth official victory was recorded on April 13. He was looking forward to it after recently having had two victories that he was sure of but were not recognized. He flew for four hours that day. Suddenly, as he was flying at an altitude of 4,000 meters, he spotted an LVG flying at 2,000 meters. As the gunner tried to hit him, the ace placed himself in his enemy's blind spot, approached at full speed, shot, and triumphed after just one round of fire. The German plane, now in flames, crashed northwest of Saint-Quentin with its passengers, Lieutenant Mathias and Vizefeldwebel Rüger.

On April 15, during a flight between Saint-Quentin, Moy, and La Fère, Lufbery descended to 300 meters to fire at some enemy troops just as Lieutenant de Laage de Meux was winning a double victory above Saint-Quentin.

TWENTY

The United States Comes to the Rescue of Our Rights and Liberties

THE UNITED STATES was horrified by repeated acts of German cruelty and destruction. It decided to follow the chivalrous lead of the Lafayette Squadron and join the fight on the side of the Allied powers.

On April 20 the illustrious crew sent a delegation to Paris. It included Captain Thénault, Lieutenant Thaw, Lufber—who was still sergeant major—Corporal Bikelow, and Corporal Hinkle.[1] On April 22 a spectacular gala was organized to celebrate American involvement in the war. People cheered enthusiastically for the pilots, who stood in a place of honor near the statue of General Lafayette.

It was a beautiful celebration of patriotism and friendship. As soon as it was over, Lufbery went back to his squadron. He was eager to prove that the US pledge to fight for France was not an empty gesture.

On April 24 he notched his ninth victory. He was standing guard during a defensive flight when he saw a camouflaged Rumpler plane. "It was a cloudy day. The absence of sun meant I could not resort to my usual tactic. So I decided to act like my enemy's camouflage was doing its job, and kept going as if I hadn't seen him. I started gaining altitude—but slowly so that he wouldn't suspect anything—and kept an eye on him. I could see he was eyeing one of our reconnaissance planes. He was waiting for me to get high up enough for him to attack the other plane without anyone standing in his way. I was obviously interfering with his plan. I decided to go for it. I pretended to fly away and slowed my engine. My trick worked. He quickly maneuvered to get closer to the French plane and attack him from behind. That was what I was hoping for.

"I immediately changed course and took off toward him at full speed. I dove and charged at him, putting my 175-horsepower engine to good use. I fired my first round

Lafayette Escadrille pilots at Lafayette's monument in Paris, 22 April 1917, during a gala event celebrating the US entry into World War I. Lufbery is seated far left. US colonel Billy Mitchell is seated third from right.

of bullets when I was 100 meters away from him. All he seemed to care about from then on was to get himself out of this tight spot. After attempting an inversion he rushed back toward his lines. I followed him, firing quick rounds every time I could get him in my line of fire. He was a tough one! Finally, I fired the round that finished him off, and he crashed heavily just north of Moy, almost exactly where two members of the Lafayette Squadron (a pilot named Hoskier and a gunner named Dressy) had fallen the day before. The next day, Thaw and Haviland took out another enemy plane near that same spot. Our friends were avenged."

Another Citation à l'ordre de l'Armée:

A pilot from the Lafayette Squadron. Skilled and fearless. A veritable example to all of his companions. Forced an enemy aircraft to land on April 8. Took down his eighth enemy plane on April 13, 1917 and his ninth on April 24.

Lufbery is still only sergeant major!

---

1. Corporal Stephen Bigelow

Although he was treated unjustly by the leadership, who continued to refuse to promote the American squadron's great ace to sublieutenant, our young hero's ardor and courage did not waver. Between May 1 and 5 he was involved in seven fights and attacked the *drachens* on two occasions.

On May 10 he traveled to Paris. A delegation from the Lafayette Squadron was invited to attend a banquet organized by the Aéro-Club and presided over by Mr. Daniel Vincent, the undersecretary of state in regard to aeronautics. Over dessert, Mr. Henry Deutsch, the Aéro-Club's president, who hailed from the Meurthe region, awarded Lufbery the Aéro-Club's Great Golden Medal to the crowd's thunderous applause.

However, feasting wasn't the only point of this trip. The great American ace took advantage of it to order and try out a new 200-horsepower SPAD plane.

"This bird, which can reach a speed of 250km/h, is going to allow me to play hide-and-seek with the enemy. It puts their 175-horsepower Benz and Mercedes engines to shame."

The fighting resumed. Lufbery had several encounters that ended in likely victories, although they were not officially recognized. On May 20 he became the first American to receive the English Military Medal.

On May 23 the squadron suffered another loss. "Lieutenant de Laage de Meux died during a freak accident that robbed us of an admirable leader and a true friend. He had just received a SPAD that was similar to mine, and wanted to try it out that afternoon. He was a remarkable pilot, although he had a tendency to rise *en chandelle*; that is to say, vertically. It's a dangerous technique, even for an experienced pilot, because the slightest engine failure can mean big trouble. That is what happened. When the plane reached 50 meters, the engine suddenly stopped working. The plane started losing speed and crashed on the field. De Laage died instantly.

"We were all stunned by this fatal accident. Although he seemed more like our friend than our superior, we all admired and respected de Laage. He was an accomplished French officer. He constantly put himself on the line. He got involved in everything, be it the management of our squadron or actual missions. He was indefatigable, and nothing ever got past him.

"He had only four official victories, but he should have long been considered an ace. I am convinced that he actually won more victories but that they always happened too far from our lines for him to get credit. Two months earlier, he had received the Legion of Honour

Adjudant Raoul Lufbery in London, 20 May 1917, after receiving the British Military Medal for bravery from the King of England. It hangs on his tunic, far right, *with his three French decorations.*

for the double victory he won on April 8. He had also received the Croix de Guerre and five impressive mentions."

After this loss, the Lafayette Squadron was sent south of Soissons, in Chaudun, where they were tasked with protecting five French reconnaissance and liaison squadrons.

On 12 June 1917 Lufbery won his tenth victory as he was patrolling along some new French posts near the Chemin des Dames.

He was northwest of Reims, near Berry-au-Bac, when he saw seven enemy planes that were helping set up artillery shots while five fighter planes were protecting them. He was alone and flying at 5,000 meters. He kept flying in front of the sun, waiting for an opportunity to strike. Suddenly he saw a fighter plane stray away from the others. He charged at him. After one burst, the enemy plane broke into pieces—the wings separated from the body—and dropped from the sky, crashing near Sapigneul, on the new French lines.

Just as he had shot his twenty-fifth bullet, though, Lufbery's gun jammed, so he quickly had to fly away before the other enemy planes avenged their companion. He gained some altitude and peacefully cruised back to Chaudun.

"Captain René Doumer—the head of the Fifth Army's photographic division—was flying his SPAD at that same moment and witnessed the enemy plane's fall. As soon as he made it back to base, he wrote a report detailing what he had seen. When I landed, one hour after my victory, I found out that it had already been officially recognized. I couldn't believe it! I wasn't used to have my victories validated so quickly.

"Here is what happened: After having written his report, Captain Doumer had someone phone the squadrons of his army to find out who had been flying a SPAD near Sapigneul around 8:45 A.M. Naturally, he was told that there hadn't been anyone flying a SPAD there at that time. So when I went to report to Captain Bernard, the head of our army's aeronautic service, he told me: 'I am already aware of your newest exploit. Let me congratulate you!'"

Lufbery received his sixth palm. That wasn't a lot for ten victories!

> Wonderful fighter pilot. His boldness, self-control, and dedication make him a fine example to be followed by the other members of his squadron. Downed his tenth enemy plane on June 12, 1917.

This would be Lufbery's last award as a sergeant major. Finally, after three years spent fighting heroically as a volunteer, Lufbery was promoted to sublieutenant. Why did it take so long for him to receive this well-deserved honor? It probably has to do with the fact that every rule has two dimensions. There is the letter of the law, and then there is the spirit. It turns out that the people who are tasked with enforcing the rules do not always understand both aspects.

Lufbery was promoted the day after his tenth victory. General Maistre summoned him, congratulated him, and invited him to lunch.

"I was pleased to have become an officer," Lufbery wrote, "but I was moved even more deeply by the way this great leader—who is among the French military's most illustrious commanders—honored me. I had actually been recommended for a promotion to sublieutenant as early as last December, but it had been denied to me because the general that was at the head of the army our squadron belonged to had noticed that I had been suspended for thirty days because of an infraction that I had been blamed for under ridiculous circumstances.

Adjudant Raoul Lufbery standing before his Spad s.VII fighter on the Chaudun airfield, 12 June 1917. Lufbery is wearing his flying tunic with all insignia removed to allow him to slip into his flight suit. His mechanics are clustered behind him.

"The previous August I had obtained a leave of absence and had been to the aviation school in Chartres. On the day I was supposed to go back to my squadron, I ran into a friend at the train station. He was about to board a train. We started chatting, and I followed him to the platform. I didn't have a ticket, so when I saw the ticket inspector I let him know that I was not planning on going past the door.

"At the same time, I took a couple of steps forward to shake my friend's hand and bid him farewell. Suddenly I felt someone grabbing my left arm really hard and abruptly pulling me back. It was the cantankerous inspector. He started yelling: 'People who do not have a valid ticket cannot cross.'

"I didn't let him finish. I sent him flying with a straight right to the jaw. Not only did he let go of my arm, which he was holding so tightly that he was hurting me, but he fell flat on his back. He got back up, squealing like a pig getting slaughtered, and ran to the station's military supervisor.

"The supervisor was an elderly lieutenant-colonel. He started viciously ranting against aviators. I have to admit that he wasn't completely wrong and that some bird-brained pilots have a tendency to do very silly things, but I did not enjoy being put in the same bag as them.

"Colonel, you are wearing the same uniform as me. You are decorated like me. I would like to know what you would do if some oaf laid his hands on you for no reason.

'Of course, of course,' he said, 'that is very upsetting. I'm not saying you're the only one to be in the wrong. However, you should not have struck a civil servant who was only carrying out his duties. He filed a complaint. The whole town is going to hear of this and gossip about it. I'm going to have to take action, make an example out of you.'

"Anyway, he ended up giving me a fifteen-day suspension and the *commandant-general de la place* upped my sentence to thirty days. In the end, I really did not care. I didn't even observe this suspension. Trying to enforce such a penalty against a subofficer on active duty would be like trying to catch the moon in one's teeth. But it did end up on my record and delayed my promotion to officer for several months."

Lufbery hadn't changed since Bombay!

About a week after his tenth victory and his promotion to sublieutenant, he went to see his brother Julien, who was serving as sergeant-secretary at the headquarters of an army corps stationed about 10 kilometers from Sapigneul.

"Do you know who you took down on June 12?" Julien asked his brother.

"I have no idea. I just know that's one less thing to worry about. It's all that matters."

"It was Captain von Seel, the commandant of the fighter squadron number 17."[2]

"Really? Good!"

"That squadron has eleven planes that are split into two groups. Their training grounds are located in Valenciennes. The pilot you killed had papers containing all this information on him."

"That was reckless of him."

That year, the French people enthusiastically celebrated Independence Day. For the occasion, the pilots of the Lafayette Squadron were invited to attend a gala at the Hotel des Invalides.

When he headed back to the battlefront, Lufbery continued to fly every day, but he had trouble adapting to new combat methods, which required that several pilots go on patrol together. Lufbery was a virtuoso who preferred performing alone.

He continued to regularly challenge enemy planes but had to wait until September 4 to notch his next official victory. Here is what his seventh citation says:

"Fighter pilot who has been involved in sixteen fights over the last two weeks. During those altercations, he has forced six enemy planes to retreat after successfully firing at them. He shot one down on September 4 (eleventh victory). His plane was seriously damaged by enemy fire on five occasions."

Soon, there was another citation:

Wonderful fighter pilot. Attacked two enemy planes on September 22, 1917. Shot one down (twelveth victory) and forced the other one to retreat. Took down an enemy two-seater on October 16. It went up in flames and crashed behind enemy lines . Had two bullets perforate his engine during the altercation (13th victory).

He received one more citation—his ninth—only a few days later:

Remarkable pilot. His bravery, stamina, and audacity are exemplary. On October 24, just as the enemy troops who had been defeated the day before were preparing to retaliate, he went above and beyond and challenged the enemy in close combat seven times over the course of three successive flights. During one of those altercations he shot down his fourteenth enemy plane and overcame five more planes, which were forced to retreat.

Aren't those citations moving? They are so concise, although the situations they describe are so full of drama. Don't they wonderfully encapsulate the fortitude of the great aerial warrior who always fought like a lion?

Of all the awards he received, Lufbery was most proudest of his tenth—and last—citation.[3] He received it after his double victory over Lieutenant Grauert, Vizefeldwebel Löffl, Lieutenant Pöhl, and Lieutenant Heilmann:

Pilot driven by a relentless desire to dominate his adversary. Always in the air looking for any opportunity. Remarkable skill and endurance. Downed his fifteenth and sixteenth enemy planes on 2 December 1917.

Why such pride? Why such great joy coming from the victor?

"I want you to realize that Pourpe fell on the battlefield exactly three years ago," Lufbery wrote. "Every year, on the anniversary of his death, I try to avenge him. I dedicate my victims to him. On 2 December 1917 I finally succeeded, and, this time I didn't shoot down just one plane, but was fortunate enough to get two of them. Our great friend must be happy with the way I honored his memory. But whatever we do, we will never honor him as much as he deserves."

---

2. French ace adjutant Rene Fonck is credited with downing Captain Eberhard von Seel, commander of Jasta 17, over Montigny on 12 June 1917. It was his sixth victory. Lufbery downed a two-seater observation plane that same day over Sapignal.

3. Lufbery's air action was mentioned in an official French dispatch. The first mention or citation entitled the pilot to the Croix de Guerre medal. Each subsequent mention or citation was recognized with the issuance of a small palm or star, which was attached to the ribbon of the medal.

TWENTY-ONE

Lufbery's Method of Combat

THANKS TO HIS REMARKABLE intelligence, Lufbery had developed his very own method of combat, but, because he was so humble, he liked to say that he had been inspired by famous fighter pilots.

"In my opinion," he wrote, "Guynemer's and Nungesser's methods are different only because their temperaments are different. No matter how many victories are won by the people avenging him, Guynemer will always be the quintessential fighter pilot. If you were to try to picture the ultimate warrior of the sky in your head, he would be it. Aviation being a new weapon, people need a fighter whose example they can follow. Guynemer is that timeless example.

"I met Nungesser when I started out as a bomber pilot with the V.B.1 06 Squadron. In those days, he already had four citations and a military medal. He left us to join the N.65 Fighter Squadron. In his new role he has continued to deploy his usual bravery and energy. He has spent a lot of time in the air and knows every trick in the book. What I find most remarkable about this man is the strength that emanates from him. On two occasions he could have left the service because of serious injuries, but he always came back and has continued to put himself on the line. He never lost his title as the second-best ace. That achievement shows how much stamina and dedication he possesses. On top of that, he is remarkably skilled and has nerves of steel, although he always acts with appropriate caution. That's Nungesser!

"Now that I think of it, he is probably the pilot that inspired me the most. Indeed, good old 'Nunge' is a sportsman who knows that the outcome of the war will not be determined by a single encounter.

French ace Lt. Charles Nungesser beside his Nieuport 17 fighter while with the Lafayette Escadrille at Bar-le-Duc, July 1916

"A fighter pilot doesn't fight only once. He has to carry out a myriad of fights. Once he is done with one (hopefully he has managed to end the confrontation as quickly as possible), he has to be ready to fight again the next day —or in the same hour if necessary. A fighter pilot must endure and therefore had to be prudent. We have to defend our cause. We can't weaken it by mindlessly putting our lives at risk. You don't hunt Boches like a gladiator walking to his own death.

"I know that death lies in wait for us and that there are many opportunities for it to strike. That's all the more reason for us to be careful —very careful—in order to dodge its many claws.

"The fact is that the machine that is allowing us to travel at 250 kilomteres per hour and fly at an altitude of up to 6,000 meters is extremely fragile. Therefore, we must understand it very well and be cautious. We can't ask more of it than what it can do, and not do anything foolish.

"Personally, I like to fly as high as possible and try to avoid nasty surprises by maneuvering constantly so that I can see everything underneath, above, and behind the line I'm following. When I detect an enemy—usually because he is being fired at by our antiaircraft artillery—I approach him as carefully as possible. I don't rush things, and make sure to keep an eye on the horizon, especially on clouds.

"Once I have spotted the planes—enemies rarely fly alone these days—I count them, study their maneuvers, and wait for the right time to strike.

"Of course I try to hide as well as possible by using the sun and the clouds—if there are any—while not losing sight of my targets. At the same time, I keep track of where I am. My worst fear is to have an engine failure above enemy territory. My main concern is not to get stuck with the Boches. Once the pack is on my heels, I will not have time to try to figure out where I am and where I can land, so I have to take care of those details in advance.

"Once that is taken care of, I only rarely have to wait in vain. There's always an opening, a vulnerable spot. When I get my chance, I don't hesitate. I maneuver quickly to get into the blind spot of the plane I chose. I do this while trying not to lose altitude so as not to be spotted by the enemy too early. Then, I charge at him as fast as I can. I fire at him and leave, using the trajectory I thought up in my head, based on the position of the other enemy planes. As soon as I feel I'm outside the reach of my adversaries, I position myself in a way that allows me to watch them at my leisure. How much time did it take me to do all this? Five to ten seconds—as long as I benefit from the element of surprise. If my prey is mean and fights back, I have to make my plane 'dance.' I'm actually pretty good at it. I feint, I dive. Most importantly, I climb as fast as possible and keep myself out of reach of their machine guns. It's not always easy.

"You don't have to worry too much about being chased when you have a fast plane and are good at maneuvering it. The Germans are quick to realize what kind of adversary they're dealing with. They have good fighter pilots. They're skilled and disciplined. When you don't take them by surprise, they fight well. But they won't usually start a fight with a pilot they feel could give them trouble, even when they are superior in number. They're crafty. They'd rather target a pilot who is lagging behind his crew.

SPAD S.VII fighter no. 1777 on the Chaudun airfield, July 1917. On October 24, Lufbery scored one victory and four probable victories while flying this aircraft.

"A straggler is often experiencing some engine trouble, so he's at a disadvantage. Woe betide him if there are any 'birds of prey' in the area! They'll soon surround him. The leader—usually an ace—will fly above him while his suordinates start the offensive. They'll fly around the isolated plane, maintaining various altitudes, and take turns firing at him. Their goal is to throw him into a panic. When the pilot looks like he's starting to become distressed, the German ace steps in and, alas, often manages to finish him off.

"In such situations, it is necessary to keep a cool head and be prudent. If you're flying above your own territory or are close to the lines, the best thing to do is to quickly escape by using one's maneuvering skills. When one is flying above enemy territory, then it is important to be even more prudent so as to match the level of danger one is in. One should always directly face an enemy when that enemy is becoming too insistent, but it is important to show restraint and not waste one's ammunition. I have encountered that kind of situation several times. I never let a spurious sense of pride get in the way. I'm not the kind to continue fighting at any cost when I'm outmatched. I'd rather wait for a better opportunity.

"In short, what you need above all is reflection, self-control, and caution. Those are the best keys to success."

Lufbery's expertise was remarkable, and, as you can see, his incredible mind did not leave anything to chance.

When the American military sent their air force to France, its leaders asked the Lafayette Squadron's pilots to join them.

After thinking it over for a while, the ace of aces took their offer on 5 January 1918. He was glad to have done so because he was immediately promoted to major and technical director. The Americans were especially interested in employing him as an instructor. He was sent to the aviation school in Issoudun, but such a sedentary life did not suit him. "I miss the battlefront," he wrote in a letter to a relative. "I have to get back as soon as possible."

He wasn't the kind to enjoy frivolous paperwork, commands, rules. He would rarely respond when he received notes and reports. He kept asking to be sent back. "And I don't want to be in charge of a squadron! I want to fight!" he demanded.

He had another bout of rheumatism in February and blamed it on his removal from the battlefield. He was sent to Villeneuve, Marne, to join the 1st Fighter Pilots Group.[1] Another disappointment—they didn't have any planes yet. Lufbery was forced into inaction again.

"They must think I'm dead. I can't do anything. I'm looking forward to getting my hands on a fast little birdy I can use to chase the Boches around!"

Later, his unit was moved from Villeneuve to Toule.[2] It was too quiet a place for him. I received another letter. "No Boches. Meanwhile, everyone else is working. It is infuriating to be forced to stand down!"

---

1. The 1st Pursuit Organization Center
2. The 95th Aero Pursuit Squadron, USAS

TWENTY-TWO

"I Will Not Burn to Death"

ADVENTURE KEPT FINDING LUFBERY wherever he went. When one experiences the exhilaration of the great hunt it becomes difficult to stay away from it.

He was teaching and coaching remarkable men. The ace was happy to train pilots. He endeavored to impart his heroism to them, teach them his ingenious ruses, prepare them to make swift decisions, and share with them everything there is to know about hunting enemy birds, but he wanted to show by example. He had no interest in drawing on a blackboard.

Instead of staying within the strictly educational role that people wanted to assign to him, he kept flying and was always the first one to take off.

Major Jean Huffer, left, *commander of the U.S. 94th Aero Squadron, and Major Lufbery, standing beside a Nieuport 28 fighter at Toul, 18 April 1918*

On 12 April 1918 he shot down his first enemy plane as an American soldier. A few days later, on April 27, he had another victory, but it was not officially recognized. Then he ran into a string of setbacks. His gun kept jamming and the weather was perpetually bad. He was restless. He saw his young American companions rise through the ranks. Their names were Putnam, Baylies, Luke, Rickenbacker, et al. He wanted to make it to twenty victories.

During his free time he calmed his nerves by spending time with the local peasants and the few people who still lived in Toul. Everyone loved this American officer, who not only spoke French without a trace of an accent but also actually cared about their lives, gave them advice, and always remembered everything they told him. They felt that this good man who had so many decorations did not come to see them just to kill time but sincerely cared about them. Being among people who work the land reminded Lufbery of his childhood. It made him happy because he had always had simple tastes.

On May 17 he came to see me for the last time. He had insisted on chatting with me before returning to the front. We had so many memories in common! I can still see him sitting by my side, his athletic silhouette standing out against the gray walls of my office. I wanted to have a long conversation with him, get my taciturn friend to open up.

It was 6 P.M. I asked him to stay for dinner. He turned me down. His train was leaving at 8 P.M.

"No. I really want to take down more adversaries. I will come back only when my twentieth victory will be confirmed. Then we can toast to that together."

I insisted. "No, not tonight. But I will come back soon." Then he said, word for word: "I don't think anything will happen to me . . ."

It was the first time I heard him allude to the possibility of something happening to him. During our talk, he had mentioned his victims whose planes had caught on fire.

"I will never burn to death," he told me. He was looking at me with intense eyes. When you peered into them you could imagine the horrible spectacle they had

108

seen again and again: men falling from the sky trapped in flaming planes.

He left. Two days later, on 19 May 1918, he was dead. He had been hit and his plane had caught on fire 800 meters above the ground.

When he descended to about 400 meters, he stood up. Flames were enveloping him. Without hesitating, he jumped from the burning plane. He had stayed true to his word: he did not burn. But how brave he must have been to carry out such a desperate act!

If he had been a German pilot, he could have lived because they had parachutes. But the French hadn't thought of using these yet. The people who were in charge of safety did not fly!

Some peasants rushed to the place where he had fallen to help him. They were hoping for a miracle! When they realized that all that was left of the great hero was a mangled corpse, they brought bunches of their brightest and most beautiful flowers from their gardens.

Captain Edward Rickenbacker became the new American ace of aces after Lufbery and had twenty-six recognized victories by the end of the war. He described Lufbery's fatal encounter: "It was about 10 A.M. when the antiaircraft cannons started firing over Saint-Mihiel. We were on high alert. An enemy reconnaissance plane equipped with a camera had been spotted. Soon it was flying above our camp.

"Lufbery's plane was unavailable, so our friend rushed to another one.

"Five minutes later he was flying at 800 meters and was catching up to the enemy. Our observation posts witnessed the clash. Lufbery attacked first by firing short bursts. He was about to fire at point blank range when his gun seemed to jam. He circled back and attacked again—probably after having fixed his gun. He positioned himself behind the enemy and fired, but all of a sudden, his plane was engulfed in flames. He passed the German plane and flew straight ahead for three or four seconds. Then, he leaped off his plane. His body landed in a peasant's garden in Maron.

"About 100 meters from that spot, there was a small river. We speculated that Lufbery might have aimed for it hoping that the water would break his fall."

We took the hero to the Evacuation Hospital No. 1 in Toul. His funeral was held at 4 P.M. on May 20.

The shoemaker's garden where Lufbery fell after exiting his burning Nieuport 28 fighter. He landed on the picket fence behind the peasant woman in the village of Maron, north of Nancy. She holds the end of a picket wrapped in paper which she pulled from Lufbery's throat."

The morning of the ceremony, the nurses went to pick flowers in the woods. They found some lilies of the valley in shaded areas, gathered bunches of flowering hawthorn branches, and picked a few cornflowers. They arranged those flowers Lufbery had loved so much around his coffin, which was shrouded in the American flag.

As the final touches were added to Lufbery's funeral chamber, his orderly appeared on the doorstep. He looked distraught; tears ran down his face. He was awkwardly holding a gorgeous bunch of lilies of the valley he had picked himself. He timidly entered the room, said a short prayer, and deposited the flowers. He had tied a card to the bouquet. The clumsily handwritten note read: "To my dear friend, Commandant Lufbery, in acknowledgment of everything he did for me." Pourpe's former mechanic and avenger received a heartfelt homage from his own mechanic.

At 4 P.M., after a succession of French and American public figures paid homage to the pilot, his funeral cortege headed to the cemetery as a military band played funeral marches. It was a small cemetery consisting of two rows of brown crosses near some woods. During the procession, the nurses, clad in gray uniforms, formed a single line. A large crowd of men walked slowly. The guard of honor was made up of two American infantry companies and a French one. Lufbery's orderly walked behind the coffin, which was draped in the star-spangled banner. His head was down, and he was sobbing. Next came the members of Lufbery's squadron, walking two by two. They were followed by a long column of French and American officers, notable civilians, and peasants from all of the surrounding villages.

The squad that was going to fire the salvo in Lufbery's honor got in position next to the tomb. Reverend W. Billing held the service. Just as he ended his speech, the audience heard the sound of an engine. A plane from Lufbery's squadron was flying through the sky, drawing tight circles. The pilot boldly dove toward the ground, and just as he reached the top of the trees in the neighboring woods, he straightened his plane and leaned out of it to throw flowers on Lufbery's tomb.

After the service and the prayers, General Passaga and General Edwards each gave a speech. The armed squad fired three salvos and a bugler played a funerary song. Another bugler who stood farther away, at the edge of the woods, softly echoed it.

Finally, the coffin was lowered into the ground, and people threw enough flowers on it to cover it completely. After that, the procession headed back to the hospital to the sound of music.

Few ceremonies have been as moving. In a letter sent the next day, American lieutenant Kenneth P. Culbert wrote: "My only wish is to do as much for my country as he did, even if I must pay for it with my life." He died in combat the next day.[1]

A few months later, Miss Marie-Gertrude Brownell, a nurse at the hospital in the American military base in Toul, noted:

> Although there are now four rows of brown and green crosses in our cemetery instead of only two, Major Lufbery's tomb still dons the biggest wreath. On Sundays, French mothers take their children to visit the resting place of the great American ace.

In 1921 Toul decided that it wanted to show its gratitude to Major Lufbery, but since they did not have enough money to erect a grand monument, they decided to include Lufbery's name among the names of the local men who had died for their homeland.

This is how young and heroic Lufbery reunited with young and heroic Pourpe, the friend he had so dearly wanted to avenge, in the heaven of great warriors.

Those two heroes who lived parallel lives and had similar fates shared the same earnest love for their country and will be remembered as some of the most glorious figures of the war and of aviation.

Noble hearts! Admirable knights of adventure! You teach us to love humanity in spite of its most odious elements.

---

1. Lt. Kenneth P. Culbert, USMC, aerial observer, and his pilot, Lt. Walter V. Barnaby, 1st Aero Squadron, USAS, were returning from an aero observation mission on 22 May 1918 when their aircraft was struck by German antiaircraft fire near St. Mihiel. Their aircraft crashed just inside Allied lines, instantly killing Barnaby and seriously injuring Culbert. Culbert was transported to the American hospital at Sebastopal Farm, near Toul. He died at midnight without regaining consciousness. In a 21 May 1918 letter to C. T. Copeland, his Harvard professor and mentor, Culbert described Major Lufbery's funeral.

"Perhaps you'd like to hear of Major Lufbery's funeral—you doubtless know that he was shot down, and fell from his burning plane into a courtyard. He had done a great deal in uniting the French and Americans—he was the greatest of our airmen and seventh on the list of French aces—he had all the qualities of a soldier, audacity, utter fearlessness, persistence, and tremendous skill—in every way, sir, he was a valuable man.

"As we marched to his interment the sun was just sinking behind the mountain that rises so abruptly in front of Toul; the sky was a faultless blue, and the air was heavy with the scent of the blossoms on the trees surrounding the fields. An American and French general led the procession, following close on to a band which played the funeral march and 'Nearer, my God, to Thee' in so beautiful a way that I for one could hardly keep my eyes dry. Then followed the officers of his squadron and of my own—and after us an assorted group of Frenchmen famous in the stories of this war, American officers of high rank, and two American companies of infantry, separated by a French one.

How slowly we seemed to march as we went to his grave, passing before crowds of American nurses in their clean white uniforms, and a throng of patients and French civilians! He was given a full military burial; with the salutes of the firing squad, and the two repetitions of taps, one answering the other from the west. General Edwards made a brief address, one of the finest talks I have ever heard any man give—while throughout all the ceremony French and American planes circled the field. In all my life I have never heard taps blown so beautifully as on that afternoon—even some of the officers joined the women there in quietly dabbing at their eyes with white handkerchiefs. France and the United States has truly assembled to pay a last tribute to one of their soldiers. My only prayer is that somehow through some means I can do as much as he for my country before I too wander west—if in that direction I am to travel."

(Memoirs of the Harvard War Dead in the War against Germany, 1922, Vol. III, 95–96)

Major Lufbery's funeral procession transporting his casket to the American cemetery, Sebastapol Barracks, 20 May 1918

PART TWO

Essays and Articles

The Arrival of the Lufberys in France by Raoul Lufbery III

Present-day Lufbery family members would say that Major Raoul Lufbery's birth in France in 1885 came about only as a result of a family member's great business acumen. In fact, having any Lufbery members residing in France can be attributed to a risky and bold entrepreneurial gamble starting in 1866 by Major Lufbery's uncle George Freeman Lufbery Sr., from Rahway, New Jersey. If Raoul's uncle had failed at his attempt to establish his industrial mega-company, it is doubtful that any member of the Lufbery family would have established a lasting residency in France, thereby eliminating the possibilities of any Lufbery offspring being born in that country (including Major Raoul Lufbery). George Freeman Lufbery Sr. was the older half brother to Raoul's father, Edward Lufbery. Both were born in America and both were citizens of the United States.

Before the story is told of how the Lufberys relocated to France, it is helpful to share a brief overview of the Lufbery family genealogy. Lufbery is not a French name. It originated from descendants living in the village of Newport, Essex, England, in 1493. The first family relatives arrived in America in 1637 at Plymouth, Massachusetts. In 1659, some Lufbery family members moved to Woodbridge, New Jersey.

As with most family genealogy, as decades pass by, the last name can have numerous spellings. Records show "Lufbery" was spelled as "Luffberry," "Loofborrow," "Lufberry," "Lufbury," and "Lufborough." Major Raoul Lufbery even spelled it "Lafberg" to pass for French when he first met Marc Pourpe. Raoul wanted to impress Pourpe with his French-born heritage, to increase his chances of employment with Marc's spectacular flying exhibition tour, which was performing in Calcutta in January 1913.

In 1695 the first Lufbery family member established a connection with the state of Connecticut. Major Raoul Lufbery had always considered the community of Wallingford, Connecticut, his adopted hometown in America. Numerous family members still live and work in Wallingford today.

Two New Jersey family members, Abraham Lufbery and Isaac Lofborough, both volunteered and served in the Continental army during the US Revolutionary War of 1775 to 1783. Andrew Lufberry was a private with the Pennsylvania Volunteers during the War of 1812.

Charles Sampson Lufbery and Elizabeth Fitz (Weaver) Lufbery were the parents of George Freeman Lufbery(Raoul's uncle), who was born in 1839 in Hoboken, New Jersey. After the passing of Elizabeth, Charles Sampson Lufbery married Ann (Phebe) Lufbery, and they had one child, Edward Lufbery (Raoul's father). He was born in 1854 in New York City. Thus, George and Edward were half brothers by the same father.

Charles Sampson Lufbery and his son George Freeman Lufbery Sr. both fought in the US Civil War. George was wounded at the battle of Antietam, Maryland, in 1862 and was discharged from the army for disabling wounds on 2 April 1863. Edward Lufbery was only nine years old at this time and was living with his mother in New York City.

Charles Sampson Lufbery prospered and became financially wealthy selling construction materials to real estate developers during the great growth expansion of New York City in the first half of the 1800s. Other New Jersey uncles, aunts, and cousins also catered to this building boom by providing building products and furnishings during this time period. One family business, known as the "Lufbery & Ayres Lumber Planing Company," did extensive lumber sales in the region for about 25 years. John H. Lufbery, who was part owner of this lumber company, was elected mayor of the city of Rahway, New Jersey, in

1860 and served in the state legislature in 1872 and 1874. He was an uncle to George Freeman Lufbery.

George Freeman Lufbery, at age 26, aspired to create his own business opportunity. He had a background in chemistry and had made the commitment to put all his know-how, effort, and personal wealth into formulas to produce synthetic rubber. In the late 1860s, the world was well into the Industrial Revolution, with consumer demands creating colossal needs for rubber due to the inventions and development of electricity (wire coating insulation), sealants, hoses, personal protective outerwear (rubber boots and raincoats), and hundreds of other home and business rubber products. Natural rubber from tree plantations in South America could no longer meet the worldwide demand. George saw the opportunity to become an industrialist in this new and emerging synthetic-chemical rubber industry.

In 1866, George teamed up with American industrialist Hiram Hutchinson, and his son, Alcander, in France. The two had recently refurbished an old paper mill there into a chemical rubber factory to break into this new and promising industry. This father-and-son team had ties to New Jersey and the Lufbery family. Both men had lived in New Jersey, and Hiram Hutchinson was married to a cousin of George Lufbery. The factory management and operation between these men were professional and successful for the next five years. Alcander Hutchinson was "Factory Director & Chief" and George Freeman Lufbery was the "Chemist & Director of Operations."

In 1871, George decided to try a new business venture and partnered with the dynamic industrialist Charles Daumy from the Marseilles-les-Aubigny region. His factory manufactured hydraulic lime for cement. They formed the "Daumy and Lufbery Company," but George Lufbery became discontented with this line of work and wanted to return to the rubber industry. Regional land purchase records showed George had been acquiring commercial properties in Chauny, France, between 1870 to 1873 to start his own manufacturing business.

In 1869 George's fifteen-year-old half brother Edward, who would be Raoul Lufbery's father, traveled from America to Europe to study chemistry in Germany. After Edward graduated from university in 1873, George hired him as assistant manager and sent him to his small and modest chemical factory in the city of Chauny, France. At this time, a local news story noted both brothers seemed to be adventurous and ambitious for success and wished to increase the size and value of their business. Both had

Edward Lufbery with his daughter Yvonne in Wallingford, Connecticut, in 1925

expertise as chemists, and George lead the way with his friendly and jovial personality. Local French citizens were somewhat amazed that the young Americans were investing resources and building a factory in this new and promising synthetic-rubber industry in Europe.

Edward Lufbery worked for his brother in the Chauny synthetic-rubber chemical factory for the next three years and then relocated to Chamalieres, France, in 1876 to work for the J. B. Thorillon Rubber Clothes Company. While there, Edward met and married Anne Vessiere on May 21 of that year. She became the mother of Raoul Lufbery and his two older brothers, Julien and Charles.

No one knows why the brothers ended their partnership in 1876 and went their separate ways. It appears that for the rest of their lives, there was little interaction between them and their family members. History revealed that George had a phenomenal business career and superb lifestyle. Conversely, Edward's family experienced hardships and financial difficulties.

George Freeman Lufbery Sr. continued with his rubber business into the late 1870s. In the following decades he demonstrated an entrepreneurial spirit, savvy business practices, and unwavering determination to succeed. He guarded his manufacturing secrets and chemical formulas in order to maintain his leadership role and the domination of the industry's European market. He developed and improved the chemicals and processes needed for the vulcanization of rubber. He also invented the industrialized manufacturing equipment used by his rubber business customers while acquiring numerous patents on his many inventions.

In 1884, George formed a partnership with Leonard Chardonnier to mega-size the factory complex to 92 buildings spread over 29 acres. In addition to the existing two cargo transport boat canals, a train railway was built to improve transportation to Paris and beyond. By the early 1890s, George Freeman had achieved his liflong goal and had became a rubber chemical industry titan with very profitable worldwide sales. He was viewed in the Chauny region as a caring and helpful philanthropist who contributed to education scholarships to students and provided donations to numerous community organizations for many years.

In 1901, George Freeman Lufbery Sr. semiretired with his second wife, Elizabeth Pitts Weaver, of England, and spent winters in Port Orange, Florida. Still having the zest for entrepreneurship, he became the owner of a large orange tree plantation and "dabbled" in America's orange juice market. He also built a factory to process palmetto leaves into fiber for commercial uses. While a chemist and inventor in France, George had developed fertilizers and insecticides that would became the catalyst for his agricultural ventures.

1898 Lufbery automobile

In 1902, George Sr. transferred a portion of the Chauny factory business management to oldest son, Charles Edouard. Charles was given the title "Chief Director of the Factory." Before this promotion, Charles had been operating a sodium-chloride processing plant and had created a small automobile company that produced the luxury "Lufbery Automobile" in France starting in 1898.

On 7 August 1910, George Freeman Lufbery Sr. departed France for the last time and returned to the United States to begin a full retirement. Even after all his time in France, he remained a loyal American and never gave up his US citizenship. George Sr. passed the full operation of the massive Chauny, France, chemical rubber factory onto son Charles Edouard. Charles Edouard had been born in France in 1869 and was 41 years old at the time. His mother was George's first wife, Jenny Campbell, of New York.

In 1910 George Sr.'s youngest son, George Freeman Lufbery Jr., was living in Elizabeth, New Jersey, where he was constructing his own factory on a 9-acre parcel of land. He had been born in Marseilles, Cher, Centre, France, in 1874. He soon began manufacturing chemicals for the rubber trade for the North American market.

In November 1910, George Freeman Sr. and his second wife, Elizabeth, left Florida and moved to San Diego, California. He died there on 19 April 1911 at age 72 and was buried in San Diego's Greenwood Memorial Park.

The synthetic-rubber factory complex in Chauny, France, continued to do well for the

The Lufbery mansion in Rahway, New Jersey, photographed in the late 1800s.

Lufbery family under the direction of Charles Edouard Lufbery through the spring of 1914. The local city residents noted that Charles Edouard inherited his father's spirit, business acumen, industrial aggressiveness, and tradition of generosity.

However, in August 1914 the start of World War I changed everything. The war brought catastrophic events to the city of Chauny and to the Lufbery rubber factory.

The city was occupied by German forces for a substantial part of the war because it was close to the front lines. The German military demanded war materials from the factory throughout the three years of its occupation there. Chauny was extensively destroyed by dynamite during March 1917, when the Germans did a strategic withdrawal of the Hindenburg line as the region and the city of Chauny were recaptured by Allied forces. Of the 92 buildings within the Lufbery rubber factory complex, only 13 were classified as repairable after the war.

Aviator Raoul Lufbery, while with the Lafayette Escadrille, visited the chemical rubber factory site in April 1917. Raoul wrote a letter home to his brother saying, "During my stay in Ham, I took advantage of the proximity of Chauny to go and see—the status of my cousin's factory." Raoul found the unfortunate city looted, burned, and destroyed by Cheddite (explosives). "I witnessed nothing but ruins from the factory," he said. He jested that the Germans had blown up the family factory in retaliation for his destruction of their military aircraft.

After the war, a French business journal noted the following: "This rubber factory establishment by George F.

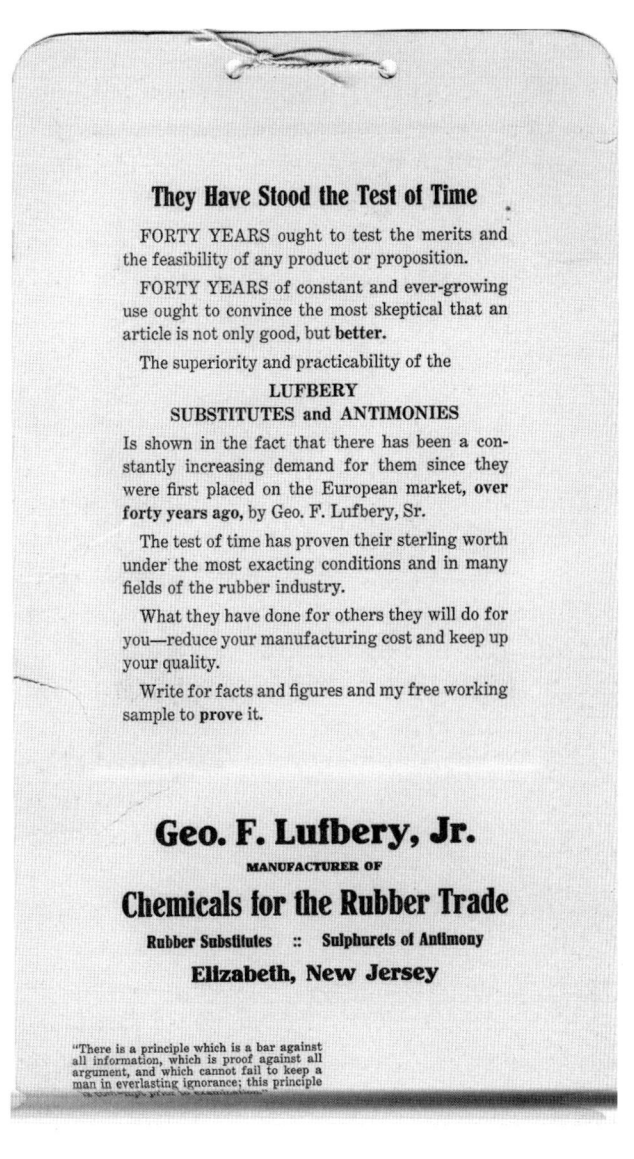

The front and back of the September 1914 calendar advertisement for George Freeman Jr.'s New Jersey rubber business

The 29-acre rubber chemical factory complex in Chauny during the spring of 1914

Housing in Chauny for Lufbery factory employees

Lufbery Sr. manufactured oils, coloring materials, and special chemicals for the making of synthetic rubber. These highly demanded products, before the war, were exported all over the world. In 1914, the factory employed 200 workers. The site included 92 buildings spread over 29 acres. This plant was almost completely devastated and annihilated by the invasion, but its reconstruction is being accelerated and the work must resume soon." In addition to the rubber factory destruction, the beautiful Lufbery family mansion in Chauny was also dynamited into ruins.

The 11 November 1918 end of the war did not stop the New Jersey and Chauny, France, Lufbery family difficulties and hardships. First and foremost, Major Raoul Lufbery died in aerial combat seven months before the signing of the armistice.

George Freeman Lufbery Jr. also died in 1918 at 44 years of age in Elizabeth, New Jersey, and was buried in Valparaiso, Indiana, where the family of his wife, Bertha (Miller) Lufbery, resided. There is no doubt the wartime factory difficulties, financial hardships, and the ultimate destruction of the Chauny rubber factory complex created stress and serious health issues for both of George Freeman Sr.'s sons.

Charles Edouard Lufbery was delegated sole administrator and director of rebuilding the entire factory complex after the war. His father, George Sr., had taken thirty years to build the manufacturing complex before the war. Charles attempted to rebuild the factory site in five years. Unfortunately, there were many challenges and complications. Charles Edouard committed suicide in Chauny on 13 June 1924. A French newspaper article made note of this:

> Charles Lufbery, 55-year-old son of George F. Lufbery Sr., committed suicide this morning by throwing himself under a 6-ton ejector cylinder. When the workers saw it, they could only remove the body, whose head lay a little farther away, separated from the body. Mr. Lufbery was highly esteemed in the area, and he was married to the daughter of one of the most important jewelers in Paris. He was very tired in his effort to reassemble the rubber factory, which had been destroyed by the Germans, and the crisis of the 1920s was hard. He suffered from depression.

On 23 September 1924, in a general meeting of shareholders, the Lufbery & Chardonnier Company was dissolved. From that point forward, a series of other companies owned the rebuilt portions of the factory complex, and chemical products produced there ranged from linoleum to fertilizer. As the decades went by, a decline of the factory's operation and production output occurred until its final closure in 1992. Most of the factory buildings were dismantled and removed soon after, leaving little evidence that the George Freeman Lufbery Sr. mega chemical rubber factory had ever existed.

A room in the Lufbery mansion at Chauny before it was dynamited

The destroyed Lufbery Chauny mansion in 1917

Raoul Lufbery's Early Life and Adventures: March 1885 to July 1914 by Raoul Lufbery III

This addition to Jacques Mortane's 1937 book is intended to provide an overview of Major Raoul Lufbery's life before his outstanding military aviation career in World War I. Many interesting details about Raoul's young life are shared for the first time with the reader. Much of the information comes from thirty years of research by family members and is generally not found in history books. It is believed this is the most comprehensive collection of information ever compiled about Raoul's childhood and young adult life.

Raoul Lufbery was born on 14 March 1885 in Chamalieres, France, to Edward Lufbery, an American father, and Anne Vessiere, a French mother. Anne had been born in Chamalieres on 20 August 1859, the loving daughter of Pierre and Madeleine Vessiere. Edward and Anne had married on 21 May 1876 and had two sons prior to the birth of Raoul. Oldest son, Julien, was born on 6 April 1879, and middle son, Charles, was born on 15 October 1881. Raoul's mother, Anne, died on 8 June 1886 at twenty-seven years of age while giving birth to a stillborn child. Raoul was fifteen months old at the time of her passing.

Edward Lufbery tried to raise the three young boys, manage his job, and do the domestic chores. but he soon found the workload overwhelming. He arranged with Madeleine Vessiere, his deceased wife's mother, to place Raoul and his two older brothers in her care. Grandmother Vessiere did her best to raise the three boys under difficult and impoverished times. Her husband, Pierre, had passed away seven years earlier at age 52 in Chamalieres, where he was working as a grocer. Madeleine continued on with the grocery business for some years to support the family. The oldest brother, Julien, six years older than Raoul, had to assume the father role for the family until his late teenage years.

After Edward Lufbery placed his three sons in the care of their grandmother, he moved to Blois, France, to work as a chemist at the Poulain chocolate factory. Over time, the relationship between Edward and Madeleine grew strained and difficult, and visits between Edward and his sons were few during that time period. In 1890, Edward married Marie Bosdevore and moved her to America, where he worked as a chemist at a New Jersey rubber company and later at the New York Insulating Wire Company in Wallingford, Connecticut. Their only son, Rene Lufbery, was born on 19 September 1891 in Wallingford.

In 1893, Edward, Marie, and baby Rene returned to France. From 1893 to 1899 their next three children were born in either Blois or Tours. Daughter Yvonne was born on 1 December 1893, Marie-Louise was born in 1895, and Germaine was born on 7 September 1897. Their fourth daughter, Bertha, was born on 29 December 1899 in Champagne-Ardenne, France.

Edward revealed some years later in an interview with a newspaper reporter that his son Raoul was sent to the Cevennes Mountains, in the hill country of France, to board with a peasant family for part of his grade school years. Edward noted, "The course black bread, sour wine, savory ragouts, and freedom of the open sunlight country strengthened his slim, colt-like limbs and gave him a muscular heavy body. Somewhere in these hills the wandering spirit for adventure was instilled into the young soul of Raoul."

Edward further noted that Raoul had a profound interest in analyzing the details and idiosyncrasies of

Raoul Lufbery's brothers in World War I, from left to right: Sgt. Julien Lufbery, French army, artillery; Rene Lufbery, US Navy seaman; Sgt. Charles Lufbery, French army, infantry

children's games popular at that time. However, he lost interest upon fully understanding their mechanical workings, thereby exhausting their possibilities of amusement. Raoul was a prolific reader of adventure stories, which likely influenced his worldwide wandering spirit. He also enjoyed reading about worldwide travel, gymnastics, wrestling, boxing, and target shooting.

Raoul's father had been a frequent traveler all his life between America and Europe. Edward sold and traded rare postage stamps and traveled from America to Europe forty-six times. At some point in Raoul's early teens, these factors gave him the motivation and a mindset to get on with exploring the world.

In 1897 twelve-year-old Raoul left school in Chamalieres to help support his grandmother and two older brothers. His first job was an errand boy at the Maitre Corre notary company, where his brother Julien worked as a clerk. Julien had persuaded his employer to hire Raoul. From there, Raoul then sold shoes at Pradier, on rue des Gras, then worked as a laborer at the Bergougnan Rubber Factory. He boarded with Julien, who continued to provide Raoul with guidance and support.

A bit later Raoul, a sturdy and self-sufficient lad, began his adventuring exploits by roaming the countryside of France. When he grew weary, he slept in fields or under trees. He worked for food when he was hungry and roamed from village to farm exploring the beautiful landscapes, vineyards, mountains, and forest. He periodically kept in touch with his father in Bois. Raoul would roam for a time and then briefly return home. He repeated this cycle of adventure but always remained within the boundaries of his birth country. His father noted that Raoul was a confident and a likable teenager with a determined drive who didn't exhibit any sensational qualities.

In 1900, according to brother Charles, Raoul left his grandmother Vessiere's care and went off to see the big city of Paris. For the next year he continued his roaming and traveling.

In 1901 Edward's second wife, Marie, died in Blois, France, at age 29, leaving him with five young children to care for. Edward admitted that raising five children alone was too much for his paternal resources. He summoned Raoul to Blois to help with their care. Raoul, now age 15, helped Edward raise the children for nearly three years, acting as nursemaid and doing the household chores. Edward noted that Raoul found the responsibility extremely boring and drab, but he did his duties well. In 1905, with his father's permission, Raoul departed Blois and set off to travel the seven seas and to visit over thirty countries.

On 28 February 1901, oldest brother Julien, age 21, married Marie Puyfoulhoux, age 18, from Vertaizon, 20 miles from Clermont-Ferrand. Their first daughter, Germaine, was born on 3 September 1903, making Raoul an uncle.

On 7 April 1906 Edward Lufbery moved back to Wallingford, Connecticut, from France to establish a bakery. His sons Charles, age 24, and Rene, age 15 accompanied him and worked with him on and off. The bakery thrived until Edward gave it up. Later that year Charles's wife, Laurence or Laurie, arrived in Wallingford from France. The couple had married three years earlier in Clermont-Ferrand. Laurie had been born in France on 15 September 1878 to Benoit Colly and Jeanne (Mege) Colly. Her father had operated a truck transport company for many years.

Starting in 1900, Raoul, Charles, and Julien had assisted Edward financially for a four-year period while he raised his five children from his second marriage. Edward always said he was very appreciative of his three sons for their support and consideration. Julien was the first son to end financial support to his father once he married Marie Puyfoulhoux and they had their first child.

In March 1905 Raoul, age 20, began globetrotting. He started his worldwide adventures by visiting and working in the following countries:

- Algiers (dock cargo worker and nursing aide), April 1905 to March 1906
- Tunisia, Tunis (cook trainee and railway track worker), March 1906 to April 1906
- Egypt (worker for the Suez Canal Company), May 1906 to June 1906
- Egypt (declared his American citizenship at the French consulate of Cairo), June 26, 1906
- Aegean Sea (cook on a cabotage sailboat), July 1906
- Turkey, Istanbul (manufacturer of iron fruit baskets and waiter), August 1906
- Balkans (peddler), September 1906
- Germany, Fulda (beer brewer), Sept. 1906 to April 1907
- Germany, Hamburg (dock worker), April 1907

Brother Charles and father, Edward, noted Raoul greatly enjoyed his time in Egypt. They said he loved the freedom of the burning sands, the golden glory of the skies by day, the purple haze that shrouded the ancient ruins by night, the odd companionship of desert roving bands of Arabs and their swift wild horses. While in Egypt, Raoul wrote home and said he "could wish to live there always if he could wish to live always anywhere."

In May 1907 Raoul, age 22, arrived in New York City from Hamburg, Germany, on the ship *Ascan Ubermann*, where he had served as a cook. He reached Wallingford a few days later. As it happened, the day Raoul arrived in New York, his father, Edward, boarded a ship traveling to France to pursue his stamp collection and its dealership opportunities. Because of their separate travels, followed by the advent of World War I, Raoul and Edward never saw each other again. Raoul moved into an apartment with brother Charles and his wife, Laurie, in the old Wallace block at 35 North Main Street, Wallingford. Both men were employed at the Simpson, Hall, and Miller silver factory. Raoul worked at the factory making casket handles and other hardware for coffins.

Raoul was very sports oriented and enjoyed boxing, wresting, weightlifting, and gymnastics at the local gyms. Occasionally he wagered a few dollars on boxing matches with other young men from Wallingford. As word spread of Raoul's prowess as an amateur boxer, the opportunity for matches became difficult. Charles had a second job baking in nearby New Haven. He arranged boxing matches in that larger city. Raoul would catch the trolley the day of the fight to meet his foe in New Haven. Raoul rarely lost a fight, and both brothers split the winner's purse of a few dollars per match.

Meanwhile Raoul and Charles attended the Colony Street night school to improve their English-speaking skills. After a few months, both men felt the teacher's lesson plan was moving forward too slowly. They dropped night school and taught each other English at home after completing their day's factory work. Raoul and Charles would often go mushroom hunting in the wooded areas of Wallingford. Raoul had no love for the hustle of the big cities of Europe and Asia and thought Wallingford was a lovely place with its majestic hills, scenic landscapes, and flowing streams. He enjoyed small-town life with adjoining open country.

Raoul also thoroughly enjoyed meeting up again with his siblings in America. He become reacquainted with three of his four half sisters—Marie-Louise, Germaine, Yvonne—and his half brother Rene, from Wallingford, and from Yalesville (all from his father's second marriage). Raoul had a good relationship with them, and together they shared in family outings and recreational activities. Charles noted that Raoul had the closest relationship with sister Yvonne. Raoul appointed himself "protector" of her well-being and whenever possible played jokes and teased her in a friendly way. This sibling teasing with Yvonne was his exclusive privilege, and he curtailed any other family member from attempting to do the same.

Raoul and Yvonne also enjoyed sharing their musical talents with other family members. Raoul was a good amateur mandolin musician and enjoyed playing a tune while Yvonne pleasantly sang the lyrics. One favorite song of the duo, titled "When My Father Was Combing His Beard," had a sweet and melodious tune.

Sister-in-law Laurie remembered young Raoul as a dedicated factory worker who came home tranquil and tired. After dinner he went to bed like an old man, and at breakfast he was quiet. She used to say to her husband, Charles, "Is that boy [Raoul] someone who killed tigers in India, who saw the world from Calcutta to Paris? No, no I cannot believe, he is so quiet!"

According to Charles, Raoul was very fond of all pet dogs, especially springer spaniels. Raoul bonded with pets for their unwavering companionship and loyalty. Raoul noted that most dogs had a faithful allegiance to people and could be counted on as part of a helpful working team. Their unconditional acceptance remained true in spite of human flaws or social shortcomings. Raoul also noted that humans could not always be counted on to do the same as their pets under similar circumstances.

In September 1908 Raoul departed Wallingford following a year and a half there, for more globetrotting adventures. He corresponded with his father and American siblings from numerous locations around the world for the rest of his life. Raoul viewed Wallingford as his adopted hometown. He often said he would return to Wallingford after the war to settle down. Edward Lufbery noted in an interview after Raoul had been killed in action that his time in Wallingford must have been the most mundane, uneventful period in his adventurous and colorful life.

Raoul worked with other teenage boys at the Simpson, Hall, and Miller factory. But his coworkers did not remember young Raoul as being exceptional or distinctive. They did remember a steady worker and a silent lad who occasionally played a joke on someone during coffee break. But as soon as break time was over, he returned to work producing his fair share of hardware for coffins. Edward recalled that Raoul did not like regular work hours, redundant piecework jobs, or smoky factories.

In October 1908 Raoul worked in New York and New Orleans. He also toured Mexico and Quebec, Canada. He then traveled to San Francisco and worked as a hotel waiter. From his workplace at San Francisco's White Palace Hotel, Raoul wrote his brother Charles in Wallingford that he was a waiter there and that it was somewhat better than his former job in New Orleans, as a baker putting raisins in bread.

On 20 November 1908, while still in San Francisco, Raoul enlisted in the US Army at Fort McDowell and was deployed to Honolulu, Hawaii, in December. In March 1910 the army sent him to Manila, the Philippines, where he became a rifle marksman. He had excellent eyesight and "nerves of steel." These qualities gave him the ability to function extremely well under demanding or difficult situations and would play an important role in his sharpshooting abilities on the ground and later in the sky. Raoul received his honorable discharge from the army on 12 July 1911.

Raoul, now 26 years of age, again starts his globetrotting adventures by traveling to

- Japan (tourist), July 1911
- Hong Kong (customs agent), August to October 1911
- Sri Lanka, Colombo (concessioner for a *hevea* or rubber tree plantation), October 1911
- India, Madras, and Calcutta (tourist), October to November 1911
- Malay Peninsula, Singapore (tourist)
- India, Bombay (tiger hunter expedition assistant)
- India, Bombay (merry-go-round worker), December 1911 to February 1912
- India (ticket collector on the Great Indian Peninsula Railway), March to August 1912

The following copy of Raoul Lufbery's original military discharge document from the Army of the United States dated 14 July 1911 offers a brief description of his physical appearance. The discharge indicates that he had "Blue #10 eyes," "D [dark] Brown" hair, and "Ruddy" complexion and was "5" feet "5-1/4" inches in height. His discharge erroneously states that he was born in "Paris" and that his occupation at the time of his enlistment was that of a "laborer." In the section marked "Character," Lufbery's character is listed as "Excellent."

On the back of his discharge document under the section for Marksmanship, Lufbery is listed as a "Sharpshooter" with two qualification dates, one being 27 February 1911. His physical condition when discharged is listed as "good." And his company commander has written on the document that his "Service [was] honest and faithful" and that he had "no unauthorized absences."

During his three-year military enlistment, Lufbery served at a time of relative peace in a nonhostile setting. Under the section "Battles, engagements, skirmishes, expeditions," the remark written in is "None." For all intents and purposes, his service had been unremarkable. But in three short years, Lufbery would return to military service in the then-unimagined capacity of air fighter, winning many accolades before returning again to the United States Army as a highly decorated commissioned pilot at the rank of major.

In the spring of 1918 Raoul Lufbery made an agreement with the nationwide McClure Newspaper Syndicate to pen a series of ten newspaper articles about his prewar aviation adventures and his outstanding military career. He was able to complete only four of those articles before he was tragically killed in aerial combat on 19 May 1918, bringing an abrupt end to the remainder of the series. The *Indianapolis News* published the first four installments beginning with part I on 29 June 1918. They were written in Lufbery's own words and covered

The front of Lufbery's discharge

his experiences from August 1912, when he first met Marc Pourpe in India, and through his enlistment in the French Air Service, when he joined Pourpe's Escadrille Reconnaissance MS 23 at the airfield at Toul, France. Those four articles will now follow and will expand upon Lufbery's adventures.

The back of Lufbery's discharge

Raoul Lufbery's American Newspaper Articles

[The following dispatches written by Raoul Lufbery were published in four issues of the *Indianapolis News* in 1918. The newspaper described the articles as "The own story of the American Ace of Aces, left uncompleted by his tragic, but glorious, death in France on May 19, 1918." Corrections and clarifications have been added, in brackets, by the contributors.]

Part 1: How I Broke Into the War Game

It was on the racecourse at Calcutta, transformed temporarily into a flying field, that I made my debut in aviation, if so odd a beginning may be called a debut. One hot August [December] day, in the year 1912, while I was strolling along the banks of the Ganges river, my attention was attracted by a great crowd of natives who were talking and waving their arms in the wildest excitement. Near by there was a little group of Europeans, who were perhaps equally excited, but, after our Western custom, more restrained in their manner of showing it. I joined this gathering—curious as to the meaning of it.

"The French aviators are coming," some one told me. The others, eager to give information to a newcomer, pointed out a boat which was coming into shore. On the deck were two large yellow cases.

"Do you see them? They are crates containing their machines. They are Bleriot [Blériot] monoplane.""

Shortly afterward the boat came to anchor and two young fellows, Marc Pourpe and Joseph [Georges] Verminck, the aviators, disembarked and were received by their compatriots.

The natives waited patiently while the enormous boxes were being carried ashore. Most of them had heard of aeroplanes, but they had never seen them, and their curiosity was aroused to the highest pitch. A crowd of a dozen or more coolie women, standing near me, were discussing this new event. I understand enough of their language to be interested and amused at their remarks. People the world around are a good deal alike and the skeptic in America who used to say, "No, sir! You can't tell me that them pesky things will ever fly! had his counterpart in that crowd of Indians on the banks of the Ganges. Finally, one of them, a woman more daring then the others, stepped forward and cautiously touched the tip of a forefinger to one of the boxes.

"Funny bird," she said, turning to the others, who were horrified at her boldness. "No wings, no tail, only the devil could make it fly."

First Aeroplane in India

Although I had never before seen an aeroplane, I had followed, from a distance, the progress which had been made toward the mastery of the air. I knew, by reputation, all of the pilots of the period. Their names, their achievements, the facts of their lives, all this was stored in my memory. I eagerly read all that I could find upon this fascinating subject of flying. Unfortunately, however, I had no technical knowledge. But I have always believed that my love of adventure and the experience which I gained in seeking it in odd corners of the world, compensated to me for my want of schooling in the ordinary sense. This, I felt sure, would hold true in aviation. All that I wanted was an opportunity. Meanwhile, I passed hours and hours poring over maps, making imaginary aerial voyages. At the time of the arrival in Calcutta of the French aviators my ambition to become an aviator, a king of the air, was at its height.

I had no qualifications of any kind for work connected with aviation. Nevertheless, I decided to offer my services to the French pilots. "I will never have another chance like this," I said to myself. "I must make the most of it." Therefore, I went boldly up to Mr. Joseph [Georges] Verminck and made known to him my wishes.

He thanked me and said that at least a dozen offers of service had been made before mine. "Everywhere we go", he said, "it is the same story." We are overwhelmed with offers. At present we do not need anyone. I am very busy. You will excuse me, monsieur?"

This rather cool reception was a little disheartening. Nevertheless, there was still hope for me. After a few moments of reflection, I decided to try my luck with Marc Pourpe.

I found him at work on the field, with his mechanics and a gang of five coolies, three Sinhalese and two Bengalese. While waiting for a favorable opportunity to approach him, I did some quick thinking, trying to find some inducement to offer to make him accept my services. At last, seeing him at leisure for the moment, I decided that it was now or never. After introducing myself I asked him when he expected to begin his flights.

"Haven't any idea," he said, somewhat gruffly. "In three or four days, perhaps. Depends on how long it will take me to erect my hangars with this coolie labor. I tell them to do one thing and they do another. I explain to them how I want something done and they do it in exactly the opposite way."

Then I said, "Will you let me ask you another question?"

"Fire away."

"How long will it take you to assemble your two Blériots?"

"Half a day," he replied.

"Very well," I said. "I have lived in this country for a long time. I speak the language and know the customs of the natives. You are a stranger here and will never be able to get them to do your work in the way you want it done. It is now 8:30. If you will allow me to help you, I promise that before evening your two hangars will be erected and that you will be able to start flying tomorrow afternoon."

To my great joy he accepted and, as I assured him, he was able to give his first exhibition flight the following day. This little triumph not only gained the friendship of the two aviators, but it brought as well the opening for which I have so long been waiting. As a reward for my assistance in erecting their hangars they gave me a position as lecturer upon aeronautics! It was not exactly a logical promotion, but they felt that they owed me something. "Therefore," said Marc Pourpe, "we'll make him a lecturer, and he can tell the natives what he doesn't know about aeroplanes."

Begins to Lecture

I, who had never in my life before seen an aeroplane, found myself under the necessity of explaining to visitors, the functioning of the machines! I had to describe the mechanism of the motors, and the construction of the bodies, tell how and why these strange craft were able to overcome the law of gravity. And all I knew of these matters I learned through the local Calcutta papers. Several of these had printed articles about the Blériot monoplane and the Gnome motor. I studied these accounts, of course, and more carefully perhaps—then the average reader. With this knowledge as a basis, and with a few large technical terms with which to awe the ignorant, I would have been a poor lecturer had I failed to convince them of my wisdom as a professor of aero-dynamics.

At 3 o'clock on the day when I was to begin my new duties—the great Indian capital gradually awakened from the afternoon siesta. As though by some enchantment, the empty sunlit streets, checkered with deep patches of shadow, were suddenly filled with people—hundreds, thousands, tens of thousands of them, a human tide, murmuring, many colored, slowly moving. It poured from every tiny street and alley. The grand route, leading to the race course where our little blue hangars were, was packed, as far as the eye could reach, with incredulous natives, who had come to see for themselves if it was true that men could fly in the air. As I saw this multitude approaching, I went to my place in one of the hangars and there awaited our first visitors, to whom I was to explain the mysteries of this strange new bird, as strange to me, almost as it was to them.

About twenty Bengalese entered first. They were wealthy men, and wise with the wisdom of the east. But they knew nothing about aeroplanes and listened gravely to my explanations. They were very attentive, too attentive perhaps. I was so much encouraged by the impression I seemed to be making that I went on more boldly—more eloquently. I gave free play to my imagination, told them things about the Gnome motor which the builders themselves did not know, and from this plunged into a learned discourse upon the monoplane itself, air currents, air resistance, how these forces act upon planes, etc.

While I was in the midst of my lecture a group of English officers entered and I was compelled to put a check upon my too fertile fancy. Nevertheless, after they were all gone, I was very well pleased with myself. And the Indians, I am sure, felt that they had more than the worth of their two rupees.

Learning the Ropes

Two months after my meeting with the two French aviators, we arrived at Saigon, a large commercial center in Cochin-China. During the intervening time I had not only improved upon my first "lecture," but tried hard to make myself useful in other ways. I picked up much information about aeroplanes which was to be helpful to me later.

At Saigon our flights were attended by a sad accident. Joseph [Georges] Verminck was killed in giving an exhibition flight for the natives of the town of My Tho, on the River Mekong. Shortly after this his mechanician [mechanic] fell ill and was compelled to return to France. I was left alone with Marc Pourpe and his Blériot, "La Curieuse." He had now no one to depend on but myself. Therefore, I worked with increased energy, eager to convince him that I could replace my imaginary knowledge about monoplanes with more practical wisdom, of which he was then in far greater need. At this time, we started on a grand tour of the capitals of all the provinces of Cochin-China and visited many of those in Cambodia as well.

Arriving at Phnom Penh, we found the city bright with banners. Everyone was in holiday dress, in honor of the celebrated airmen. His majesty, the old king Sisowath, commanded his elephants to be brought forth to form the guard of honor for La Curieuse, which was taken from the boat, as at Calcutta, with wings and tail dismounted. It was placed behind the elephants, near the head of the procession, and was pushed by six robust natives. They, too, must have thought it a "funny bird." I would have given much to have known their thoughts as they pushed it along, on the wheels of its landing chassis, through the crowded gayly decorated streets. Following these came other coolies carrying the wings and elevating planes. Despite their burdens, they held themselves very erect, proud of the honor of bearing parts of the marvelous "man-kite."

Flying Fete in Cochin-China

Riding in a jinrikisha [rickshaw] I formed the rear guard of this strange procession. My "homme-cheval" threw out his chest, disdainfully regarding his comrades in front of him, who carried only the mechanical parts of the wonderful bird. He shouted to them from time to time. I did not understand what he was saying but I could guess from his manner.

"It is I who is carrying the hero."

And I, too, gazed proudly from side to side as we slowly moved along; for although I was not the hero, I was his chief and only mechanician, which was honor enough for me.

We made a triumphant passage through the city and continued our way to the field selected for the exhibition. At the edge of the road I saw a group of country women who stood gazing at "La Curieuse" with their mouths wide open and their eyes staring out of their heads. I asked the Annamite Sargent-Interpreter what was the matter with them.

"Oh," he said, pointing to one of the coolies who was helping to push the body of the Blériot, "him very much a liar. Him say to country woman, 'See big fish we catch in Mekong River.'"

It was evident that the women believed this. They were literally stiff with terror.

At last came the hour for the exhibition. The little monoplane was ready for flight, and an enormous crowd had gathered to witness the incredible event. With the help of a gang of coolies, I had assembled it for the first time. I was very uneasy and examined every wire and bolt carefully several times, fearing that I might have overlooked some small but important thing.

Marc Pourpe walked hastily out from the tent[,] looking at me with an air not entirely of assurance. Nevertheless, without a moment's hesitation, he climbed up into the seat and gave me the signal to start the motor.

Coolies Held On

Now I had arranged beforehand with some coolies that they were to hold the tail of the La Curieuse while I spun the propeller. I was afraid that they would let go and run the moment they heard the roar of the motor, before Pourpe could try his reglage [réglage, master switch]t o see if the engine was running properly. Therefore, I had threatened them, saying that if they did so, I would give them an awful beating and report them to king Sisowath, who would certainly give them another one. This threat succeeded beyond my hopes. I was greatly relieved to see them hold on, even though the motor roared, in what must have been to them, a very terrifying manner.

Marc Pourpe raised his left hand, the signal for "all clear," but the coolies paid no attention. They hung on with all their strength, their black hair streaming out in the wind from the propeller. As many as could find a grip were clinging to the machine, and the others had their arms locked around the bodies of their comrades, their feet braced and their heads bent down. I shouted, motioning them to let go, but they only took a firmer hold. It was necessary to pry them loose from the machine[,] which I did with the help of Europeans who come out to witness the flight. Coolie by coolie, we had to unlock their fingers.

La Curieuse, being at least free, rolled swiftly along the ground, gathering speed, rose gracefully into the air. A murmur of surprise, delight, incredulity arose from the crowd, then a great shouting and huzzaing. The man-kite could really fly! The natives were wild with joy. Their high guttural voices sounded like the gurgling of water in a swift mountain stream.

With Marc Pourpe

As for myself, I could hardly believe my eyes. I had assembled the machine carefully, but being inexperienced,

I feared that something would go wrong. As I watched it circling over the town, responding perfectly to the wishes of the pilot, my joy must have been plainly visible. This day was one of the proudest and happiest of my life. I shall never forget it.

Gliding gently down over the crowd, Pourpe landed, jumped from his seat and came looking for me. I guessed that he was as relieved at the happy result of his flight as I was myself, and, bighearted man that he was, wished to compliment me for assembling La Curieuse without error. Before I could reach him he was surrounded by a crowd of Europeans and upper-caste natives who were eager to shake hands with him.

The old king, wishing to honor a so distinguished guest, had given orders for a series of native dances. The dancers now took their places, their faces grotesquely masked, wearing enormous headdresses, tall and tapering and many storied, like Chinese pagodas. Whether awed or frightened at the thought of performing before the flying man I can't say. But they did not dance. They stood motionless in the space which had been cleared for them. Other natives were ordered to urge them into their dances, which they did with rods, beating them lustily on legs and backs. The effect of this was hardly notable. A few of the dancers raised their arms and extended them in the sinewy gesture which marks the beginning of the dance, lifting one leg in unison with the movement. But there they stood, incapable of further movement. Others stood on both feet taking their punishment stolidly. At last the persuaders, exhausted by their efforts[,] gave up in despair.

One other picture remains fixed in my memory. It is that of King Sisowath, followed by his ministers, descending from the royal box at the closed end of the fete. He motioned for the little French aviator to approach him, and then, with hands trembling with emotion, he pinned upon his breast the Grand Cross of Cambodia.

An Accident

Having gone from success to success in Cochin-China, we set out for Tonkin. There the French authorities had prepared a program for us: two exhibitions at Hauphong [Haiphong], a flight from this city to Hanoi, two exhibitions there, followed by a second flight to Langson and the frontier of China. Nom Dim was also to be visited by La Curieuse.

On a memorable day of fine clear weather, when the blue sky of Tonkin was filled with thousands of kites, fashioned in the most bizarre shapes, La Curieuse might have been seen flying toward the east. She looked like a great queen bee, which senses by instinct the approach of night, and flies fast and far toward the distant hive lest her delicate wings be weighed down with dew. Over rice fields and forest, she went until the mountains of Kaakin. majestic and imposing, rose before her.

On the other side of the mountains is the city of Lang Son situated in a vast plain, and only a few miles from the Chinese frontier. It was here that the voyage of La Curieuse was to end.

A field close to the city has been chosen for landing ground. A gang of coolies filled in the holes dug by the water buffalo. Then they built a hangar of bamboo poles and covered the roof with palm leaves.

Long Overdue

It is 6 o'clock in the evening. A large crowd composed of several hundred of Europeans and thousands of natives, waits, with impatience, the arrival of the man-kite. I am here, too[,] and while waiting I have been picturing to myself the groups of wandering natives in the rice fields and in the remote mountain villages, looking into the sky when they hear the roar of the strange flying thing, which is neither bird nor kite. But the moments pass. The sun, already low, slowly disappears behind the jagged peaks of the Kaakin Mountains. I am impatient—then anxious. Frenchmen and the Native nobles gathered around me, all asking the same question: When do you think he will arrive?

"Alas," I tell them[,] "it is already very late—he is overdue. He left Hanoi two hours and a half ago."

I search the sky and listen intensely for the familiar sound of the motor. It is to no purpose. La Curieuse does not come. The enthusiasm, the eagerness of the people gives place to restlessness. A murmur of discontent rises on all sides. Night falls and the disappointed crowd dwindles slowly away.

Several hours afterward I received the following telegram: "Motor trouble, landed and turned over in rice field. La Curieuse slightly wounded. Come at once to make repairs. POURPE."

I was curious to know of what the natives thought of the unfinished journey. Therefore, the next morning before leaving Langson, I made inquiries of several of them who spoke a little English. The replies I received were about the same in every case.

"Oh" they would say, "we know very well Marc Pourpe ride a big kite. Coolies pull on string. Coolie very much tired. Very much hot. Let go of the string. Stop drink tea. Marc Pourpe—him fall with big kite in rice field. "

This was the opinion of all the natives everywhere. They thought La Curieuse was a very wonderful man-kite which was pulled along by the end of a string by coolies. In some places which we visited, they were not convinced, even though they saw Pourpe's Blériot flying without any apparent help from the ground. The string was concealed very well but nevertheless they were sure that coolies as well hidden, pulling it along. The Chinese are master kite builders. In one town they made a kite which was an exact model of Pourpe's Blériot. It would fly beautifully but it was silent. It didn't sing when it flew, like La Curieuse. So they tied on a box of bees to simulate the sound of the motor. The bees did their best. They made a fine buzzing noise on the ground, but high in the air the Chinamen could not hear them although they listened very intently. This was a droll incident. The Chinese were jealous [envious] of us Europeans. They did not like to admit that anyone, least of all "foreign devils," could make kites better than theirs.

Several days later the Blériot, having been repaired, and the persevering little aviator started on his voyage a second time. It was a very successful flight and gained for him the title "The Eagle of the Kaakin." The natives were forced to admit that he had a mechanical man-kite and had no need for coolies to pull it along by a string. A few of them still doubted, however. After Pourpe landed they came to ask my permission to examine the machine. At first, they stood gazing at it from a distance. Then, getting a little bolder, they approached cautiously and touched the wings with their fingers. Finally, squatting down on their haunches, they worked themselves under the fuselage, and searched carefully for the mysterious string. Not finding it, they crawled out and stood gazing at La Curieuse for a moment. They were up a stump and could only give vent their wonder and perplexity with their favorite expression "Tyah" [to shape things to your own liking].

The exhibitions at Tonkin over, we left Annam[,] where, as in all our travels, we astonished and delighted the native population. At Hue, the capital, we met the young king, who decorated both of us. To Marc Poupe he gave the Kim-Kam, the highest honor of the kingdom. I received the Kim-Tien, called the Golden Sapec. He could not have pleased me better. I am very proud of it, for it is my first medal. [Published 29 June 1918]

Part II: Flying Adventures in Africa

He Tells of thrilling trip From Cairo to Khartoum and Back by Marc Pourpe, Noted Birdman—Lufbery as Mechanic

After many adventures in Indochina, Marc Pourpe, "The Eagle of the Kaakin," returned to France, where for several weeks he remained quietly with his family. But the lure of adventure, the longing for new experiences, soon made itself felt again. The memory of glorious days in the far east, of his aerial voyages in strange lands, only urged him to set out anew. He loved the uncertainty of the life of an airman, its endless variety and the demands which were made upon him by the unforeseen event. But more than this, he wished to prove the usefulness of aviation in the colonies where roads and railroads were few, and the methods of communications were still very primitive. He had already done valuable work toward this end, and he could not be satisfied until he had completed the task which he had undertaken. Therefore, although his mother, who was very fond of him, urged him to stay longer at home, he was not to be persuaded and said good-by.

I was not expecting that he would so quickly tire of the pleasant life in Paris, but for this reason was somewhat surprised to receive a hurried call from him one evening. I had been sitting alone in my lodgings, stretched out comfortably before any open fire, feeling content with life and the world at large. Half asleep and half dreaming, when I heard a sharp knock at the door.

"Enter" I said, and Pourpe entered in his brisk and energetic way. I knew immediately that he had something important to tell me. But first, knowing that I had been very ill, he asked how I was.

"Very much better," I said.

"Et bien! We are going to start on another long journey."

The Map of Africa

Very much surprised, I asked him where. He replied by drawing a map from his pocket, which he spread out on my table. It was a map of North Africa. Then he said: "Now listen[,] Lufbery—to what I am going to tell you. My reputation as an aviator depends upon the success of the journey which we are about to undertake. We've got to succeed! I have thought of everything. I have made allowances and deductions for every unforeseen event. We are now in the epoch of a long aerial voyage.

"Brindejono has made a circuit of all the capitals. Roland Garros has crossed the Mediterranean. We are going to fly from Cairo to Khartoum and back, following the borders of the Nile. It is a journey of 1,400 kilometers, but if everything goes well, it ought easily to be made in fifteen days. I have left nothing to chance. I have carefully measured my distances and have chosen my landing places. Leaving Cairo, with a favorable wind, I will land first at Luxor, then at Assouan [Aswan], then here at Wadai Halfaya [Wadi Halfa], to Abu

Almed [Abu Hammad], at Dela [Ed Debba?]. A last coup d'aile—viola! [voilà] the capital of Soudan."

He was very enthusiastic, and I said that the plan seemed plausible enough.

"Of course, it is plausible" he said. "It is a quite possible voyage and we are going to accomplish it. Now, in the matter of supplies, particularly of oil and gasoline, of course they will be very difficult to find in Egypt and the Sudan. But you need not worry about this. I have made all arrangements and at all the important towns on our route you will find everything which a little Morane plane needs to drink."

"A Morane! I said, so you are not going to fly your Blériot?"

"No, a Morane: [with] a sixty-horsepower Gnome motor. You don't know much about it, I imagine?"

I said that I was not familiar with it in detail, but that having kept his Blériot in running order when we were in Indochina, I saw no reason why I should not succeed with a Morane. At any rate, up to the present, we have both been favored by chance. Very likely our good fortune would continue. He had no doubt. "We were born under a lucky star," he said. Then, in the manner of all airmen who agree to such a broad statement, we both rapped on wood.

Flying in the Blue Egyptian Sky

We arrived at Cairo without incident and early one morning, under a blue Egyptian sky, the little Morane plane called "le taillar" by the Arabs started on the long voyage. [Lufbery misspelled the Arabic word for bird. The correct spelling is "al tuyur" or "al tayir."]

I watched it mounting higher and higher above the towering minarets of the old citadel. It was a curious sight in that setting. Much more curious it must have been to the inhabitants of the city, many of whom were aroused from sleep by the sound of the motor. Women hastened out on the terrace without waiting to adjust their veils, their children huddled around them, not knowing whether to laugh or cry. The men were much calmer. They gazed at the aeroplane silently, without any apparent emotion. "The Flying Infidel." With this expression they both explained and damned this early morning disturber of their devotions.

Some of them were already on their knees at prayer. They continued passively, now lifting their eyes to the east, now bending down to the ground, but when they had finished they rose slowly to their feet and looked sullenly, bitterly at the "Roumi aile." One could easily read the meaning of those angry looks. They believe that the tomb of Mohammad floats in the depths of space. "Let this infidel dare to disturb his slumber!"

Like a pigeon which takes its bearings before starting on a long journey, "le taillar" with the white wings circled for a moment over the city, then turned in the direction of the pyramids. Having arrived there, I saw the machine suddenly point nose down, and dive rapidly, as if it wished to alight on the summit of those great historical monuments. It redressed, however, a few meters above them and climbed swiftly again. Although I was far distant, and had not been told of his purpose, I easily guessed the meaning of Pourpe's maneuver. It was his salute to the Sphinx and the pyramids and the ancient Egyptian civilization. Then he continued his flight toward the South and little by little disappeared in the blue distance.

Forced to Land

Four hours have passed since the departure, and as of yet no news. Luxor, the first stop, is not very distant, 400 kilometers at the most. He should have arrived by this time. I wait. I still wait. It is midday. No word from the little aviator. At last, about half past five in the evening, I receive a telegram, very brief, saying: Forced to land near Menshieh. Come at once to make slight repair.

After having to travel all night by train, I got down not at Menshieh but at a village a little further on. I was immediately accosted by an Arab, who with many sweeping gestures and pointing at the sky, tried to explain to me the arrival of le taillar. Seeing that I did not appear to understand, he took me by the sleeve and led me to the edge of the road. There were two camels kneeling, and my guide explained, by means of further gestures, that they were at my disposal. With his brown hand he pointed out to the village at the summit of a distant hill.

"Mamour taal hone," he said. This time I understood. Mamour, the mayor chief dignitary of the village, was expecting me. I mounted one of the camels, and the Arab loaded my baggage on the other one. Then they rose to their feet and swaying from right to left started in the direction of the village.

Mamour was a venerable old man with a long white beard. He had received orders from Lord Kitchener, saying, "Give assistance to the aviators in case of need," and was very hospitable. After having given me some refreshment, coffee and a dish of small peas he asked me to tell him about some of our adventures. He loved stories, he said. I told him, politely, through the interpreter, that I had only come here in order to repair the aeroplane. I said that I would be very grateful if he would take me, as quickly as possible, to Monsieur Pourpe, who was doubtlessly waiting impatiently for me.

"Can you tell me if he is far from here? And has he made a good landing?"

Landed Beautifully

"He is close at hand," he replied. "On the sand bar in the middle of the Nile, and he has landed beautifully. A bird could not have done it better."

After losing much available time in talking, he decided to accompany me. Donkeys were gotten ready and we set out followed by several servants. The road wound this way and that, but we arrived at last at the bank of the great river. In that region the Nile it is very broad, not deep, and dotted with islands and sandbars. The boat, which was to ferry us, was anchored in the river near one of these. We shouted and waved our hands but no one came, all the boatmen having gone to look at the aeroplane. From time to time, boats, heavily loaded with grain, passed us, floating lazily along with the current. The mamour and his servants would hail, one by one, making signs to them to approach, but they continued calmly on their way, the boatmen regarding us indifferently as though we were a part of the landscape. Then the old man and his servants would shake their uplifting hands cursing them as long as they were within hearing.

Boat followed boat. Each time there were the same polite, earnest entreaties, the same placid indifference, the same raving and cursing. I was amused at first but finally I too began to lose patience. One last appeal and this time a successful one. A boat, not so heavily loaded as the others, consented to approach us. A long conversation followed, in which I heard the name of Kitchener pronounced many times. The master of the boat, giving in to the arguments of the old mamour, took us on board. He looked at me very curiously. I believe that old mamour told him that I was an intimate friend of Lord Kitchener. Whatever his argument, it had the desired result, and with a sigh of long deferred relief, I set foot on the island.

Crowd of Natives

From a distance I saw the upper part of "le taillar." The rest of the machine was hidden by a fold in the ground. Even here, on the lonely island in the middle of the Nile, the aeroplane was surrounded by a crowd of several hundred curious natives. Pushing my way through, I found Marc Pourpe seated quietly on the sand, under the shade of one of the wings. He was devouring an enormous leg of chicken, without in the least minding the many curious glances which were fixed upon him.

"Well, I said, "how goes the appetite? Not too bad?"

"Tiens? C'est vous, Lufbery! How in the world did you find me? Not without a good deal of trouble, I'll wager."

I then made a hasty examination of the aeroplane.

"You see," he said, "nothing serious, only a few wires broken and several dents in the capot [hood]. Pure luck that I didn't turn over. Let me tell you how it happened. Yesterday, the visibility was very bad, and this forced me to fly low over the river. Up to this point everything went beautifully and then suddenly something happened to the motor. There was nothing to do but land. I was directly over the river but luck was with me. I saw this island beckoning me with open arms. Without looking a second I cut the contact, maneuvered and landed like a flower at first, then kept rolling. Wheels sank into the sand. Result—and a superb pylone [vertical drop] onto my nose. I was broken-hearted. I climbed out sadly regarding my poor old cuckoo. A bad beginning, with 1,100 kilometers yet to go in order to reach the junction of the Blue and White Nile. Le taillar remained with her tail in the air for a good hour until the arrival of some of mamour's and other notables of the surrounding villages. They were much surprised to hear me speak their language. They thanked me warmly for having the courtesy to fly over their country and you should have heard their praise of my landing. They thought it was nothing short of wonderful. I wasn't exactly of their opinion, but I hadn't the heart to disillusion them."

Dinner on the Nile

The Morane being repaired, we willingly accepted the hospitality of mamour. He appeared to be very happy to have us as his guest and did everything possible to make the occasion a memorable one. A dinner was given in our honor to which he invited all the natives of mark from the surrounding villages.

I was very hungry for I had nothing to eat since early morning. Therefore, no one was happier than me when the dinner hour came. As soon as we were seated a servant entered carrying an enormous roast turkey on a wooden platter. It was everything that a roast turkey should be— brown, piping hot, done, evidently to a turn. Another servant, this time a Nubian with a skin as black as coal, and shining like ebony, followed carrying a copper tray loaded with finger bowls of perfumed water. Crowded about the open door I saw a crowd of beggars. They[,] too, had come to the banquet, but without an official invitation. Although the feast had not yet begun, they were waiting patiently for the fragments which might remain. I felt sorry for them. If all the guests are as hungry as myself, I thought, they are going to be badly disappointed.

Meanwhile we all sat there, looking at the smoking turkey, waiting—hungrily waiting. I began to be restless. I wondered why they didn't start. Marc Pourpe was telling stories as affably as though he had just finished a most satisfying meal. I marveled at his self-control and then remembered the leg of chicken I had seen him eating on the island. I questioned him with my eyes and at last he told me that the mamour had sent for something which was very essential to the comfort of his guests. What it was he didn't know--but whatever it was it had not yet arrived.

While he was explaining this to me, the door burst open, and an Arab, very much out of breath, covered with dust, streaming with perspiration, entered.

Thoughtfulness of Host

"Voila!" he said, in French, throwing two knives and two forks on the table. Then he made a low bow and went out.

We were deeply touched at the thoughtfulness of our old host who had sent this poor devil on a camel to Menshah [Menshieh], for knives and forks so that his guests might not have to eat with their fingers.

Then with the servant's clean brown hands, he took up the turkey which he tore in pieces, placing large morsels on our plates. An expert carver could not have done it more skillfully with a knife. We fell to with a will, the poor beggars outside the door watching the rapidly disappearing turkey with mournful eyes.

A second dish was passed which Pourpe explained to me was liver, fried in Arabic fashion. He had the stomach of an epicure, and so, very prudently, he waited for me to try it first, looking at me, meanwhile, out of the corner of his eye. I did my best, but with indifferent success, for the meat was burned to a cinder. Hungry though I still was, I had to forgo this dish, which the other guests appeared to think a delicacy. Pourpe, too, declined it, cleverly covering his refusal by telling another story.

So the banquet drew to a close, and when all had finished, our venerable host, rising gravely from his seat, turned to Pourpe and said: "My friend, to look at your white skin, I can guess that your father is a rich man. I know, too, that you are brave, and that, if ever in your travels in the skies you should meet a flock of eagles you will destroy them. May god lead you!"

I did not know, until later, the meaning of his words. But I was impressed by his manner of saying them. And in brevity, that after-dinner speech might serve as a model to all the world.

Guest of Government

Nine days after leaving Cairo, Pourpe landed in Khartum. There, as everywhere, he was warmly welcomed, and, for nearly a week was a guest of the governor, Pasha Smith. After so trying a flight, a little rest was necessary both to the pilot and to the mechanician. Although Pourpe had taken the precaution to wear smoked glasses, his eyes were badly injured by the reflection of the sunlight on the sand. As for myself, my eyes gave me no trouble, but I was very tired and greatly in need of sleep. It is probable that during the trip I had used every means of transportation which exists in Low Egypt, High Egypt, and the Sudan. I traveled by locomotive, passenger train, freight train, cattle train, on camels, on donkeys, by water in shallops [light sailboats] and barges. I had eaten all sorts of strange food to which I was not accustomed, and had so many bizarre experiences that I felt the need of some leisure in order to think them over.

On the evening before the departure for the return journey another dinner was given in our honor. All the English colony and the elite of the Arab and Sudanese society were invited and drank to the success of Marc Pourpe and to the entente cordiale [agreement for improved Anglo-French relations]. Near the close of the dinner Pasha Smith called his old Arab servant Ali, and said to him:

"Ali, in order to reward you for your many years of faithful and devoted service, I am going to present you to the pilot of the le taillar. He seemed to be very much pleased, although he was a little shy at being brought so suddenly to the center of attention. He stood motionless for a moment.

"Well, Ali, what do you think of the aviator?" the pasha demanded.

He lifted his hand gravely and replied: "Marc Pourpe is not only a birdman. He is also a good son and loves the memory of his father who is dead. It is in search of him that he flies over the deserts and in the air. May God protect him."

Over the Desert

One day, in the month of January, the tranquil existence of the old mamour of Wadi Halfa was disturbed by an unusual event—the arrival of a telegram which read:

"To the Mayor of the town of Wadi Halfa:

"Will you please select and prepare a landing field for the aeroplane which will visit you the day after tomorrow? If possible, select one near the town. Dimensions, 400 meters square. Mark center with a white circle 20 meters in diameter. Light a fire at one end of the field as soon as you are informed of my departure from this place. This is to help me find the direction of the wind. When you see me coming, guard the field with soldiers, keeping it clear of spectators. Respectfully, MARC POURPE."

The news of the expected arrival of the birdman spread rapidly through the town. Men discussed it in the cafes, around their Turkish pipes, telling of what they had heard, enlarging and embellishing the rumors according to the liveliness of their fancy.

The mamour called together his advisers, discussing with them the measures which they should take. He was anxious to follow the orders given in the telegram, but unfortunately, of all those present, not one had ever seen an aeroplane at close hand. Several days previously they had seen a little Morane flying toward the south, but it was so high and traveling so fast, that in spite of all their attention they were not able to note any of the details. To them it was simply a mechanical bird. But they followed Pourpe's directions to the letter. The field was chosen, soldiers were summoned to guard it, and a fire lighted. Then, wishing to meet the requirements of the occasion in grand style, the mamour ordered out a band of native musicians. While waiting the arrival of the mamour the crowd listened to the beating of the tomtoms and the wailing of the flutes, as the musicians played the best selection of their repertory.

GUARD IT CAREFULLY

Meanwhile, leaving behind him for a second time the great Nubian Desert, Pourpe approached nearer and nearer to the town. At last he saw it a tiny speck on the landscape, but growing larger and larger until he discovered, near a clump of palm trees, a column of black smoke rising from one end of a broad field and blown by the wind toward the west. He cut his motor and descended in wide spirals. Soon he could see very plainly the white circle in the middle of the field, but he was at a loss to explain a larger circle of small black points at its outer rim. Approaching more closely he saw that they were soldiers, with fixed bayonets, the guard that he had requested of the mamour. It had not occurred to him to ask that an approach to the field be kept open. The natives evidently expected that he would drop perpendicularly out of the air and land directly on the circle. Great was their astonishment and disappointment when he landed at some distance outside the circle of bayonets. In order to reward them for their faithful efforts I gave them the privilege of guarding his avion which, because of a strong wind, I had anchored to the ground by means of ropes tied to the wheels and fastened to stakes in the ground.

"Guard it carefully! I told them. Don't let any one touch it!"

One of them put his hand on a long knife which he had in his belt. "No one touch le taillar! But if he goes away by himself, no can help."

I explained to them that there was no fear in this, but they were not convinced. If there was no danger, why had I fastened it to the ground with ropes. Their belief was that when Pourpe wanted it to fly he merely told his bird to start and off it went.

The voyage was continued the following day and Pourpe arrived safely at Cairo, the first aviator to make this long and, at that time, dangerous aerial journey. [When Pourpe made his nine-day, 870-mile flight from Cairo to Khartoum, he carried the first airmail letters in Egypt. The official letters and cards, each bearing a special commemorative frank, are among the most collectible pieces of airmail to this day.] From Cairo he flew to Suez, where he met several members of his family, who wept with joy and pride to see him. They had known him as a little fellow in short trousers and had not seen him for many years. It was at Suez that he had passed his boyhood and where he learned the Arab tongue.

Leaving this city with many regrets, he flew to Port Said. I am following him by train. Here our travels in Africa came to an end and a few days later the little Morane plane being carefully packed, we sailed for Marseilles and Paris. Where we should go from Paris—it will be for chance to decide. [Published 6 July 1918]

Part III: At War—I Join the Air Service

NOTED ACE TELLS OF EFFORTS TO BECOME AVIATOR IN TRENCH SERVICE—FEARED WAR WOULD BE OVER BEFORE HE COULD ENLIST.

THE FIRST DAYS OF AUGUST, 1914. Everywhere in Paris—in the boulevards, in the streets, in the cafes, in the theaters—we heard the same rumor. War against Germany was on the point of being declared. In spite of all this, the Parisians did not take the matter seriously.

Meanwhile a feeling of anxiety was present in the air. Sometimes they joked, sometimes they talked gravely, but always the discussions were in harmony with the tone of the morning and evening newspapers. Some of them had seen the trains crowded with troops being rushed toward the frontier. Of course, this means something.

"Bah!" responded the other: "you will see that everything will be arranged satisfactorily as in the past. At Agadir, did we not come within a hairbreadth of having a rumpus? And Fashoda! At Fashoda, also, our misunderstandings with the English were quickly settled. Everybody thought things would turn out badly, still you see at the present time they are our best friends."

Marc Pourpe and I sided with the optimists: that is to say, with those who did not think it would come. Notwithstanding, we worked diligently on our future project. Everything was in disorder in our little workroom. Here and there on the floor lay maps of eastern Asia and the neighboring oceans, alongside were rulers and dividers, as well as pencils, red, blue, and yellow.

Long Trip Planned

This time we had in mind a long trip that would last for perhaps ten months or a year. We expected to visit many of the oriental countries starting at Sumatra, then Java, later the Philippines and Japan, coming back towards the southwest through southern China, Indochina, Siam and Burma. After all this we would return to France to enjoy a little well-earned rest.

At the time of studying the routes and itineraries, we had also chosen the airplanes. For the voyages from province to province and from city to city we would use the 60-horsepower Morane—the same that had made the trip from Cairo to Khartoum. Exhibitions and acrobacy would be performed on the smaller 50-horsepower Deperdussin. The long trips over the rivers and streams and between the islands of the archipeiago would be made on the 80-horsepower Nieuport hydro-monoplane. We also expected to take along a Fabre glider equipped with an air propeller. This machine was to be used for making tests and we hoped to be able to organize a postal service flight between Cambodia and Laos. The means of communications between these two countries leaves much to be desired, no roads, no railways and only the Mekong River and its tributaries and a few other small rivers which are navigable during certain periods of the year. During the dry season there is so little water in some localities that even the smallest river boats can not pass. The glider would be able to go everywhere, as it drew only ten inches of water.

Already for a good hour my mind had been wandering in the east. With eyes fixed on the map, deep in thought, studying the possibilities of an aerial voyage from Bangkok to Rangoon. I was lost in the midst of the peaks and ravines of the big chain of mountains separating Burma and Siam, looking for a convenient pass for our plane, when suddenly my thoughts were interrupted by the voice of Marc Pourpe.

War Declared

"Say[,] Lufbery" he called, "you have lived in the Philippines and know a little about the country. What do you think of a trip in the hydro from Borneo to Manila?"

"Very feasible, very feasible," I replied: "the distance from—" I was unable to finish the sentence. At that moment we heard a formidable bing! bang! The door flew open and in tumbled our old concierge.

"Well! Father Pierre!" we shouted. "What's the matter?"

Too exhausted by his rapid ascent to the second floor, he was unable to say a word for several seconds. Finally, he recovered sufficiently to speak, in a voice that seemed to come from the bottom of his stomach. "We're in it. It's time! War has been declared."

A few days later Marc Pourpe was called up and left for his post. On a Morane-Parasol, he with a few other pilots was designated for the defense of Paris. As arms on their planes they carried steel darts and old cavalry muskets.

Before leaving, Pourpe, to whom I had confided my intentions of enlisting, had said, "Good luck, Lufbery; perhaps I will see you in Berlin within a few days."

Tries to Enlist

Full of enthusiasm, I departed for the recruiting office in Rue St. Dominique, hoping to be received with open arms. Upon arriving there I found myself in the presence of an enormous crowd, men of all nationalities and all ages, having come, like myself, to offer their services to France. Lost in the midst of this masculine gathering, which obstructed the greater portion of the streets, I could discern a few women. Very likely they were the wives, sisters, or fiancés of the future legionnaires. Those with tender hearts were crying outright, while others were dabbing at their eyes with the corners of their handkerchiefs.

In vain I tried to sneak into the yard, but it was effort wasted, as outside the men were tightly pressed, one against another.

Suddenly my attention was drawn to a small gathering on the opposite sidewalk. As I approached them I discovered a French major, surrounded by a few impatient volunteers, those who wished to leave immediately. They plied him with all kinds of questions concerning the necessary formalities for enlisting and showed their soiled, creased military books, many of them written in foreign languages. The brave officer answered as best he could and did all that was possible to satisfy everybody.

To a tall old man with white hair and flowing mustache, whose paper he had examined, he said "Sixty years! A little old for service in this campaign. You should ask to be enrolled in the ambulance corps to aid in caring for the wounded."

"But I want to go to war as a fighter," protested the old man. "I want to fight the boches!"

Aviators Needed

Later, it was a small hunchback who advanced. Swaggeringly he stepped forth, showing to anyone who would pay attention a diploma for first prize in shooting. He also wished to kill some Prussians.

"Hum! Hum!" said the major. "I fear that your deformity will hinder you in carrying your knapsack. It would be much better if you looked for a clerk's job in some office."

I went forward in my turn and complacently asked the Major what the proper course was to follow and who must I see in order to enlist. Rapidly he glanced through my papers and in throwing back his head looked me in the eye and said "Aviation! American! Young! Go over there!" and pointed with his finger toward the office. "They will take you: we need aviators."

These words did much to stimulate my ardor and enthusiasm. Pushing and shoving with elbows and shoulders from right to left, I finally edged my way as far as the center of the yard. Arrived there, it was impossible to proceed farther in spite of all my efforts.

Before long a low outcry was heard, a kind of "Hah," a sigh of relief coming from everybody's chest. It was a captain who showed himself at one of the windows at the ground floor. He raised his hand motioning for silence. He was going to say something.

"Gentlemen, "he said, "it is utterly useless for you to waste your time waiting here. This is the sixth time I have come to the window to tell you this; besides, you are blocking up the office yard, much to our inconvenience. Soldiers? For the first time being we have more than we need, more than we can feed, more than we can equip. Also, most of you are not Frenchmen, and as yet there is no law authorizing strangers to enlist in the French army for the duration of the war. At present the government is trying to solve this question. Come back in a fortnight or a month. Now, if among you there are some from Alsace-Lorraine, they can enlist in the Foreign Legion for five years' service in Africa. Good-by, gentlemen and thank you."

This little speech has the effect of a cold shower bath on the mob, dispersing them crumbling and growling among themselves. An hour later I happen to be passing along the Rue St. Dominique again and saw the same officer at the same window, probably repeating his little speech for the seventh time!

Successful

About the 22d or the 23d of August the law authorizing strangers to enlist in the French army was passed. In the meantime, I had become acquainted with several Americans, future soldiers of fortune, who, like myself, were impatient to be off, on their way to fight for France.

We had only one fear—that the war would be finished before we could take a part in it. To be able to say, "We were there! We fought against the enemy!" That was our sole ambition. Alas! But very few people at that time thought that this gigantic struggle started between Prussia militarism and the democracy of Europe would last for many years.

Two of my new companions belonged to a club which had been formed at 11 Rue de Valois, but in reality was the recruiting office of the American volunteer corps. One evening I went there with them and was introduced to the president of the organization, who after words of welcome took my name and gave me a questionnaire to fill out. Among the questions which I answered by a simple "yes" were three readings as follows:

"Do you accept from the start all the severities of the discipline and the hardships of the war?"

"Do you promise absolute obedience to French officers of the active army?"

"Are you ready to swear loyalty to the French flag until death, if that is what is necessary?"

"Why?"

To this last question instead of "yes," one was supposed to write: "For the cause of justice and liberty."

I wrote it down, feeling rather foolish, but serious about it as well.

Big Day Arrived

At last the big day arrived and it was decided that all of us should go together to enlist, this time for good, because the papers that we had filled out at the office of the American Volunteer corps were nothing more or less than preliminary measures. There were about 40 of us. Coming from the club we formed in columns of fours with the French and American flags at our head. We marched like veterans as far as the [Hotel] Invalides, followed by a crowd that cheered: "Vive l'Amerique! Vive les volunteers! Vive la Americans!"

The yard of the Invalides was crowded with a mob of new recruits of all nationalities. Patiently we waited our turn to take the physical examinations while the president, who on this occasion had performed the duties of the lieutenant, captain, and even a general, gave us his last advice.

"Americans, come in!" cried a voice, and in less time that it takes to tell it we were in the examining room standing before the doctors. Profiting by the disorder, several South Americans had slipped in with us.

Only Three Turned Down

The examinations lasted about half an hour and only three volunteers from our entire band were turned down. One on account a flat feet, another for myopia, and the third because he was too thin for his height. This last man they told to eat well and come back in a fortnight.

The physical examination finished, there remained nothing more to do but to sign the enlistment papers lying upon the large table in front of us. However, I read mine carefully before putting my name at the bottom.

"This is not it! This is not it at all," I told the noncommissioned officer on service. "I want to go into the aviation, not into the second regiment of the foreign legion."

"Don't you worry about that," he growled at me. "Sign it and everything will be alright."

But this was not my idea at all, because I had firmly decided not to go into the infantry unless it was absolutely impossible to enlist as an aviation mechanic. I bid my comrades good-bye, wished them good luck and went home, naturally without signing the papers.

Later, after looking all around, my lucky day came, and I stumbled into the right path. Going to the "Permanence de L'Aeronautique" my papers were examined, a few questions were answered and then I was sent to St. Cyr for the mechanical examination. Arrived there, I asked to be taken to the superintendent of the workshop, who proved to be a captain. He questioned me further.

"Yes, my captain" I replied. "For almost two years I was with Mark Pourpe on all his flights in the far east and the trip from Cairo to Khartoum."

"Then you are well acquainted with the rotary engine."

"Yes, my Captain."

"Do you know how to line up an airplane?"

"Certainly," I answered," but it is especially with the Blériot, the Deperdussin and Morane with which I have had experience having worked on all these types."

"Yes, all that is very good," he replied, "but at this moment we need sailmakers more than anything else. Do you know how to put on the cloth and make splices?"

"Although not being an expert in that line of work," I told him, " I do not think it would be very difficult. Naturally, however, I would not be able to work as fast as an expert."

"Well, we shall see," he said, and handed me a piece of seven-strand steel cable. "I shall give you half an hour to make a splice. That is about as much time as one should need.

"You may commence now," he continued, glancing at his watch.

Twenty-five minutes later the job was finished, and I showed it to the Captain.

"Not too bad, not too bad," he admitted, examining close to it. "At present there are only three things for you to do. First, go back to the Permanence de L' Aeronautique and sign your enlistment papers. Second, go to the clothing depot at Versailles and get a uniform. Third, to be off and that's all."

"To be off where?" I demanded.

"I can't tell you" he said, shaking his head and walking away: "probably where they need you most. You'll find out when you have our transport order."

The next day, arrayed in a brand new uniform of the engineers, one day's travel rations, consisting of a minute box of tunny fish and an immense loaf of war bread in my haversack, I boarded the train for Dijon, where at this time a large aviation center and supply depot was located. I departed without regrets and with a light heart, though to be sure I would much rather have gone direct to the front.

Rumors of Wonders

Comfortably installed in a third-class compartment I watched the scenery with merriment as it drifted past softly, humming one of my favorite songs.

Suddenly an old woman, seated beside me on the bench, remarked, "And there is somebody who is indeed very happy to be going to war."

To which a rather stout man opposite added "He is very likely a young artilleryman."

"You are an artilleryman, are you not?" he said, addressing me directly.

"Not on your life," I replied, with a touch of pride in my voice: "I belong to the aviation."

The word "aviation" produced quite a flutter in the compartment. A young girl who since the departure of the train had been deeply absorbed in a novel, lifted her eyes and looked at me with an inquisitive expression on her face. The old woman became more and more curious and wished to know everything.

"Tell me," she inquired, "is it true aviator Roland Garros had brought down a Zeppelin by ripping its gasbag from end to end with the tip of one of the wings on his plane?"

"Even so," she continued, with admiration in her voice, "What courage it must take to do things like that." I was going to reply that such a trick was not very feasible, although I did not doubt for a single moment that Garros was able to accomplish wonders.

But the fat man opposite did not give me time. Crossing his hands on his ample waistline and setting his lower chin well over a collar of doubtful color, he butted in with, "Nothing truer Madame. A friend of my son who knows the noted aviator very well has told me the story of the combat, and, furthermore, it was so well done that his airplane was not in the least bit damaged."

"And [Jules] Vedrines, madam," he continued, "have you heard tell of the deeds of Vedrines? He also has done his Mounted on his armored plane La Vache. He has brought down three boches in three minutes without firing a single shot. Like a bird of prey, he swoops down full motor and rams them amidships."

[Note: The armored plane "La Vache" was a 160-horsepowered machine built in the Blériot shops. It was armored throughout, but after several flights was declared unsuccessful.]

I did not deem it expedient to dispute what I had heard, for it would have been effort wasted. The enthusiasm during the first days of the war was much too great. On the other hand, these imaginary stories were not the inventions of the fat man, for I had already heard them many times. Even one day in discussing the subject with a policeman, I tried to convince him of the impossibilities of doing such things with an airplane without damaging it. That had no more effect that to raise his detective instinct.

"Tell me, you," he said, twisting his enormous moustache with his left hand, "you are young and sturdy. How is it that you are not yet at the front? Show me your papers!"

He looked at them attentively and in a voice which he tried to make severe, said, "You speak French very well for an American."

Then, turning his back, he walked away, twirling his club. [Published 20 July 1918]

Part IV: At the Front—His Initiation

THE AMERICAN "ACE OF ACES" FAREWELL ARTICLE, FINISHED THE NIGHT BEFORE HE DIED

CONTRIBUTORS' NOTE: This final installment of Major Lufbery's narrative of his career in aviation ended on 18 May 1918. The following day he was shot down and killed. His last written pages were left lying on his table the next morning as he rushed to the airfield to respond to an alarm and rose to aerial combat for the last time. An hour later his machine came down in flames, and the American "ace of aces" met a terrible but glorious death. Major Lufbery intended to write ten stories about his adventures, for the sake, he said, of capitalizing on whatever reputation he might have, to rouse interest at home in the air service. He began his narrative in April, but the German offensive and the fine weather made such demands on him and his fellow pilots that they were up nearly every day flying combat patrols. Rarely could he spare more than half an hour writing in the evening before turning in. Lufbery's own complete story will never be told. But he has left as a legacy the simple, unpretentious tale of his love for France and for aviation. This final newspaper installment is preceded by Marc Pourpe's written recommendation at Lufbery's request to help his friend secure a position in French aviation.

Lufbery writes: "At my request, Pourpe had given me the following note, which, in my mind, and given the justified fame my friend had acquired, should facilitate my entrance into French military aviation. I transcribe it here in full, in memory of one for whom I had an almost fraternal affection."

Juvisy, August 2, 1914

Before departing for the center at Saint-Cyr, where I am posted as a pilot, I leave this note for my mechanic, Raoul Lufbery, an American, who would like to be assigned to an aeronautic center. Lufbery has been my mechanic for three years; he went with me on all my raids (flights) in the far east, and that from Cairo to Khartoum and back to Cairo. He wants to be, and can be of great help to our country in this moment, and he will be sincerely devoted to us. He wishes to be detached to Villacoublay at Voisin [the Villacoublay airbase at Voisin, France, is now operational as a NATO airbase] as he knows all of their flying machines.

May this note be useful to him, and thank you to those who will consider him.

Marc Pourpe
Engineer aviator
Stationed at the center of Saint-Cyr

A WEEK PASSED at this center of aviation at Dijon without my having to exert any talents as a sailmaker. The battle of the Marne was at hand, but our placid existence was undisturbed. The greater portion of my working time was spent as "pilotes des caisses d'essence," an aviation term applied in unloading the auto trucks bringing in the sixty-liter cases of aeroplane gasoline and carrying them to the storeroom on one's back. This was not a very interesting occupation, but it had to be done. Moreover, it was useless to object, the military regulations requiring that one perform the duties assigned to him without any dispute. To those who complain they invariably reply with a shrug of the shoulders and a "Qu'est-se que vous voulez? C'est la guerre!" My only consolation was in finding there a friend whom I had known before the war. Captain James N. Hall, who was with me the other day when he was shot down and captured. He was an author and had won the academic palms. He, also, struggled at "pilotage des caisses d'essence," but lacked the inclination and the training for this kind of work and I do not think that I made a mistake when I said that he would never be an expert in that line.

After the day's work was finished, we invariably spent the evening in the barracks, reading the papers and discussing the news, which at that time was very discouraging.

"It's going bad. It's going very bad," said one. "The boches continue their march toward Paris! It appears that they're not very far from there now."

To which another replied, "but, old top, don't you see, that's the idea. We let them advance is order to beat them all the worse. Besides, I've got the latest dope, my cousin works in the Ministry."

Time to Win Another

Then the shrill, rasping, voice of our pessimist broke out, "You're all of you way behind the times. Don't let anyone pull the wool over your eyes like that. Can't you see that we've been betrayed, sold out to the boche as we were in 1870! What do you think of it? You, the American!"

"What do I think of it?" I replied, reflectively. "Well, I think that although we have lost the first battle, we still have enough time to win another."

This reply, almost heroique, did not please my interlocutor the least bit for he shouted in a voice louder than before, "Hey, there! You guys look at the Yank who's trying to put something over on us. That's all been hashed over long ago. General Desaix made that same little clap-trap speech the year before you, and he at least was an ace of his time, while you—why! You'll never be one or I'll miss my guess."

I was going to answer, when suddenly "Taps" were sounded, putting an end to the discussion, and we all went to bed.

An Aeroplane Graveyard

The center of aviation at Dijon, like all large centers which were up to date, had its cemetery: except that this one did not exist, as one might be led to believe, to serve as the last resting place for the remains of the pilots and mechanics of the camp. No, indeed! It was simply a chosen patch of ground, or rather, a very bizarre dump heap, where rested in common the remains of aeroplanes of all types and all makes.

This graveyard made a lasting impression upon my memory. Often during a few leisure moments, I would stroll over there and rest my elbows upon the top rail of the fence that separated these derelicts from the outer world. I would think how much like human beings were these discarded machines. Only a few months ago they had been alive, although it was only a mechanical life, and had been able to defy the laws of gravity and soar with the birds. And now they were in the discard, left to rot and ruin, not worth the space they occupied.

The flat surfaces of the wings were covered with dust: the fabric had been torn in thousands of places and here and there pieces dangled by more threads, swaying in the breeze: the cables and stay-wires especially appealed to the spiders looking for a home, and in many cases were veritable panels of cobwebs: and occasionally there was to be soon a motor, rusty enough to have been at the bottom of the ocean for a dozen years.

In looking over the ghostly and motley collection of derelicts I had much the same feeling that I imagined the good people who first saw Rip Van Winkle must have had when he burst upon them after his 20 years of sleep.

Many Different Types

I could distinguish many of the different types, while others were smashed and wrecked beyond all recognition. Just before me lay a Blériot that had been through a bad wing slip. The right wing was broken off close at the fuselage and its tip crumpled and torn, much as one wads up a newspaper before throwing it into the fire.

In one corner I could make out an old Breguet that had experienced a "pancake," or loss of speed from a height of about thirty feet. Its landing gear had been pushed away up between the wings. Among us mechanicians this type of machine was familiarly called a "McCormick" because when in the air the sound of its motor could be very easily mistaken for the thrashing machine at work in the adjoining field.

Near the entrance lay an ancient Farman, type 1913, with the elevating planes sticking away out in front. In loving terms, we always spoke of this type of apparatus as a "cage poule" because with its many struts and interlaced stay wires it did greatly resemble a fenced[-]in yard where the better portion of our ham and eggs originate. Also, this pet name, at times, got under the skin of pilots riding these buses.

Occupying a center place in the sacred plot, drooped one over another, were several Morane-Parasols. One in particular I recognized. Its nose was smashed in, its tail gone, and the fuselage broken off square just back of the pilot's seat. Only a few days previous the pilot had lost control of this machine and rammed into the ground headfirst: one of the worse [worst] smashes I have ever seen. It made me shiver to look at it.

Frequently my reveries were disturbed by the arrival of a new victim. Then I would jump over the fence, examine it carefully, trying to ascertain, if possible, the cause of its downfall and later discussing the accident with my comrades.

Chief Mourner

The day following my dispute with the pessimist, I was assigned with my friend, the academician, to carry the tail of a smashed Blériot to its last abode. A corporal was in command of the detail, that was to say, he was the "master of ceremonies."

"Hey, corporal! Director of the cortege," cried my friend, "don't you think that a little march from Chopin would be appropriate on this occasion?"

The corporal, good boy that he was, found the idea very amusing and set the example himself, by striking up the opening strains in his deep base [bass] voice.

Being unable to sing or at the most singing very badly, I contented myself to be the chief mourner. But this did not add to the harmony. My wailings resembled more the yelping of a dog when you step on his tail.

The funeral procession was slowly approaching the cemetery, when suddenly a loud voice arose above our hub bub. I heard someone calling "Lufbery! Lufbery!" I turned around and found a figure coming towards us gesturing widely. Looking again I recognized Marc Pourpe. "Well! Luf, old man! How's everything going?" he said, shaking hands. "You certainly have been interested in your work here. I have been hollering at you for more than five minutes and you never even turned your head."

"Qu'est-ce que vous voulez?" I replied. Shrugging my shoulders. "C'est la guerre."

"C'est la guerre. Yes!" he shot back. "And now you are going to fight in a slightly different fashion for I am taking you to the front with me! We leave tomorrow, in my double-seater Morane Parasol, to join the Escadrille M. S. at Toul. I have seen the commanding officer of the camp, asked for you, and everything is arranged. Nothing more for you to do but pack. Does that suite you?"

"Hip! Hip! Hip! Hooray," I rousingly replied.

The next day I was ready long before the hour of departure. Very carefully I had packed my equipment in all the spare corners of the fuselage. There was a blanket, a haversack, very fat and bulging, holding my mess kit, toilet articles, etc, a bag of tools and lastly a "fusil Gras," a relic of the days of 1870 with which I proposed to bring down the first boche who would be unfortunate enough to cross our path.

The visibility was good, the clouds were high, and the winds favorable. "We must take advantage of these excellent conditions," remarked Marc Pourpe upon approaching his machine, "and get underway. Bundle up well because it is a long trip and you know how cold it is up high. You haven't forgotten the least little thing?"

Then, glancing toward the rear seat, he saw my luggage.

"Well! Well! He explained, "you certainly have a nerve. What's all this junk? A fusil Gras! Why not a "soixante quinze"? [see page 176] But no, this time I object. Do you take my Morane for a wheelbarrow? If we are able to leave the ground with all this junk, we'll certainly be fortunate, and our lucky star which has always favored us, will still be there, watching over us, keeping us in the right path, safe, from all harm." And more of the same.

Fly to the Front

Nevertheless a little later, the Morane Parasol, in spite of its overload, driven by its pilot, defended by its mechanician, majestically took the air and headed northwest, leaving far behind a checkerboard of forests, towns, and green fields, interlaced here and there by the smooth hard-packed roads, standing out in the sunset like silvery ribbons.

That evening towards 5 o'clock, after an uneventful voyage, we landed on the aviation field of Toul. There we found a few friends whom we had known before the war. Among them the aviators Gilbert and Garros, who also belong to this famous "Escadrille de reconnaissance M. S. 23," commanded by Captain de Vergnette.

Being as yet unaccustomed to long aerial trips, I admitted frankly that I was rather tired, and it was more than pleasant to find, in the mechanics dormitory, an unoccupied bed with several blankets. Arranging things as comfortably as possible I was preparing to enjoy a well-earned rest when suddenly in the next room, separated from ours by only a wooden partition, I heard some voices and recognized that of [Roland] Garros.

"My captain," he said, "I declare openly that it's getting to be terrible. Again, I was almost brought down by French bullets! And this time it wasn't too far away. It hit my rear gasoline tank and just grazed the observers back. Don't you think that this is ridiculous? It would be much preferable if they did not shoot at all. This time, there was absolutely no excuse, I was flying low enough for them to see my cocardes, if they took the trouble."

"Yes" replied the captain. "This is happening too frequently. We must look for a remedy. But it is not all together the poilus' fault that they shoot at us, they mean all right. I think that, above all, the newspapers are responsible for these disagreeable mistakes. Look here! Not lately than last Monday, I read an article that said that all airplanes having a covered fuselage and a fishlike tail were German. You will admit that this is stupid, although nothing is truer. But one thing is evident: that the reporters who write this foolishness have always ignored, and still ignore, the existence of the Morane-Parasol.

"Mechanicians, attention! I demand absolute silence. I have a very important message for you!" It was the Adjutant Pilote Pinsard who burst into our room and spoke thusly:

"Wait for these orders, and above all, let no one move unless I say so," he continued in gasps, due no doubt, to his rather violent entrance. By the flickering light of the lantern he read the following message apparently received by telephone:

"To the Commanding Officer of the Escadrille M. S. 23:

It has been reported that forty Uhlans [cavalrymen armed with lances] are advancing toward Toul, probably with the intention of making a raid upon the aerodrome. Prepare for defense of the camp as rapidly as possible."

VOLUNTEERS TO MEET THE ENEMY

After having read the message, the adjutant quickly lifted his head, looked around and inquired: "Are there some brave ones among you? I must have four volunteers immediately!"

As rapidly as possible I slipped into my clothes, put on my shoes, and without loosing a minute, offered my services to the pilote Pinsard.

"Excellent! That's very good," he said. "See the gun over there in the corner? Take it and come with me. I am going to post you as an advance sentry."

"You will wait here," he said, addressing the three other mechanics. "I'll come back for you. Put out all lights and above all, make no noise."

We went out into the night together, stealthily slipping along, grazing the walls, and taking a thousand precautions to avoid being seen. Finally, we arrived near a large tree which was to serve as the strategic position. Already somebody was there. That somebody proved to be Marc Pourpe, a revolver in his right hand, and a dagger in his left. His eyes were trying to pierce the darkness in the direction from which the enemy would appear. Upon seeing us he let out a sigh of relief.

"At last" he whispered hoarsely, "the relief. It's not too soon. Certainly it is more than a half an hour that I have been on the alert."

"The relief! Not yet!" answered Pinsard. "This is the only reinforcements that I have brought you.

"You understand, Lufbery," he added, turning toward me. "You are to remain here until your ammunition is exhausted. See that haystack near the road?"

"Yes, I see it," I replied.

"Well! When the enemy arrives there, commence firing. "

"But," I protested to him. "I have examined the magazine of my Label rifle and there is not a single cartridge in it."

"That makes no difference," he assured me, "remain here just the same. I will send some." And he was gone.

Five minutes passed, then ten, and the ammunition did not show up. In reality, I was beginning to find the time a trifle long.

"All the same, this is too much negligence. Don't you think so?" asked Pourpe.

"So much the worse," I replied, putting on a resigned air. "A la guerre, comme a la guerre! If the Uhlans come, I'll hit 'em on the head with the butt of my gun."

"You'd better go back and get some cartridges," advised Pourpe in a subdued voice. "What can you do with an empty gun, against forty? Go! I'll remain here alone."

I hastened over to the dormitory and, throwing open the door, cried as loud as possible, "Cartridges! "For the —" But—I could not finish. Loud peals of laughter came from all corners of the room. The joke was so evident that I could not help from joining in the general hilarity.

"Don't say a word to any one," confided a mechanic near me. "That's how we initiate all the new arrivals. Now we're going to play it on another." [Published 27 July 1918]

Raoul Becomes a Pilot

The following is a portion of an article that appeared in issue no. 160 of the French aviation journal *Icare,* titled "Raoul Lufbery: A Life Well-Filled." Most of the material in the article had previously been published in the four-part *Indianapolis News* syndicated series and in Jacque Mortane's book. However, the following material on Lufbery was not covered in the newspaper's final installment. Jean-Xavier Lufbery, grandnephew of Raoul, helped prepare the manuscript with an *Icare* editor. The primary source is Lufbery's autobiography, which had been passed down through the family by Raoul's brother Julien. Lufbery's story continues just after he has volunteered for sentry duty, part of an elaborate initiation prank that was pulled on him by Pourpe and the other pilots.

This was the seriocomic episode that marked my entrance into the campaign. I thought it was interesting to note here, because it is a proof of the playful spirit that characterizes the French. This gaiety abandons him but rarely, even in the worst circumstances, which makes of him a quite agreeable and kind companion.

I become a pilot

At the time we arrived at the Front, Marc Pourpe and I, military aviation was far from having the degree of perfection that she has attained afterward. It was the start of the campaign. The several escadrilles, therefore, did not have a well-defined tactical role. We knew neither the hunt nor the bombardment. The war was not yet stabilized everywhere, the role of pilots consisted notably of surveying the movements of the enemy. These reconnaissance missions were relatively easy because machines in use did not surpass a speed of 100 kilometers an hour, and an altitude of 2000 meters. The armament was simple. The pilot or the mechanic was armed with a musket with which to defend himself in case they were attacked by an enemy airplane. This situation seemed improbable. The pilots were thus more sportsmen than soldiers, and so when they met with but two adversaries, they usually continued their flights without paying attention to each other.

Yet, in the early days of October 1914, there were several machines equipped with Hotchkiss machine guns, but it was much later that we had them in the *M. S. 23*. This did not stop Gilbert, a pre-war hero who took one of the first aerial victories by taking down, with musket fire, an enemy plane on the second of November 1914, an exploit that he repeated twice on the eighteenth of November and on the tenth of January 1915.

With Gilbert, our escadrille also included another famous pilot from peacetime, Garros, a veritable soldier of the air, who had the first idea to shoot through the propeller, and, finally, my friend and master, Marc Pourpe.

That one, starting at our arrival at *Escadrille M. S. 23,* won the admiration of everyone, bosses and comrades. He carried in the war the same devotion, the same spirit of sacrifice, the same ardent faith he had shown in executing his perilous raids in the colonies.

Like Marc Pourpe, Gilbert and Garros wanted very much to honor me with their friendship, even though I was nothing more than a simple mechanic at this time. It is thanks to the advice and councils that they lavished on me by these heroes so justly celebrated that I made a place among the fellowship of combatants of the air. I accomplish a duty that is sweet to me by expressing here to them my hearty and profound gratitude.

Alas, I would not profit for long from the lessons of the glorious Marc Pourpe. In his desire to demonstrate the advantages to which aviation could be put in the war, this strong spirit in a body that appeared frail and delicate accomplished marvels of energy and heroism. In less than four months, Pourpe had totaled more than 78 hours of flight above enemy lines. At that date, it was a remarkable feat. As prudent as he was brave, neither bad weather nor danger would stop this admirable young man who accomplished his duties like an apostle. Even though he was injured in a fall in September 1914, and even though he returned multiple times from reconnaissance with his machine riddled with bullets, nothing could diminish his valor, and it took a brutal death to stop the soaring career that promised to be so beautiful and which would have finished in apotheosis. The tragic event which took him from the affection and admiration of his numerous friends occurred on December 2nd, 1914, when we were in the Somme. Despite the fact that the weather was unfavorable for flying, Pourpe decided to leave for a reconnaissance mission. He took off at about nine in the morning, despite a sky covered in thick clouds and in cold, humid weather of which he was well aware.

In returning from his mission, as he was coming out of the clouds, his machine slid on one wing and crashed on the ground, instantly killing pilot and passenger.

I rushed to the site of the catastrophe as soon as I knew of it. On my way there, I still hoped that I would not have to mourn the irremediable loss of my dearest friend for whom I had the most sincere and complete admiration. Alas, I had to accept this terrible truth.

Poor, dear Pourpe! After three years, it is with the same sad feeling that I recall the poignant hours that I lived that day. My grief was boundless. With his death, France not only lost one of her most modest and skillful pilots, but I was robbed of a sure and devoted friend who had many times given me proof of his trust and concern.

Adieu to the future projects we had so joyfully planned. A cold anger made me hate even more an enemy that had ruined our hopes. I resolved to make the enemy pay dearly and, swearing to avenge my friend, I immediately drafted up a demand to become a student-pilot. It was the only means at my disposal worthy of proving how profound and durable were the feelings of gratitude and fraternal affection that I had dedicated to the one who was, to me, the living model of energy, courage, and duty.

It was not until the spring of 1915 that my request to become a student-pilot was approved. I thought that I would not receive a favorable response. To calm my impatience, I absorbed myself in my work as a mechanic; but if I continued to fulfill my task conscientiously, I felt that the enthusiasm that had made me accept this secondary role was now fading.

I realized that to be a mechanic was good, but to become a pilot would be better. I desired to involve myself more actively in the fight, and to have a bigger part in the danger. Not that the post of mechanic was restful. It is far from my thoughts to diminish the merit of these precious auxiliaries. Coming from their ranks, I know the fatigues and the often-intense labor of mechanics, who, without fail, jealously cared for their pilots' machine.

A pilot is called to fly at dawn; the plane needs to be ready at the moment at which the pilot will take flight. If the flights of the previous day make it necessary, the pilot will work all night to make the machine runs perfectly. Too bad if that night is clear and the filthy German aviators take advantage of this clarity to come and *bombard* the barracks and hangars. In this case, the danger adds to the fatigue of a precise, minute task.

A pilot who does not have a competent, serious, and devoted mechanic cannot do much. If it is up to the pilot to ensure, before each flight, that his mount will not get weaker before his return to the hangar. It is up to the mechanic to execute the multiple delicate and indispensable operations to obtain this result.

Without entering into the technical details which will only mildly interest my readers, I am going to limit myself to quickly quoting some of the tasks that fall to the mechanic.

A good mechanic must, before and after each flight, clean, check, and maintain the motor, propeller, tank, frame, wheels, tires, controls, ribs, stays, and rudders. He must know how to tune an engine, know and check all the parts (cylinders, pistons, crank shaft, rods, valves, springs, locks), know how to look after the carburetor and ignition system, constantly clean the magneto and ensure the state of the spark plugs. To be able to maintain a machine, he has to know why it swoops, veers, rears, and leans. He needs to know how to find and remedy an unexpected breakdown, even a complicated one. He needs to know how to maneuver the plane from the hangar to its starting ground, tighten or replace a piece of canvas, adapt a spare part, repair a piece of broken wood, etc., etc.

All of these operations and more require not only a professional knowledge which cannot be acquired except with much willingness and an innate taste for things mechanical, but also furnish a considerable amount of work.

Let us, the pilots, recognize that a great portion of our success is due to the zeal and devotion of our faithful, modest mechanics.

At school

I arrived at the Military Aviation center of Chartres on 18 May 1915. Starting the next day, I took my first lessons on a dual-control Blériot, a school machine in which the future pilot was placed under the supervision of a monitor who, by counseling and guiding his student, gave to him, bit by bit, more liberty in controlling the maneuvers, while always ready to intervene at the slightest error.

[According to the *Icare* article, "There is a passage missing here; after training to be a pilot, Lufbery was accepted into a bombing escadrille."]

Bombardment of the enemy cantonments at Cemecey

This was a most arduous journey. I stayed in the air for three hours. The low, thick clouds did not permit me to fly at more than 1300 meters, and, also, the Kraut [antiaircraft] artillery was having a field day in full swing, which did not stop us from accomplishing our mission and returning without harm.

Our area was calm, as the bad weather that was raging prevented any incursion from enemy planes. And yet, on the tenth of February, we spotted several of them, and I was designated to carry out an observation flight at Nancy. I left, bringing my mechanic along as a machine gunner. The rain fell without end and the clouds flew by very low, pushed by a violent wind. A flight in these conditions is excessively troublesome because one must fight without ceasing to maintain the stability of the machine. I tried to penetrate the clouds to see what was happening below, but I could not get through. The wind, the cold, and the rain were preventing my motor from functioning fully and I could not rise to more than 1300 meters. We had to return after an hour and a half, shivering from the cold, our limbs tense, without having anything to report.

The squadron was grounded for a dozen days due to unfavorable weather. On the twenty-first of February, we received the order to bombard the station at Pagny-sur-Moselle. Despite dreadful weather, we departed with twenty machines. I was accompanied by Sergeant Allard and we carried five bombs. I made every effort to climb to 2700 meters despite this reduced cargo. When we arrived at that altitude, there were only four machines left, the others having been unable to cross the very thick layer of clouds.

The flight leader gave the signal to depart, and we all four set off toward the designated target, guiding ourselves solely by the compass, as we were completely cut off from the ground by the clouds.

A flight above this chaos of humid, white, and grey masses rolling pell-mell, interweaving and flying at tremendous speed under your feet, is a veritable enchantment when you pass over it. Up there, it is the sun, luminous clarity, and purity of the azure. One glides in an atmosphere that has infinite charm and gentleness. From time to time, through several holes that form here and there in the sea which you command, you can spy a village, a waterway, the green of the prairies or of a forest, but the breaks are not sufficient to allow you to find certain landmarks. The compass is not a sufficient means to guide one's self with certainty. It is necessary to cross back over the layer of clouds to find your path with the aid of the ground and the map.

We were doing just that when our flight leader judged that we had nearly arrived above Pagny, and, effectively, we were not far from it. We arrived above the station without any problems, and, after our shells had been dropped, we took the path back, flying yet again above the sea of clouds.

Our return to the squadron's airfield was greeted with exclamations of joy from the ground. Our crew had believed that we had been lost in the turmoil, and we received the congratulations of the captain of the Group and of the captain commanding the escadrille. Following this happy raid, I was promoted to sergeant, the first official recognition of the mastery I had acquired as a war pilot.

Several days later, on 21 February 1916, on a grey, foggy Sunday, we undertook a new bombing raid. It was to bomb the station and bivouacs at Chambley, the capital of the township, located 26 kilometers from Briey, the center of a basin of iron ore, the object of the Krauts' greed. I had on board Captain Jacquin, his first outing with me. It came close to being fatal for both of us.

As soon as our group crossed the enemy lines, we were heavily shelled. I was among the first machines, and I was trapped by a Kraut [antiaircraft] battery that had been made invisible by its camouflage and the fog, but which was firing spectacularly well and quickly. The explosions surrounded me from all sides and as I was advancing, the shots became more and more precise despite the feints and detours I frequently made.

Suddenly, a terrible shock, followed immediately by a sudden lurch in which I avoided, with great difficulty, the plane completely overturning. What had happened? It was a shell from the cursed battery that had burst a few meters in front of our machine. We had only narrowly escaped it! A few meters more and we would have been annihilated.

But we were not unscathed. An explosion had caught the propeller; it was a fatal blow, fully behind enemy lines. Since it was impossible to go any farther, there was no choice left but to land at whatever cost and no matter where.

Thanks to the speed we had acquired, I succeeded in doing a half-turn, executing a spiral. I had to keep my machine airborne as long as possible, to try to return to our lines. I therefore summoned all my energy and will and, putting the nose toward the south west, I continued gliding until I found suitable terrain. Finally, after long minutes of perplexity and anguish, I noticed a field where I could descend with my poor, wounded bird. *We* landed safe and sound, my passenger and I, but where were we? In France, or in Hun territory? Cruel confusion! There was a big city very close-by, but first the fog and then the attention that I had needed during the maneuver had prevented me from identifying it on the map. Captain Jacquin estimated that we must be near Bar-le-Duc, but our ignorance about the path we had followed and the distance traveled, as well as the ignorance of the precise place where the accident that had almost cost us our lives had happened, augmented our uncertainty.

There was no one in the vicinity. A rapid examination of my machine had convinced me of the impossibility of putting it back in working order; the propeller needed to be replaced. We headed toward the first houses and, when we arrived, we were overjoyed to learn that we were, effectively, in the suburbs of Bar-le-Duc. The captain returned to our sector by the railway and sent my mechanic back with a spare propeller. For my part, I was able to return to Malzéville by air two days later, on the twenty-ninth of February.

I was warmly congratulated for the calmness I had shown in the occasion, and Captain Jacquin promised to go out again in my company, assuring me that he was untroubled by the success of our next exploits.

We executed a bombardment together the following week, Thursday the second of March, on the railway hub of Bensdorf, an important communication hub situated in Lorraine, which had been annexed, along the line from Strasbourg to Metz. We had dropped five great bombs on it with full success. However, the return was difficult. I strayed on the sea of clouds and had great difficulty returning to our territory because of poor performance by the motor. This would be my last raid as a bomber pilot.

Raoul Lufbery Joins the Lafayette Escadrille by Raoul Lufbery III

Five months after Marc Pourpe's death, Raoul Lufbery requested and was granted a transfer to the French aviation pilot school. He began pilot training in Chartres on 18 May 1915. He received his pilot *brevet* #1286 on 29 July 1915. In early October of that year, he was assigned to French flying squadron VB 106, where he performed bombing runs in a two-man Voisin bomber.

On 10 April 1916 Lufbery requested and was returned to the Nieuport Division of the GDE (Groupe de Division d' Etrainement) at Plessis-Belleville, northeast of Paris, for retraining as a fighter pilot. After completing fighter training on Nieuport scout planes, on May 24 he was assigned to what was known at the time as the Escadrille Americaine, Nieuport 124.

This unit was composed of young American volunteers from all socioeconomic backgrounds. More than half were from well-to-do families. Eleven were scions of millionaires. Their backgrounds varied from college students to playboys, from soldiers of fortune to professional and amateur aviators, to young men with a sense of curiosity. Their average age was twenty-six, about five years older than the average age of the Allied pilot at twenty-one. However, the common thread that bound the group together was a thirst for adventure and a desire to defend France against Germany.

On 15 April 1916 the French government agreed to the creation of this all-American air squadron under the command of French captain Georges Thenault. Over time, thirty-eight American pilots became members of this elite volunteer fighter unit destined for international fame and notoriety through their aerial exploits.

Lufbery became the eighth volunteer member of the group, joining the squadron at Bar-le-Duc in the Verdun sector. He soon became an indispensable addition to the squadron. During his tenure with the Escadrille he scored sixteen confirmed victories while flying 295 combat patrols (100 more than any other single member of the squadron), and in the process accumulated 477 air hours over the front.

The American pilots downed a total of thirty-five confirmed enemy aircraft during the squadron's twenty months at the front. Lufbery accounted for sixteen of those victories. The total number of enemy aircraft destroyed by the American pilots far exceeded that number. But France's Service Aeronautique established two strict rules for confirming victories, which kept the pilots' total down. In order for an enemy aircraft (plane, dirigible, observation balloon) to be listed as confirmed, it had to fall within French lines, or its destruction had to have been witnessed either from the air or from the ground by someone other than the pilot himself. Also the haphazard manner with which records were kept at the front further denied the pilots additional victories.

The pilots paid a heavy price to secure their victories. Eight would be killed in aerial combat while serving on the roster, including four of the original founding members. Four others, including Lufbery, would pay the supreme sacrifice before war's end.

Upon reaching "Ace" status, Lufbery began to be cited by name in the official communiqués of the French army. As a result, his fame grew in the French and American press. As the war ground on and the Lafayette Escadrille sustained losses and celebrated victories, Lufbery became the steady hand of the unit, leading multiple daily patrols over the front, teaching new members the skills needed to survive aerial combat and the harsh weather while piloting fragile aircraft.

Despite a five-year age difference and a vast socioeconomic gulf that stood between Lufbery and his fellow pilots, he quickly won his comrades over with his self-effacing demeanor, while securing their respect through the dedication to his trade: shooting down German aircraft. It seemed incongruous that this thirty-one-year-old pilot of simple means, and with no formal education, would have as his closest friend fellow pilot Norman Prince, a Harvard Law school graduate and the scion of one of America's wealthiest industrialists.

More than once Lufbery swooped to rescue an ounumbered fellow pilot in a dogfight, often in disregard for his own safety. Squadron mate Edwin Parsons would later write this of Lufbery:

> Without exaggerations, those of us who flew and fought with him and appreciated his dexterity believed that few could equal and none could surpass him. His air work was incomparable. It didn't come easily, for he wasn't a natural[-]born flyer. He gradually and literally "pulled himself up by his bootstraps" till he became the master craftsman. Then his plane became a part of himself, a thing that can be said but of a few airmen. He flew as the bird flies, without any thought of how it was done. His record of seventeen [sic; 16] is impressive, but it represents only a fractional part of his actual destruction. Many of his combats and victories took place so far back of the enemy lines that no official confirmation was possible. With his plane showing the evidences of a savage leaden duel, the lone eagle would glide down from the cloud-flecked skies, make a terse report, and that would be the end. He cared little for the credit, but there was certainly an inner satisfaction that he must have felt, but never showed, that he had chalked up another victim of his vengeance.[1]

Parsons continued:

> He had no particular method of attack. He flew alone a great deal and waited patiently for opportunities. He not only waited for them but worked for them as well. Except in emergencies, when he gave or accepted combat, he was in the most favorable position.
>
> Having been a mechanic, he gave his motors his personal attention. He spent hours at the butts, firing and regulating his guns, so there would be no jams. He had his cartridges triple calibrated, thus eliminating to the greatest possible extent the chances of an oversized shell case sticking in the breech block.

> In a patrol, Luf was always on the job, and many a youngster like myself had him to thank for our continued existence. He had a happy faculty of being on the spot at the right moment to rescue some unhappy buzzard who had gotten himself into a jam. His cool head, steady nerve and unerring aim were worth a whole squadron.
>
> Oft-times sacrificing a sure kill of his own, with his uncanny faculty for watching everything that transpired in a dogfight, he'd swoop through the lead-filled sky to some isolated spot where a desperate youngster was waging a losing fight. Making a lightning decision as to his best method of attack, he would dart here, there and everywhere, till it seemed as if the whole sector were full of Lufbery-piloted planes. Twisting and turning in a succession of amazing acrobatics, firing a short burst at one, then another, he bewildered and confounded the enemy hornets. No odds were too great in an emergency.

A *Washington Post* newspaper article dated 12 July 1916 and titled "U.S. Men in Air Fight" was the first time aviator Lufbery received press coverage since joining the Lafayette Escadrille some forty-nine days earlier. During the autumn of 1916, Lufbery generated considerable coverage in newspapers and magazines both in the United States and in France. Many of the media stories focused in on his growing aviation combat victories and military citations.

During October 1917 a reporter for the *Philadelphia Public Ledger* interviewed Lufbery and asked what type of young man would America need for her military air fleet? Lufbery responded:

> It will take the cream of the American youth between the ages of eighteen and twenty-six to man America's thousands of airplanes, and the double cream of youth to qualify as chasers (fighter pilots) in the Republic's new aerial army. Intensive and scientific training must be given to this cream of youth upon which America's welfare in the air must rest. Experience has shown that for best results the fighting aviator should not be over twenty-six years old or under eighteen. The youth under eighteen has shown himself to be bold, but he lacks judgment. Men over twenty-six are too cautious. The best air fighters, especially a man handling a "chaser," must be of perfect physique. He must have the coolest nerve and be a temperament that longs for a fight. He must have a sense of absolute duty and fearlessness, the keenest sense of action and perfect sight to gain the absolute "feel" of his air machine. He must be entirely familiar with aerial acrobatics. The latter means life or death.

---

1. Edwin Parsons, *Flight iinto Hell: The Story of the Lafayette Escadrille* (London: John Long, 1938), 66–67.

Lufbery continued to explain:

> Fighting at twenty-two thousand feet in the air produces a heavy strain on the heart. It is vital, therefore, that this organ show not the slightest evidence of weakness. Such a weakness would decrease the aviator's fighting efficiency. The American boys who come over here for this work will be subject to rapid and frequent variations in altitude. It is a common occurrence to dive vertically from sixteen thousand to ten thousand feet with the motor pulling hard.
>
> Sharpness of vision is imperative. Otherwise the enemy may escape or the aviator himself will be surprised or mistake a friendly machine for a hostile craft. The differences are often merely insignificant colors and details.
>
> America's aviators must be men who will be absolute masters of themselves under fire, thinking out their attacks as their fight progresses. Experience has shown that the "chaser" men should weigh under one hundred and eighty pounds. Americans from the ranks of sports—youths who have played baseball, polo, football, or have shot and participated in other sports—will probably make the best chasers.

Lufbery's description for the "best type of men to be fighter pilots" in this era of early combat flying mirrored many of his traits and life experiences. With the exception of age, he exemplified all the physical, mental, and emotional attributes. Most importantly, he had nearly two years of combat flying experience in hostile airspace with numerous victories. Who better to explain the needed qualifications of our nation's first fighter pilots for future sky battles than the only American double ace of the day.

Lufbery was, by far, the most successful pilot throughout the existence of the Lafayette Escadrille. Caporal Benjamin Stuart Walcott, an American pilot in France's Service Aeronautique assigned to Escadrille SPA 84, wrote this about Raoul's final two official victories on 2 December 1917—the third anniversary of the death of his friend Marc Pourpe.

> An hour after we were back, they said that Lufbery had just brought down another machine, his 15th, in flames. He was using a new machine and the gun was not properly regulated—seven balls were in each blade of the propeller, yet it held together and brought him home. I was down at the Lafayette hangers talking to Bill Thaw and here comes the mighty man in a hurry from reporting his flight. With fire in his eye he got in his old machine and off again for the lines. At noon he had brought down another, which hasn't yet been officially homologue (tallied), but is none the less sure for that.[2]

Lufbery's 2 December 1917 double victories made him America's first triple ace. This remarkable military aviation accomplishment surely had to be one of Raoul's proudest, even though he would never dwell or boast about it. Raoul instead used that day to remember Marc Pourpe, who had given the ultimate sacrifice on the battlefield, exactly three years earlier to the day of his victories. Raoul said: "Our great friend should be satisfied with the manner which I now honor his memory, although never on God's green earth will he receive all the honor he deserves."

On 28 December 1917 Raoul penned a letter to his father, Edward, who was residing in Wallingford, Connecticut. Raoul mentioned his latest military decoration, his commission as major in US aviation, and his two recent aerial victories. The full body of this letter—in which he informs Edward he will not be coming home for Christmas, and how he is helping Edward in his stamp business—appears on pages 234–235. It is interesting to note the formal manner with which Raoul closes his letter, signing off with his full name, rather than concluding with, for example, "your son, Raoul."

---

2. Benjamin Stuart Walcott, *Above French Lines: Letters of Stuart Walcott, American Aviator; July 4, 1917 to December 8, 1917* (Princeton, NJ: Princeton University Press, 1918), 85.

BERT HALL	WILLIAM THAW	*(center portrait)*	ELLIOT C. COWDIN	CLYDE H. BALSLEY

DIDIER MASSON	CHOUTEAU C. JOHNSON	KIFFEN Y. ROCKWELL	NORMAN PRINCE	VICTOR CHAPMAN	FREDERICK PRINCE, JR.	LAWRENCE RUMSEY

DUDLEY HILL	ROBERT SOUBIRAN	RAOUL LUFBERY	JAMES R. McCONNELL	CHARLES H. DOLAN, JR.

HAROLD B. WILLIS	WILLIS B. HAVILAND	JAMES NORMAN HALL	EDWIN C. PARSONS	RONALD W. HOSKIER

DAVID McPETERSON	KENNETH MARR	JOHN A. H. DREXEL	WILLIAM E. DUGAN, JR.	ROBERT L. ROCKWELL	EDMOND C. C. GENET	PAUL PAVELKA

WALTER LOVELL	CHRISTOPHER FORD	RAY C. BRIDGMAN	DOUGLAS MacMONAGLE	HENRY S. JONES	STEPHEN BIGELOW

THOMAS M. HEWITT, JR.	JAMES R. DOOLITTLE	THE VALIANT 38	COURTNEY CAMPBELL, JR.	EDWARD F. HINKLE

+ original — Dead

Lafayette Escadrille Roster

Pilot	Tenure With The Squadron
F.* Chapman, Victor	20 April–23 June 1916 (Killed In Combat)
F. McConnell, James	20 April 1916–19 March 1917 (KIC)
F. Prince, Norman	20 April–14 October 1916 (KIC)
F. Rockwell, Kiffin	20 April–23 September 1916 (KIC)
F. Thaw, William	21 April 1916–18 February 1918
F. Cowdin, Elliot	28 April–25 June 1916
F. Hall, Bert	28 April–1 November 1916
8. Lufbery, Raoul	24 May 1916–5 January 1918
9. Balsley, H. Clyde	29 May–18 June 1916
10. Johnson, C, Choueau	29 May 1916–31 October 1917
11. Rumsey, Laurence	4 June–25 November 1916
12. Hill, Dudley	9 June 1916–18 February 1918
13. Masson, Didier	19 June 1916–15 February 1917 and 15 June–8 October 1917
14. Pavelka, Paul	11 August 1916–24 January 1917
15. Rockwell, Robert	17 September 1916–18 February 1918
16. Haviland, Willis	22 October 1916–18 September 1917
17. Prince, Frederick	22 October 1916–15 February 1917
18. Soubiran, Robert	22 October 1916–18 February 1918
19. Hoskier, Ronald	11 December 1916–23 April 1917 (KIC)
20. Genet, Edmond	19 January–16 April 1917 (KIC)
21. Parsons, Edwin	25 January 1917–26 February 1918
22. Bigelow, Stephen	8 February–11 September 1917
23. Lovell, Walter	26 February–24 October 1917
24. Hinkle, Edward	1 March–12 June 1917
25. Willis, Harold	1 March–18 August 1917
26. Marr, Kenneth	29 March 1917–18 February 1918
27. Dugan, William	30 March 1917–18 February 1918
28. Hewitt, Thomas	30 March –17 September 1917
29. Campbell, A. Courtney	15 April–1 October 1917 (KIC)
30. Bridgman, Ray	1 May 1917–18 February 1918
31. Dolan, Charles	12 May 1917–18 February 1918
32. Drexel, John	12 May–15 June 1917
33. Jones, Henry	12 May 1917–18 February 1918
34. Hall, James	16 June–26 June 1917 and 3 October 1917–18 February 1918
35. MacMonagle, Douglas	16 June–24 September 1917 (KIC)
36. Peterson, David	16 June–18 February 1918
37. Doolittle, James	2 July–17 July 1917
38. Ford, Christopher	8 November 1917–18 February 1918

French Officers

Thenault, Capt. Georges	20 April 1916–16 January 1918
DeLaage De Meux, Lt. Alfred	20 April 1916– 23 May 1917
Nungesser, Lt. Charles	14 July–15 August 1916
Maison-Rouge, Lt. Antoine Arnoux de	28 May–6 October 1917
Verdier-Fauvety, Lt. Louis	6 October 1917–18 February 1918

*F indicates founding member

Lafayette Escadrille Squadron Locations

The Lafayette Escadrille was transferred eleven times and served in nine different locations in its twenty-three months of service at the front, in order to be near the heaviest fighting. Consequently, it flew over every sector of the western front.

1. Luxeuil 20 April–19 May 1916
Vosges Sector

The seven pilots of the Escadrille Americaine and their two French officers first took to the field at Luxeuil-les-Bains, an ancient spa at the foot of the Vosges Mountains, near the Swiss border. The squadron was designated N.124 for the Nieuport pursuit planes it would fly. The pilots were quartered in a villa adjoining the hot baths of Luxeuil. The Luxeuil aerodrome was the most expansive and beautiful in France. The 2-mile-long airfield was flat and was surrounded by high hills. The French aviators occupied one end of it, and the British aviators of the RNAS the other end. The Vosges was a relatively quiet sector, and the squadron was assigned to protect Captain Maurice Happe's Farman and Breguet bombers while on missions.

The squadron flew its first official patrol on May 13. Kiffin Rockwell scored the first victory on May 18, when he downed a German LVG reconnaissance plane. The only casualties the squadron suffered were the deaths of four mechanics who were killed by enemy bombers during a night raid. The "Boche" struck again on the night of May 19 as the squadron was leaving Luxeuil for Bar-le-Duc. There were no further casualties, but the enemy bombs destroyed four automobile tractors.

2. Bar-le-Duc 19 May–14 September 1916
Verdun Sector

The squadron had been ordered to Bar-le-Duc to take part in the raging battle of Verdun. There, it would become part of Groupe de Combat 12. The pilots were quartered in a comfortable villa between the village of Bar-le-Duc and the Behonne airfield. The aerodrome was situated on a plateau surrounded by deep ravines to the southeast and northwest, which caused the pilots considerable difficulties as they flew continuous patrols over the battlefield.

On 24 May Caporal Raoul Lufbery was assigned to the squadron. On 30 July he scored his first confirmed aerial victory after sixteen unsuccessful combats by downing a German two-seater aircraft west of Etain in the Verdun sector. On 31 July he scored his second victory when he shot down a German two-seater reconnaissance plane above Fort Vaux. On 4 August he downed a two-seater above Aboucort for this third confirmed victory. On 8 August he shot down an Aviatik C. near Douamont for his fourth confirmed victory. On 16 August he was awarded France's Medaille Militare and Croix de Guerre, with palm for his aerial feats as a bomber and fighter pilot.

In mid-September the pilots were ordered back to Luxeuil to fly cover for Captain Maurice Happe's bombing raids. During their participation at Verdun, due to constantly clear weather, they fought 146 combats, with thirteen confirmed victories. On June 23, ilot Victor Chapman was killed in aerial combat, and three pilots were wounded. Before leaving Bar-le-Duc, the pilots were ordered to turn over their worn-out Nieuport 11 fighters to Escadrille N.12, the unit replacing them there.

3. Luxeuil 14 September–18 October 1916
Vosges Sector

Nieuport 16 and Nieuport 11c.1 fighter aircraft on the airfield at Luxeuil

While in transit to Luxeuil from Bar-le-Duc, the American pilots made a three-day Paris stopover. While there, they purchased a lion cub, which they named "Whiskey" and made the squadron's mascot. On September 19, six new Nieuport 17 fighters arrived at the squadron's aerodrome. The pilots were ordered to fly protection for both French and British bombers stationed there. On September 23, Kiffin Rockwell was killed in aerial combat near Rodern.

> On 26 September Lufbery was promoted to adjudant (warrant officer).

On October 12, Norman Prince was mortally injured when he crashed on the Corcieux airfield while returning from an Allied bombing raid against the Mauser factory at Oberndorf, Germany. He died on October 15.

> Lufbery claimed his fifth aerial victory and became America's first ace on the 12 October bombing raid when he downed a Roland C.II Walfisch near Oberndorf. He was awarded a second Palm to his Croix de Guerre on 28 October 1916.

The escadrille was ordered to Cachy, its mission completed at Luxeuil.

4. Cachy   18 October 1916–26 January 1917
Somme Sector

The squadron's pilots arrived at Cachy in support of the Somme offensive on 23 October and were assigned to Groupe de Combat 13 under Major Fequant. The squadron remained a part of that group for the rest of its war service. Shortly after its arrival, pilot William Thaw suggested the American pilots adopt the Indian head of a Seminole chief as their squadron's aircraft insignia. Thaw

Lafayette Escadrille pilots inside barracks staying warm, November 1916. Left to right: *Pavelka, British pilot, Robert Rockwell, McConnell* (foreground), *DeLaage, Haviland, Lufbery, Hill* (foreground), *unknown, unknown, unknown, unknown.*

Lafayette Escadrille pilots at Cachy, 25 January 1917. Left to right: *Soubiran, Johnson, Hoskier, Thaw, Fred Prince, Bigelow, Parsons, Genet.*

had spotted the Indian head trademark on a Savage ammunition box and upon the men's approval had ordered French caporal Suchet, an N.124 squadron mechanic, to adapt the image onto the sides of the pilots' Nieuports. Conditions were appalling at Cachy: constant rain, fog, mud, and snow.

> On 9 November Lufbery scored a probable victory near Ablaincourt. On 10 November he scored a second probable victory over Haplincourt. Both enemy aircraft fell too far behind enemy lines to be officially confirmed by a second witness.

From mid-November to mid-January only twelve days were fit for flying. The pilots were quartered in a sieve-like barracks. The airfield came under attack from enemy bombing raids. The first SPAD S V11 fighter aircraft arrived at Cachy. On November 16, in yielding to German diplomatic protests, the squadron became the Escadrille des Volontaires at the request of the US secretary of state.

> On 4 December Lufbery scored a probable victory east of Chaulnes. On 6 December the squadron was renamed L'Escadrille Lafayette at the instruction of France's Minister of War. On 27 December Lufbery scored his sixth confirmed victory by downing an Aviatic C southeast of Chaulnes. On 24 January Lufbery scored his seventh confirmed victory by downing an Aviatic C near Chaulnes-Peronne. On 29 January he was made a Chevalier de la Legion d'Honneur and was awarded a third palm to his Croix de Guerre.

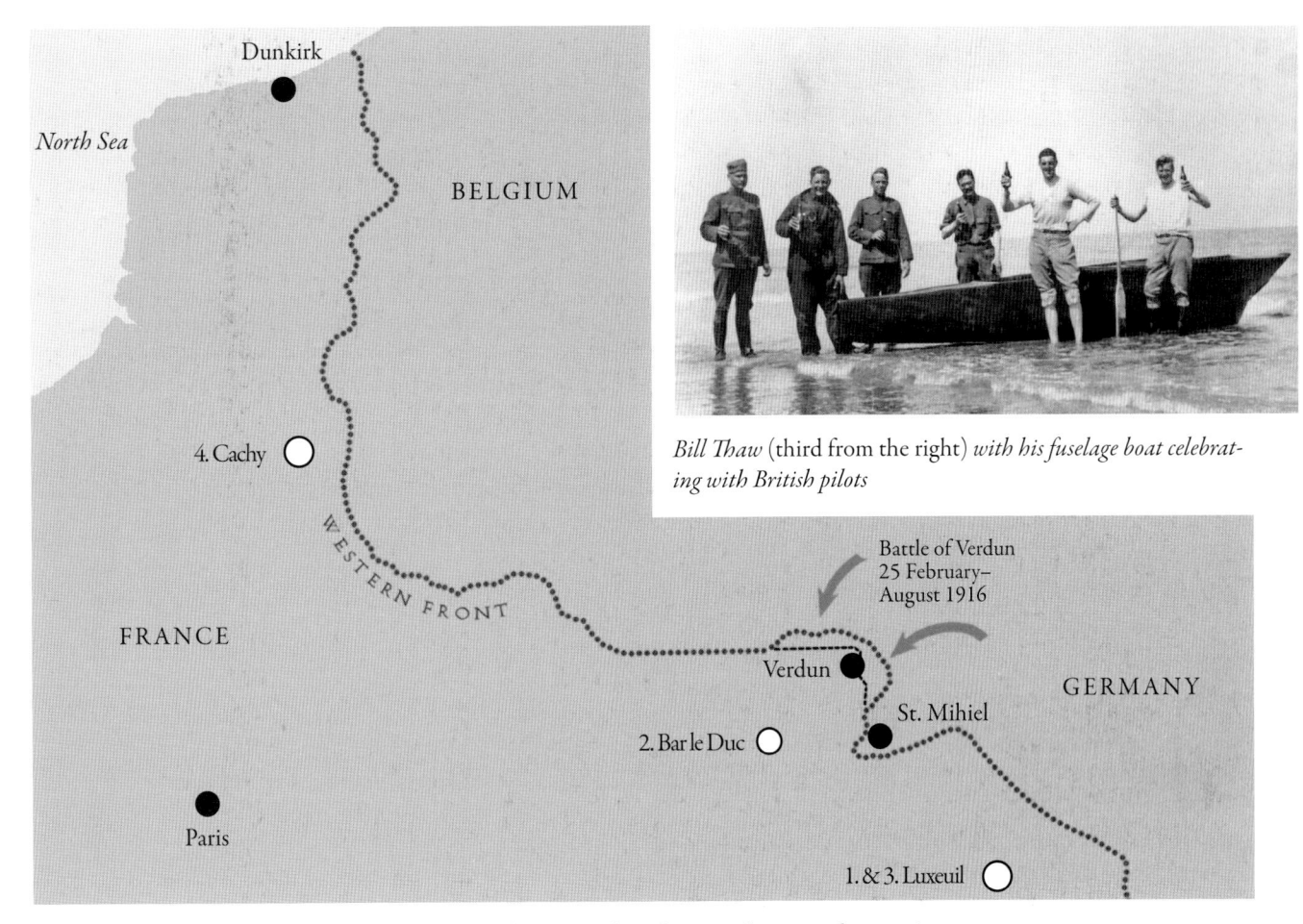

Bill Thaw (third from the right) *with his fuselage boat celebrating with British pilots*

Squadron locations of the Escadrille Americaine on the western front from April to December 1916

5. Saint-Juste (Ravenal) 26 January–7 April 1917
OISE AND AISNE SECTORS

The squadron was ordered to Ravenal to prepare for a planned spring offensive. Edward Hinkle, who joined the squadron on March 1, described the bleakness of Saint-Juste: "Ravenal was a wretched place. Icy winds and snow blowing across the field. We'd go out on patrols, stiff as corpses in our cockpits . . . the prop wash chilling us to our bone marrow. The off-duty pilots hibernated in underground shelters, sleeping under mounds of covers."

On March 16, pilot William Thaw took the lion "Whiskey" to Paris to see an oculist. He brought back a female lion cub with Whiskey, who was soon named "Soda." On March 19, pilot James McConnell was killed in aerial combat. The enemy had begun an "elastic retreat" toward St. Quentin and the Hindenburg Line, burning everything behind them. The Allies pushed forward under French general Nivelle, with the squadron flying reconnaissance. Ravenal soon proved too far from the front, and the squadron was ordered forward to the former German airfield at Ham.

6. Ham 7 April–3 June 1917
SOMME SECTOR

Edwin Parsons described the purpose for the squadron's relocation to Ham. "The French advanced so quickly and so far that in order to be anywhere near the front, we moved our field nearly forty kilometers further toward Germany, at the edge of the ravaged village of Ham, which had been for nearly three years in German hands . . . ruined villages, torn-up railroad tracks, blasted bridges." Pilots Harold Willis and Edward Hinkle collaborated to produce a new Indian head insignia, a fierce Sioux warrior with a brown face and a full red, white, and blue bonnet.

On 8 April Lufbery scored a probable victory over an enemy aircraft near Mont Sapignerel. On 13 April he scored his eighth confirmed victory over a two-seater reconnaissance plane northwest of St. Quentin.

On April 16, pilot Edmond Genet was killed by German antiaircraft fire. On April 23, pilot Ronald Hoskier and his French gunner were shot down and killed while flying a Morane Parasol reconnaissance plane.

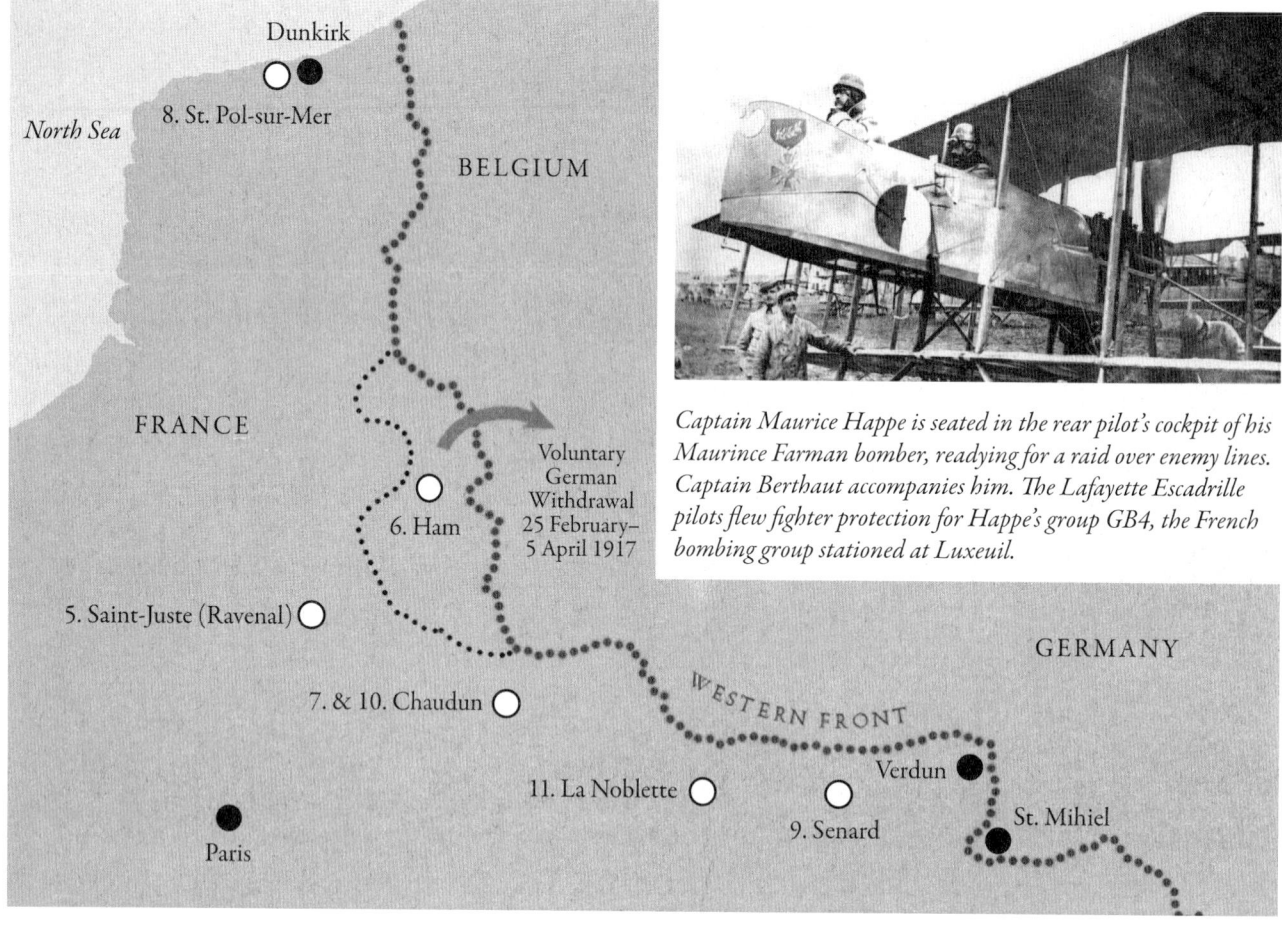

Squadron locations of the Escadrille Lafayette on the western front from January to December 1917

Captain Maurice Happe is seated in the rear pilot's cockpit of his Maurince Farman bomber, readying for a raid over enemy lines. Captain Berthaut accompanies him. The Lafayette Escadrille pilots flew fighter protection for Happe's group GB4, the French bombing group stationed at Luxeuil.

On 24 April Lufbery scored his ninth confirmed victory over an Aviatic C east of Cerisy. On 8 May he was awarded the British Military Medal. On 15 May he was awarded a fourth palm to his Croix de Guerre for his April 8, 13 and 24 probable, and two confirmed victories. On 19 May he was awarded France's Medaille Militaire for his outstanding bravery.

On May 23 the squadron's French adjutant, Lieutenant Alfred delaage deMeux, was killed when he crashed his new SPAD fighter into the ground near the Ham airfield. The pilots fought sixty-six air combats with the enemy in a two-month period, officially destroying seven enemy planes.

7. Chaudun 3 June–17 July 1917
AISNE SECTOR

As pilot Edwin Parsons remembered Chaudun: "In the beginning of June, the Escadrille was ordered from the unlucky field at Ham to a newly-created drome at Chaudun, behind Soissons . . . Chaudun proved to be as lucky as Ham was unlucky. The field was large and smooth, with plenty of landing space for all the six escadrilles."

Shortly after the squadron arrived at Chaudun, its designation was changed from N.124 to SPA 124 since it had become equipped predominately with SPAD S VII fighters.

On 12 June Lufbery became a double-ace when he scored his tenth confirmed victory over an enemy two-seater near Aguilcourt. He received his fifth palm to his Croix de Guerre for his 12 June victory.

Parson's French mechanics beside his flipped Nieuport scout at Ham, March 1917.

The Lafayette Escadrille pilots at Chaudun surround their mascots, Whiskey and Soda, on the lions' last day with the squadron. 15 October 1917. Left to right: James Hall, William Thaw, Dudley Hill, Kenneth Marr, David Peterson, Raoul Lufbery, Robert Rockwell, Ray Bridgman, and Dr. Manet, the squadron's doctor.

8. St. Pol sur Mer (Dunkirk) 17 July–11 August 1917
FLANDERS SECTOR

On July 17 the squadron was ordered to Dunkirk, to the far northern end of the lines at the edge of the North Sea. From there the squadron was to assist the combined French, English, and Belgian armies in a great drive in Flanders. The aerodrome, with its smooth, long, narrow airstrip, was right at the ocean near the village of St. Pol sur Mer, 1.5 miles from Dunkirk. Pilot Edwin Parsons remembered how "the stay at Dunkirk provided a very pleasant interlude for the tough months to follow. It was a continuous round of sea bathing, poker and drinking parties with the pilots of several English squadrons near whom we were billeted."

9. Senard 11 August–28 September 1917
VERDUN SECTOR

Following the brief respite at St. Pol sur Mer, the squadron returned to its previous area of operations, to the airfield near the village of Senard, there to fly patrols and bomber escort during the Verdun Offensive. It was a busy time, as pilot Edwin Parsons related: "There, based at the flying field of Senard, we went in for some really intensive air work, the most exhausting of all our campaigns. After our arrival, we had twenty-four days of brilliant sunshine, and the total flying hours piled up in that one month alone was staggering . . . three shows a day . . . nightly incursions of the German bombing squadrons. Destroyed one or two hangars with several ships."

On 4 September Lufbery destroyed an enemy aircraft east of Cheppy for his eleventh confirmed victory. On 5 September he scored a probably victory near Louvermont. On 6 September he scored another probable victory near Louvermont. He would receive the sixth palm to his Croix de Guerre for these actions. On 22 September he scored his twelvth confirmed victory, destroying a two-seater east of Cheppy. That same day, 22 September, he scored a probable victory over an enemy aircraft near Cheppy. Following these aerial actions Lufbery was promoted to sous-lieutenant, joining pilot William Thaw as a commissioned officer in France's Service Aerounatique.

Lafayette escadrille pilots at Chaudun, 10 July 1917. Standing, left to right: *Soubiran, Campbell, Parsons, Bridgman, Dugan, MacMonagle, Lovell, Willis, Jones, Peterson, Maison-Rouge.* Seated, left to right: *Hill, Masson and "Soda," Thaw and "Whiskey," Thenault, Lufbery, Johnson, Bigelow, Rockwell.*

On September 24, pilot Douglas MacMonagle was killed in aerial combat. On September 25 and 27 the enemy bombarded the aerodrome, setting fire to a hangar. The squadron engaged in 150 fights above Verdun.

10. Chadun 29 September–3 December 1917
AISNE SECTOR

The squadron was ordered back to Chaudun to take part in the Malmaison Offensive. On October 1, pilot Andrew Courtney Campbell was killed in combat. October proved most active for the pilots. The Malmaison Offensive was launched on the 10th. On October 15 the Escadrille's two lion mascots, "Whiskey" and "Soda," were taken to a Paris zoo, where they remained until their deaths soon after the war.

> On 16 October Lufbery scored his 13th confirmed victory by downing a two-seater near Vauxillon. On 24 October Lufbery destroyed a two-seater near Urcel for his 14th confirmed victory. He also had four probable victories that same day near Urcel downing two enemy scouts and two two-seaters. On 29 October he was awarded a seventh palm to his Croix de Guerre for his 22 September and 16 October actions. He was awarded his eighth palm to his Croix de Guerre for his 24 October action.

11. La Cheppe and La Ferme de la Noblette
3 December–18 February 1918
CHAMPAGNE SECTOR

Upon their arrival north of Chalons, at La Noblette, the American pilots were advised to obtain their releases from the French Service Aeronautic in order to receive their US military commissions.

> On 2 December Lufbery scored his fifteenth confirmed victory over a two-seater south of Ployart. Later that day he scored his sixteenth confirmed victory over a two-seater near Laval. Lufbery was pleased that he destroyed these two enemy aircraft on the third anniversary of the death of Marc Pourpe.

All American pilots were released from the squadron on December 25 with the exception of Edwin Parsons, who was in the US on leave. Since December 1, until their paperwork had been processed, the Americans had been flying as civilians. By 18 February 18, all the pilots' commissions had come through. On that date the Lafayette Escadrille officially passed to US jurisdiction and became the US 103rd Aero Pursuit Squadron, having served admirably in every sector along the entire western front.

The Aircraft

"The evolution of the airplane is marvelous. A machine is out of date in two months. First the Germans have one that the French can't touch, and then the French have one that the Germans can't get near. When I first came down here they had just got out a new machine that was supposed to beat everything up to that time. Now a new model of another machine is about to displace that. The way they keep cutting down the wings I think soon they will have nothing but a box and a motor."

—Lafayette Escadrille pilot Robert Rockwell

In the first week of May 1916, six Nieuport 11C.1 fighter aircraft and two Nieuport 16 fighter aircraft were delivered to the Escadrille Americaine's aerodrome near Luxeuil. These tiny single-seater biplanes, France's first real fighter plane, soon became the answer to the German Fokker Eindecker fighter, which had ruled the sky since the previous summer. With only 16 square yards of wing surface, this Nieuport was nicknamed the Bebe because of its diminutive size.

Wood and wire furnished the basic ingredients of this new fighter. A silver spruce or ash skeleton was held in place by high-tensile Swedish wire, which was then covered by a skin of unbleached flax linen. On its nose was a propeller of black walnut or Spanish mahogany.

Three of the squadron's new fighters had 80 hp nine-cylinder Le Rhone rotary engines, and three featured the 110 hp model. Its top speed was approximately 100 miles per hour. Its armament consisted of a single .303 caliber Lewis machine gun with a forty-seven-round drum mounted above the top wing on brackets, which enabled the pilot to fire it over the arc of the propeller.

The two manufacturers of the Lewis gun were the British Birmingham Small Arms Company (BSA) and the Savage Arms Company of New York. The squadron's pilots adopted that company's logo as their official insignia, the image of a fierce Indian head blazoned on the firm's wood ammunition crates. Their mechanics painted the Indian heads on the sides of the fighter aircraft.

Several devices were employed to utilize the machine gun. The two most practical were the Godfrey folding post mount, and the Foster adjustable gun mount. The Foster mount allowed the pilot to bring the gun down on a curved rail for reloading and upward firing. The pilot could fire the machine gun while seated in his fighter through the use of a Bowden cable, which extended from the trigger of the Lewis gun down into the cockpit.

The Lewis gun armament system proved inferior to the enemy fighters' synchronized L.GM.08/15 Maxim "Spandau" machine gun. The Lewis gun's ammunition came in single-capacity drums of forty-seven rounds and double capacity drums of ninety-seven rounds. The drums could be emptied in a five-to-ten-second continuous burst and required frequent reloading in combat, a difficult procedure, while the Spandau machine gun was belt-fed and had a continuous supply of ammunition. Capitaine Georges Thenault later wrote of the difficulty of reloading the Lewis gun in combat.

"It was a far from easy job to substitute a full drum for an empty one with your fingers frozen and hampered by thick gloves, and one needed a lot of practice to do it properly, especially as one had to use one hand for piloting the ship for fear of getting into a spin.

"Only a practiced pilot could repair a machine gun jam in the air, so that in flight there was always the danger of being disarmed against an adversary who could fire 500 cartridges at a clip."

Then there was the problem of jamming. Edward Hinkle remembered how: "The Lewis gun usually jammed after the first burst was fired. Then we'd have to hold the stick between our knees while we reached up to yank the gun breech back and clear the jammed cartridge. It was a primitive weapon . . . a real wonder that we ever hit anything with it."

Aircraft vibrations presented an additional problem. Capitaine Thenault stated that vibration caused the Lewis gun to jam in three-quarters of the squadron's attacks upon enemy aircraft.

When the Nieuport 11s left the aircraft factories for the front, their varnished skins would have been painted one or two colors: aluminum or light yellow. Once the planes arrived at the squadron, they were repainted to the preference of the pilots who flew them. Combinations of yellow, olive green, and red predominated in an effort to conceal the planes from overhead observation, by having them blend in with the agriculture of the French countryside. The underside of the machines were painted silver gray or sky blue to serve as concealment when viewed against the sky.

Lafayette Escadrille pilot Sgt. Dudley Hill in his Nieuport 17c.1 fighters at Cachy in October 1916. His post-mounted Lewis gun drum is loaded with a 97-round drum magazine. A Bowden firing cable extends into the cockpit. A Vickers machine gun is mounted in front of him on the fuselage.

The escadrille pilots first flew the Nieuport 11 in combat from the Luxeuil aerodrome. They later flew it from the Behonne aerodrome through the summer and early fall of 1916. When they again returned to Luxeuil in mid-September, they left their Nieuport 11s at Behonne. On September 19 the first of their new Nieuport 17C.1s arrived there.

The Nieuport 17, with wings of increased span and surface area, soon proved a more durable machine than its predecessor. Powered by a 110 hp Le Rhone rotary engine or by a 130 hp Clerget engine, it developed an air speed of between 110 and 115 miles per hour despite the fact that it was 200 pounds heavier than the Bebe. A flatter wing created less wind resistance, and an additional 20 square feet of wing surface more than compensated for its added weight. Its maximum altitude was 18,000 feet, less than some German planes. But it stood unchallenged in its climbing ability for the first 10,000 feet, which it accomplished in 10½ minutes.

The Nieuport 17 was also a better-armed fighter than the Bebe. In addition to the Lewis gun mounted on its upper wing plane, it also had a British Vickers gun mounted directly in front of the pilot, which fired through the plane's propeller by aid of the Birkigt synchronizing gear connected to the motor. This gear timed the firing of the Vickers gun so that it would shoot only when the propeller had cleared the barrel.

The belt-fed Vickers gun, with its 350–500 rounds of .303 caliber ammunition, represented for the first time a weapon comparable to Germany's sychronized Spandau machine gun. However, it jammed more frequently than the enemy's Spandau and would accept only perfect ammunition. Because of this drawback, the Allied pilots carried brass hammers in their cockpits to pound a bulging cartridge case from the gun's breech.

In October 1916 the French introduced their SPAD S.VII fighter plane into the Lafayette Squadron. Its name came from the initials of the company that constructed it, Louis Blériot's Socie'te' Anonyme pour l'Aviation et ses Derive's. This plane was to counter the German Albatros D.I, which had restored to Germany the air supremacy it had lost that previous July during the Battle of the Somme.

Over a period of months the SPAD gradually replaced the Nieuport 17's in the Lafayette Squadron. By early June 1917 only two or three Nieuports remained. At that time the official classification of the squadron was changed from Nieuport 124 to Spad 124.

The SPAD S.VII soon proved an effective fighter, equal to anything the Germans had in the air. It was a flat-winged, sturdy aircraft that developed a top speed of 120 mph through its fixed, water-cooled V-8, 150 hp Hispano-Suiza engine (later increased to 180 hp) It was armed with an Alkan-synchronized Vickers gun with a ring-sight system. It was mounted between the plane's cylinder banks. In June 1917, when the 200 hp Spad was introduced at the front, this model was armed with two Vickers guns. It presented an awesome weapon in a swift dive and could take punishment that would have torn the Nieuport's lower wings away. Nevertheless, the Nieuport could still outclimb and outmaneuver the SPAD. Also, when the SPAD's engine died, it took on "the gliding angle of a brick," and an accident in the fighter too often proved fatal.

The machine guns' Constantinesco hydraulic synchronizer was tied directly to the camshaft that turned the propeller. If the gun jammed, the pilot was at the mercy of his adversary, since if the engine should quit, it could not be restarted in the air. For those reasons the Nieuport was preferred over the SPAD by several of the Lafayette pilots.

But despite the SPAD's drawbacks, its great ability to stand up in a dive most impressed its pilots. As Capitaine Thenault noted: "The SPAD was the only machine which enabled one to dive without fear of the consequences and often when diving on an enemy plane, which in turn dived to escape, one had the pleasant surprise of seeing it come to pieces in the air without a shot having been fired."

When comparing the Nieuport and SPAD fighters, each plane demonstrated its own positive characteristics and drawbacks. The Nieuport was more pleasant to fly than the SPAD, which demanded the pilot's full attention. The Nieuport also had a better outlook than the SPAD, particularly downward, because of its narrow lower wing. The Nieuport was also a superb climber, and because of its great maneuverability, it was unsurpassed in a dogfight, which required close fighting and sharp turns.

Conversely, the Nieuport had structural weaknesses, and its rotary-engine controls could prove difficult to the inexperienced pilot. Since the engine could not be throttled down, the pilot controlled his airspeed through the use of a "Blip Switch" cutoff button on the control stick. This allowed him to switch the engine off for brief intervals in order to reduce power, as for landing. The Gnome rotary engine, in addition to a thumb switch on the stick or dash, also had buttons on the control stick, which the pilot could employ to cut out one or more cylinders for continuous running at low speed.

Another drawback of the Nieuport's rotary engine was that it constantly spewed burnt castor oil (its lubricant), with its nauseating smell blowing back into the pilot's cockpit. Some pilots claimed the fumes had a laxative

Lafayette Escadrille pilot Sgt. James Ralph Doolittle beside his SPAD S.VII fighter at Chaudun in July 1917

effect, which they tried to counter by carrying milk and brandy on patrol. Still, in all, the Nieuport proved one of the most effective fighter planes of the war.

The Spad, while quick to respond to the pilot's commands, was also a durable fighter and better armed than the Nieuport, particularly the 220 hp SPAD XIII with its two Vickers machine guns. For this reason it was preferred and flown by the great French aces: Guynemer, Fonk, and Nungesser. However, not all pilots liked this aircraft, and as pilot James Norman Hall recalled, while they were very fast and had a high ceiling, "they were less manoeuverable and far less reliable than the one-eighties I was accustomed to. Many of their engines lasted only twelve or fifteen hours at the front."

Also, the instruments on the dash in front of the pilot's seat were rudimentary. Edwin Parsons said of them: "Our instruments were of the crudest and only the most essential. We had only a compass; a fairly reliable altimeter which showed us at least approximately our altitude from the field where we had taken off; a tachometer to show engine revolutions; an oil pulsator to show oil was flowing; a clock and a map. That was the complete equipment."

If the ultimate merit of any particular fighter aircraft was judged by how many pilots survived the war in it, then as far as the Lafayette Escadrille was concerned, the Nieuport and the SPAD would have rated nearly equal. Approximately an equal number of the squadron's 38 pilots lost their lives or were shot down and captured in Nieuports and SPADs.

THE ENEMY

WHENEVER THE Lafayette Escadrille pilot faced his German adversary in the skies above the western front, invariably the odds stood in the enemy pilot's favor. It was not that the German foe was a braver or more skilled fighter pilot than his American counterpart. However, he was often better trained, with a minimum of six months' fighter training over and above his training in two-seater machines. This course was followed by three weeks of close scrutiny under the critical eye of top German aces. What gave him the decisive edge was his superiority of aircraft armament, the fact that he did most of his aerial battles over his own airspace, and the strategy employed by his squadron.

The German Flying Corps remained one step ahead of the Allies in the development of its aircraft and armament. It had first gained air supremacy in the summer of 1915, with the introduction of its Fokker E.1 and E.III fighters with their belt-fed machine guns firing through the propeller disc. Because of the Fokker's high ceiling, the German pilot could pick his target, then make a diving attack, while fully utilizing the additional advantage of extra ammunition and longer bursts of fire.

By the spring of 1916, at about the time the Escadrille Americaine had arrived at the front, the French Service Aeronautique had regained the edge in fighter supremacy with the introduction of the Nieuport 11 fighter. But by fall that edge had dissipated when the Germans introduced in great numbers their Albatros D.I, and the improved D.II fighters with twin 7.92 Spandau guns and 160 hp Mercedes engines. Again, Germany stood unmatched in speed, altitude, and fire power until the autumn of 1917, when France began employing in large numbers its SPAD S. XIII fighter, armed with twin, belt-fed Vickers machine guns.

But even with this improved weapon, the German Spandau and Parabellum machine guns still proved more dependable and smoother to operate than the Lewis and Vickers guns, which France employed on its own fighters. And by 1917 the enemy held additional advantages when it began to utilize as standard equipment electrically heated flying suits, parachutes, and liquid oxygen.

The second advantage that the German air force held was in the method of its tactics. Unlike the American pilots of N.124, the German fighter pilots flew no regular patrols but would be quickly moved about in tent hangars to any part of the front, which allowed them to confront the small Lafayette patrols with large numbers of aircraft.

The pilots of the "Flying Circuses" would remain on the ground scanning the sky with binoculars for approaching enemy fighters. Or they would sit in their deck chairs awaiting orders to pilot their gaudy-colored fighters the instant forward observation posts warned of approaching enemy.

Throughout most of their service on the western front, the duty of the German fighter Jagdstaffein (squadrons) was to protect their air space from enemy incursion. Few of their fighters sought combat over Allied territory. Since they were defensively deployed and accomplished the majority of their combats over their own lines, they held the advantage in numbers and in altitude, and through the use of ruse and decoy, with a lumbering two-seater observation plane often serving as bait.

Woe to the novice pilot who attacked the solo two-seater. When he closed in, a flock of German fighters that had been hiding in the sun, waiting for such an opportunity, would swoop down spewing bullets into their victim's plane. Canadian ace William Bishop related how his foe had developed pack hunting into a refined art.

"Almost every morning we would find well-laid traps set for us. It required careful manoeuvering to avoid falling into them. Several times we did and it took a lot of trouble to get out safely. Four or five Huns would come along and we would engage them. Then suddenly as many as fifteen or twenty would appear from all angles and join in the fight. This happened every day and the Huns were evidently out to get us."

But even the straight-flying German two-seaters performing reconnaissance patrols within Allied lines were no easy prey. They often flew too high for the squadron's aircraft to reach them. As one pilot lamented: "If you want to go to heaven, the easiest way I know is to dive on a two-seater."

The Fokker E.III Eindecker fighter with its forward-firing Parabellum or Spandau machine gun quickly earned it the title "Fokker scourge" after its introduction into combat in the winter of 1915–1916.

The Albatros D series fighter was introduced into the service by Germany in the autumn of 1916 and soon proved a formidable foe against the French Nieuport with its Mercedes power plant and twin 7.92 Spandau machine guns.

The German LVG reconnaissance aircraft was a frequent target for the American Lafayette pilots. But it was no easy prey with its observer-manned, free-firing machine gun in the rear cockpit, causing one American pilot to lament, "If you want to go to heaven . . . dive on a two-seater."

German 40-victory ace Captain Oswald Boelcke. Boelcke may have inflicted Victor Chapman's deep scalp wound during a 17 June 1916 aerial engagement above the right bank of the Meuse River. On 9 October 1916 Raoul Lufbery and Boelcke probably fought an inconclusive aerial duel north of Mulhouse. Shortly after he disengaged, Lufbery's Nieuport 17 no. 1830 was shot to pieces by a German observation aircraft, forcing him to make an emergency landing on the Fontaine airfield.

Boelcke's body beside the wreckage of his Fokker E. IV monoplane near German-held Bapaume, France, following his 28 October 1916 aerial collision with his wingman, Lt. Erwin Bohume. Boelcke was 26 years of age at the time of his death.

The Front

"I've had five hundred hours over the lines. You don't know what that means, not yet. I'm no good anymore. It's strain. Let me give you some advice. Save your nervous energy. You will need all you have and more. Above everything else, don't think at the front. The best pilot is the best machine." —*High Adventure*

The American pilot chosen as a squadron replacement at the GDE (Groupe des Division d'Entrainement) pilot pool by Capitaine Thenault arrived at the Lafayette Escadrille aerodrome either by flying in a new fighter plane or by taking a French military train from the GDE to the village nearest the squadron's aerodrome. Often this village, from which the aerodrome had taken its name, was merely a row of makeshift structures with rough pine walls and corrugated iron roofs, facing the length of a dusty street. Directly behind the village stood the battered remains of the original French village, its stone edifice long pulverized into heaps of rubble.

A squadron chauffeur driving the staff car greeted the replacement pilot as he stepped off the train. With his gear stored in the vehicle, the new pilot was driven down the dusty road toward the aerodrome through rows of stooped and sweating *permissionaires* departing from or returning to the trenches.

The Lafayette Escadrille's aerodrome, located 15 miles from the front, between the war zone and the infantry rest zone, consisted of a cluster of portable canvas hangars squatting on the edges of a 300-yard-square airfield. Upon his arrival there, the replacement pilot was greeted by Captain Thenault and the other American pilots.

The squadron's fighter planes occupied hangars on the same airfield shared with three other pursuit squadrons. Together the four squadrons formed Groupe de Combat *13*, with a specific sector of front to cover. In flying weather, through a series of overlapping patrols, they protected their sector from daylight to dusk. Circumstances dictated the number of patrols flown and the amount of aircraft in each patrol.

The replacement pilot soon learned his duties. In a *chasse* squadron like *N.124*, his daily mission was often predesignated, such as protecting the aircraft of the Corps d'Armee: i.e., the Allied photographic machines, the artillery *réglage* machines, or the bombing formations. But with no specific assignment, he patrolled the lines unrestrained. And if he had a malingering nature, he could employ a myriad of excuses—a boiling radiator, a stuttering motor, a jammed gun block—which could keep him out of harm's way. However, the majority suppressed their fear and served dutifully, attacking enemy planes at every opportunity, or ground-strafing enemy trenches, transports, and troop concentrations.

Under normal conditions a pilot was required to fly two two-hour daily patrols. During an Allied offensive he might be required to fly six hours daily, but rarely more than that. The constant strain in the air was too taxing for the normal pilot to function beyond this limit.

Invariably a new pilot, unfamiliar with the strain of combat flying, would ask if he might be allowed to fly voluntary patrols. The veteran pilots, upon hearing this oft-repeated question, merely shook their heads and told their newly arrived comrade that within six weeks' time, he would fly no more than the required limit and would fly voluntary patrols only when the situation demanded it.

One pilot was the exception. Raoul Lufbery relished every opportunity to be fighting in the air. To Captain Thenault, his pilot was "a superman" who had to be ordered to rest. "To fly high is very fatiguing," Thenault noted, "as the sudden changes of altitude quickly tire the heart. But never have I met a pilot with more endurance than Lufbery. When the sky was clear he would go up three or four times a day to eighteen thousand feet just for his own pleasure, in a dilettante fashion. Never was he at all ill from it."

Lufbery lived to fight. With no concept of fear, the prospect of death could not dissuade him from his missions. And during his relentless hunts, he took as much as he gave, often returning to the squadron's airfield, his plane a testimony to his fierce combats.

But if he suffered no ill effects from oxygen deprivation, one of his frequent rheumatic attacks could keep him out of the sky, attacks that at times became so severe that Lufbery required hospitalization. Often he flew half-crippled, in great pain from his inflamed muscles and swollen joints.

The most dangerous time for the novice pilot was his first month at the front. He had only a fifty-fifty chance of surviving that period and was of little value to the squadron because of his inability to spot the enemy in the air. But if he survived those first thirty days, his odds of living improved, since 80 percent of the casualties were suffered by pilots with fewer than twenty missions.

When not flying patrols, the pilots often slept. One German pilot called sleep "the food of the nerves," and it was not uncommon for pilots to sleep up to twelve hours a day as their bodies demanded relief from the intense fatigue and nerve strain brought on by combat flying.

The British Royal Flying Corps allowed their pilots a three month rest period following six months of combat flying. But the American pilots in France's Service Aeronautique served until they were killed, seriously wounded, or physically and emotionally used up. When the pilots were not sleeping, they read, played poker or bridge, or took walks. If the squadron was not flying around the clock during an offensive, evenings were devoted to drink and music from the piano and phonograph.

Every American replacement arrived at the front as a *caporal* pilot. He was promoted to *sergent* following thirty flying hours over the lines. When he had accumulated one hundred air hours and had participated in a number of combats and victories, he was promoted to *adjudant*. Only two Lafayette pilots, William Thaw and Raoul Lufbery, attained the commissioned rank of lieutenant.

The pilot's pay consisted of nine sous a day and an additional franc a day for flight pay. That sum totaled twenty-five cents in US money. In addition, a pilot was paid one hundred francs (later increased to two hundred francs) a month from the William K. Vanderbilt Lafayette Flying Corps Fund for his mess expenses and to see to other necessities. The fund also distributed cash prizes and Paris leave whenever a pilot received a French decoration or was credited with the destruction of an enemy aircraft. The prizes were distributed as follows:

Raoul Lufbery seated in the back seat of the squadron's staff car

Legion of Honor: 1,500 francs ($300)
Medaille Militaire: 1,000 francs ($200)
Croix de Guerre: 500 francs ($100)
Citation (palm): 250 francs ($50)
Downing an enemy aircraft: 1,000 francs ($200)

The squadron carried no more than nineteen pilots on its rolls at one time. Initially, when the roster was small, a patrol consisted of one to three pilots. But later on, as the roster grew, the pilots were divided into three flights of six pilots each, including the flight commander. However, it was rare that the patrol ever consisted of more than four pilots, due to the unreliability of their aircraft.

The total personnel of the Lafayette Squadron consisted of eighty men. This included the pilots, the armament officer and his assistant, the medical officer, two

French mechanics watching a SPAD fighter depart on patrol while other mechanics work on a SPAD S.VII aircraft

mechanics for each plane, twelve chauffeurs to drive the squadron trucks and *camions*, squadron and officer orderlies, the mess cooks, and secretaries.

Every night at 10 P.M., orders reached the squadron from headquarters of the army containing the following morning's assignments. These assignments were coordinated with the general in charge of the army in the groupe's sector.

Under normal conditions the squadron's daily routine of three flights consisted as follows: When A Flight patrolled the front, B Flight was on alert. This meant that a pilot on B Flight was dressed in his flying clothes, his plane out of the hangar, and its engine kept warm by his two mechanics, who continually turned it over. Lufbery passed the time while on alert discussing with his mechanics some particular plane malfunction he had noticed on his previous flight, or hand-gauging and loading cartridges into his machine gun magazines. *Lafayette* pilot Edward Hinkle said this of Raoul:

> Lufbery was a wonderful mechanic and his plane was always the best in the Escadrille. Anyone would rather have a secondhand Lufbery machine than a new one, anytime."

As the pilots of B Flight killed time, the pilots of C Flight were on *repos* (sleeping or resting). This dull routine was followed day after day, including Sundays and holidays, except for special occasions when Paris leave might be granted.

The only time the routine was altered was during an Allied offensive, and then the pilots flew from daylight to dusk, pushed physically and mentally to their limits, until the conclusion of the assault. Gasoline flares were put on the airfield for pilots who returned after dusk to land by.

Weather dictated whether the pilots were to fly patrols. Often the squadron was kept grounded by inclement weather, rain, sleet, or an impassable airstrip alternately frozen or oozing clay.

When weather permitted, the pilots flew two types of daily patrols: *offensive* and *defensive* patrols. *Offensive* patrols were patrols flown over enemy territory to protect Allied observation or bombing aircraft, to seek out and destroy enemy aircraft, to spot enemy troop movements, and to conduct ground strafing. *Defensive* patrols were flown to protect Allied balloons, aircraft, and ground installations, and to knock down enemy aircraft which penetrated allied air space.

A *defensive* patrol was normally flown at three different altitudes. The Lafayette squadron, when flying a defensive patrol, was accompanied by two other patrols flown by other squadrons of the Groupe de Combat.

The area over which the squadrons patrolled was divided into three zones. The *rear zone* consisted of a 5-mile area extending from the Allied observation-balloon lines to the Allied frontline trenches. The *zone of advance* consisted of the area between the Allied and German frontline trenches and up to 5 miles inside enemy territory to their observation-balloon lines. The *third zone* was that area over German territory that was behind the enemy's observation-balloon lines.

A normal patrol over these zones usually lasted two hours, the fuel limit of the Allied fighter. The *low patrol* was the first patrol off the airfield. It flew at 3,000 feet just in front of the Allied balloon lines, and its duty was to protect the balloons and to intercept enemy bombing, observation, or pursuit aircraft. The second patrol off the field was the *intermediate patrol,* which covered an altitude of between 10,000 and 12,000 feet. The *intermediate patrol* was to protect the *low patrol.*

The last patrol off the airfield flew *high patrol,* which was at the highest altitude the fighter could attain, depending upon the air pressure and temperature of any given day. For the Nieuport 11C.1 aircraft, this was at approximately 15,000 feet. For the Nieuport 17C.I and the SPAD S.VII fighter, this was between 17,000 and 18,000 feet, although some pilots coaxed their SPADs beyond 20,000 feet under favorable atmospheric conditions.

The *high patrol* left the airfield last, since it normally required a half hour to reach its altitude before it could level off and begin patrolling back and forth across the sector. A fighter plane was mushy and unstable at that height. The air was bitterly cold, "a pure agony of mind and body," and because the pilots carried no oxygen supply, the slightest exertion, such as the cocking of a machine gun, caused one to pant. The duty of the *high patrol* was to protect the *intermediate patrol.*

Patrolling was done in an open V formation, with the flight leader taking the point and with the deputy leader nearest him, both in clearly marked fighters with flight streamers attached to their wings or rudders. The newest pilots were usually placed toward the front of the patrol, with the experienced pilots covering the rear, the likely point of enemy attack. A patrol never flew in a straight line but continually altered its path to prevent surprise attack by enemy fighters and bracketing by enemy antiaircraft fire.

No pilot was placed on *high patrol* for two consecutive days, because of the physical stress and the resulting severe headaches. When a pilot came off *high patrol*, his next assignment following *repos* and alert status was to *low patrol,* then to *intermediate patrol,* before being assigned again to *high patrol.*

When Allied ground gunners spotted German formations, they signaled the enemy' location to the Lafayette patrol overhead through antiaircraft fire. Using a high-explosive shell that emitted white smoke, the Allied battery fired in front of the Lafayette patrol, setting the round to explode either above or below the formation to let the Americans know that the enemy patrol was either above or below them. The battery used armor-piercing shells that emitted black smoke to indicate which sector the enemy patrol was flying. A single black explosion indicated Sector One; two explosions indicated Sector Two, etc.

Whenever a patrol spotted an enemy aircraft, the usual response was to climb above the German formation with the sun at the pilots' back. This provided the advantage of striking an adversary while coming out of the blinding rays of the sun. But if both patrols spotted each other simultaneously, both would climb for advantage. As pilot Carl Dolan remembered:

> We were interested in getting up behind them and getting a crack at them. But they had the same idea, you see. So if we spotted each other at the same time, we'd both climb. I have never been high enough to be above the Germans. No matter how high we'd go, the Germans always seemed to be a couple of hundred meters above us. They'd come diving at us. Of course, if we could get the sun at our backs we'd turn and face them. Otherwise we'd run and attempt to outmaneuver them.

The Patrol

The light from the candle in the orderly's hand made the pilot's heart stutter. Saying, "*C'est l'heure, monsieur,*" the *caporal* placed the candleholder on the table in the pilot's cubicle, then went out and quietly closed the door as on a room where someone had died. The pilot had slept little since turning in, despite his terrible weariness, and then only to dream the same nightmare and to break out of it sweating. As before, he had been falling in a burning bus.

"If this war lasts much longer, none of us will get home," he thought. "I don't want to die. I don't take chances. But will my sense of duty, or is it the shame of being thought a coward?—I can't tell which—will this override my fear and keep me on my course?"

The pilot sat up and looked to the window square with its oilcloth covering, which offered a glimmer of light. Outside his cubicle the squadron's phonograph pulsed out an oft-played tune throughout the barracks. His tongue felt metallic from last night's cognac. He remembered the empty chair, how everyone had tried to ignore it. But it was as if their dead comrade had occupied his place.

The pilot left his cubicle. The fall chill had entered the barracks. The pilots were gathered about the mess room stove. He watched a veteran pilot who had flown many patrols raise a match to his cigarette. His hand shook badly, and he clutched it with his free hand as he furtively glanced about. His months with the squadron had taken their toll, and his usefulness as a combat pilot had been lost. Still, he hung on and did the best he could. Behind him a young replacement, a skilled pilot, appeared as calm as the Sphinx. But the other pilots knew that once the patrol reached the Allied balloon lines, he would again turn his fighter back. What, he wondered, would be the young pilot's excuse today? And yet, he could not condemn him. Even after many patrols, he too had to fight the urge to turn homeward.

The previous day Capitaine Thenault had handed each flight commander his assignment. Together they had gone over the large-scale map of the sector, hanging

Spad fighters lined up before the Bessonneau hangars on the squadron's airfield

on the wall of the groupe's bureau, studying each square to be covered by the patrol. "At dawn a second assault begins. Again, our duty will be to support the advance of our troops. Seek out and destroy enemy ground emplacements. 'A' flight will leave at dawn."

The American pilots hurriedly gulped their chocolate as they pulled on their combination flying suits over a variety of clothing. Two wore French service uniforms; another, slacks and an oil-soaked sweater; a third, pajamas. The pilot at the door peered into the sky then grimly recited the RFC poem their British comrades had taught them.

> *He left the mess room early before the break of dawn.*
> *Greatly to his horror the weather promised fair.*

Too quickly it was ten minutes to patrol time, one hour before sunrise. Last night it had rained and the airfield was still soft.

The pilots strapped wooden clogs to their military shoes, and with their fur-lined flying boots under their arms, they tumbled into the darkness and across the field toward the hangars. With feet like lead, it was an exhausting journey. The hangar's wooden supports groaned with the weight of their canvas sides flapping and billowing in the morning air. Toward the front a low sky painted red from cannon flashes rumbled with the deadly storm of exploding artillery.

The fighter planes were lined up outside the Bessonneau hangars, wing to wing in a perfect row. In the darkness the sleek little Spads appeared identical. But a closer look revealed that a couple were new and clean while others were oil-stained and battle-scarred, their fuselages and wings covered with patches where they had taken enemy fire. Each plane bore the squadron's insignia on its fuselage, a fierce Sioux Indian head. In addition each pilot's personal insignia had been painted on the fuselage of his fighter near the Indian head..

The French *mechaniciens*, men of great skill and patience, huddled over the machines as they cleaned winscreens and idled motors at 350 revolutions. While the pilots had slept, their *mechaniciens* had been up about their duties, always cheerful as they worked, checking motors and bracing wires and cleaning and arming machine guns.

The pilot frowned as he saw the Dupont ammunition crates, American-made cartridges. Brass casings that would split and bulge and jam the breech of the machine gun, leaving one defenseless. Too much of it had been defective of late. How many air battles have been lost from

Spad on dawn patrol

faulty American-made cartridges?

While his two French mechanics finished their work, the pilot buckled on his fleece-lined flying boots, then checked the pocket of his combination for his small box of matches. These, he carried to ignite his plane should he be downed inside enemy lines. He also checked his "French parachute," an 8m m military revolver he would put to his head if his recurring nightmare proved true, if his fighter became a "flamer." He and his comrades pulled silk stockings over their heads to keep sweat from their eyes before donning their fur-lined caps and goggles. They put on paper and silk gloves for added warmth before slipping into their mittens.

The flight commander shouted out the final instructions for the rendezvous point. Then the pilot's first mechanic motioned that his bus was ready, and he climbed into the cockpit and adjusted his goggles as his second mechanic buckled his seat straps.

The flight commander briefly gave his motor full gas. His little fighter quivered and shoved against the wheel

French mechanics checking out their pilot's Spad before patrol

chocks. Upon his salute, the mechanics jerked the chocks away and the flight commander taxied across the airfield and turned into the wind, where Capitaine Thenault stood pointing the direction for takeoff with his cane. Upon Thenault's signal the flight commander applied full throttle. The fighter's tail fishtailed, then lifted into the air, and the plane skimmed across the field and rose swiftly into the fading darkness.

The pilot taxied to his spot, the rest of the patrol in single file behind him. He pulled the throttle wide and his revolution counter soared to 1,800, producing a tremendous prop rush and roar from his motor. His pulse leapt. His throat muscles tightened. The mechanics pulled his wheel chocks away, and his Spad shot across the ground and climbed upward..

Gradually the patrol assembled in the sky as the pilots fell into formation above the rendezvous point. They tested their machine guns, then turned in unison and headed east for the front, picking up speed. A steadily increasing blast of air forced its way into the pilot's throat and nostrils. Only now that he was in the air and committed did his nerves settle down and a calmness envelope him.

Five miles from the front, the patrol flew across the staggered row of Allied observation balloons. As the American pilots neared the crisscross of lines that were the trenches, hundreds of gun flashes and exploding artillery shells arched upward through the fading darkness. Clouds of smoke rose high into the air as the battlefield, an inconceivable pockmarked desolation, took a further savaging from the cannon fire.

Soon after the patrol had passed over the forward German trenches, puffs of coal-black smoke stained the air before him. The pilot's mind flashed back to his cubicle, to his foot locker containing the "To whom it may concern" letter with his instructions in the event of his death. "Is this my last patrol?" he wondered. "Will I soon die?" Fear gripped his heart and he fought the compulsion to turn his ship around. A missfiring engine. A jammed gun block. Who could blame him? His face flushed hot with shame despite the tremendous blast from his propeller. Glancing quickly about at his comrades, he flew on toward the ever-increasing wall of German antiaircraft smoke.

To reassure himself, the pilot remembered that a speeding *chasse* is rarely downed by antiaircraft fire. At that instant, a German 105 round burst very near and he suddenly lost control of his machine as the concussion lifted then dropped him violently to the bottom of the vacuum the *eclatement* had created. Four other explosions

Battle in No Man's Land.

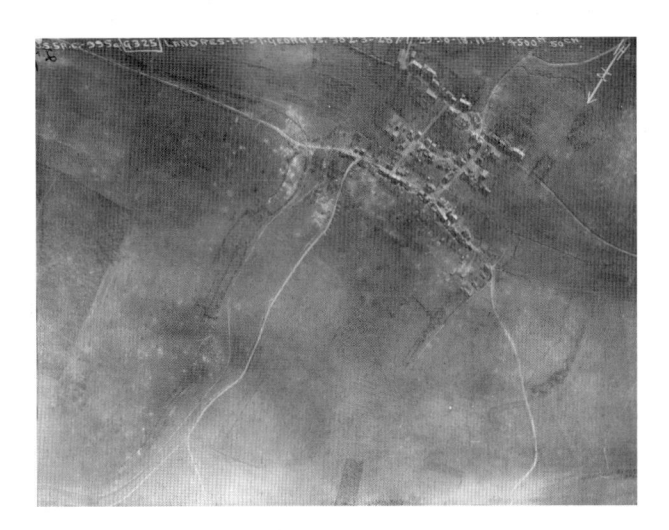

Above German-held territory

quickly followed, terrific bursts that shook his bus and surrounded him with black sooty smoke. He immediately implemented the instructions he had been taught.

"Never fly in a straight line for more than fifteen seconds. Change direction constantly, but be careful not to fly in a regularly irregular fashion. The German gunners may leave you alone at first, hoping you will become careless, or they may be plotting out your style of flight. Then they make their calculations and let you have it."

The antiaircraft fire stopped as quickly as it had begun, and the pilot knew now that he must be ever vigilant. Only at 6,000 meters or above was a patrol safe from attack by enemy *avions*, and the patrol was well below that altitude. There were too many blind spots from the cockpit of a fighter, which could hide the approach of enemy aircraft. He continued the weaving flight, which allowed him to see in all directions. At the same time he regulated his throttle to maintain his position in formation, while following his map, and keeping watch on the instruments on his dashboard to make sure they were functioning properly. The steady nerve strain proved very fatiguing.

By now the patrol had penetrated well to the rear of the attacking German army, their field guns filling the air with concussions that rocked his bus and made him feel nauseated. Suddenly, the flight commander, his rudder marked with a streamer, held up his arm and, with a turning dive, descended rapidly toward the roads below. The pilot dropped with him near to the ground, pulled up and leveled out, and was soon skimming a ruined village and shell-pocked earth. Then the pilot saw what the flight commander had seen, a row of blocky gray *camions* with helmeted men pouring out of them, their forward movements toward the Bosche lines abruptly stopped by the appearance of their aircraft..

He followed the flight commander's rapidly skimming bus as the muted staccato of his machine gun penetrated the air. Then he framed the rear camion within his ring sight and triggered the firing button on the top of his joystick. The row of vehicles quickly consumed his deadly fire before disappearing beneath his zooming Spad. As he raked the road, ground machine gun fire sprayed the sky with smoking tracers. The concussion from field guns cracking beneath him violently rocked his bus.

The pilot followed the flight commander's banking fighter as it swung wide right then passed over the murdered debris of dead horses and men, wagons, and gun limbers. He was now down under 60 meters, suddenly alone. Through the blast of his engine he imagined the screams of the thrashing horses. To his right he spotted a small clump of trees and immediately saw the square-helmeted gun crew aim up at him. Ground fire pierced the skin of his bus with a sudden unnerving *flac! flac-flac! flac!* He banked sharply and swung his Spad around, then began a straight run at the trees. He dropped the fighter's nose. The gun crew filled his sight. They fired up at him as he closed to within 90 meters before he pressed his gun trip, sweeping them with fire, then zoomed past them over the treetops. Glancing back, he saw them toss their arms into the air, then collapse against the sides of their fortification.

Overhead in the distance the pilot noticed the violent rocking of the flight commander's bus, the signal of enemy aircraft nearby. The pilot quickly gained altitude as he rushed upward to join the other Spads of the patrol. He put his thumb up against the sun and closed one eye and quickly saw the reason for the flight commander's frantic gestures, a layer of rainbow-colored Fokkers 1,200 meters above and to the east. The lead Fokker's nose had already dropped, its guns rattling, the pack quickly following. As smoke from their tracers shredded the air around the small American patrol, the Lafayette pilots scattered. Now it was every man for himself.

The instant the pilot had spotted the fast-closing enemy formation, he knew it was hopeless to continue to rise and face them. He opened his throttle wide and turned tightly toward home, following the rest of the patrol.

His ears filled with the sharp cracking *raffle* of the enemy's guns as pencil lines of blue smoke stabbed the air beside his head. Glancing back, his heart clenched when he spotted a fast-closing blue nose. With a loud *whang-g-g* one of his bracing wires was shot through. He kicked his rudder bar, flapping the rudder back and forth to throw off the German pilot's aim.

Hurling forward with diving momentum, the Fokker swiftly shot under the pilot's Spad. Its lozenged fuselage of light-pink, purple, deep-blue, green, and yellow resurfaced before his gunsights not 30 yards away. The German pilot, his goggles reflecting the sun, glanced frantically back over his shoulder, his mouth wide with surprise.

The American pilot lined his sights on the Fokker's fuselage just behind the pilot's head and pressed his gun trip. His tracers blasted harmlessly past the enemy bus. He released a second burst. His Vickers gun popped, then jammed, and he frantically hammered the gun's crank handle with a mallet to free the bulging cartridge.

With the American pilot's focus now broken, the enemy pilot swoop upward and away. As he pounded on the crank handle, the Fokker quickly returned, looming large in his mirror. It had rolled in behind him and fired. He knew he was a dead man.

Now dangerously unarmed, the American pilot dropped his nose and flew full throttle toward the safety of Allied lines. Panic stricken, he fought the urge to fly a straight course but kicked his rudder bar continually, zizagging to keep the enemy's sights off his back. For a second time the Fokker overshot him. Unarmed, he could do nothing but flee homeward. At that instant a Spad fighter penetrated his field of vision from the right. He heard its guns *raffle* as it hurled across his nose, just meters from his propeller.

Out the side of his cockpit, he watched a cloud of white vapor issue from the enemy bus. The Fokker's fuel

Pilots decompressing at Chaudun following a dawn patrol. Sitting, left to right: *Lovell, Willis, Masson, Johnson, Haviland, Dugan, Parsons.* Standing, left to right: *Soubiran, Bigelow, Peterson, Hill, Lufbery.*

tank had been hit, and it heeled over violently, then exploded, filling the air with fragments. Its fuselage plummeted vertically at tremendous speed, trailing blackish smoke until it struck the earth. As his rescuer followed it down, he quickly checked his clock and altimeter, then glanced all about him. No enemy aircraft was visible, only the lone Spad in the distance with an Indian Head on its side. Who, he wondered, had been his rescuer? By now, the other pilots of the patrol should have neared the Allied balloon lines.

In the closing distance he could see the enemy frontline trenches and no-man's land. The artillery barrage had stopped and the two armies clashed in desperate action. The murdered strip of brown earth between the trenches suddenly appeared. And when the entire sky before his Spad blackened with bursting shrapnel, he knew no enemy buses would be following him. The *rang! rang!* of closely bursting shells and the concussion of antiaircraft fire lifted his machine, then dropped it with a sickening motion. Once free of the storm, he rubbed his goggles with his mitten, then rechecked his instruments.

Once over French airspace, when he spotted the Allied balloon lines a calming enveloped him. Above was the sun and the dazzling white clouds; below, the alternating lights and shades of cloud patterns on the earth.

He skimmed the top of a row of fortified hills. Soon he passed a cathedral spire and closely clustered red-tiled roofs, then woods and quilted green and brown pastures and fields with peasants working them.

The pilot cut back his motor. Immediately the air grew warmer and less noisy. He pointed his nose earthward and banked as hills and irregularities grew visible. Moving forms became men as he neared the Nissen huts and Bessonneau hangers.

He continued to circle the aerodrome until he had lined up his approach. Then he dropped down just above the sheds, gliding swiftly over the muddy field at 50 miles an hour. He felt the sudden, slight jar as the Spad's wheels joined the muddy airfield. His tail quickly dropped and dragged for a quarter mile before his fighter stopped. He sped up his motor and taxied back toward his hangar and his two waiting mechanics.

The mechanics rushed to meet him once he had fully stopped and had cut his motor, their faces at once showing concern and happiness. They spoke quickly as they unbuckled his safety harness and helped him from his cockpit. But the engine's roar had temporarily deafened him, and he could not hear their words. And yet he knew what they were asking him, as they had before. He assured them he was all right as he removed his flying cap. His weakened legs nearly buckled as he dropped to earth. Rivulets of sweat coursed down his face as he and his crew surveyed the battle damage to his fighter.

The pilot counted the Spads parked on the tarmac. All but one was in its place. Who, he wondered, would be absent for mess? His hearing had gradually returned, though his ears ached horribly from the sudden changes in altitude.

Moments later he gathered with the other pilots of the patrol at the Bureau du Groupe. He was surprised and grateful to see that everyone had come home. He suddenly felt very thirsty and ravenously hungry. The pilots began filling out their reports, their faces dirty, pale, and nerve strained. The room quickly filled with frantic gestures and excited voices as his comrades recounted combats and narrow escapes, which sounded like impossible fiction.

The pilot had been all right in the air. But he grew panicky now that he was on ground and safely home. The room constricted around him. A bottle of cognac and glasses were passed about. He grabbed the bottle and poured a glassful, needing both hands to bring it to his lips. He drank deeply, then snatched up bread and tore at it with his teeth. The effect of the alcohol on his stomach was immediate. He grew relaxed and very tired. He quickly scribbled out his *Compte Rendu*, his summary of the events of his patrol. In the "Remarks" column, he wrote "*Rein a' signaler*"—nothing to report. He couldn't think now. He would correct it later. He had to get out.

Once out the door, he heard an approaching aircraft. He looked up and followed a squadron's Spad coming in from the east. Was it the missing one from the tarmac? The Spad swooped down, touched the ground, taxied in, and quickly stopped. He didn't recognize the pilot until the pilot faced him and lifted his goggles. Then he knew immediately who it was but was surprised to see that it was Lufbery.

Days earlier, the cold and damp had doubled Lufbery up with rheumatism. And the captain had ordered his premier pilot to southern France in hope that the warm sunshine would bake it out of him. There had been no forewarning of his return to the squadron. The pilot later learned that Lufbery had arrived that morning shortly after the patrol had left the field. He had quickly donned his flight suit, climbed into a parked Spad, and immediately rose to air. The grateful pilot now knew who had saved his life, just as Lufbery had saved Bobbie Soubiran's life a few weeks ago by diving on and scattering four enemy machines, thus allowing Soubiran to escape.

Lufbery returns to the squadron unannounced. Left to right: *Major Fequant, Captain Thenault, Thaw, Lufbery.*

Lufbery held up a gloved fist. The pilot smiled and acknowledged his gesture. Then he watched as Lufbery swung his Spad around, taxied down the runway, and rose swiftly east in the direction of the front.

The pilot staggered wearily back to to his barracks cubicle, where he would try to sleep until the afternoon patrol. He collapsed upon his cot, still in his flying suit.

"It's not death I fear," he thought. "Once it was, but not now. It's the constant flinching from it that is making me a coward. I'm twenty-seven years old. I look forty. And I have no purpose in life beyond the next patrol."

He fought to put all thoughts away, to sleep. He had nearly won the battle when someone in the messroom had begun humming that damned British tune a 54 Squadron pilot had taught them. He knew the words as well as he knew the pounding of his heart, and he turned to the wall and covered his ears.

"For a batman woke me from my bed;
I'd had a thick night and a very sore head
And I said to myself, to myself I said:
"Oh, we haven't got a hope in the morning!"'

Lafayette Escadrille Pilot Combat Patrols

Raoul Lufbery joined the Lafayette Escadrille at Bar-le-Duc on 24 May 1916, approximately one month after the seven original pilots arrived at the front. He flew more combat patrols and accumulated more hours in the air than any of the other thirty-seven American pilots on the squadron's roster. He scored sixteen of the squadron's thirty-five confirmed victories while flying 295 patrols, a ratio of one victory for every eighteen patrols. The other pilots scored nineteen victories while flying 3,280 patrols, or one victory for every 172 patrols.

Lafayette Escadrille Pilot	Patrols	Duration
Lufbery, Raoul	295	477 hours, 5 minutes
Thaw, William	190	275 hours, 40 minutes
Bridgman, Ray	178	284 hours, 45 minutes
Hill, Dudley	158	216 hours
Rockwell, Robert	155	211 hours, 25 minutes
DeLaage deMeux, Alfred	147	240 hours
Jones, Henry	142	184 hours, 30 minutes
Marr, Kenneth	134	187 hours, 10 minutes
Soubiran, Robert	131	206 hours, 50 minutes
Parsons, Edwin	128	177 hours, 20 minutes
Peterson, David	121	171 hours, 35 minutes
Johnson, C. Choteau	112	139 hours, 5 minutes
Willis, Harold	112	172 hours, 10 minutes
Dugan, William	111	145 hours, 55 minutes
Lovell, Walter	104	137 hours, 25 minutes
Rockwell, Kiffin	100	185 hours, 40 minutes
Thenault, Georges	98	150 hours, 25 minutes
Prince, Norman	94	175 hours, 45 minutes
Campbell, A. Courtney	90	117 hours, 30 minutes
Dolan, Charles	90	120 hours, 15 minutes
McConnell, James	89	109 hours, 15 minutes
DeMaison Rouge, Antoine	88	96 hours, 15 minutes
Haviland, Willis	79	110 hours, 40 minutes
Hall, James	74	99 hours, 45 minutes
Masson, Didier	73	115 hours, 50 minutes
Ford, Christopher	61	69 hours, 35 minutes
Hewitt, Thomas	59	70 hours, 10 minutes
Hall, Bert	51	86 hours, 25 minutes
Hoskier, Ronald	42	60 hours, 10 minutes
Genet, Edmond	39	65 hours, 10 minutes
Chapman, Victor	37	71 hours
Rumsey, Laurence	36	65 hours
Pavelka, Paul	34	48 hours, 30 minutes
MacMonagle, Douglas	33	48 hours, 25 minutes
Hinkle, Edward	25	27 hours, 35 minutes
Drexel, John	23	29 hours, 45 minutes
Doolitte, James	16	28 hours, 15 minutes
Cowdin, Elliot	15	20 hours
Balsley, H. Clyde	11	18 hours
Prince, Frederick	?	?
Bigelow, Stephen	??	

Raoul Lufbery Official and Probable Victories

1916	Aircraft Type	Location
1. 30 July	two-seater	Foret d' Etain (W. Etain) Verdun Sector
2. 31 July	two-seater	Fort Vaux
3. 4 August	two-seater	Aboucort
4. 8 August	Aviatik C.	N.E.. Douaumont (S. Douaumont)
5. 12 October	Roland C.II	Oberndorf
(P) 9 November		Ablaincourt
(P) 10 November		Haplincourt
(P) 4 December		E. Chaulnes
6. 27 December	Aviatic C	S.E. Chaulnes

1917		
7. 24 January	Aviatic C	Chaulnes-Peronne
(P) 8 April	enemy aircraft	Mont Sapignerel
8. 13 April	two-seater	N.W. St. Quentin
9. 24 April	Aviatic C	E, Cerisy
10. 12 June	two- seater	Sapignal (Aguilcourt)
11. 4 Sept.	Rumpler C	E. Cheppy (Cheppy)
(P) 5 Sept.	enemy aircraft	Louvermont
(P)* 6 Sept.	enemy aircraft	Bezonvaux
12. 22 Sept.	two-seater	Bois de Cheppy (E. Cheppy)
(P) 22 Sept.	enemy aircraft	Cheppy
13. 16 October	two-seater	Vauxillon (Hurtebise)
14. 24 October	two-seater	Courtecon
(P) 24 October	two-seater	Chaignon-Urcel
(P) 24 October	scout	Urcel
(P) 24 October	two-seater	Urcel
(P) 24 October	enemy aircraft	Urcel
15. 2 Dec.	two-seater	S. Ployart
16. 2 Dec.	two-seater	Laval

1918		
(P) 12 April	Albatross DIII	Xivray
(P) 27 April		

Confirmed Victories: 16
Probable Victories: 13

* *Journal des Marches et Operations Escadrille N.124* shows no flight for Lufbery on September 6, but it does show one on September 7.

(P) Indicates Probable Victory

Source: Frank W. Bailey and Christopher Cony, *The French Air Service War Chronology, 1914–1918: Day-to-Day Claims and Losses by French Fighter, Bomber and Two-Seat Pilots on the Western Front* (London: Grubb Street, 2001).

The Bottle Of Death

On the morning of 18 May 1916, Caporal Kiffin Rockwell, on his fourth patrol, flew a history-making sortie over the front. Upon crossing the enemy lines near Thann, his engine began to cough and sputter. As he turned back toward his aerodrome, he spotted a German LVG reconnaissance plane 2,000 feet beneath him. Kiffin prepared to fight his first combat. He immediately pushed in his throttle and nosed his Nieuport downward.

As he swooped down on the enemy bus, he watched the gunner quickly alert the pilot. The pilot sped toward his lines as the gunner trained a burst of fire on Rockwell's Nieuport.

Kiffin felt his fighter shudder as he closed the distance. His main wing spar had been struck by an enemy round. But as he later described it, "I didn't pay any attention to that and kept going straight for him, until I got within 25 or 30 meters of him."

Only when Kiffin thought he would ram the enemy plane did he fire four rounds from his Lewis gun and swerve sharply right at the last instant to avoid a collision. Incredibly, Rockwell's shots did mortal damage. Glancing back, he saw the German gunner fall backward toward the pilot, who was already crumpled up in the forward cockpit.

The LVG fell off on one wing, then dropped into a vertical dive. Three minutes later it hit the ground in flames, billowing a plume of black, greasy smoke just inside enemy lines. The victory, the first for Rockwell, and the first for the American squadron, was confirmed by a French observation post, which quickly telephoned the news back to Luxeuil.

The Lafayette Escadrille Kentucky Bourbon "Bottle of Death," 4 August 1989. It had just been removed from the attic of the Franco-American Museum at Bleranouurt, France, where it had been stored for three decades.

By the time Kiffin had returned to the aerodrome, his comrades were on the tarmac waiting to congratulate him. They rushed his Nieuport, and, cheering, they lifted him from his plane. And as his friend, James McConnell, noted with envy, "All Luxeuil smiled upon him—particularly the girls." Word of his victory soon reached Paris, where it also caused "a tremendous wave of excitement."

Kiffin's brother, Paul, was working in Paris as a correspondent at the time of the announcement. He rushed a congratulatory letter to his brother, then mailed him a bottle of Kentucky bourbon. Once it reached Luxeuil, Kiffin poured himself a shot, then handed the bottle to Victor Chapman. Chapman declined to drink and instead suggested that the bourbon be saved "for rare occasions."

Chapman went on to explain that each pilot who shot down a German plane should be "entitled to one slug." Thus, a ceremony was instituted that saw a number of pilots drink from what was later called the "Bottle of Death" until the bourbon bottle was finally drained. The name of the victorious pilot and the date of his kill were written on the back of the label. A total of twenty-eight slugs were drunk from the bottle. But if the French pilots in the squadron were also allowed a slug, Lt. DeLaage would have gotten three and Lt. Charles Nungesser would have gotten one.

Raoul Lufbery was awarded sixteen slugs for his numerous victories. Here is the list of the squadron's other pilots who swallowed the vintage bourbon from the Bottle of Death:

Kiffin Rockwell at Behonne, summer of 1916, seated in the cockpit of his Nieuport 11 fighter N.1148, regulating his Lewis machine gun. A mechanic, far left, *loads one of Rockwell's forty-seven-round magazines with .303 caliber ammunition.*

- Bert Hall, three slugs
- James Normal Hall, one. He took the last drink from the bottle for his 1 January 1918 victory.
- Willis Haviland, one
- Charles Johnson, one
- Walter Lovell, one
- Kenneth Marr, one
- Didier Masson, one
- Ted Parsons, one
- David Peterson, one
- Kiffin Rockwell, two
- Norman Prince, three. He was entitled to one more slug but died of injuries before he could drink it.
- William Thaw, two

When the squadron disbanded, Major Thaw took possession of the bottle. After the war he returned to Pittsburgh and stored the bottle with the rest of his war mementos in the attic of Morewood Place, the Thaw family mansion. Not long after William's father, Benjamin Thaw, passed away, the mansion was boarded over. William, its last occupant, took up residence in the Schenley Apartments.

In April 1934 Thaw had gone to the mansion to sort out his war mementos, which had lain dusty and neglected in the attic. Among the artifacts were an Indian Head insignia from Lufbery's fighter plane, and the Bottle of Death. A lethargy permeated Thaw, the result of Bright's disease. Of late he had been feverish, and when he returned to his apartment, he collapsed into unconsciousness. He died on 22 April 1934. He was forty years of age.

Over time, the bottle found its way to the Franco-American Museum at Blerancourt, France, where it was stored in the attic for many years. When it was brought out of storage in 1989, it was in poor condition. Not knowing the significance of the bottle, a museum staff member discarded it into a wastebasket. An American historian doing research at Blerancourt at the time recognized the significance of the bottle and retrieved it. He informed the staff of its significance, and eventually the museum put the bottle on exhibit.

Paris

Paris remained an ever-popular destination for the Lafayette Escadrille pilots *en repos*. The aviation groupe bar and the cafés in the villages near the aerodrome offered pale relief from the war's drudgery. And as pilot Edwin Parsons noted, they were no substitute for the good food, fine wine, and loose women of Paris: Parsons later recalled:

> Taking it all in all, our squadron life was very quiet, and we existed only for times we could wrangle a leave to go to Paris. Then we tried to crowd all the excitement and general hell-raising we could into a few short hours. I'm far from being the only man who has mournfully remarked after a hectic 48 hours among the houris and bright lights of the Big Sinful City, "Gosh, I gotta go back to the front to rest." Despite its hazards, it was a haven of rest for the weary."

But not all of the American pilots sought escape through female companionship or through drink and conversation at the Chatham Bar or at Harry's Place, the favorite rendezvous spots. For Edmond Genet, Paris leave gave him the opportunity to attend religious services. Other pilots visited relatives who were a part of the American colony or who were involved with Paris-based relief agencies such as the American Red Cross or the American ambulances services. Ronald Hoskier's parents both worked for the Red Cross, as did Minnie MacMonagle, the mother of Douglas MacMonagle, who owned a Paris apartment. Sadly, both grieving mothers would attend their son's funerals.

Pilot Willis Haviland's mother, Grace Haviland, left the United States when he entered aviation school at Pau. She settled in Paris so she could see her son when he took leave. William Thaw's sister, Henrietta Thaw Slade, also had a Paris apartment at 148 Rue de Longchamp, which served as a hangout for the pilots. Victor Chapman spent many hours there reading books from her library.

The Paris apartment of Alice Weeks became another gathering point and temporary shelter for American volunteers *en repos*. In 1915 Mrs. Weeks had taken up residence in Paris in order to be nearer to her son, Kenneth, who had joined the French Foreign Legion. He was killed in combat on 16 June 1915. Following his death, she served as the hostess and benefactor to many American volunteers, including the squadron's pilots. The American volunteers serving in the Foreign Legion officially voted her "Mother" because of her tireless work on their behalf, which was all done at her own expense.

Raoul Lufbery often chose to leave Paris to his comrades except when he was required to attend an official event. This stemmed partly from an incident in late August 1916 that led to his arrest after he punched a train station ticket taker in the jaw for grabbing his arm then was turned into the *gendarmes* by the station master.

Had Lufbery chosen to do so, he could have lived lavishly on the monetary prizes he had earned from the Lafayette Flying Corps fund for the downing of so many enemy aircraft. Instead, he journeyed to Chamalieres, the home of his youth, to reconnect with family members. Or he visited Princess Ghika, the mother of his deceased friend Marc Pourpe at Clos Marie, her stone villa, which sat in the Roscoff commune in Brittany in northwestern France, five hours from Paris by rail.

Special celebratory events or funerals also provided the opportunity for old comrades to gather together on leave, such as the 2 April 1917 morning service held in James McConnell's honor at the American Church in Paris, or the 14 June 1917 event at France's Aeronautique League, when six of the squadrons pilots were presented with the Aero Club of France medal, or the 1917 Fourth of July celebration in honor of America's Independence Day.

Lafayette Escadrille and Flying Corps pilots at the funeral of James McConnell at the American Church in Paris, 2 April 1917. Left to right: Robert Donze, Granville Pollock, Frederick Prince, Paul Rockwell, Charles Johnson, Robert Soubiran, Didier Masson.

American Foreign Legionnaire Paul Pavelka on leave with Paul Rockwell at Place de la Concorde, Paris, November 1916. Pavelka had just left the trenches in Champagne. His uniform is soiled from the mud and blood of the battlefield. Nearly a pound of shrapnel was picked from the lining of his greatcoat. Pavelka joined the Lafayette Escadrille on 11 August 1916.

Some American Legionnares who hoped to transfer to the United States Army at Place des Etats-Unis, Paris 4 July 1917. Front row, left to right: Christopher Charles, Eugene Jacob, Fred Zinn, Adj. Albanel(Zinn's French pilot), Raoul Lufbery, Andrew Walborn. Back row, left to right: Jack Moyet, Algernon Sartoris, Guy Agostini, Robert Mulhauser, Paul Rockwell, Willis Haviland, Jack Moyet, William Parington.

Lafayette Escadrille pilots on cannon barrel in front of Hotel des Invalides, Paris, 4 July 1917, celebrating Independence Day. Left to right: *Robert Rockwell, Charles Johnson, Dudley Hill, Edgar Bouligny (LFC), Didier Masson, William Thaw, Raoul Lufbery, Robert Soubiran, Paul Rockwell.*

Lt. Raoul Lufbery in Paris at the wheel of his Hispano Suiza Alfonso XIII roadster. The auto was a 1917 gift from the Hispano Suiza company, which made the engine for his Spad fighter. Raoul's association with the firm was via his success with their engine in aerial combat. His picture and combat profile appeared in their July 1918 instruction manual for the Hispano Suiza aeronautical engine.

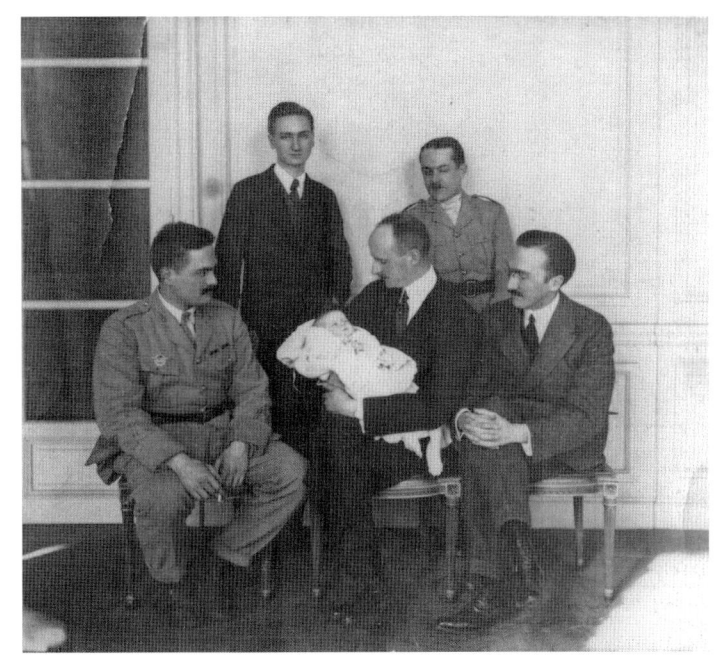

William Thaw at the Paris apartment of his sister, Henrietta Thaw Slade. Left to right: *William Thaw, brother Alexander Blair Thaw, Lawrence Slade holding daughter Elma, Charles Johnson, brother Benjamin Thaw. Alexander Blair Thaw would later become the commanding officer of the US 138th Aero Squadron at age nineteen. First Lieutenant Thaw would be killed in a plane crash in France on 19 August 1918.*

Right to left: Alice Weeks, William Thaw, Edward Hinkle, Walter Lovell, Harold Willis. Paris, 1917.

Herman and Harriet Hoskier, the parents of Lafayette Escadrille pilot Ronald Hoskier. Herman was a section chief with Richard Norton's Ambulance Service. Harriet served as a Red Cross volunteer in Paris.

Gathering at Aeronautique League of France, Paris, 14 June 1917, for the presentation of the Great Medal of the Aero Club of France to French pilots and American volunteer pilots. Standing, left to right: Adj. Jailler, Sgt. Lovell, Lt. Lufbery, Sgt. Johnson, Sgt. Haviland, Capt. Thenault, Willis, Lt. Henri Languedoc, Lt. Tourday, Lt. Hector Vardin, Lt. Thaw. Seated, left to right: Lt. Albert Deullin, Capt. Alfred Heurtaux, Capt. Georges Guynemer, Lt. Paul Tarascon, Capt. Andre Watteau. By war's end, the pilots in this photograph had destroyed a total of one-hundred fifty enemy aircraft.

The Lafayette Escadrille Mascots

Raoul Lufbery had a fondness for all pet dogs, especially springer spaniels. He bonded with them for their unwavering loyalty and companionship. Raoul noted that most dogs remained faithful to their masters and could be counted on as part of a working team. They offered unconditional acceptance and were free of human flaws and social shortcomings. Raoul also felt that humans could not always be counted upon to do the same as their pets under similar circumstances.

Raoul was the caring master to the numerous mascots that shared the Lafayette Escadrille's airfield and barracks. Canines frequently appear with the pilots in many images. The most ubiquitous was "Fram," Captain Thenault's police dog. Other canines who provided companionship to the pilots were the Captain's two spaniel pups. Then there was "Pete Black," William Thaw's Belgian police dog; "Tiny," the fox terrier whom Lt. DeLaage had found taking refuge in the ruins of Soisson; and "Juzo," the chow chow who no one seemed to claim and who thought of himself as a lion.

A diverse menagerie of wild animals also populated the squadron's aerodrome. Bert Hall owned an African genet, a catlike mammal that had been gifted to him by a Senegalese chief who was serving in the French army and was encamped with his tribal warriors near the squadron. William Thaw owned a pet fox that was killed by a soldier while playing on the airfield. But the squadron's two most famous pets were "Whiskey" and "Soda," their two African lions who had free range of the squadron's airplane hangars and airfields.

On 13 September 1916 the squadron was in transit from Bar-le-Duc to the Luxeuil airfield. Its pilots made a seventy-two-hour Paris stopover. While Dudley Hill was perusing the classified section of the Paris edition of the *New York Herald,* he spotted an ad offering a four-month-old lion cub for sale. The pilots were later to learn that the dentist who owned the cub and who had placed the ad had initially bought the animal to entertain his patients. But his clients had become unnerved by its roaring and the baring of its claws. The cub had been born in the Marseilles harbor. Its mother belonged to a lion tamer who was on his way to the United States.

Hill discussed the purchase of the cub with fellow pilots Bert Hall, Chouteau Johnson, Kiffin Rockwell, and William Thaw, and all agreed that such an exotic pet would make an ideal mascot for the American squadron.

Raoul Lufbery holds Captain Thenault's two spaniel pups.

They pooled their resources to reach the five-hundred-franc asking price. After purchasing the cub, the dentist informed them that the lion required 8 quarts of milk a day, which he had been feeding to him from a baby bottle.

Once the pilots had taken charge of the lion, they took him on their rounds as they celebrated their leave. As William York Stevenson, an American driver in the Ambulance Service, noted in his diary entry for 23 September 1916:

> Culby ran into the American Flying Squad in Paris. They were in the process of being transferred from Verdun to the Vosges and were celebrating. They had somewhere purchased a young lion cub, which they dragged around from hotel to hotel for five days, much to the consternation of the inhabitants and to the annoyance of the lion, which kept up a steady stream of growls and snarls. He had only just been weaned and liked to have a finger to suck: but if the owner wished to withdraw it, there was nothing doing until the lion wanted him to. Culby had to sit perfectly still with his finger in its mouth for an hour, and he said it was the worst experience he's had since Verdun.

When the pilots' leave had expired, the problem became how to get their new mascot from Paris to their quarters at Luxeuil. Thaw decided they would pass it off as a dog and purchased a dog's fare, then got the lion onto the train without difficulty. But when the conductor came by the Americans' compartment to punch their tickets, he looked quizzically at the cub and asked Thaw what kind of animal it was.

"An African dog," Thaw replied. But at that instant the young lion released a loud roar and bared his claws, terrifying some female passengers. The station master appeared and ordered the lion off the train. As the other American pilots headed back to Luxeuil, Thaw was forced to seek out a carpenter to construct a cage for his "dog," who later rode to Luxeuil in a luggage car.

One evening while the pilots were in their quarters shortly after their return to the squadron, someone had filled a saucer with whiskey, then placed it at the lion cub's feet to test its reaction. Upon first taste the cub drew back but then approached the saucer and had soon lapped the plate dry, whereupon "he roared like a lion should." Someone immediately christened him

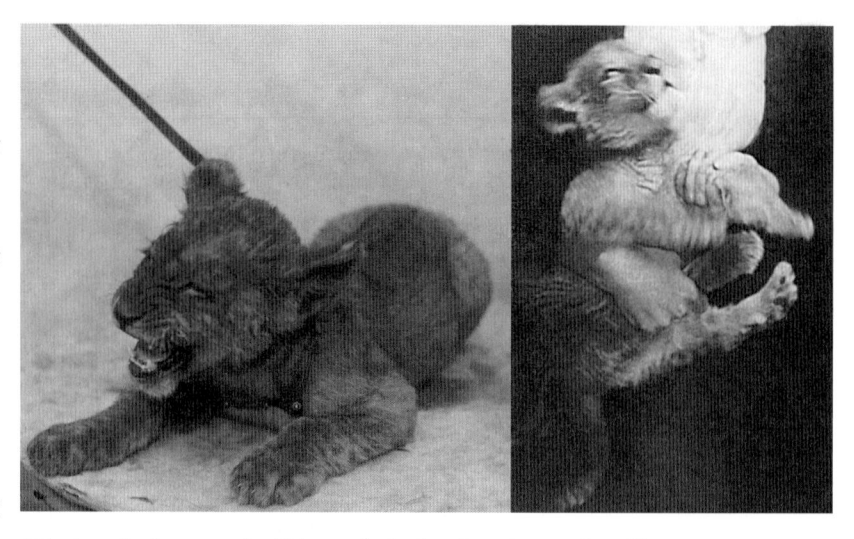

Whiskey, the four-month-old lion cub the day the pilots purchased him in Paris, 13 September 1916. On the right is Soda, the cub lioness, the day she was purchased by William Thaw and Lt. DeLaage in Paris, 17 March 1917.

"Whiskey," and before long his reputation had spread the full length of the western front as he attracted hordes of visitors to the squadron during his tenure there.

Whiskey was immediately accepted by the American pilots, who petted and pampered him and found constant amusement with him. And because of the steady attention he received from the pilots, he was soon following them around, a docile and lovable playmate rarely known to bite and scratch. However, on 14 March 1917 Whiskey did deeply scratch Edmond Genet's left wrist, forcing him to have the wound cauterized to prevent infection.

Whiskey and Soda with "Juzo", the chow chow who thought he was a lion

As the lion matured, it bonded with Captain Thenault's dog, Fram, and to the other dogs of the squadron and would roll and frolic on the floor with them. Edmond Genet wrote this of Whiskey in a 13 February 1917 letter to a friend:

> He really don't know whether he's a lion or a dog. More than likely he thinks he's the latter, for all the animals he has ever seen or played with have been dogs and his real companion is this terrier who sleeps with him every night.

That was "Tiny," the fox terrier. Genet also noted that

> Whiskey is some lively pup and quite playful though he growls as though he was angry at everyone including himself. We can take him up in our arms and fondle him, and while we are eating at the table he goes racing around the table from one to the other and climbs up with his great clumsy paws on the table's edge to beg loudly for his share.

One annoying habit that the lion would never outgrow was his natural instinct to gnaw on whatever was available. As pilot Edward Hinkle remembered, Whiskey was "particularly fond of gold braid and fancy uniform decorations." Approximately a month after the squadron's move to Cachy, Whiskey paid a severe penalty for "this annoying habit of chewing up things." On one bitter evening in mid-November 1916 as the pilots were huddled around a table playing cards, Whiskey made short work of Laurence Rumsey's kepi. Enraged, Rumsey struck the lion with a walking stick, severely damaging the optic nerve of its right eye. The next day William Thaw took Whiskey to a Paris oculist, but in spite of his efforts to save his vision, the lion's eye soon clouded into a milky orb.

But even this painful lesson failed to curb Whiskey's omnivorous appetite for "expensive fur coats, hats, leather jackets, etc.," and in order to save their wardrobes, the pilots were forced to keep their belongings in their footlockers or on shelves near the ceilings of the barracks.

As Whiskey reached 200 pounds at full maturity, his fur developed a malodorous air. This odor was hidden under *eau de cologne* whenever he served in an official capacity. Edwin Parsons also remembered how the lion had an extreme case of halitosis, which Parsons nevertheless overlooked in his desperate effort to find warmth in the leaky Cachy barracks. As Parsons later remembered:

Above: *Elliot Cowdin and Captain Thenault putting his German shepherd "Fram" and William Thaw's Belgian police dog "Pete Black" through their paces*

> There weren't enough blankets to go around in Cachy. That is where I learned to sleep with the Lion to keep warm. It had its advantages but also its disadvantages as his fur smelled pretty high and he had a definite case of halitosis. I would put him at my feet to keep them warm and would eventually wind up using him as a pillow as he would work his way to the top of the bed.

While the squadron was at Saint-Juste the men decided that Whiskey needed a female companion. Eventually they located one in Paris, and with everyone chipping in, William Thaw and Lieutenant deLaage purchased her and brought her back to the squadron on 18 March 1917. The men named the cub lioness "Soda." However, Soda soon proved fickle, with a temperament the antithesis of Whiskey's. As Edward Hinkle later recalled:

> While Whiskey and Soda were compatible as their names imply, the lioness was surly to humans and never became a favorite with the crew. In fact, she was "always spitting, clawing, and scratching" and would not allow herself to be petted or fondled by anyone but Lufbery, the only pilot for whom she was "good and gentle." As Whiskey before her, she too had adopted the great pilot as her master and immediately recognized him amongst the others. Lufbery was the one person that could always control and play roughhouse games with Whiskey. The enjoyment and bond shared by this "king of the jungle" and by this outstanding "hunter" combat pilot was truly remarkable.

With the acquisition of Soda, public interest in the mascots compounded. James Norman Hall noted that:

> hundreds of Chasseurs have visited our aerodrome during the past week, mainly, I think, for a glimpse of Whiskey and Soda, our lions, who are known to French soldiers from one end of the line to the other. Whiskey is almost full-grown and Soda about the size of a wild cat. They have the freedom of the camp and run about everywhere.

When the two lions were not roaming free or sleeping in the pilot's quarters, they were kept near the squadron's kitchen in an open airplane engine box surrounded by chicken wire. During the day they provided amusement for the pilots. Once Whiskey was pitted against a boar, another squadron's mascot. But he soon proved a cowardly lion and, as Carl Dolan remembered, "was too scared to fight much of a match."

Whiskey's favorite pastime was to wrestle with Lufbery. A kinship had immediately developed between the great hunter, Lufbery, and the "Whiskey Man" who adored him, and with an absolute devotion the cub would instantly come running at Lufbery's command. As Captain Thenault later recalled:

> It was a sight to see the brave Whiskey, when he spotted Lufbery, hurl himself upon him at full gallop as if to devour him, but it was to devour him with the caresses of a lion who can hide its terrible claws so as not to harm his friends.

One trick the two performed together was for Lufbery to plant Whiskey in an ambush against some unsuspecting *poilu* who had been visiting the squadron for the purpose of viewing the mascots. On Lufbery's command, the lion would bound from his hiding place and pounce on the terrified visitor, usually driving the unfortunate soldier to the ground, whereupon Whiskey would "put his head back and open his mouth wide, showing all his yellowed fangs in a silent laugh."

It was Whiskey's dubious fondness for "gold braid and fancy uniform decorations" that ultimately forced the expulsion of the two lions. In October 1917, when the squadron was at Chaudun, Whiskey had picked the wrong victim, Commandant Philippe Fequant, the commander of Groupe de Combat 13. The lion had playfully knocked Fequant to the ground, then had proceeded to chew up the front of his tunic and his visor cap. Enraged, Fequant had first ordered both lions shot but had then

Raoul Lufbery and Didier Masson bathing with "Fram," Captain Thenault's German shepherd

Paul Pavelka holding "Miss Tiny," the fox terrier who was discovered hiding in the ruins in Soissons by Lt. DeLaage. She became the lion Whiskey's sleeping companion.

relented and instead had ordered them to the Jardin des Plantes, a Paris zoo. Edward Hinkle, who was no longer a pilot with the squadron but paid frequent visits to the aerodrome, later recalled the sad ending to the lions' legacy, which occurred on 16 October 1917.

> After the gnawing session on a French officer's uniform while the officer was still inside it, we got the ultimatum from the Command to get rid of both lions. Luf and Whiskey were great pals, so Luf volunteered to take Whiskey to the Paris Zoo. I went along. It was a great lark for Whiskey, who loved to ride. He sat between us in the front of the truck. It was a sad thing to see the cage door close on him. We visited Whiskey whenever we had Paris leave, and he always recognized us. Both Whiskey and Soda died soon after the war of rheumatism, or maybe loneliness.

But before Whiskey passed on, he had the opportunity to destroy one more French uniform. Pilot Dudley Hill made a trip to a Paris tailor shop to pick up a new Horizon Blue French uniform to replace his old oil-soaked service uniform. Once he had donned his natty threads, he decided to pay a visit to the Jardin des Plantes zoo to visit Whiskey and Soda.

Once at the zoo, Hill explained to Whiskey's keeper his relationship with the animals and managed to talk his way into the lion's cage. The instant the half-blind Whiskey spotted the half-blind aviator, the lion was so overjoyed at seeing his old squadron mate, he bounded up to him, planted his huge paws on Hill's shoulders in a welcoming embrace, and drove the unprepared Hill in his new uniform into the mire at the bottom of the cage. There, Whiskey continued to express his affection by mauling Hill with his teeth and paws, much to the delight of the gathering crowd who viewed the spectacle as an act staged for their benefit. The crowd acknowledged their appreciation and delight through raucous laughter and applause.

Whiskey gently nuzzles Raoul Lufbery while Dr. Manet, the squadron's doctor, looks on.

Whiskey and Soda express their affection for Raoul Lufbery, Chaudun, October 1917.

Raoul Lufbery's Medals

Listed here are the Civilian Awards and Military Decorations that Raoul Lufbery received up until the date of his death in aerial combat on 19 May 1918.

Kim-Tein, the "Golden Sapec"

This was the first decoration awarded to Raoul Lufbery. Following an aerial exhibit at Tonkin, he and Marc Pourpe left Annam (central Vietnam) for Hue, the capital of the Nguyen dynasty, where they met young King Duy, who decorated them both on 28 June 1913. As Lufbery recalled:

> To Marc Pourpe he gave the Kim-Kam (Kim Khanh), the highest honor of the Kingdom. I received the Kim-Tein called the Golden Sapec. He could not have pleased me better. I am very proud of it, for it is my first medal.

Lufbery considered this medal his lucky charm and always kept it with him.

Great Medal of the Aero-Club of France

This medal or medallion with its accompanying certificate was presented to Raoul Lufbery and fifteen other French pilots and American volunteer pilots at the Aeronautique League of France, Paris, 14 June 1917.

Kingdom of Montenegro Silver Medal For Bravery

This medal was awarded to Lufbery on 18 December 1917 for bravery in battle. On 27 December 1917 he proudly wrote the following to his brother Charles in Wallingford.

> Now, I am looking like a Christmas tree, medals all over my chest. The last one I was decorated with is a Montenegrin order, with a ribbon, red, blue, and white. Though it has not the value of the French Legion of Honor or the Military Medal, I am awfully proud to wear it.

He followed up with a letter the next day to his father.

> Ten days ago, I was decorated with a new medal. It was a Montenegro Order which has a ribbon red, blue, and white, awfully nice that little decoration and I am very pleased to wear it.

British Military Medal.

This medal was awarded to Lufbery on 20 May 1917. It was instituted as a gallantry award on 25 March 1916. The medal was awarded to other ranks (enlisted men) of the

Sous-lieutenant Raoul Lufbery wearing his military medals in late December 1917

British army and Commonwealth Forces, and to some Allied troops to recognize gallantry and for devotion to duty when under fire on land. The legend "For Bravery In The Field" appears on the reverse of the medal. Recipients are entitled to use the letters "M.M." at the end of their names.

French Legion of Honor

This medal was awarded to Lufbery on 29 January 1917. The medal was instituted by Napoleon I on 19 May 1802 and was awarded for distinguished military and civil services. The Order is divided into five grades: Grands Croix, Grands Officiers, Commandeurs, Officiers and Chevaliers. Lufbery received the Chevalier grade medal.

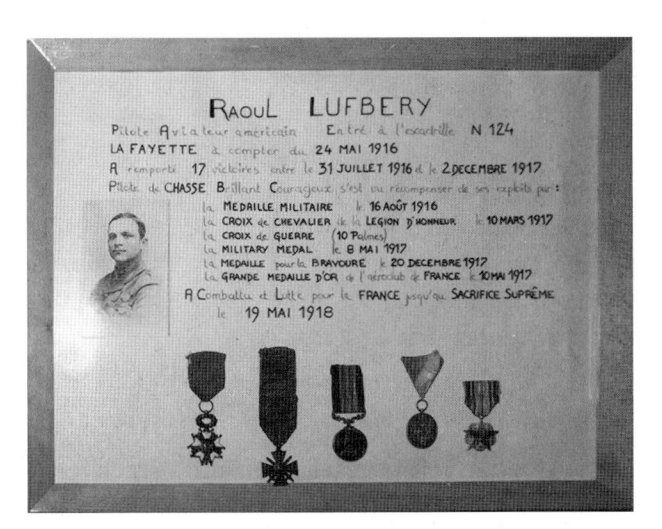

French Medaille Militaire.

This medal was awarded to Lufbery on 16 January 1916. The medal was instituted as a gallantry award in 1852. It was awarded to general officers in command of armies or admirals in command of fleets, and to noncommissioned officers of the army and navy who specially distinguish themselves in war.

French Croix de Guerre Medal

Lufbery received ten Croix de Guerre citations and awarded ten brass palms to apply to his medal ribbon, one for each mention in the Order of the Army. The medal was instituted in April 1915. It was awarded to soldiers and sailors of all ranks who were mentioned in dispatches by a general or commanding officer.

Some of Raoul Lufbery's medals on display in the clubroom of the postwar French Lafayette Escadrille at Luxeuil-les-Bains, France, as of 15 May 1980.

Raoul Lufbery's Kim-Tein Golden Sapec award presented to him by King Duy Tan at Hue, Vietnam, on 28 June 1913. This was Lufbery's first decoration.

Raoul Lufbery's medals. Top row, left to right: French Legion of Honor, French War Cross with ten palms, French Medaille Militaire. Bottom row, left to right: Kingdom of Montenegro Bravery Medal, Aero Club of France Gold medallion, British Military Medal.

LISTED HERE are the brief summaries of Raoul Lufbery's heroic achievements as they appeared on his official award documents that accompanied his medals.

FRENCH MEDAILLE MILITAIRE, issued 16 August 1916

> A model of skill, sangfroid, and courage. He has distinguished himself through the long[-]distance bombardments and by the daily combats which he has with enemy planes. On 31 July [1916] he never hesitated to attack at close range, a group of four enemy planes. He downed one of them near our lines. He succeeded in downing another on 4 August 1916.

This appointment involves the award of the Croix de Guerre, with Palm. Citation in the Order of the Army.

CROIX DE GUERRE WITH PALM issued 26 September 1916. Citation to Order of the Army. Extract from General Orders No. 410.

> A remarkable pilot. On 4 August 1916, attacked an enemy aircraft which fell on the lines. On 8 August he repeated the same exploit, the enemy machine fell in flames near Douaumont.

CROIX DE GUERRE WITH PALM issued 28 October 1916. Citation to Order of the Army Extract from General Orders No. 28.

> Brave and skillful pilot. Downed his 5th plane on 12 October during an important mission.

FRENCH LEGION D'HONNEUR CHEVALIER, issued 29 January 1917.

> Was appointed in the order of the Legion of Honor to the rank of Knight. Enlisted under the French flag for the duration of the war. Displayed remarkable skill as a fighter pilot and defeated until 27 December 1916, six enemy aircraft. Already twice cited in the Army Order and Military Medal.

This appointment involves the award of the Croix de Guerre, with Palm. Citation in the Order of the Army.

CROIX DE GUERRE WITH PALM, issued 15 May 1917. Citation to Order of the Army Extract from General Orders No. 87.

> Pilot of the Escadrille Lafayette, skillful and intrepid, a true model for his comrades. On 8 April he forced an enemy plane to ground, Shot down an enemy aircraft on 13 April 1917 and an aircraft on 24 April.

Adj. Raoul Lufbery at Cachy, France, having just been awarded France's Legion of Honor, March 1917. Lufbery supports himself with a cane due to the rheumatism in his back.

CROIX DE GUERRE WITH PALM, issued 15 June 1917. Citation to Order of the Army Extract from General Orders No. 487

> Wonderful fighter pilot. For his squadron he is a living example of cold-blooded audacity and dedication. Shot down on 12 June 1917 his tenth enemy aircraft.

OROIX DE GUERRE WITH PAL, issued 13 October 1917. Citation to Order of the Army. Extract from General Orders No. 937.

> Fighter pilot who fought sixteen battles in two weeks during which he confronted and knocked down six enemy planes and shot down another. On 4 September 1917 he scored his eleventh victory. Has seriously damaged five aircraft in these fights.

CROIX DE GUERRE WITH PALM, issued 29 October 1917 Citation to Order of the Army Extract from General Orders No. 520.

Wonderful fighter pilot. On 22 September 1917 he attacked two enemy planes, shot down his twelfth plane, and forced another to land helpless in the lines.

On 13 October he shot down a biplace in flames behind enemy lines. During the combat he received two bullets in his engine while scoring his thirteenth victory.

CROIX DE GUERRE WITH PALM issued 9 November 1917. Citation to Order of the Army. Extract from General Orders No. 526.

Remarkable pilot. The most beautiful example of bravery, energy, and daring. On 24 October 1917 as the enemy, defeated the day before, tried to react, he made a splendid effort; delivering during three successive flights, seven close combats in which he shot down his 14th adversary and knocked down another five German planes.

CROIX DE GUERRE WITH PALM issued 21 January 1918. Citation to Order of the Army. Extract from General Orders No. 1151.

Pilot animated by an implacable will to dominate the adversary always in the air to seize the slightest opportunity, remarkable for his skill and endurance, shot down on 2 December 1917, his 15th and his 16th enemy aircraft.

BRITISH MILITARY MEDAL, presented 8 May 1917. By General Order No. 10 of 8 May 1917, of G.Q.H.,S.M., the King of England bestowed the Military Medal (M.M.) on the pilots whose names follow, who stood out for their bravery during the campaign.

MONTENEGRO GOLD MEDAL FOR BRAVERY, issued 18 December 1917.

SOURCE: James Norman Hall and Charles Bernard Nordhoff, *The Lafayette Flying Corps*, 2 vols. (Boston and New York: Houghton Mifflin; Cambridge, MA: Riverside, 1920).

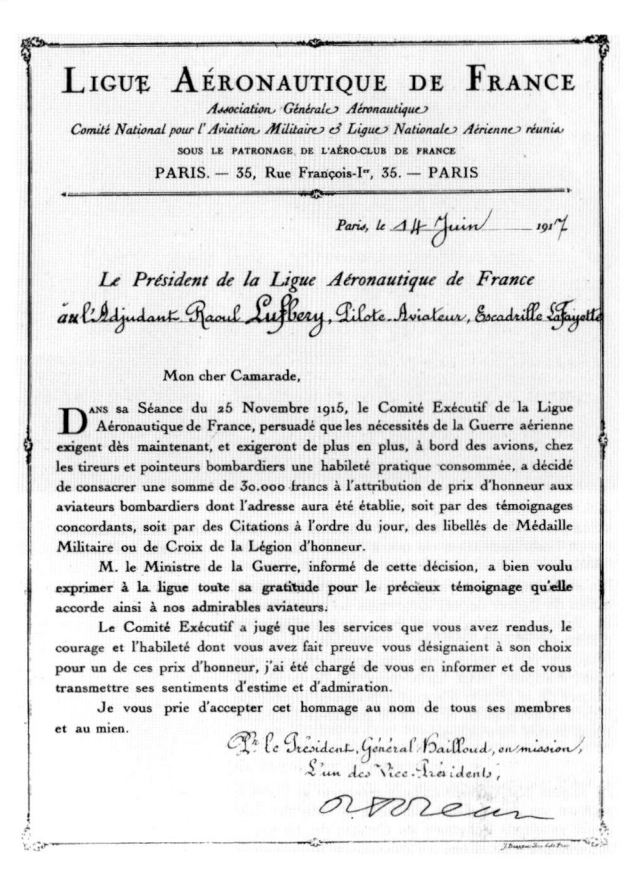

Lufbery's Ligue Aeronautique de France certificate presented to him on 14 June 1917

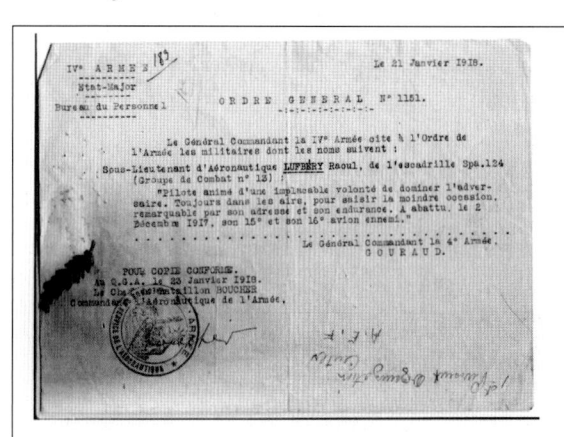

IVth Army Headquarters
Bureau of Personnel

21 January 1918

GENERAL ORDER No.1151

The General commanding the IVth Army awards the citation of the Order of the Army to the soldiers whose names follow:

Sous-Lieutenant of the Aeronautical Service Lufbéry, Raoul, of Escadrille SPA.124 (Groupe de Combat no.13) :

"[He is a] spirited pilot with an unrelenting will to dominate the adversary. [He is] always in the air, seizing the slightest opportunity [to fly], and is remarkable for his skill and endurance. He shot down, on 2 December 1917, his 15th and 16th enemy planes."

The General Commanding the 4th Army
GOURAUD

Certified True Copy
At Army Headquarters, 23 January 1918
Major BOUCHER
Commander of the Aeronautical Service of the Army
[signed] Boucher

Right: *Raoul Lufbery's Official French citation issued to him on 21 January 1918 in recognition of his 2 December 1917 aerial victories. The document has his tiny brass palm affixed to it, which would be placed on his Croix de Guerre ribbon.*

Raoul Lufbery's Winter of Discontent

The Lafayette Escadrille finished its last combat patrol on 23 December 1917. Two days later, on December 25, it was officially disbanded, and a period of great confusion followed for the pilots. In early December 1917 the French Service Aeronautique had told the men to seek their US Army commissions, and all but two pilots had been released by the French Army by December 21. In fact, pilot Carl Dolan discovered that when he received his commission as a first lieutenant in the US Army in January 1918, the document had been issued and dated on 7 November 1917. However, he had no knowledge of it and had yet to take his US oath of enlistment.

The most confusing time for the pilots was the period between their release by the French but before they had been completely taken over by the US Army Air Service on 18 February 1918. Most were in a state of limbo and were flying patrols as civilians and either had no US commissions or, like Dolan, had no knowledge that they had been commissioned. Dolan later recalled:

> The Americans didn't take us over as a unit. They took us over individually. Some of us were in American uniforms and some of us were in French uniforms. After we transferred, the Americans left us with the French, but we were getting orders from the Americans and the French.

Too often the pilots didn't know which orders to follow, particularly if a French commander's order contradicted an American commander's order, and the American commander outranked the French commander.

Although the pilots had been dropped from the SPA 124 roster, they continued to fly patrols with the squadron, with pilot William Thaw commanding. But Thaw would not receive his US Army major's commission until 26 January 1918. No longer with the French, and yet to be commissioned by the Americans, from 21 December 1917 until the date of his commission, Thaw had been flying as a civilian.

Five other volunteer American pilots who had been flying with other French squadrons joined SPA 124 and had begun flying patrols in January 1918. *Sergent* Phelps Collins of Escadrille SPA 303 was assigned on January 7 and was commissioned a captain in the US Army two days later;

Major Raoul Lufbery in Paris awaiting reassignment, 19 January 1918

Charles Biddle was assigned on January 10 and had been commissioned a US captain on 7 November 1917 while still flying with Escadrille SPA 73; Paul Baer of Escadrille SPA 80, also assigned on January 10, had been commissioned a first lieutenant in the US Army on 5 November 1917; Charles Wilcox of SPA 80 was assigned on 25 January 1918 and had received his US commission as a first lieutenant on 9 January 1918; George Turnure Jr. of SPA 103 joined Spa 124 on 12 February 1918 and had been commissioned a US first lieutenant on 2 January 1918.[1]

It is likely that these five pilots were unaware of the fact that they been granted US Army commissions, and only on a later date did they take their oaths of enlistment. It wasn't until 9 January 1918, when Charles Biddle had gone to Headquarters in Paris, did he learn that he had been released by the French and had a US commission waiting for him.[2]

---

1. It is likely that these five pilots were unaware of the fact that they been granted US Army commissions, and only on a later date would they take their oaths of enlistment. Not until 9 January 1918, when Charles Biddle had gone to Headquarters in Paris, did he learn that he had been released by the French and had a US commission waiting for him.

2. All these men were outstanding pilots. However, none of the original thirty-eight Lafayette Escadrille pilots who survived the war considered these latecomers to be members of their exclusive group, the *Valiant 38*.

190

James Norman Hall in the French uniform he was wearing on 1 January 1918, the day he shot down an Albatros fighter near LaCheppe, in the Champagne sector. At the time he was flying as a civilian, having been released by the French and without a US Army commission, which wouldn't arrive until 7 February 1918.

Pilot James Norman Hall, who had been released by France's Service Aeronautique on 25 December 1917, destroyed an enemy Fokker fighter on New Year's Day 1918 after leaving the aerodrome at LaCheppe, in the Champagne sector. His victory was confirmed after the aircraft crashed in no-man's land. But it wasn't until 7 February 1918 that Hall received his captain's commission in the US Army. Thus, he had been flying as a civilian the day he downed the German aircraft. And oddly enough, his victory would be the last confirmation added to the victory tally of the old Lafayette Escadrille, even though the squadron had been disbanded six days earlier.

Meanwhile, sous Lieutenant Raoul Lufbery had been languishing while his old comrades continued to fly patrols with SPA 124. He complained to his friend Jacques Mortane: "Everyone else is working. It is infuriating to be forced to stand down."

The squadron's top ace had been given no explanation as to why he hadn't been allowed to fly with his comrades. Perhaps that decision was based on his age. He was nearing thirty-three, making him the oldest American fighter

Captain James Norman Hall in his US Army Air Service uniform standing beside his SPAD SXlll fighter, US 103rd Aero Squadron, LaNoblette, France, late February 1918.

pilot. On 5 January 1918 the US Army finally offered him a commission as major. On 10 January 1918 he accepted the commission in the US Army's Aviation Signal Corps and was ordered by Headquarters American Expeditionary Forces to report to Paris "for assignment to duty."

On January 22 he was sent to the headquarters of the 1st Pursuit Organization Center at Villeneuve-les-Vertus and was ordered to wait for a telegram from the US Signal Corps. On January 30 he received the telegram ordering him to the headquarters of the Third Aviation Instruction Center at Issoudun. There, his great talents as a combat patrol leader were squandered by his superiors, who gave him a writing desk, a pad, and a pencil and ordered him to produce a pamphlet on "How to Kill Germans."

When a comrade visited Raoul at Issoudun he found a pilot sick, feverish, bedridden, and overwhelmed with boredom. He received no satisfactory answer when he questioned Lufbery about his health. Raoul's friend suspected his sedentary situation was a plausible explanation for his illness. Sadly, this great combat pilot who lived only to fly and fight faced a fate similar to his "Whiskey-man" lion mascot who sat trapped in his cage in the Jardin des Plantes Paris zoo.

SOURCES: James Norman Hall and Charles Bernard Nordhoff, *The Lafayette Flying Corps,* 2 vols. (Boston and New York: Houghton Mifflin; Cambridge, MA: Riverside, 1920).

Charles Biddle, *Fighting Airman: The Way of the Eagle* (Garden City, NY: Doubleday, 1968).

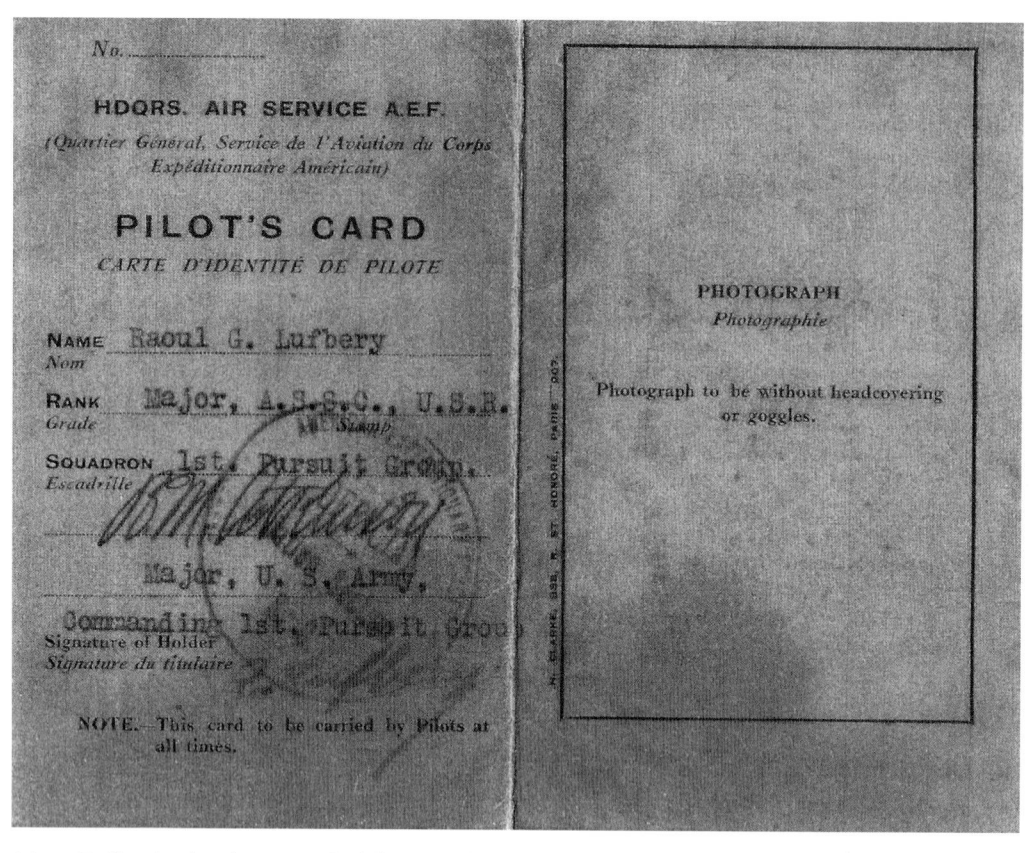

Major Lufbery's pilot identity card while assigned to the First Pursuit Organization Center at Villeneuve-Vertus, France, 22 January 1918

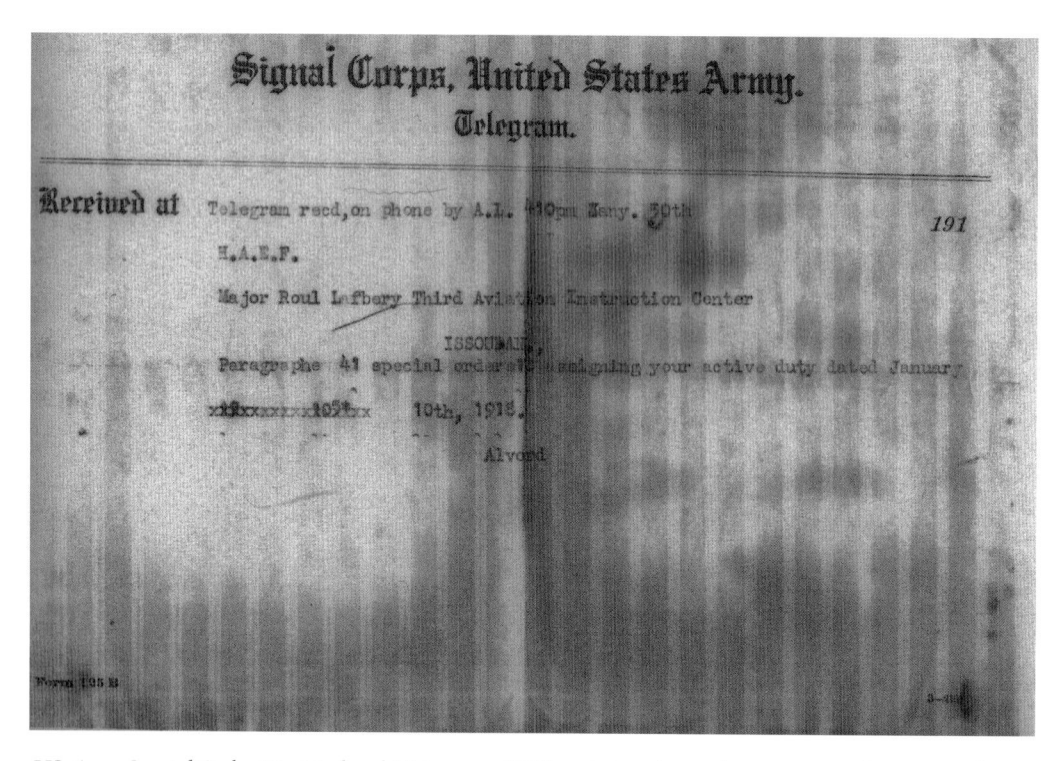

US Army Special Order No. 10, dated 10 January 1918, ordering the newly commissioned Major Lufbery to Paris for assignment to duty

HEADQUARTERS AMERICAN EXPEDITIONARY FORCES

Copy-Hd.

Special Orders,

No. 10

    Extract.

*   *   *   *   *

 41. Pursuant to instructions contained in War Department Cable No. 376, Major Raoul Lufbery, Aviation Section, Signal Officers' Reserve Corps, is assigned to active duty and will report to the Commanding General, Lines of Communication, Paris, ~~Framocy for assignment to duty.~~

True copy.
H. J. Lewis
Capt. S.C.

*   *   *   *   *

By command of General Pershing:

Official: ROBERT C DAVIS,

JAMES G. HARBORD,
Brigadier General,
Chief of Staff

30 January 1918, US Signal Corps telegram ordering Major Lufbery to the Third Aviation Instruction Center at Issoudun, France

The Death of Major Raoul Lufbery

The veteran Lafayette Escadrille pilots, with hundreds of hours of combat flying, were placed under the command of newly commissioned US Air Service staff officers, "who didn't know a prop from a tail skid." Because these officers often outranked the experienced Lafayette veterans, they implemented many ridiculous decisions, such as assigning Major Raoul Lufbery, the squadron's top ace, to a desk and ordering him to write a pamphlet on aerial tactics, or requiring the veteran pilots to wear cavalry spurs on their military boots.

The vast experience of the seasoned pilots was nearly lost to the newly forming AEF squadrons as a result of the initial decisions of the American Air Service medical staff. Having put the pilots through the tests required of flying candidates, they had deemed most of the men physically unfit for a variety of maladies, including blindness and crippled limbs. This had prompted Major William Thaw's caustic response that the staff physicians had every tool in their medical kits "but an instrument that measures guts."

It was only through the direct intervention by General Billy Mitchell to General John Pershing, commander of the AEF, that their physical infirmities were officially overlooked when Mitchell convinced the general that the experience and expertise of the old Lafayette pilots was vital in the forming of the new American squadrons. Mitchell's decision proved correct, as fifteen of those veterans went on to become instructors, flight commanders,

Major Lufbery standing on the Gengoult airfield shortly after his assignment to the 94th Aero Squadron, USAS

First Lieutenant Edwin Green sighting in the Vickers machine guns on his Nieuport 28 fighter

and AEF squadron leaders while destroying an impressive number of enemy aircraft.

On 18 February 1918 the pilots, now all commissioned US officers in US uniforms, severed ties with SPA 124 and joined the roster of the 103rd Aero Squadron, USAS, with Major Thaw in command. The 103rd became America's first frontline aero squadron. Meanwhile SPA 124, with its all-French personnel, was named Escadrille Jeanne d'Arc. Both squadrons continued to operate out of the La Noblette aerodrome, with the 103rd still attached to Groupe de Combat 13.

Coincidentally, on February 18, Major Lufbery escaped his confines through the intervention of Major Thaw and was assigned to the newly formed US 95th Aero Pursuit Squadron which had just arrived in Villeneuve des Vertusto. It became the first American-trained pursuit squadron to enter the Zone of Advance. Lufbery was very anxious to get back into the cockpit of a fighter. When leaving Issoudun for his new assignment, Lufbery said: "I have done my duty for France, but I still have to do my duty for America."

On March 5 the US 94th Aero Pursuit Squadron also arrived from Issoudun. Major Lufbery served as combat instructor as he helped to prepare the novice pilots in the intricacies of patrolling.

On March 28, 1918, Major Lufbery led Lieutenants Douglas Campbell and Edward Rickenbacker on the 94th's first combat patrol. Rickenbacker, soon to become America's top ace in World War I, later would write that "everything I learned, I learned from Lufbery." On March 29, Lufbery also led the 94th's second patrol accompanied by Lieutenants Thorne Taylor and John Wentworth. He continued to lead patrols when he was not in the air hunting solo.

On March 29, Captain James Norman Hall left the US 103rd Aero Squadron and was assigned as a flight commander to the US 94th Aero Squadron, then at Epiez. On April 29 he scored his fourth confirmed victory, which he shared with Lt. Edward Rickenbacker (his first) when they shot down a Pfalz D.III fighter near St. Buassant.

On April 7, the 94th, now under the command of Major Jean Huffer, was placed under the VIII French Army as an independent unit and was moved to the Gengoult airdrome, 4 kilometers northeast of Toul. The squadron's first aerial combat occurred on April 12 near Xiveray, when Major Lufbery single-handedly attacked three Albatros fighters and almost assuredly shot one down, adding yet another German plane to his list of "probables." He had

First Lieutenant James Meissner supporting the damaged upper wing of his Nieuport 28 fighter, which shed its fabric on his 3 May 1918 flight

Left: *First Lieutenant Edward Rickenbacker seated in the cockpit of his Nieuport 28 fighter.* Right: *Rickenbacker supporting the damaged upper wing of his Nieuport 28 fighter, which shed its fabric during an aerial combat against an Albatros DV fighter near Ribecourt. It was his third victory.*

successive combats on April 23 near St. Baussant, and on April 27, when he scored another probable. On May 18 he would fight it out with six German fighters over Norrey until his guns jammed and he would be forced to withdraw.

The 94th Pursuit Squadron was equipped with the French-manufactured Nieuport 28 fighter. The plane was powered by Gnome 160 horsepower rotary engine, which produced a maximum air speed of 122 miles per hour. Its armament consisted of two Vickers .303-caliber machine guns mounted on the port side of the fighter. The American pilots liked the fighter. Captain James Norman Hall, now a flight commander with the 94th, said of it:

> It was thought to be an advance on the Spad, and it was, indeed, a splendid little ship equipped with a rotary motor, and so fast in its pickup of power that it could be pulled off the ground as soon as the wheels were rolling. It was superb for "acrobacy" and had wonderful maneuverability: in Air Service parlance, it could be turned on a dime.[1]

But Hall soon learned that the fighter had a fatal flaw. A Nieuport 28 flown by Lt. James Meissner on 2 May 1918 had revealed an alarming defect. The fabric on its upper wing surface had split under pressure along the leading edge and had ripped back in great strips. Meissner had just managed to control the Nieuport and to bring it safely to ground. At the time of the incident, it was thought that the defect had been unique to Meissner's fighter. It was not. Lt. Rickenbacker's Nieuport would suffer the same fate during a successful aerial combat with an Albatros DV fighter near Ribecourt.[2]

On the morning of May 7, 1918, Captain Hall left the Toul aerodrome in the St. Mihiel sector with Lieutenants Rickenbacker and Green to challenge five enemy fighters in the air near Pont-a-Moussan. Their patrol located the enemy group above the village of Armaville, south of Metz. Holding an altitude advantage, the Americans dove to the attack. Hall had his foe squarely within his gunsights and was about to open fire when he heard an ominous ripping overhead. Instantly large pieces of shredded fabric began flapping above him. He immediately broke off the attack and turned toward Allied lines.

Hall nursed his Nieuport homeward and throttled to the slowest possible speed to stay airborne and yet keep

Captain James Normal Hall leaving on his last patrol, 7 May 1918

A Rumpler C.1 reconnaissance plane as flown by the German crew that downed Major Lufbery

German observer-gunner in the rear cockpit of a German reconnaissance plane

---

1. Lt. Rickenbacker lost the fabric on the upper wing surface of his Nieuport 28 on 17 May 1918 during a victorious aerial combat against an Albatros DV Fighter near Ribecourt. It was his third victory.

2. James Norman Hall, *My Island Home: An Autobiography* (Boston: Little, Brown, 1952).

The remains of Major Lufbery's Nieuport 28

Major Lufbery's flag-draped coffin in repose shortly before his funeral, 20 May 1918

his fighter in a straight level descent. He continued to lose altitude and came under fierce antiaircraft fire. Unable to take evasive action, his plane shook violently from a direct hit. At 1,000 meters he dropped out of control.

Closing quickly to earth near Pagny-sur-Moselle, Hall reefed back on the stick. His landing gear sheared away as he slammed to ground and skidded across an open field. Almost immediately he was surrounded by German troops, who lifted him from his fighter.

As Hall touched the ground, shooting pain in his ankles told him that one or both had been broken. Also, for a second time, he had broken his nose. A German artillery officer informed him that the mortal blow dealt his plane had been the result of a direct hit by a 37-millimeter round from an antiaircraft battery. Miraculously the round had failed to explode on contact but had pierced the engine and had stuck fast in one of the cylinders.

On 19 May 1918, at approximately 9 A.M., the antaircraft batteries on top of Mont St. Michel began firing, their white puffs breaking at high altitude. Almost immediately Major Huffer received notice that a German photoreconnaissance plane was heading toward the 94th's field. Seconds later it appeared. It was a Rumpler C.1 reconnaissance plane of Reihenbilduz Nr. 3, piloted by Unteroffizier Otto Kirchbaum, with Leutnant Kurt Scheibe in the observer's cockpit.

First Lieutenant Oscar J. Gude, the only pilot on the squadron's airfield who was ready for flight, climbed into his Nieuport fighter N6154 and immediately rose to meet the enemy.[3] As he gained altitude, the German biplace appeared to be struck with shrapnel. It fell into a spin and headed groundward, but at 200 feet it recovered and its pilot turned back toward his own lines.[3]

Gude followed the German bus over the Foret de Haye. Through inexperience he began firing at the enemy while it was still far out of range. He emptied his machine guns in a continual four-hundred-round burst, causing no damage to the observation plane.

Major Lufbery, who had been following the engagement from the officer's barracks, jumped onto a motorcycle and sped to the hangars as the enemy biplace again fell under a violent artillery barrage but still managed to maintain a steadily retreating course in the direction of Nancy.

Lufbery soon discovered that his own Nieuport fighter N6193, with its well-maintained machine gun, was out of commission. Second Lieutenant Philip Davis's Nieuport N6178 sat on the airfield.[4] Assured by the mechanics that the plane was in good order, Lufbery slipped into his fight suit, climbed into the machine, and, with no time to check the machine gun, sped off and rapidly ascended to attack.[4]

---

3. First Lieutenant Oscar Gude's reputation with his fellow 94th pilots was one of a shirker and coward. He joined the squadron on 1 March 1918 and departed on 7 July 1918. On 4 August 1918 he was assigned to the US 93rd Aero Squadron, then under the commanded of Major Huffer. On 22 October 1918, while on patrol flying Major Huffer's Spad, Gude landed on a German airfield and surrendered his aircraft to the enemy. A fellow pilot said of him: "He not only knew he was yellow in combat but would admit it."

4. Following Major Lufbery's death, on 23 May 1918 Second Lieutenant Philip Davis replaced his destroyed aircraft Nieuport 6178 with Lufbery's Nieuport 6193. On 2 June 1918 Davis fought a fierce combat with a German patrol over enemy lines. His plane was struck and burst into flame. Davis crashed just behind German lines and burned to death in Lufbery's Nieuport 6193.

Left to right: *First Lieutenant Oscar Gude, First Lieutenant Edward Rickenbacker, Second Lieutenant Alan Winslow, Major Raoul Lufbery, Gengoult aerodrome, May 1918*

Five minutes later he had reached an altitude of 2,000 feet. Pilots and ground crew near the hangars watched him close the distance with the Rumpler C.1 reconnaissance plane, some 6 miles distant. Lufbery attacked the enemy bus from under its tail. He fired several short *rafales* before swerving away, evidently in an attempt to clear a jammed round from his machine gun. Circling overhead, two minutes later he again attacked the enemy bus from the same position, then flew straight past it. Almost immediately his Nieuport burst into flames. A round from the German observer's guns had shot away Lufbery's right thumb as he clutched the joystick, then pierced his full fuel tank. The cockpit instantly exploded. Lufbery attempted to put the fighter into a slip to force the flames away from himself, but the wind from the rapidly plummeting plane only fed the inferno.

His flight suit on fire, Lufbery exited the burning aircraft. To this day, the question remains. Did he fall out of the Nieuport fighter, or was he fulfilling his May 17 pledge to his friend Jacques Mortane when he told him, "I will never burn to death"? Weeks earlier he had also told a group of novice pilots what he would do should his plane catch fire. "I should always stay with the machine," he said. "If you jump you certainly haven't got a chance."

Did he see the stream beneath him that promised a remote chance for survival, and desperately jump toward it from a height of more than 200 feet? His body missed the stream by a hundred yards and landed on a fence sur-

Maron (Merthe-et-Moselle). Major Lufbery fell in the garden behind the first house on the right. There is a brass plaque mounted to its wall with this inscription "Raoul Lufbery, Major, Air Service, United States Army. Killed in aerial combat, May 19, 1918."

rounding the garden of a house in the little town of Maron, 12 miles southeast of Gengoult. Lufbery's Nieuport sped on at 120 mph in a steep half-mile glide, then hit the ground and incinerated. The German Rumpler was almost immediately shot down by Sgt. Dupree of SPA 68, 1 mile inside Allied lines near Mars-la-Tour. The two-man crew survived and was taken prisoner.

Some thirty minutes later, Lufbery's comrades arrived at the scene where he had fallen. Already his charred body had been carried by the villagers to the town hall, where they had covered it with flowers from their gardens. Lufbery's friends gently transported it to the American hospital near the squadron's aerodrome. The next day, following a full military funeral and eulogy by General Clarence Edwards, commander of the US 26th Division and Lufbery's former commander in the Philippines, the great pilot was buried in the American Cemetery, Sebastopol Barracks. He was thirty-three years of age at the time of his death.[5]

Gone was the great Lufbery of whom Edwin Parsons, his Lafayette Escadrille comrade, had said, few could equal and none could surpass. "His cool head, steady nerve, and unerring aim were worth a whole squadron," Parsons said. "He flew as the bird flies without any thought of how it was done." Captain Georges Thenault, Lufbery's Lafayette Escadrille commander, would later write of him:

"His Spad was always the highest and every day he won new victories. He seemed to hardly care about having them confirmed. Calmly he reigned as a sovereign lord in his chosen element and beat down his foes to accomplish his duty and not for the sake of glory."

Edward Lufbery, Major Lufbery's father, would say the following after learning of his son's death in aerial combat: "It was the war that Raoul waited for as he wandered all over the world to find. He walked on the ground, lived on the ground, and worked on the ground. All the time it was the sky where he belonged! The war had been Raoul's mother, sweetheart, and wife to him."[6]

---

5. John B. Kane, of the US Army Graves Registration Service, witnessed the aerial combat of Major Lufbery on May 19, 1918. He recorded the events in his memoir which was published in 2017 by his grandson under the title The Khaki Road of Yesterday. Kane had just left Sunday morning Mass when he heard explosions and saw the sky over the hill at Toul dotted with anti-aircraft smoke. Kane caught a glimpse of an enemy aircraft glistening "like a silver bird" in the sun as it banked to avoid the explosions. As it passed out of view, Kane heard the roar of a fighter plane departing the 94th Aero Squadron airfield. When the plane, (a Nieuport 28), gained altitude, it engaged the German invader. The combatants fired at each other as they circled in wide loops for advantage. Kane recorded that the "maneuvering for position kept on and on" until the combatants disappeared in the direction of Nancy. Kane evidently did not witness the death of Lufbery, but he did record that Lufbery's fighter exploded and that he jumped out of the flaming inferno as it plummet between Toul and Nancy before crashing to earth a hundred feet from a small stream. However, Kane was present later that morning when Lufbery's "charred and broken body" was brought to a small room on the hospital grounds where a member of Kane's unit embalmed the corpse. Captain Rickenbacker arrived with Lufbery's dress uniform, allowing Kane to view the body as they dressed it. Kane stated that "his legs to the hips were badly burned, but fortunately his face was in good condition. His closely cropped mustache and eyebrows were singed slightly, and one hand had a machine gun bullet wound." The condition of Lufbery's legs, and the fact that his face was relatively unscathed, may lend support to the conclusion that Lufbery jumped from, rather than had fallen out of his flaming cockpit.

6. Edward Lufbery made forty-six trips between France and America in his lifetime. He traveled from Connecticut to attend the inspiring dedication of the Lafayette Escadrille Memorial on 4 July 1928 in honor of his son Raoul. As he often did on previous trips, he would remain in France for up to two years visiting friends and collecting rare European trading stamps for his collection. In November of 1929, Edward fell ill and died in Blois France at seventy-five years of age. He had lived and worked in that city for many years some four decades earlier. He was buried in an unmarked grave in a Blois cemetery.

Inventory of Major Lufbery's personal effects located in his room at the Gengoult officer's barracks, 20 May 1918

A Real Soldier of Fortune

The following article was written by a reporter for the *New York City Sun* and was published on 19 May 1918—the same day that Major Raoul Lufbery was killed in aerial combat in France.

American Ace Has Had Adventurous Career Since He Left Home When 15 Years Old

First Hand Talk With Flier's Relatives in Connecticut Reveals Charming Personality of the Man

Charles Lufbery had forgotten that he must go back to the factory at 1 o'clock and that he had had no luncheon; for he was telling with affectionate pride all he knew of his brother, Major Raoul Lufbery, now famous as an aviator in France.

He could not give a complete record, a "dossier," he called it, of his brother. Indeed nobody but Raoul Lufbery himself could do that, for his life has led him through many unknown, sunlit byways. And then Charles had not seen him since he was in Wallingford, Connecticut, ten years ago.

Charles served with the French army from July 10, 1915, until he was discharged on March 23, 1917. Once he was within fifteen miles of where Raoul was stationed, but his commanding officer said they must go right on and so he missed seeing his brother.

People in Wallingford say that Charles is of the same general appearance as his brother. He is slight, not more than five feet eight inches in height, with straight, brown hair and sad luminous brown eyes. He must have got this sadness in his eyes during those nineteen days he served without relief in the trenches at the battle of the Somme. And here he was, unknown and undecorated, telling stories of his brother with more joy than if they had been his own.

Family Never Understood Him

Raoul was the member of the Lufbery family whom none of the rest ever quite understood. But for this very mystery and the quiet charm of his personality they loved him more than they did any of the others.

"We were never surprised at anything Raoul ever did, and sometimes," Charles said, "when we were alone he was as good as a storybook. But you could not get him to talk if there was company."

At that noon hour in Wallingford we sat in the kitchen of the little brown cottage. Noise from the factory next door came like a liberal pizzicato of basses in a Puccini opera. Laurie, Raoul's sister-in-law, searched through boxes for old letters, while Marcel, the nine-year-old son, gallantly spun his top in the hope that somebody would look that way. Little moving shadows from the great apple tree were on the floor. And there was a scent, as ever in Connecticut in May, of wood smoke and flowers and ferny meadows.

I do not know just what time of year Raoul Lufbery came to Wallingford, but it should have been May, and I think he must have stood there on the common, looking off at the wooded hills and taking deep draughts of the rustic air when he said to himself that Wallingford should always be his home wherever he happened to be.

He was in Connecticut only a year and a half in all his life. His father was American, born in New York City, and spent most of his life in Wallingford, and his mother was French. He himself was born thirty-three years ago in Clermont-Ferrand, France.

Seldom Wrote to Home Folks

Just when Raoul learned to fly Charles didn't know, but certainly he did learn, and they were very glad, for now they could hear of him through the newspapers. He hated to write, and when he was in Wallingford he used to tell them that when they did not hear from him they would know he was dead. However, some said vaguely that he learned piloting in Indo-China, and his sister Yvonne knew for sure the celebrated Marc Pourpe was his teacher.

And after that conversation you can understand that Major Lufbery had to take to the air, as he had exhausted everything land and water had to offer by way of adventure.

"He was always ready to risk everything," Charles said. "And the moment's joy was all he wanted from it." Ah, he is splendid for the army! He could dress wounds or cook or comfort the wounded, and do all those simple things which so few know how to do at all. He ought to know them. He has made his living ever since he was 15.

"You know," Charles continued, "when he thought he might come home, they talked of giving him a great banquet. Well, Gerve (so they called him), if he should hear of such an intention beforehand would slip home incognito. He wouldn't know what to do with a banquet. "

"Yes," Mrs. Lufbery said, "but he'd manage that better than the girl in South Dakota. This girl wrote and wanted to know when Raoul would be at home and where she could send something she had knitted him. He'd be terribly worried over this; so I sent the letter to Yvonne. You see they all think I am his mother and I'd be so honored—only I hope I don't look so old. He was never the one to be popular with girls, or men, either. He liked to be alone, and sometimes he would sit looking, and say nothing."

Raoul Always Most Modest

Charles said that in Paris he had seen aviators splendid in their decorations and uniforms, the most admired men in the hotels. But Raoul wouldn't cut much of a figure among them. Indeed, he'd sooner face twenty German airplanes than try, "because he does not care much about how he looks," Charles said.

To show you what sort of family Lufbery came from, Julien, his oldest brother, Charles, and Raoul all went to help France, although two are American citizens. Major Raoul's family are poor, but when you know them you understand that culture and hospitality are not the exclusive property of the rich. Raoul got his taste for high adventure early in life. His mother died when he was about two years old, leaving the three brothers to their grandmother's care. According to all accounts, she found it the hardest work in her life. For Raoul was always restless.

Like a true Frenchman—or an American of the world, as he really is—he decided when he was 15 that he just couldn't live another day unless he saw Paris. So, he left his grandmother and set off.

He never saw her again. When Charles was in France, he went to Clairmont-Ferrand to see her, and found "to my great sadness that she was dead and we had not heard of it."

Meanwhile, the boys' father married again. From this marriage they have four sisters, Yvonne, Marie-Louise, and Germaine, nurses in Boston, and Bertha, who is married and with whom Raoul's father now lives in Yalesville, Connecticut. There is another brother, Rene, who tried to enlist in the aviation service last spring, with what fortune I do not know.

Unlike most great men from the provinces Raoul was unimpressed by Paris. It was well enough, he used to say, for people who liked the order of the city. But obeying the police, dining in cafes, toiling and paying your rent wasn't his idea of life.

He sailed for Algeria. But the voyage was a very hard one, and he fell ill upon arriving in Algiers. While in the hospital, he became a great favorite with the doctors and nurses, as he always did with people whom he came to know. And, having no prospects, they made him an orderly in the hospital. Here he stayed for two years.

From there he went to Egypt, where he says to this day he would like to settle, if he were compelled to settle anyplace, because the climate is so congenial to a vagabond.

Told of Entertaining Adventures

In Wallingford on Sundays and when he was not working in the silver factory, Raoul would entertain his brother and sister-in-law with tales of these early adventures which he remembered more vividly than any of the later ones.

One night in Garah, for the sake of his personal preference and also his purse, he decided to spend the night sleeping in the sand near a ruined castle. "Just as he is sleeping," his brother said, "he sees a man crouching with a knife in his mouth, waiting for a chance to stab him. Raoul had nothing to fight with, but he wrestled with the man, and the noise they made brought some soldiers from the patrol and they both were arrested.

"The chief was very angry and threatened to send Raoul to torture and prison. But luckily Raoul had money and the other fellow had a bad record, and they released my brother."

Even in Egypt the people respected the person who had money. But this dollar, and that's all that Lufbery had, was exceedingly valuable, because by its means he got into the first military uniform he ever wore. It came about this way:

After that escape the moonlit nights of Egypt lost their charm for our hero aviator. So he decided to go back to Constantine, Algeria. It was more French and less ungodly there. Accordingly he set out until he reached the beginning of the desert, where nobody could travel without a guide, though the way was short, only about a two days journey.

Here he met a young Canadian, also bound for Constantine. Presently, a man with three donkeys put in an appearance. The man wanted the boys to help with the merchandise, but he inquired where they were going and if they had any money. Raoul produced his dollar and the Canadian had about that much. The man took it all and they started.

Way Laid by a Robber Band

They had traveled one night without adventure, resting during the day. But the next evening, just as they started, they were surrounded by a band of robbers. The owner of the donkeys laid about them with a club and killed two of the thieves. The others killed him and one donkey.

When they saw that the two boys had no money, they took their clothes, every stitch, and left some bread and water for them and the two remaining donkeys, which were too slow for the robbers' trade.

By riding all night in the chilled desert, the boys reached a settlement of two houses early the next morning. The people said they had no food to give, but they purchased the donkeys from the boys and let them spend the five francs to buy two empty grain bags from them.

Lufbery, always quick to put to use what was at hand, cut a hole in the bottom of each bag for their heads and one in either side for their arms. The two adventurers donned their costumes and set out for a French Foreign Legion barracks which was about an hour away. When the soldiers saw the boys approach they screamed and howled. And though the boys' sense of humor had been dulled by hunger and their own plight, they had only to look at each other to see what the joke was.

Strange Objects Taken In and Fed

Seeing that the strange objects were well disposed and so merry, also that they knew the French language, the soldiers took them in, fed them, and gave them some clothes. And this was the first time the future American ace had worn the military uniform. Of course, it possessed great variety, and some of the garments were a trifle large, but one cannot be too squeamish in the matter of attire right after coming out of a grain bag.

Here Raoul and the Canadian parted, and Raoul went for a while to Constantinople, through Romania and through Switzerland. After various unrecorded adventures he arrived at Fulda, Germany, where he worked for two years in a brewery. From the eternal dampness of the place he contracted rheumatism, from which he is never entirely free.

While at Fulda he learned to speak and read German, but he became so ill from rheumatism that he had to be taken to a hospital. For a while after his release he taught gymnastics. With the little money he got from that he went to Hamburg. There he helped load a ship, for which he got the $40 necessary to pay his fare to America.

The gymnastics set him up wonderfully and he was skilled in athletics. The neighbors who lived downstairs in the house which his brother occupied in Wallingford could have told that, for he'd make a dumbbell of a broomstick with two stones tied to the ends, and not infrequently one of these would fall off and raise a great noise downstairs.

Some time in 1906 he reached America, where he thought he would find his family again, for, though they had been separated, there was a strong affection among them all. When he got to Wallingford he found that his father had sailed for France two days before. But Charles and his wife were there to welcome him. Yes, and the half-brother Rene, and these two boys set up housekeeping on their own account in a non-committal red brick building called the Wallace block just below the railroad station.

Later he lived with his brother Charles. He was very eager to learn English and went to night school for a while. But he liked to be alone.

"And he was beautiful then," Mrs. Lufbery said. "He had such nice eyes." Perhaps there was some of that look of divine purpose which artist Farre has since discovered in his eyes.[1]

Among his friends there was Joe, a young Italian with a passion for music and all beautiful things. From

---

1. Famous French artist Henri Farre painted a distinguished portrait of aviator Lufbery on 6 January 1918 that was widely published in newspapers during that time.

him Lufbery learned to play the mandolin, which he has never given up. There were not many exciting events in Lufbery's life in America. Only one, in fact. And that was the day upon which his favorite sister, Yvonne, came from France and he met her in New York. She had spent her whole life up to that time in a convent, for her own mother had died while these children were very young.

She and her brother were always close chums, and she was eager to please him, but though he gallantly insisted upon carrying a little black basket—very old fashioned even in France—which she used as a suitcase, she wouldn't give it to him. Not being able to sing a single note in tune, she tried to please him by rendering a piece called "When My Father Was Combing His Beard."

Raoul appointed himself to tease this sister, a privilege he would allow none of the rest to do. In writing to Yvonne from Manila, P. I., on April 23, 1910, he said: "I still remember about the little black basket which you had as a suitcase when you first came in Wallingford. At that time you were very proud of it and thought no basket in all the world could beat yours. But now I believe you have changed your mind and do not take very good care of that poor little devil."

He compliments her upon her good English and is most "satisfied" that both will be able to write and speak it correctly soon. He can't resist bringing up the song: "I remember that famous song 'When My Father Was Combing His Beard,' which was so sweet and melodious that even Rene, although not a musician at all, was charmed, if not hypnotized, every time you gave the beautiful serenade. I do not know the words, but I sometimes play the tune on my mandolin."

But though he was fond of his sister, he got restless in Wallingford. He went to New Orleans, then to Mexico and finally to San Francisco. In New Orleans he was in a bakery, but he wrote a card in French that he didn't consider this his life's work. From the White Palace Hotel, San Francisco, he wrote that he was a waiter there and that it was somewhat better than putting raisins in bread, his former job. In the same year, 1908, he wrote home from Honolulu, Hawaii. And then the letter from the Philippines where he served with the American army for 18 months.

"And Charley" (his brother), Raoul asked in this same letter to Yvonne, "is he still working in the factory? Has he now a small garden around his new house? I know it was his dream to have something like this when I left over there. He was also crazy for chickens. I hope he has all these things now and is satisfied. I wish so little could satisfy me.

"Very often, generally in the evening when I am alone, studying or reading in my room, I think of my little sister Yvonne. I have a good idea that we are not separated forever, but that we are able to meet again one of these days." But Yvonne has not seen him since.

According to Elliott Cowdin, Lufbery joined the Lafayette Escadrille when it was sent to Verdun sector early in May 1916.[2] There were no letters to the Wallingford Lufberys about that. Only a postal card from Hong Kong in 1911, saying that Raoul had a position in the Imperial Chinese Customs in Canton, "which I like tolerably well."

But on December 27, 1917, now possessing the Croix de Guerre, the British Military Medal, the French Medaille Militaire, and the Legion of Honor, Raoul wrote this to his brother:

"Now, I am looking like a Christmas tree, medals all over my chest. The last one I was decorated with is a Montenegrin order, with a ribbon, red, blue and white. Though it has not the value of the French Legion of Honor or the Military Medal, I am awfully proud to wear it.

"You certainly have heard through the newspapers about my commission in the American Aviation, but the truth is I have been appointed to the rank (Major) a month ago, but I cannot wear the uniform yet, as the French are still holding my discharge.

"I now have sixteen official German machines to my credit, and many others unofficial. On December 2, I brought two of them down.

"Well, how is everything up at the old Wallingford? I would like very much to see it back again. Unfortunately, I must give it up for the present. For I should like to organize some sort of a little flying circus for the Germans before I leave here."

But here in Wallingford it was 1 o'clock, and the whistle had blown. so Charles Lufbery took his sandwiches and started back to the factory.

"We're very proud of all Raoul's honors," he said, with a certain wistfulness, "but the best thing would be if America had a medal for great bravery then Raoul would win it, and he'd come back here, and the President himself would pin the medal on."

---

2. Elliot Cowdin was one of the original founding pilots of the Lafayette Escadrille.

A Letter from Princess Ghika

[The following is a copy of the letter Princess Ghika, mother of Marc Pourpe, penned to Edward Lufbery, expressing her profound sympathy for the loss of his son.]

(here for 1 month)
Le Clos-Marie Roscoff Finistere

27 May 1918

Monsieur,

I am Marc Pourpe's mother and your son Raoul became the son of my heart. That splendid boy revenged my son killed at the front the 2nd of December 1914.

Since, you know what he gloriously accomplished! You know what became of him. My husband, second husband, and I, we used to love him tenderly, and every day more and more. He was a real hero, in acts, soul and feelings, he was straight and strong, he who in pure gold, that poor dear Raoul,—and no words can express our despair! He came to see us here the 14th of May. He was ill, and that dear boy crossed all France from east to west—to be at my call and to come and see me.

The 16th at 6 of evening. I parted from him at Morlain—and three days after, at his first "vol" [flight] he was gloriously killed.

It seems to me that my own son is killed twice. Monsieur, we had spoken about you and Wallingford where he thought to go after the war with us.

I want to know if you or Wallingford City will ask to receive his ashes to bury him there. If not, will you send me a paper with the permission to claim him after war and to bury him in Lorient/Bretagne where my son will be buried. Amongst my family, my son, who from he was the best friend, the pupil—he brother.

I am in bed—so deeply sad and wounded.

If you want to know a lot of exactly about Raoul ask it from me, but excuse my English speaking, if you speak French, I will write to you in French and—it will be better.

However, you are the father of a hero, of my dearly beloved Raoul who used to call me "little mother."

Let us share hearts with yours,—ace of my heart to—the flying ace.

Preciously yours forever,
Anne-Marie
Princess Georges Ghika

Major Lufbery's Final Resting Place

To this day, questions arise within the Lufbery family as to why Major Raoul Lufbery's body was not returned to the United States for burial. Some relatives believe an ongoing arrangement had been made by Edward Lufbery with the L'Association du Memorial de L'Escadrille Lafayette that if the family wished, his remains could be transferred from their Memorial Monument in France for reinterment in Wallingford, Connecticut, Major Lufbery's adopted hometown. However, no documents have surfaced to date within family records that would permit the major's body to be removed to Connecticut.

At the time of Lufbery's death, and into the late 1920s, Wallingford city leaders and some family members in the United States discussed and debated about having Raoul returned to his adopted hometown. This issue has been a sensitive and concerning family matter for many years.

The first person to request Major Lufbery's remains following his death was Princess Anne-Marie Ghika, the mother of Marc Pourpe. She wrote the following in a 27 May 1918 letter of sympathy to Edward Lufbery, the pilot's father.

> I want to know if you or Wallingford City will ask to receive his ashes, to bury him there. If not will you send us a paper with the jurisdiction for claiming him after the war, and to bury him in Lorient/Bretagne where my son will be buried. Amongst my family, my son, who he was the best friend, the pupil—the brother.

It is not known if Mr. Lufbery responded to the princess. It is known that her request was not honored. In 1919 Major Lufbery's remains were transferred from the Sebastopol Forest Cemetery to the St. Mihiel American Cemetery at Thiaucourt, France, and placed in Grave #2, Row #1, Block D. But that would not be his final resting place.

Lafayette Flying Corps pilot Edgar Hamilton, who first conceived the concept of a Lafayette Escadrille monument in December 1922

On 10 April 1921, the *Boston Sunday Globe* published a brief article titled "Father Wishes Lufbery's Body to Stay in France." The article is datelined Wallingford, Connecticut. April 9.

Edward Lufbery, father of the late Major Raoul Lufbery, American ace shot down in France, does not desire that his son's body be brought here for final interment. His wish, he stated, was that the body remain in France where Mrs. Lufbery, the mother, is buried. No member of the family here had requested that Major Lufbery's body be brought to this town (Wallingford, CT).

On 5 June 1922 Edward Lufbery received a second request for his son's remains. It came from Edgar Guerard Hamilton, a former Lafayette Flying Corps pilot. After the war, Hamilton served on the American Graves Registration Committee, which helped locate the remains of missing American airmen. In the process Hamilton located all but six Flying Corpsmen. Later, he conceived the idea that all the fallen American volunteer pilots should be buried in a memorial garden near Paris.

On 20 February 1922 Hamilton met with relatives of deceased pilots and with prominent Americans residing in France and presented his idea to them. They approved of his concept. Hamilton knew that if he could secure the remains of the Lafayette Escadrille's most famous member for burial in the garden, it might prompt other relatives of deceased pilots to do the same.

In Hamilton's letter to Edward Lufbery, he is responding to a letter from the pilot's father. He makes a strong argument in an effort to convince Major Lufbery's father to keep Raoul's body in France and to have Raoul interred in the proposed Lafayette Escadrille Memorial Garden with other fallen pilots from Lufbery's squadron. To advance his argument, Hamilton stated how he had gotten a letter

Lafayette Escadrille Memorial while under construction, 10 January 1927

from Edward's oldest son, Julien, then living in Rouen, France, in which Julien stated his full support that Raoul be buried with his friends in his birth country. Julien's views carried great weight with the father in influencing the final decision as to where Major Lufbery would rest for eternity.

> My dear Mr. Lufbery:
> Your very interesting letter reached me this morning and I hasten to reply. First of all, as to your son's grave. Up to the month of February his body was still in France and unless it has been removed since, it is still there. I beg of you in this case to consider the feelings of your boy in this matter. Where would he rather lie, in France which was the country of his adoption, for whom he fought and died, or in Wallingford, a city where he lived but a short time and for him he cared nothing! Raoul was French in nature and not American. Everything about him was French and it would be almost a sacrilege to take him back to America now to satisfy the pride of the citizens of Wallingford. His place is beside that of Norman Prince, Rockwell, Campbell, Genet, and his other friends who lost their lives flying with him and who he mourned at their death.
> The committee that has the cemetery project in hand is busy getting out the literature to send to all the parents together with a drawing in color of the proposed Memorial Garden. You will probably hear from

Sergent William McKerness, Lafayette Flying Corps, in his flying gear. McKerness was killed in aerial combat while serving as an observer/gunner with Escadrille Caudron 46 on 15 August 1918. After the war his parents had his remains returned to the United States. He was buried in Arlington National Cemetery on 8 September 1921.

The completed Lafayette Escadrille Monument, July 1928

them directly as in the future all the correspondence in respect to the Memorial will pass through their hands.

If you decide, as I am sure you will, to allow your son's body to be placed in our Memorial. Will you please write to the war department to that effect and send to Mrs. Ovington, 5 Rue Desbordes Valmore, Paris, who is the secretary of the committee, or to myself, your authorization for the removal of Raoul's body from Thiaucourt.[1]

I have received a letter from your son who lives in Rouen who is entirely in accord with me in regard to the necessity of Raoul's being placed with his friends. He said he would write to you about the matter....

I come from Waterbury myself, went to school for six years in Cheshire, and know Yalesville and Wallingford well.

The father of another one of our boys who was killed in the French aviation lives in Wallingford on Longhill road. His name is McKerness. He had done the inexplicable and blasphemous thing of causing his son's body to be returned to America only to have it buried in Arlington cemetery. Imagine such a thing. His son died in the French uniform and his father brings him to America to lie among several thousand nameless and forgotten dead. If he had wished him buried in Wallingford I could have understood, but to place a member of the Lafayette Escadrille to be forgotten in Arlington.[2]

If I can at any time be of service to you, I hope that you will not hesitate to call upon me....

Believe me, very sincerely yours,

Edgar Guerard Hamilton
Morgan Harjes
14 Place Vendome, Paris

---

1. Georgina Ovington, the mother of Lafayette Flying Corps pilot Carter Ovington, who was killed on 29 May 1918 while returning from a combat patrol, became the secretary of the Lafayette Flying Corps. She gave much of her time and energy in assisting her son's comrades and helped perpetuate the history of the corps.

2. William John McKerness attended public school in Wallingford, Connecticut. He sailed for France on 26 May 1917 and joined the French Service Aeronautique. Caporal McKerness served at the front in Escadrille C. 46 as an aviation observer and machine gunner. He was killed on 15 August 1918, when his aircraft was attacked and shot down by eight enemy Fokkers. He was buried in an Allied cemetery. His family later had his remains exhumed and removed to the United States and buried in Arlington National Cemetery on 8 September 1921.

On 11 December 1922 Hamilton and the others met again and founded the Executive Committee of the Lafayette Escadrille Memorial Association. By then, Hamilton's concept of a memorial garden had evolved into a monument. He and the committee decided that the fallen should all be brought to rest in one memorial structure that would also serve to perpetuate the spirit that inspired their volunteer service in France. To this end they began soliciting financial aid from prominent American and French officials, and in March of 1923 an association called the Memorial de l'Escadrille Lafayette was formed to bring Hamilton's dream to fruition. Large donations came in from wealthy American industrialists and from some relatives of deceased pilots. Frederick Henry Prince, the father of pilot Norman Prince, donated $20,000 to the cause.

Construction of a monument soon began. Once it was completed, it would be composed of a central Arch of Triumph and the sanctuary crypt. The arch was to be one-half the size of the Arch de Triomphe de l'Etoile, and upon its stone facades the names of the dead and the surviving pilots of the Lafayette Flying Corps would be inscribed in order of enlistment.

The beautiful park of Villeneuve L'Etang, 8 miles outside Paris and midway to Versailles, was selected for the monument's site. On it would stand the Memorial de l'Escadrille Lafayette, a striking monument to be erected to the memory of the 209 American volunteer pilots of the Escadrille Lafayette and the Lafayette Flying Corps. It would also serve to perpetuate the spirit that inspired their volunteer service in France.

In 1928, as the monument was nearing completion, the association's members realized that without the remains of Major Lufbery, it would be incomplete. To this end, Lewis Crenshaw, the association's administrater-delegate and acting secretary, again approached Edward Lufbery in an effort to convince him to allow his son's body to rest there. This time Mr. Lufbery gave his approval. Crenshaw wrote the following in an 11 April 1928 letter to Lufbery.[3]

> Dear Mr. Lufbery.
>
> Thank you very much for your letter of the 5th inst. With the authorization enclosed. You can be assured that the transfer will be carried out in the most reverent

---

3. Lewis Dabney Crenshaw, the administrator-delegate and secretary for the Lafayette Flying Corps Foundation, was a graduate of the University of Virginia Law School. During World War I he was director of the University's European bureau.

Lewis D. Crenshaw, secretary of the Lafayette Flying Corps Association

The monument's central arch inscribed with the names of the deceased American pilots who died in service to France.

Former Lafayette Escadrille and Lafayette Flying Corps pilots attending the dedication blessing at the monument

Gathering of the dignitaries, former pilots, and family members at the dedication of the Lafayette Escadrille Memorial, July 4, 1928. Major Lufbery's father, Edward, stands to the left of the Monument behind the French officers seated at the rail. Dressed in a gray suit and dark fedora, his large white mustache is quite prominent. Raoul's older brother, Julien, his sister-in-law Laurence Lufbery, and her young daughter, Doris Lufbery, were also present at the dedication.

manner. It will be made under the personal supervision of a member of the committee.

Pardon the delay acknowledging this issue to the Easter vacations. As I only need one authorization I am returning the other to you.

We have made an arrangement with Mr. Bernard Lane, the undertaker of the American Cathedral of the Holy Trinity in Paris, to take entire charge of the exhumation of the bodies of our dead, and he will also provide heavy oak coffins with thick lead lining, which will protect the remains of our pilots practically indefinitely, particularly as the Crypt has been especially constructed so as to be well lighted and absolutely dry.

Every week the mail from America tells us of more people who are coming over to the Dedication and I feel sure that you will see scores of people at that time who knew and admired and loved your son.

When you do come to Paris, please be sure to let me know as far in advance as possible, as I am enormously taken with the work of the Memorial at present, having lots of details to attend to as the date of the Dedication approaches, and as Rockwell is also a fairly busy man and we both wish to be sure of having you join us at lunch or dinner on your visit.[4]

With kindest personal regards, I am faithfully yours.

Lewis D. Crenshaw, Adm. Deleg.

Once the families of the fallen had granted their approval, the effort was begun on 15 May 1928 to remove the bodies of the sixty-seven members of the Lafayette Flying Corps from their resting places in France, Belgium, Italy, and the United States and to reinter them at the memorial in time for the July 4 dedication ceremonies. There were sixty-eight sarcophagi in the sanctuary, one of which was to be left empty. In truth, a number sit empty today because of the impossibility of locating or removing several of the Lafayette pilots' remains, or because their families failed to grant their approval. Only six of the twelve dead pilots of the Escadrille Lafayette whose names appear on tombs in the memorial's crypt are truly buried there. They are Edmond Genet, James Ralph Doolittle, Ronald Hoskier, Raoul Lufbery, Douglas MacMonagle, and Paul Pavelka.

Almost from the moment of its conception the monument was fraught with controversy. Even before its con-

---

4. Paul Ayers Rockwell was the brother of Lafayette Escadrille pilot Kiffin Rockwell. Paul Rockwell was involved early on in the construction of the monument.

The tombs of the pilots in the monument's crypt. A crude lighting system has been strung along the wall below the windows.

struction began, a war broke out between former pilot William Thaw and Norman Prince's father, Frederick Henry Prince, which lasted through the years of the memorial's construction and ultimately saw the embittered Prince refusing to allow Norman's remains to rest in the memorial. On the very eve before the monument's dedication, a further dispute erupted between the former pilots it was intended to honor, which threatened to disrupt the dedication ceremonies.

The friction began when a Lafayette Escadrille pilot had objected to the inclusion of the names of the Lafayette Flying Corps dead with the names of the Lafayette Escadrille dead, for which the monument had been intended. The former pilot further complained that the Lafayette Flying Corps, which had been established in 1917, was attempting to "steal the thunder" of the Lafayette Escadrille.

Other Lafayette Escadrille members objected to the sharing of the Lafayette Flying Corps in the monument's inscriptions and in the official ceremonies and further complained that the names of living corpsmen should not be inscribed on the monument as had been planned. But their differences were worked through by 'harmonizing the conflicting views."

At the 4 July 1928 dedication of the monument, which had been made possible by the private donations of many French and American citizens, ten thousand people attended, including the American relatives of many dead airmen. Mr. Edward Lufbery attended the dedication. Also observing the ceremonies were Ferdinand Foch, marshal of

France; France's minister of war, Painleve; US ambassador Myron T. Herrick; and Georges Thenault, France's air attache to Washington and the Lafayette Escadrille's former commander, along with a number of the French and American pilots.

Today Raoul Lufbery's body reposes in his sarcophagus in the Lafayette Escadrille monument crypt. But such is not the case for Norman Prince, a founding member of the squadron. Following the death of Prince on 12 October 1916, Lufbery wrote this of him.

> The death of Marc Pourpe and Norman Prince were the two most painful events in my life. Pourpe was my friend and mentor. Prince was my best friend, my most intimate friend, and confidant.

The two pilots had seemed destined to repose side by side in the monument. But in the spring of 1937, Frederick Henry Prince, Norman's father, removed his son's body from the monument and had him reinterred in a private chapel in the National Cathedral in Washington, DC. The senior Prince had become angered at the pushback from the other Lafayette Escadrille veterans, who felt he was attempting to elevate his son's role in the squadron over the efforts of his fellow pilots. Former pilot William Thaw made their argument in 8 May 1929 letter to an editorial published in the *Pittsburgh Post Gazette*.

> It is my personal opinion that a private chapel is being purchased near the remains of President Wilson and Admiral Dewey because the surviving Lafayette pilots and the committee in charge of erecting our memorial in France refused to permit any partiality with our memorial in Paris, or any exaggeration with the Lafayette Escadrille, either in connection with its founding, operation or administration.

William Nelson Cromwell, a Paris-based American lawyer and the founder and president of the Lafayette Escadrille Memorial Foundation, had overseen the financing and building of the monument. He had personally contributed 600,000 francs to ensure its perpetual maintenance. However, his sizable donation eventually proved inadequate, and the passage of time took its toll on this burial site of America's first combat aviators. Just a few short years after its construction, water seeping from the nearby hills into the crypt area damaged it and the sarcophagi located there. With the passage of time, the edifice fell into disrepair. By the early twenty-first century the structure itself had suffered major damage.

The Lafayette Escadrille Memorial Foundation felt that the restoration of the monument was beyond their ability to repair and maintain. In 2015 the foundation reached an agreement with the American Battlefields Monument Committee to take over restoration of the structure. Restoration was completed in 2016, in time for the one hundredth anniversary celebration honoring the formation of the squadron. In January 2017 the American Commission took over ownership and responsibility for the monument, guaranteeing its perpetual care.

Copy of the approval form from Edward Lufbery granting authorization to remove his son's remains from the American Cemetery at Thiacourt for placement in his tomb in the memorial crypt

Raoul Lufbery's Posthumous Honors and Legacy

Many aviation historians consider Major Raoul Lufbery as one of the fathers of American combat aviators and certainly one of the fathers of the US Air Force. Lufbery's contributions are many and far ranging. Listed here are some of his most notable posthumous honors and achievements.

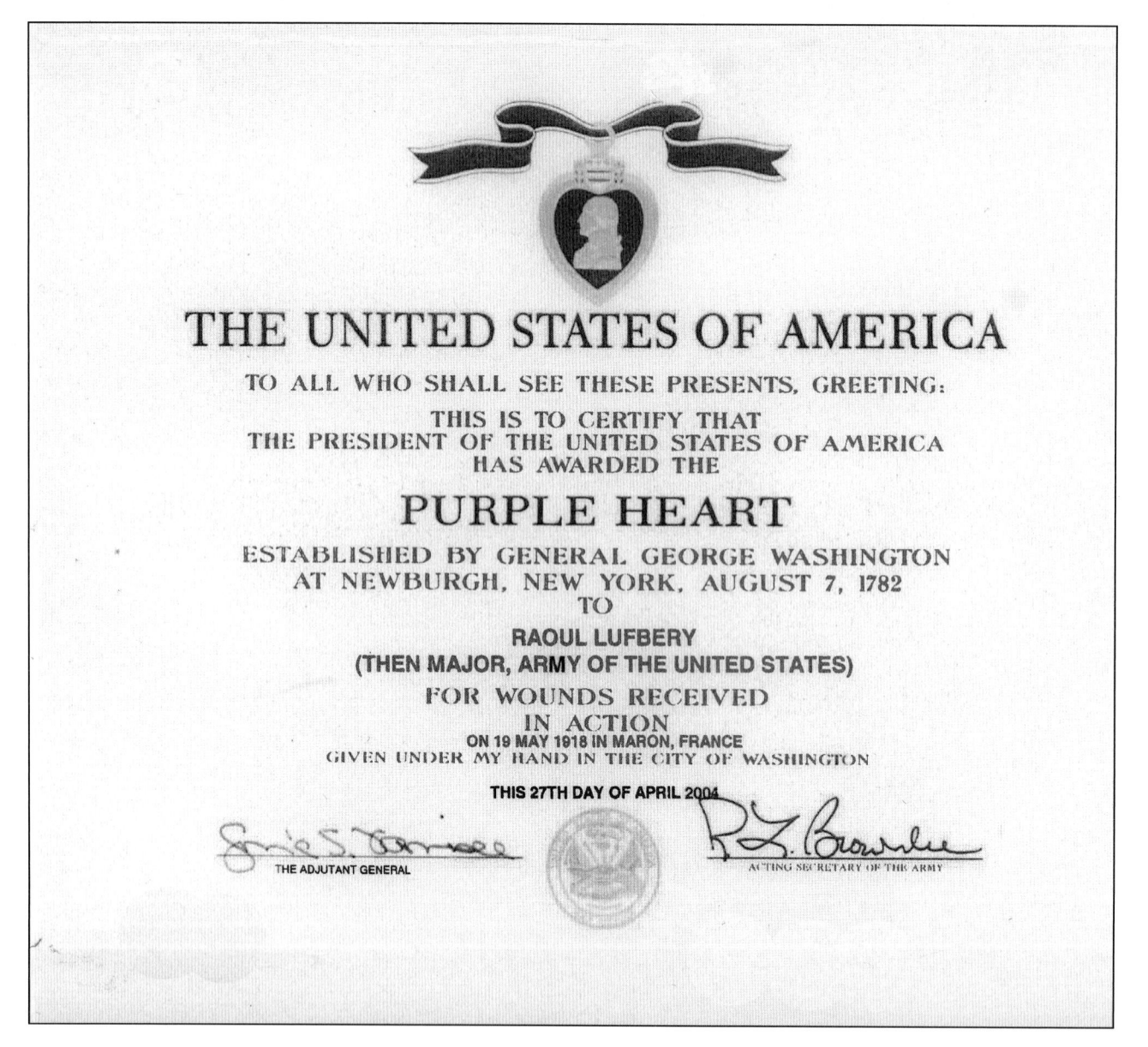

THE UNITED STATES OF AMERICA

TO ALL WHO SHALL SEE THESE PRESENTS, GREETING:

THIS IS TO CERTIFY THAT
THE PRESIDENT OF THE UNITED STATES OF AMERICA
HAS AWARDED THE

PURPLE HEART

ESTABLISHED BY GENERAL GEORGE WASHINGTON
AT NEWBURGH, NEW YORK, AUGUST 7, 1782
TO

RAOUL LUFBERY
(THEN MAJOR, ARMY OF THE UNITED STATES)

FOR WOUNDS RECEIVED
IN ACTION
ON 19 MAY 1918 IN MARON, FRANCE
GIVEN UNDER MY HAND IN THE CITY OF WASHINGTON
THIS 27TH DAY OF APRIL 2004

THE ADJUTANT GENERAL ACTING SECRETARY OF THE ARMY

The United Purple Heart was awarded to Major Lufbery and accepted by family members at the New England Air Museum at Windsor Locks, Connecticut, in 2004.

Raoul Lufbery's image on the Lafayette Escadrille Harmon Trophy, which was presented each year for the most outstanding international achievement for the art of flying. The original Harmon trophy is 24 inches tall and depicts Lufbery standing beside an eagle about to take wing. He is launching a Spad fighter plane into the air.

An Aero Club of America Medal issued in his honor

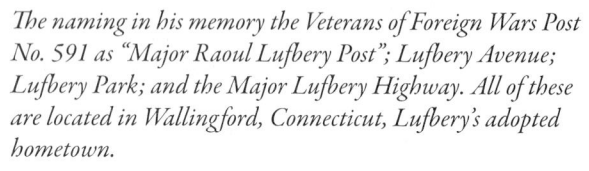

The naming in his memory the Veterans of Foreign Wars Post No. 591 as "Major Raoul Lufbery Post"; Lufbery Avenue; Lufbery Park; and the Major Lufbery Highway. All of these are located in Wallingford, Connecticut, Lufbery's adopted hometown.

WALLINGFORD, CONN., U. S. A.
HOME OF MAJOR LUFBURY
THE "ACE" AVIATOR
KILLED IN ACTION MAY 19, 1918.
THE WORLD FAMOUS AMERICAN FLYER

Raoul Lufbery
World War One
TOWN OF WALLINGFORD

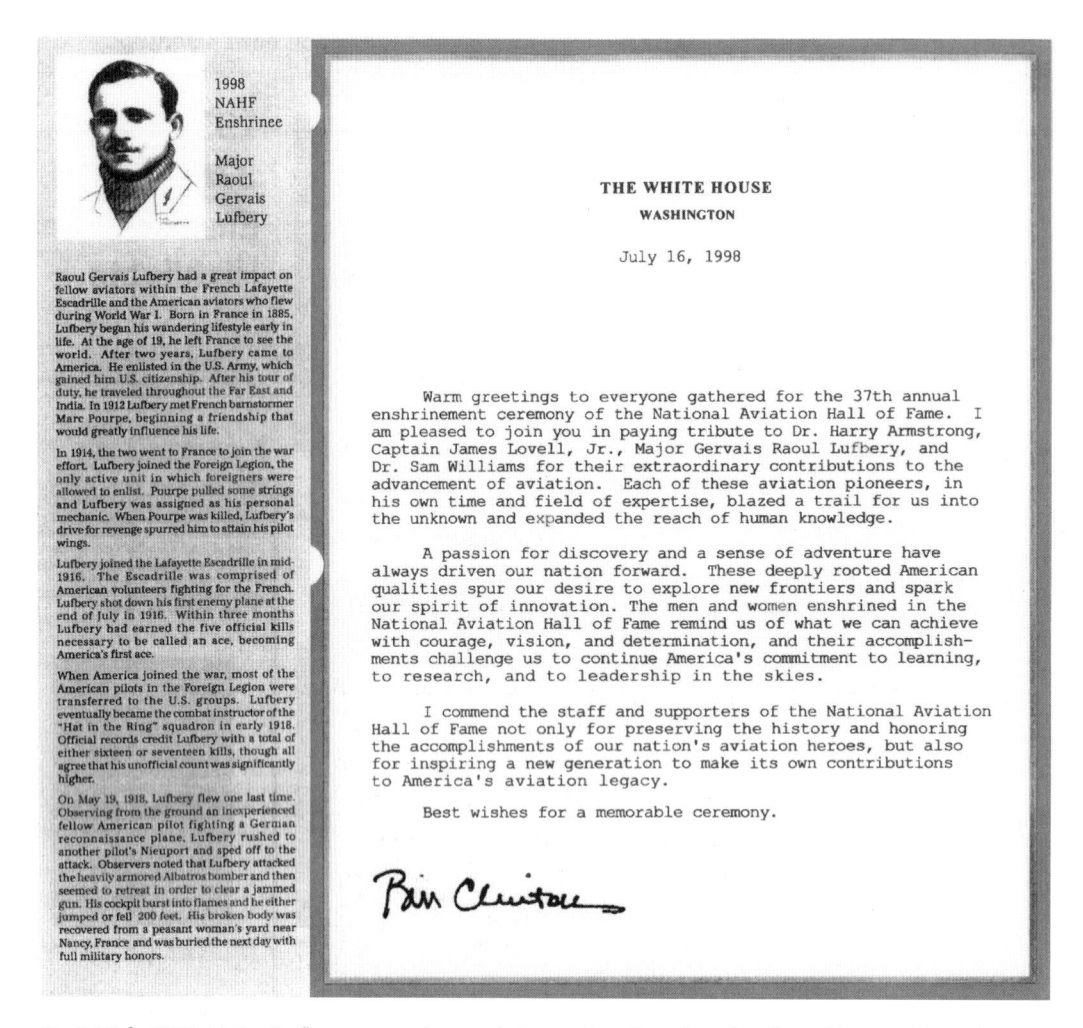

On 16 July 1998 Major Lufbery was posthumously honored, inducted, and enshrined during the 37th annual National Aviation Hall of Fame Enshrinement Ceremony in Dayton, Ohio. His enshrinee biography stated that "Raoul Gervais Lufbery had a great impact on fellow aviators within the French Lafayette Escadrille and the American aviators who flew during World War I."

The US Air Force Academy in Colorado Springs instituted the Major Raoul Lufbery Outstanding Cadet in Western Language Minor Award given annually in memory of Major Lufbery to the cadet who excels in Western language studies. The award is presented in May during the academy's graduation ceremony.

The naming of the Raoul Lufbery Aerodrome on Long Island, New York, and education exhibits on behalf of Lufbery at the New England Air Museum, at the Smithsonian Institution, and at the National Aviation Hall of Fame in Dayton, Ohio. Numerous streets and military buildings throughout the US were given his name in tribute to his World War I military aviation accomplishments.

Here are his most notable achievements:

• The mastery and understanding of the "extreme engineering and mechanical limits" of those early military flying machines under aerial combat-tested situations.

• Lufbery always demanded and accomplished the highest maintenance standards by frequent inspections of all mechanical parts and components of aircraft, machine guns, and ammunition. This kept planes in top running order for superior performance and reliability under combat operations. This was especially important during the infancy and initial start-up development years for military wing aircraft.

• "Lufbery's private formula," which he taught to the novice pilots in his squadron: *Never substitute opportunity and favorable position for reckless courage in combat. Those who do bring on an early grave.*

• Many times Lufbery instructed and mentored novice pilots in the intricacies of aerial patrolling and combat tactics. Records show that on several occasions he saved the life of a fellow pilot during aerial encounters with enemy planes.

Raoul Lufbery in Art and Print

Chalk on paper portrait of Raoul Lufbery by John Elliott (1859–1925), an English author and illustrator

Oil on Canvas portrait of Raoul Lufbery by Henry Farre (1871–1934), a French artist who served in World War I as an aerial observer-bombardier. Farre sketched and painted scenes from his combat experiences and painted portraits of French and American aces.

Sketch of Raoul Lufbery by Cyrus Leroy Baldridge (1888–1977), a New York artist, illustrator, author, and adventurer

Raoul Lufbery on the 6 June 1918 back cover of Le Pays de France, *a patriotic French newspaper of World War I*

Major Raoul Lufbery and Sous Lieutenant Eugene Gilbert on the cover of La Guerre Aerienne, *20 June 1918. Gilbert was killed on 17 May 1918. Lufbery was killed on 19 May 1918.*

Raoul Lufbery just returned from a combat patrol, supplement no. 36, La Guerre Aerienne

Raoul Lufbery on the 24 February 1918 cover of Le Pelerin, *a French Catholic weekly magazine founded in 1873 by the Assumptionist Order of priests*

Major Lufbery, The Avenger, *1942 Real Heroes Comic Book edition, published by Parent's Magazine Press*

Liane de Pougy: A Mother in Question by Dennis Gordon

When reading through Jacques Mortane's biographies of Marc Pourpe and Raoul Lufbery, the reader might ask: What was it that created the strong bond between the two men? Both were near the same age, just two years apart, and both became world travelers while teenagers in search of adventure. Marc was 25 and Raoul 27 when they joined forces in Calcutta in January 1913. Marc the exhibition flyer, and Raoul his mechanic and public spokesman. Each placed his trust in the other in order for Pourpe to perform his long and dangerous flights.

Yet the similarity in their lives preceded those days, dating back to their infancy, when both were separated from their mothers and raised by grandmothers. Lufbery's mother died when he was fifteen months old, necessitating his father to place him in the care of his grandmother. Similarly, Pourpe's father was forced to turn his infant son over to his grandmother when Marc's mother abandoned the family.

In chapter 1 of *Two Great Knights of Adventure*, Jacques Mortane introduced his reader to Liane de Pougy, Marc Pourpe's mother. He showed the reader a concerned mother dealing with a rebellious son. But there is much more to her story. Her fame and reputation far eclipsed her son's aviation legacy and it was sealed in the posthumous publication of her *Blue Notebooks*.

Anne-Marie Chassaigne was born on 2 July 1869 in La Flèche, Sarthe, France, the daughter of Pierre Blaise Eugène Chassaigne, a retired captain in the Lancers, and Aimée (née Lopez) Chassaigne, who consecrated her infant to the Virgin Mary. Her father was sixty years old and her mother forty-three at the time of her birth. Later, Anne-Marie would write how she "despised them for being old, poor, simple and having principles," and how she "disdained their advice."

Anne-Marie's elderly and indulgent parents enrolled their strong-willed daughter in a Catholic convent school to be educated. When she returned home six years later

Liane de Pougy

following the completion of her schooling, she declared, "I came back, a child no longer, I kept all my kindness as well as my smiles for the men who gravitated toward us."

At age sixteen, she ran off with Lieutenant Armand Pourpe, a French naval officer from Marseille seven years her senior. They married on 15 July 1886. On 17 May 1887 a son, Marc, was born to the Pourpes in Lorient. Anne-Marie expressed disappointment in her child's gender. She later confessed, "I longed passionately for a girl because of the dresses and the curly hair. My son was like a little living doll given to a small girl."

Anne-Marie's husband treated her with indifference from the beginning of their marriage. When Pourpe was temporarily transferred to a billet in Marseille, he placed his young wife and son in a third-floor apartment above a girls boarding school in the Rue Dragon district. Abandoned and alone, she played with the young students to relieve her boredom. She also took on lovers. Her first was a ship's lieutenant named Cronon, who served with her husband. Her second was the Marquis de Portes.

When Lieutenant Pourpe began selling Anne-Marie's family mementos to pay down their debts, she decided to free herself from her mundane life and sold her only remaining possession, a rosewood piano, for four hundred francs. Abandoning her infant son, she later stated, "An hour later I left for Paris, for my dream, for fame and for filth, for my tumultuous destiny. My husband was at Toulon and came to see me every week. When he arrived, he found the nest empty and the bird flown."

In order to fulfill his military obligations, Lieutenant Pourpe sent Marc to Suez to live with the boy's grandmother. Armand Pourpe died on 12 September 1892 at age thirty in a Marseille asylum, following his return from war service in China. Marc, just five years old at the time, continued to be raised by his grandmother.

Once Anne-Marie Pourpe reached Paris, she roomed with a female friend who introduced her to the lifestyle of wealthy pleasure-seekers who were quickly attracted to her stunning beauty. She supported herself through small acting parts. She formed a lesbian relationship with Countess Valtesse de La Bigne, whose massive brass bed served as a rendezvous for dissipated noblemen. The countess schooled Anne-Marie in the courtesan profession and introduced her to the hedonistic habits of wealthy, titled sensualists. One of them became Anne-Marie's third lover.

"At eighteen, when I sent the laws of society and the family flying, driven by my greed to know everything... I became the irresistible passion, the Ideal (so he said) of the Marquis Charles de Mac-Mahon." Anne-Marie soon cast Mac-Mahon aside "as casually as I would have swallowed an egg," but not until she destroyed his marriage and relieved him of ten thousand francs.

While she was ruining Mac-Mahon, she carried on a second affair with Evremond de Saint-Alary, a horse breeder and inveterate gambler. Before they separated, he spent most of the money she had taken from Mac-Mahon.

Following the conclusion of those liaisons, Anne-Marie met Vicomte de Pougy and soon became his paramour. Although the affair was brief, Anne-Marie took his name

Lianon the dancer at the Folies-Bergere

when they parted. Henceforth, she became Liane de Pougy. Her new given name was bestowed upon her by Valtesse de La Bigne, her decadent teacher and mentor.

Liane began working as a dancer at the Folies-Bergère. She was keenly aware of the effect her appearance had on others. She boasted, "It seemed to me natural enough that people should pay homage to my youth and beauty." She self-educated herself in art, literature, and poetry while appearing with the Folies, performing in Paris, in the French Riviera, in Rome, and in St. Petersburg.

In 1894, while playing in pantomime in St. Petersburg, Liane, then twenty-five, met Count Vladimir Miatleff, whom she called "a poet and a madman." Like other international members of the nobility, the impotent count succumbed to her beauty and charm. Liane later wrote of him, "He ruined himself for me, just for the pleasure of looking at me.... One day he summoned a Paris jeweler... so that I could choose a row of pearls and some rings." The jeweler "spread a million and a half's worth of jewels on the table.... There were ruby and diamond tiaras, emerald necklaces, diamond chains, a parure of turquoises and diamonds, etc. Mia was pacing the room—I can see him now—with his hands behind his back. Finally, I cried out: 'I simply can't make up my mind! Mia, you decide—they are all so beautiful!' Then he gave me a charming smile, looked at me with his big black eyes, and said simply: 'Take the lot.' I took the lot. He was a great nobleman."

Roman Potocki, an elderly Polish count, lavished Liane with money. While she was starring at the Folies, Potocki, another inveterate gambler, "appointed himself my *cavaliere servente*. Every day he would put aside five thousand francs from his baccarat money for the whims and the gloves of his little Lianon." She boasted, "I am Lianon the dancer at the Folies-Bergère, billed during the European tour in 1898 as 'Liane de Pougy wearing jewels worth a million.'"

At the end of the nineteenth century, Liane gained renown as Paris's most beautiful and notorious demimonde. She became the darling of the press, which continually published articles and images of her while calling her the "most beautiful courtesan of the century." She was swept up into Paris's turbulent life and used her assets to manipulate those pleasure-seekers pursuing her and casting their fortunes at her feet. Their ranks included the nobility, the aristocracy, artists, musicians, literati, politicians, financiers, and designers.

In an 11 October 1926 diary entry she summed up that period of her life: "At the age of eighteen I had a husband and a child. At that age I ran away from it all, driven by a fatal destiny. Up to the age of eighteen: family, principles, routine, and gentleness. From eighteen to thirty-six (another eighteen years), I lived in turmoil and among passion—every kind—either experienced or endured. I learned to know the world, a sad distinction. At thirty-six I met Georges."

Georges was a Romanian prince Liane had met when she was thirty-five and he was twenty-three. Of Georges, she wrote, "Oh, these Balkan types! When I first knew Georges I adored him." On 8 June 1910, Liane, then forty-one, married Georges, an agnostic, in the Catholic Church according to her faith. Prior to the ceremony, she confessed her sins, telling the priest, "Father, I have lived a very free life. Apart from killing and stealing I have done everything." Georges brought his royal title and little else to the marriage. Henceforth, Liane became known as Princess Ghika.

On 1 July 1919, one day prior to her fiftieth birthday, Liane began recording events from her past and current life in a journal that would eventually fill a series

Prince and Princess Ghika aboard the passenger liner Wisconsin, *Los Angeles, 9 October 1932*

of notebooks. She called them *My Blue Notebooks.* Her strikingly frank entries concealed nothing and exposed a woman immersed in narcissism and self-indulgence, in promiscuity with both sexes, in lavish spending on any whim. She also revealed a woman hungering for a relationship with God, who longed to free herself from her hedonistic lifestyle but lacked the willpower to do so. In one diary entry she flaunted her vices. In a subsequent entry she expressed revulsion over them.

She followed a similar pattern when writing about her relationship with her son, Marc Pourpe, applauding then admonishing her actions as his mother. In one revealing diary entry titled "Confession," she wrote this of herself: "You were a torment to your husband and an overwhelmingly heavy moral burden to your son." She then thanked God for turning her into "a real mother for my Marco."

In 1898, when Marc was eleven years old and attending London's Harrow preparatory school, his 29-year-old mother had reached the zenith of her career. In 1903 Marc was enrolled in Paris's College Chaptal, a secondary boarding school. Throughout his adolescence his mother maintained a room for him at her grand townhouse on Rue Neva. However, Liane had never been a motherly example for her son, and with all the publicity about her (with the posters, handbills, and postcards circulating her image throughout the continent), Marc must have been keenly aware of, and embarrassed by, her unorthodox lifestyle. Furthermore, as Jacques Mortane revealed, she wounded Marc with her cold formality, addressing him with the pronoun *vous,* most commonly used for someone unrelated, rather than the informal *tu,* which is customarily used to address a child or family member.

These excerpts from her *Blue Notebooks* reveal her guilt, her denial, and her pride as she recorded her relationship with her son.

3 July 1919. "My most piercing grief, the one that came near to killing me and threatened my reason (I spent fifteen months in cruel nursing homes) was the death of my son, my only child, the aviator Marc Pourpe, a volunteer who fell on the field of honour near Villers-Bretonneux on December 2nd 1914."

11 July 1919. "I did not love my son enough when he was alive. I was all woman—woman, not mother. My love was not able—didn't really want—to make a place for itself in his gloriously beautiful, excessively independent life. Oh how I have regretted it, how I have wept and been punished!"

17 July 1919. "[T]here is my Marco's dear little room, empty forever but so full of memories. I can see him now in his sky-blue pajamas, with his smooth skin, his hair, which grew so beautifully, his complete lack of mustache. He looked like a fifteen-year-old girl. I was always scolding him for not loving me enough."

17 July 1919. "My son went into open revolt against me."

16 August 1919. "Yesterday I reread the letter he wrote me for my birthday in 1914. His fame, courage, luck, and success had enlarged his spirit. He no longer resented the things about me which had wounded him. We loved each other tenderly: I was proud of him and he was glad about my marriage. Everything had become loving and sweet between us . . . my darling, how glad I am that you left me this memory of our sweetest understanding following after our savage times, and quite effacing them."

24 August 1919. "Marco had my hair, same color, quality, quantity, growing into seven little peaks all around the head. When he brushed it back he was a real beauty."

2 December 1919. "At midday it was five years since my child died for his country. . . . I had gone out, I remember, to buy something for a layette we were putting together for a poor woman whose husband was at the front. Suddenly I felt the most violent pain in my bowels."

21 February 1920. "The town of Tourane has sent me a very beautiful letter of thanks. At Lorient, where my son was born, there was to start with some question of naming a street after him. There were maneuverings and discussions. Finally this is what they came up with for me: 'We will wait for the end of the war so that we can choose among the heroes of Lorient.' Then last year the

Nathalie Barney, American playwright, poet, and novelist

mayor came to see me and gave me to understand with considerable clumsiness that all I had to do was make over a hundred thousand francs to the town of Lorient and the thing was done. . . . I . . . showed him out and left it at that. I have absolutely no intention of stripping myself because my child died for France!"

12 May 1920. "My son's birthday today; he is thirty-one. I longed passionately for a girl because of the dresses and the curly hair. My son was like a little living doll given to a small girl. I was very proud and forgot all the suffering I had been through. Yet, fate was to make me a hopeless mother; all of life called me, all the different countries drew me away.

My Marco, who was not loved enough and who didn't love me enough! During the last three years we understood each other better and drew nearer to each other.

My God, thank You for awakening me under the spur of pain. I bless You for all the suffering, which turned me into a real mother for my Marco . . . "

30 July 1924. "They have let me know that I have been granted the Military Medal in memory of my son, who had the right to it because of his two citations. The address

proclaimed 'Widow Pourpe.' I am absolutely not the Widow Pourpe, nor have I ever been, having been divorced. In law I then reverted to being Madame Chassaigne. So the Widow Pourpe, I (am) informed that she will be given the Military Medal for her son Marc Pourpe, killed by the enemy; that if she wants the ceremony of handing over she must travel to Longvic, and that she will not be reimbursed for any expenses she incurs! If she prefers, she can have it brought to her by the commandant of her local police station. I feel shocked, bruised, wounded, ruffled, and indignant. To be threatened with the police! The neighborhood will think that they are coming to arrest me."

17 October 1940. "The war of 1914: our house in Saint-Germain turned into a dressing station, devotion to the motherland, yes, but it was an unthinking sort of excitement; Marco's departure when he volunteered with Gilbert Garros; his death . . . I fell victim to an indescribable despair, a grief made far worse by remorse at not having been a good mother, at not having loved that child enough, at having preferred Georges—that is to say myself—to my son."

These excerpts from Liane's diaries portrayed a mother suffering from anguish and turmoil, who first sought justification for, then revealed her guilt about her broken relationship with her son.

Liane continued her self-indulgent lifestyle even after her June 1910 marriage to Georges Ghika and following the death of her son Marco in December 1914. She freely circulated and moved with ease among the Paris literati. Her social circle included the French poets Max Jacob and Jean Cocteau, archeologist and religious historian Solomon Reinach, stage actress Sarah Bernhardt, financier Maurice de Rothschild, and American poet and playwright Nathalie Barney, the leading sapphist of her day. Barney and Liane were often intimate together in a relationship that lasted forty years. Liane called Nathalie "my Flossie." Both later wrote and saw their works published.

Once, Liane used her former mentor Valtesse de La Bigne to torment Flossie "to the limit—both permissible and forbidden." She recalled the incident in her memoir: "I was unforgivable. One day I took Flossie to her house, went into the bedroom with Valtesse, locked the door, and refused her nothing, highly amused at the thought of Flossie speculating and suffering on the other side of the door." Eventually, the ardor between Flossie and Liane dissipated as each sought new conquests. Liane called Flossie "my greatest sin." She declared, "I was passionate and always drawn to women, nervous and disgusted in the presence of men."

In March 1926 Liane met Marcelle Manon Thiébaut, a nineteen-year-old neurotic artist who made a living selling her drawings and woodcuts, and by illustrating books. Liane was smitten by her "new little friend." She described Manon in a March 24 diary entry as a "really exquisite girl."

Liane affectionately named her new friend "My Tiny One." Strong physical impulses developed between them. On June 2 she sent Georges to the Roscoff train station to fetch Manon to their home. To Liane, she was "a joy sent from heaven." Manon was present on June 8 when the Ghikas celebrated their sixteenth wedding anniversary. Liane, age fifty-nine, proclaimed that she and Georges, age forty-two, had grown closer throughout the years and "have been kneaded and blended into one." Georges, she declared, is "my husband, my love, my all."

Liane expressed joy that "Tiny One" shared their home. On June 20 she wrote of her, "My little Thiébaut is charming, her mind is so open, so broad, so subtle, and she has pretty manners into the bargain. She is gentle and authoritative at the same time. She is perfectly well bred. Every day she thanks us for having her."

But a dramatic turn of events came fourteen days later. On July 4 Liane recorded in her diary, "Georges loves Tiny One! Tiny One loves Georges! Crack, it has happened! It is worse than cancer." When Liane confronted the pair, Georges proposed a ménage à trois. She ordered Manon to leave. However, when she did, Georges followed her out, causing Liane to lament, "My great, splendid, complete, pure happiness is over." She put away her notebooks and departed for Paris "to start another life."

In September 1926 Liane returned to her Clos Marie home in Roscoff, Brittany. On the twenty-third she resumed her diary. Nathalie Barney had brought by two lady friends to stay with her for "consolation." She described the breakup of her marriage in detail. She listed her financial and legal stipulations to Georges through her attorney and suggested Georges file for divorce.

Throughout her diary, Liane constantly expressed her desire to separate herself from her lustful passions and to build a closer relationship with God. Following Georges's departure, she sensed the opportunity had arrived.

"Alone and free," she proclaimed, "alone, I will draw nearer to You, oh my God. There lies my longing and my will." But temptation awaited her in her new friend, Mimi Franchetti, "the most beautiful, the most ardent, the most seductive of women. Is it one more test?" she wrote. "Is it consolation?"

Once again, Liane succumbed to Nathalie Barney's influence. The year 1926 concluded with Liane's intimate involvement with Mimi, with Georges pleading for her to take him back, and with their lawyers circulating divorce documents between the two.

On 1 March 1927 Liane again took up her diary. She and Mimi had separated. Inexplicably, Georges had returned to her. She felt he had changed dramatically, both physically and mentally. In Liane's mind, the Georges Ghika she had known and had lived with for eighteen years has not come back. Georges had returned a sickly creature she called Gilles, whom she described as being "shrunken, older, grinning, maniacal." Going forward, their relationship would be troubled and chaotic.

In late September 1928 Liane and Georges were on an outing near Grenoble when they motored past an "old gray house" obscured by trees. They stopped on a whim, returned, and rang the bell beside a large door emblazoned with the words "Asylum of Saint Agnes." They had stopped out of an "unhealthy curiosity," knowing the asylum housed children "who were idiots from birth." But Liane did not foresee that once the door opened, once she entered the asylum, another door would open in her heart, which would eventually lead her to the spiritual relationship with God that she had long sought.

The Mother Superior of the asylum greeted Liane and Georges. Liane described her as "a woman of impressive calm and simplicity, clearly marked by nobility and dignity . . . whose gaze could make water spring forth from a rock." Failing to see any of the "unhappy inmates," Liane and Georges asked to visit the chapel to obscure their real purpose for stopping. She put ten francs in the poor box. Liane declared that she left the asylum "shaken to the quick, vanquished by the Mother Superior."

The following day she returned alone. The Mother Superior, Sister Marie-Xavier, seemed to be expecting Liane. She found the nun's demeanor completely natural. Liane apologized for her small donation of the previous day and handed the sister fifty francs. Then she opened her heart to her and "talked a long, long time" about herself. Sister Marie-Xavier listened attentively, then asked Liane to come back that afternoon with Georges so that she could show her "her children."

When the couple returned, the Mother Superior took them to the playground. What they saw there stunned them and filled them with revulsion. Liane nearly fainted when surrounded by "sixty-seven unhappy creatures between eight and sixteen years old, scarred by the most inexorable suffering."

"Oh! Those cries, those contortions, those grimaces, that smell . . . once you have seen that, never never again can you complain of anything! I was ashamed of having talked so much about myself to Sister Marie-Xavier. I pressed the poor tremulous, rather dirty hands that reached out toward me. I searched those wandering, fixed or mad eyes for some glimmer of light. I laid my hand on those foreheads, tumultuous or stunned, feverish, so pale . . . To think that I had given them no more alms than a heedless passerby might have done! I gave five hundred francs, Georges Ghika gave a hundred, and I knew that he was more disturbed than he liked to admit."

For many days thereafter, Liane returned to the asylum. She and Mother Marie-Xavier formed a strong bond. The run-down asylum lacked even the most basic necessities. Liane was moved by the dire conditions and soon began raising funds for the structure. She decided to commit herself completely to the welfare of the children, whom she had come to know individually.

"I have written a very good letter to all my friends explaining the nature of the work in a most moving way; up to now I have collected nearly five thousand francs including my own offering, and that is only the beginning. I will move heaven and earth to help them. I will go begging everywhere." Over time, Liane became the asylum's leading benefactress and raised thousands of francs for its refurbishment and upkeep through donations from her wealthy social contacts.

Her relationship with "Gilles" continued to deteriorate. Although he physically improved, Liane declared that it "simply serves to nourish the strength of his delusion, his dishonesty, and his obscenity. He expresses himself only through that." Nevertheless, she remained faithful to him, despite the sorrow and desolation she experienced from their relationship.

It was August 1931 before Liane put pen to her diary again. Three years had passed; five years since Georges had returned to her. He had become an antithetical roadblock in her spiritual path. She calls him her torturer. She felt "purified by pain." She prayed for death to escape him. When she could bear no more, she begged God for deliverance. Her prayers were answered in an unforeseen way. Georges's mother suffered a paralyzing stroke. When he rushed to Romania to be at her side, Liane prayed that she would never see him again.

In her husband's absence, Liane doubled down on her solicitation for the asylum. It bore much fruit as her wealthy friends donated generously. One donor, Gabrielle "Coco" Chanel, "was spontaneously and splendidly generous." Liane collected nearly 300,000 francs from her contacts, enough to repair the asylum and to provide it with linen and coal. Liane declared, "This work has become my reason for staying alive. These unhappy ones and the admirable sisters are now my only family." The children of the asylum had given her the opportunity to atone for the abandonment of her own infant son, Marco.

Georges wrote daily from Romania. Liane hoped to delay his return to France by telling him she was traveling. On 16 September 1931 Georges informed her that he would be in Paris near the end of the month. She dreaded his reentry into her life.

Liane still lacked the resolve needed to secure her spiritual commitment to God. She fell in with two companions who took her to Toulon in search of opium. They entered a run-down hotel looking for Jean Cocteau, the French poet. The building was often raided by the police because of drug activity and pederasty. They found an emaciated Cocteau in a filthy room, intoxicated with opium. One of Liane's friends made a drug purchase from Cocteau's supply, then asked Liane to carry it in her purse to avoid confiscation by the police. She managed to do this without detection.

Liane continued to ignore Georges's correspondence but knew he must turn up one day. On October 11 she wrote in despair, "I feel as though I were in prison: grief and solitude. Oh to find God! My God, still beyond my reach, accept my piercing, deep and overwhelming sorrow."

On Sunday, September 25, Georges appeared at her door bearing gifts. He returned "depressed, exhausted, aching, cross." Liane resigned herself to his presence and promised to care for him "to the best of my ability."

Liane began the year 1932 worried about how she would provide the asylum with coal for its furnace. Gabrielle Chanel sent her five thousand francs for her "little invalids at Saint Agnes." On January 23, Liane, then sixty-three years old, penned a soul-wrenching confession in her diary.

"Then, quite suddenly, I felt within me, against me, a flood of bitter reproach. The flood rose, submerged me; all my life was hurled at me like stones, all my sins like mud. It became a delirium, tears poured from my eyes, I accused myself, I asked pardon, I had become nothing but repentance and desolation. I said to myself: 'What have you done since your birth, and now that you are approaching death's door, what have you done with your life? . . . Your parents lived for you and you broke their hearts. . . . You dragged your family's name in the mud. You were a torment to your husband, and an overwhelmingly heavy moral burden to your son. You had mercy on no one! Not one of those who came near you found grace in your eyes. You never loved even the most magnificent of your lovers. Kings, great financiers, poets, children, old men, scholars—they all clustered around you and you deceived them all.'"

Georges's health grew worse. He was diagnosed with jaundice and cirrhosis of the liver. Filled with remorse and despair, she prayed for God's help.

"Dear God, listen in this holy Passion week to the voice of the least of your servants, give her her daily bread, faith in You, hope in You, love in You. Accept and warm the numbness of your poor Marie Chassaigne, Marie-Anne who comes to you broken, worn out, footsore from the long road she has traveled, frantic with grief, in the throes of remorse and despair of having too often offended against you."

That summer Georges returned to Romania to visit his mother. It was a relief for Liane, finding him "difficult in so many ways." Shortly after his departure, Mother Marie-Xavier visited Liane at her Paris flat. Following their visit, Liane wrote of her and her asylum.

"Mother Marie-Xavier was here, upright and accessible, smiling with pleasure at seeing me again. Everything draws me toward her. I do so love that poor moving shelter-for-all-suffering. I foresee that it may become a refuge when I have truly succeeded in renouncing my self."

When Georges returned from Romania on September 12, he and Liane began a seventy-day sea cruise to Vancouver to help his health. They returned on November 27. On 4 January 1933 she read the obituary of Manon Thiébaut, "the woman who carried off my husband in 1926."

On April 14—Good Friday—she mentioned drawing comfort from Louis Perroy's book on Christ's crucifixion, *The Ascent of Calvary*, following the death of her beloved niece.

"Good Friday: fast, prayers, retreat. A man appeared on earth two thousand years ago and that man was the son of God. Oh Jesus, my Jesus, You who are still concealed from me, I give You my torn, calloused heart, so cold and indifferent, do with it what You will. The example of Your passion and that of the admirable devotion of my beloved sisters at the Asylum of Saint Agnes inspires me with the courage to give up everything. I am ashamed of my frivolity and triviality. I feel low and ridiculous, humiliated at never having accomplished anything big, strong, or beautiful. How could I have done that when I have never been able to conquer myself even in little things!"

On July 30 Georges left for two months to be with his ailing mother in Romania, leaving Liane alone with her "memories of vanished people and silenced voices." She reflected on her husband: "My poor Gilles with his dentures, his irresponsibility, his sparse gray hairs, his madman's meanderings . . . and the existence we are condemned to lead at each other's sides." Still, she credited him for bringing stability to her life. Her pity for him had replaced her anger. She reflected on their relationship.

"There were some men—and some women too, yes—who were never able to melt that ice. What I really did was love Love for Love's sake, and once my head had been won over, my body took great delight in giving itself. There were also a good many times when I was a little intoxicated animal with irresistible appetites. . . . Then Georges Ghika came by; what a benefactor he was! He took me and placed me where, at my age, I ought to be."

Georges continued to divide his time between Liane and his sick mother in Romania. Time healed wounds. A quiet acceptance appeared in their marriage. Liane declared, "I no longer expect anything from life; I seek God with all the strength that remains to me."

On 11 September 1934 she mentioned writing Max Jacob. She told him that "the only real happiness I can now envisage is doing the washing-up for my invalid children, escaping from the ignoble sewer in which I have lived and in which my old age is bogged down." She claims she did it cheerfully, "singing old songs."

On April 19 she wrote, "Georges arrives the day after tomorrow: back to our accustomed ways, back to hearing cynicism and blasphemy, back to the pain that comes from lack of tenderness."

On 1 August 1936 Liane returned to her notebooks after a one-year hiatus. Her mother-in-law had died in Bucharest the previous December. France was in turmoil and a European war appeared inevitable. Civil war raged in Spain, and Adolf Hitler was on the rise. Later that month, she and Georges sailed to England in anticipation of seeking refuge there.

In January 1937 she continued to work for St. Agnes, finding "charitable and generous benefactors." Her relationship with Georges had become less tumultuous. On February 8 she wrote of him, "I would detest him so much if I were not fond of him!"

On March 1 she again put pen to paper. "It is at Grenoble that I want to end my days. Will that be given to me? Will I be allowed one day to wash dishes for my invalids and the holy sisters, their poor dishes of chipped enamel? To obey the rule, within hearing of the convent bell; to play a part in that shelter of suffering—of suffering yes, but also of devotion, piety, goodness, renunciation? There, I could have opened my hands and let everything go. Am I capable of that? To be capable of it would be to be worthy of it. Lord, speak just one word . . ."

In April, Liane and Georges took a room in Grenoble's Hotel de L'Europe. For the next ten days, they visited Mother Marie-Xavier at the asylum. Liane called them "agonizing visits." They gave the sister a donation to purchase needed water rights for the asylum. They also brought sweets for the 110 children at the institution. Liane was overcome by their anguish. After viewing their suffering, she felt she could never again complain. When they concluded their visit, the couple left Grenoble for Geneva, Switzerland, for a hotel room on the lake shore in Vevey.

Then it was 15 October 1940. Three and a half years had passed since Liane last put pen to her notebook. One day, she and Georges visited the Bois-Cerf Clinic in Lausanne for treatment of their ailments. The clinic was run by an order of Trinitarian nuns, the Ladies of Bois-Cerf. She returned to "my story," writing of her remorse at having failed as a mother to Marco, of her petitions to Saint Anne, her patron saint, praying for forgiveness and help. Over time, she developed a spark of "fervent piety," which nudged her toward the faith of her youth. She strengthened her will to resist her passions. To do so, she had to abandon her friends. She felt crushed by the weight of her sins, continually asking herself "how could I, when I didn't even have the excuse of liking that frivolous life of so-called pleasure."

She read Alexei Tolstoy's *The Road to Calvary* during Lent. It awakened in her "the love for Jesus that had been sleeping in my heart." She hoped to conduct her life in a manner that would keep her "close to God every hour of the day." But she worried over Georges's spiritual welfare. She declared her love for him and prayed for his conversion, buoyed by the positive changes she had seen in his language and in his regard for the nuns at the clinic.

Father R. P. Rzewuski, a young Dominican priest and artist, entered Liane's life at the clinic. She described him as "remarkably handsome, young, attractive, full of joy of life, in demand, much liked." He soon became her confidant and spiritual adviser. She asked him, "Who or what pushed you toward God? What event brought about this vocation, your conversion? Some great sorrow, some insurmountable disgust?"

Father Rzewuski replied, "Neither sorrow nor disgust, but an immense inner emptiness that only the love of God and of my neighbor could fill." The priest had described Liane's own spiritual crisis. She opened her soul to him, revealing her remorse and "despairing repentance." Later, she said of Father Rzewuski, "He has always restored my courage; he has always found the right words."

After residing at the Hotel Carlton for eighteen months, Liane developed a skin condition. She and Georges checked into the Bois-Cerf Clinic. She was seventy-one. She hoped to remain there until her death.

"Here I became a new creature in a new life," she declared, praying "in great bursts" and working for the poor. She felt free of the threat of sin but had nothing to give back to God, having lost her "youth, beauty, strength."

Liane penned her last diary entry in January 1941. She turned her notebooks over to Father Rzewuski and the Dominican monastery at Estavayer, Switzerland. She gave them permission to destroy them, or publish them if they "might benefit some straying soul." She hoped that God's Divine Mercy would be recognized by the reader in her diaries, first through her shameful life, then through her repentance. She offered them up for publication "only in the spirit of humiliation."

She prayed constantly in the chapel before the image of the Infant Jesus for those she had offended and led into sin. Although she suffered long hours of despair and discouragement, she resisted those thoughts and viewed them as a test. "I feel my soul's spiritual life affirming my conversion" she wrote, "and yet I am only at the beginning of the way."

She ended her diary with this prayer: "My God, I believe in You, I hope in You, and I love You. May Your will be done." She signed off Anne-Marie Ghika, as though Liane de Pougy was no more.

In the mid-1940s, Georges suffered a stroke and died while visiting his aunt. His passing allowed Anne-Marie to further advance her spirituality. She enrolled in the convent order of St. Dominic as tertiary lay sister Anne-Marie Madeleine de la Penitence. She spent many days in her black-and-white habit, working with the handicapped children suffering from birth defects while spending her nights in quiet prayer seeking reparation for her past transgressions. All who interacted with her loved and respected her. A few years later, ill health drew her work to a close.

Dominican lay sister Anne-Marie Madeline de la Penitence

Anne-Marie spent her final days aspiring to sanctity at the Hotel Carlton in Lausanne, Switzerland. She died on 26 December 1950, at age eighty-one, and was buried on the grounds of her beloved Saint Agnes Asylum in Saint-Martin-le-Vinoux, France. Her memoirs were published in France in 1977.

SOURCE: *My Blue Notebooks*, by Liane de Pougy

Escadrille Morane Saulnier 23

French Escadrille 23 was formed at Brie, France, on 4 August 1914 under the command of Capitaine Auguste Le Renerend. On August 15 it relocated to the Saint Cyr airfield, where the squadron was assigned six two-seater Morane-Saulnier Type L monoplanes. These planes were initially a part of a canceled order of fifty aircraft that had been placed by the Turkish government. Once equipped, the escadrille became M. S. 23 (Morane Saulnier), a reconnaissance squadron under the command of Captain Francois de Vergnette de Lamotte.

The Morane Type L Parasol aircraft was 22 feet long and featured a 36-foot wingspan with a central cutout at the back of the wing. This allowed the pilot and observer access to their seats. The aircraft was normally powered by an 80-horsepower Gnome rotary engine. However, the squadron's planes, which had been part of the Turkish prewar order, had 50-horsepower Gnome engines. The plane's maximum speed was 70 miles per hour. The most unusual feature on the aircraft was the tall cabane, or tripod, in the center section of the wing, which supported the landing wires.

At the time Marc Pourpe was piloting the aircraft, the plane featured no armament. However, on occasion a crew member would board with a military carbine or pistol for aerial protection. In late 1914 some aviation teams were provided Lewis machine guns.

The squadron's flight personnel consisted of three pilot officers, a noncommissioned officer, and two pilot corporals. Marc Pourpe was not granted a commission despite his skill and experience. Joining him on the roster were prewar aviators Roland Garros, Eugene Gilbert, and Armand Pinsard. Gilbert and Pinsard would later become French aces.

The same day the squadron was created, it was transferred to eastern France at Villers-les-Nancy in the suburbs of Nancy. The squadron flew observation patrols for

Morane Saulnier Type L Parasol reconnaissance aircraft as flown in combat by Marc Pourpe and his observer while assigned to Escadrille MS23

the II Armée around Verdun during the battles of Picardy, Artois, and Champagne.

On 14 September 1914 it was transferred to the VI Armée sector. In October it was assigned to the IV Armée and was ordered to the Somme Front so the squadron could keep up with the hostilities. Occasionally, a pilot flew special missions depositing French agents behind the German lines.

On 2 November 1914 Sgt. Gilbert and his observer, Capitaine Marie de Vergnette de Lamotte, scored the first victory for the Escadrille 23 when the team shot down a German Taube aircraft over enemy territory. On 2 December 1914, pilot Marc Pourpe and his observer, Lt. Eugene Vauglin, were killed following the completion of their twenty-eighth mission when their aircraft crashed in bad weather near the Villers-Bretonneaux field.

On 3 January 1924 the French government posthumously awarded Pourpe France's Medaille Militaire for his September 1914 action, and for the December 2 action that resulted in his death. The medal was delivered to his mother, Princess Georges Ghika, later that summer. His remains rest in the Carnel Cemetery in Lorient, France, the place of his birth.

Raoul Lufbery Witnesses the Death of Marc Pourpe

The following is an excerpt from an article by Jacques Patin that appeared in the 15 June 1918 journal *Je Sais Tout* ("I Know Everything"). The article is titled "The Story of Determination: American Ace Lufbery." Patin based this portion of his article on an interview he held with Lufbery.

It was nearly 11 a.m. The ground crew for Escadrille Morane Squadron 23 had just finished their morning soup at the squadron's aerodrome kitchen and had begun the 2-kilometer walk to the airfield. The aircraft mechanics did not complain as they walked the road, even though it seemed very long to these men who were intoxicated with the idea of speed. They walked without envy as their officers passed by them in vehicles. They thought, if only a truck could transport them to the village, they would have a good start getting there. They would have sacrificed half their leisure time for transportation. However, these clever and speedy mechanics were glued to the road, slaves to their legs.

Raoul Lufbery, Marc Pourpe's mechanic, was unconcerned with these distinctions. His experience at world travel had taught him the proverb "Do what you have to do"—use the mode of transportation available at the hour, be it walking, bicycling, a car, the railway, an Egyptian dromedary, or an Indian elephant. At once realistic and practical, Raoul already stood on the airfield. He had skipped the morning soup with the other mechanics. Soup? He would eat later, depending on the circumstances.

It was 2 December 1914 at Treux, the small village of the Somme, not far from Villers-Bretonneux. The pilots of the squadron had risen, as they had every morning to examine the outdoors. They noted a gray winter sky and the heavy low clouds.

"Bad ceiling!" they said, in the colloquial language of men to whom the now-conquered sky was no longer imposing. They decided not to fly. Only Pourpe, despite the pilots' efforts to restrain him, had persisted in going. The Boches were a fixation with him, and he had to hunt them out every morning. Deaf to the pilots' warnings and advice, Marc had taken off at nine o'clock, despite the mist and cold.

Lufbery stood in the middle of the vast airfield, pacing the muddy ground, waiting for Pourpe to return from his morning reconnaissance flight. To allay his impatience, Raoul had taken refuge in the hangar, cleaning some parts and checking aircraft hardware. But a vague concern, nothing as yet justified, had forced him outside again. Still, his pilot had been absent for two hours. As Raoul paced, he tried to pull himself together, to dispel his apprehensions, and to stay calm.

Lufbery was a medium-sized, stocky, muscular man, a mixture of strength and flexibility. He would have projected a formidable demeanor had not a bit of modesty and timidity spread over his whole person to soften his gestures. Fair skinned, with a shaved face and a touch of mustache on his thin lips, he spoke little and smiled willingly with his clear blue eyes. Above all, he attracted and retained sympathy through his pervading naturalness. His comrades admired Raoul's cordial warmth, his genuineness, his quiet attitude, his agility and skill. But surely, no one suspected that Raoul's unfurrowed brow would one day shelter one of the most indomitable energies of that time and serve as a crucible for his iron will.

Lufbery was startled by a noise, soft at first, like a rustling of wings. A distinct sound soon followed, like bees humming. As he listened the noise grew—an airplane? He looked up and searched the horizon. Alas! Under the yellowish sky, the heavy dark clouds closed their shredded cotton wool to form an impenetrable screen. Raoul saw nothing. And yet, the joyful hum of a rotary engine, very close now, struck his ears.

There was no mistaking it! Marc Pourpe would be the only one flying over the field, since he was the only pilot airborne that morning. Lufbery felt the "screw-vice" pressure relaxing against his temples. His anxiety dissipated, and an immense exuberance of hope invaded his thoughts. However, in short order, the overhead humming noise began to subside, to vanish in the distance. The sky and countryside fell silent.

Lufbery gathered his strength and hesitated before joining a crowd of armed officers, soldiers, and peasants all rushing to the first sound of the disaster. Dumbfounded with terror, he was soon looking at the debris of a broken apparatus, crushed on the ground, a shapeless heap of twisted steel, half-charred wood, and ragged canvas. Marc Pourpe's corpse was just then being carried away, the one Lufbery loved more than himself, along with the body of his flight observer, Lt. Eugene Vaughlin. Both aviators had experienced an inexplicable fall and had died as a result. Raoul stood there frozen, eyes large with horror, but without a tear, without a complaint, without a gesture.

Alas, it was Marc and the plane Raoul had waited for out of hopefulness that was generated by its purring engine as it flew over the field. By what treachery had Marc succumbed, killed by a crash? And now gone forever!

Lufbery was inconsolable over Marc's death. In his short life, Marc had been so full of valor and heroism, and better than a friend or brother: For Raoul, Marc had been a tireless energetic teacher, a master of courage, a righteous example for every moment, for each day. From the youth that Lufbery had been yesterday, Marc Pourpe had made a soldier, and the pain came suddenly to Lufbery, the man.

The excruciating death of aviator Pourpe would separate the two friends forever. But Lufbery would not despair. His pain strengthened his resolve and reinvigorated his courage. He vowed to avenge Marc's death. Raoul made a solemn and silent oath through the distress of his torn heart, an oath to move forward. He soon requested and was accepted for pilot training.

Corporal Marc Pourpe shortly before his death, his face reflecting his fatigue from flying so many reconnaissance patrols

Raoul Lufbery's 1917 Letter to His Father

> 28-12-17
>
> Dear father
>
> No doubt you will be disapointed in receiving this letter for. I know you were expecting me to come over to Wallinford sometime around Chrismus or New year. Well! Things did not go exactly like I wanted and I am very uncertain about my trip now.
>
> Few days ago I was decorated with a new medal, it is a Montenegrin order which has a ribbon red, blue, and white. a very nice little decorations and I am very pleased to wear it.
>
> I suppose that you have heard about my commission of major in the american aviation. Well I have got it allright, but, I cannot leave the French untill I get my discharge papers.
>
> I receive nearly everyday a letter from stamps sellers. I would

Raoul Lufbery's 28 December 1917 letter from France to Edward in Connecticut

be awfully glad to help you, but
I have n't got much time left for me
when I ever go in Paris on a one
or two days leave. Any way if soon
or later I am lucky enough to obtain
a furlough for the States, I will
send the money over to E. Montenolle
whom will do the buying.

Sixteen boches to my credit this
is my actual score. On the second
of December I brought two downs,
one fell in flame on no man's land
and the other, after falling from
four thousands yards ~~crash~~ out of control
crashed to the ground, not very
far from the first lines trenches.

I have heard about one
of your nephew from Chauny
he is now living in the south
of France.

Has Rene enlisted? if yes.
in which branch of the army?
Best wishes to all
yours
Raoul Lufbery

Acknowledgments

When one begins the undertaking of trying to research and to factually document the outstanding accomplishments of a past family member from decades ago, it takes a "squadron" of relatives and friends to accomplish the task. Furthermore, and in the case with Major Raoul Lufbery, help and assistance from World War I historians and aviation experts is surely important and relied upon. In our update and expansion of French author Jacques Mortane's 1937 book *Two Great Knights of Adventure,* about Marc Pourpe and Raoul Lufbery, we did nothing to compromise his good work. Our goal was only to further complement and expand the details and accomplishments of these two amazing pioneering pilots. We diligently expanded upon facts and records, provided previously unpublished details, and added an array of visual images and documents to showcase these two flyboys' aviation achievements from the prewar and World War I time period.

The following family members from the United States contributed information, resources, and images for this enhanced book update: Lynn Lufbery, Raoul Lufbery IV, Devon Lufbery, Sharon Lufbery Welch, Richard Welch, Lisa Riotte Powers (Lufbery), Paul Powers, Laurie Riotte Ewers (Lufbery), Joseph Ewers, Robert Stickle, Ray Wolff, Jodi Tilander, Alexis Lufbery, Paul Lufbery, Steven Lufbery, Veronica Lufbery, Priscilla Sparks (Haller), Christopher DiLorenzo, and Marion Lufbery Miller.

Likewise, here are the French family members who contributed to this book effort during the past few years: Jean-Xavier Lufbery, Gisele Lufbery, Claude Lufbery, Stephanie Lufbery, Anne-Marie Lachal Vellet (Lufbery), and Bernard Lufbery.

Lufbery deceased family members from both countries over the past century contributed substantially to this new book by documenting, saving, and forwarding their personal files and records about Major Lufbery to their siblings or children. They are with us only in spirit today, and we shall recognize them for their foresight and devotion to aviator Raoul Lufbery. From France we have Julien Lufbery and Charles C. Lufbery. From the US we have Charles A. Lufbery, Laurence Lufbery, Bertha Lufbery Haller, Rene Lufbery, Germaine Lufbery, Yvonne Lufbery, Marie-Louise Lufbery, Edward Lufbery, Rene Lufbery II, Marcel Lufbery, Diane Lufbery, Raoul Lufbery II, Margaret Lufbery, and Doris Lufbery Riotte. I am forever grateful to all the Lufberys noted above for the assistance rendered.

It is with my full appreciation and thanks that I can acknowledge the following World War I, aviation historians and subject-matter specialists who aided me in obtaining information, photographs, and official documents over many years for Major Raoul Lufbery. Often, they assisted by validating data, by recommending historical sources for research, and by offering their exceptional knowledge and expertise. Their contributions were always done with kindness and encouragement.

From France, those talented individuals are Jean-Marc Simon (WWI aviation historian and writer), Monsieur and Madame Vinot (Academic Society of Chauny, France), and Jean-Xavier Lufbery (my cousin and the French family historian for Major Lufbery).

From the United States I must thank the following WW I aviation subject-matter experts and education professionals: Bill Jackson (friend and WWI aviation historian), Steven Ruffin (friend, WWI aviation historian and author), Steve Suddaby (WWI historian), Steven Tom (WWI historian and author), Jim Streckfuss (WWI historian and aviation history professor), and John Sirotiak (friend and technical-support colleague).

It is with gratitude that I acknowledge the historical and professional support I received from Dawne Dewey, Lisa Rickey, and Megan O'Connor from the Wright State University Special Collections and Archives Libraries System. Ms. O'Connor did a wonderful job with the French- to-English translations of many Major Lufbery documents.

Finally, I must thank my friend and coeditor Dennis Gordon for his wonderful passion and wisdom with WWI military aviation history. His unwavering admiration to the brave and remarkable pilots who flew during the Great War is commendable and second to none. With his effort and my desire, we have been able to shocase through this book the remarkable flying adventures of two very special pilots in my life, Marc and Raoul.

My best regards and thanks to all.

—Raoul Lufbery III

Bibliography

Bailey, Frank W., and Christopher Cory. *The French Air Service War Chronology, 1914–1917: Day-to-Day Claims and Losses by French Fighter, Bomber and Two-Seat Pilots on the Western Front*. London: Grubb Street, 2001.

Connell, Dennis, and Frank W. Bailey. "Victory Logs, Lafayette Escadrille and Lafayette Flying Corps." *Cross & Cockade Journal* 21, no. 4 (Winter 1980).

dePougy, Liane. *My Blue Notebooks*. New York: Harper & Row, 1979.

Franks, Norman. *Who Downed the Aces in WWI?* London: Grub Street, 1996.

Gordon, Dennis. *Lafayette Escadrille Pilot Biographies*. Missoula, MT: Doughboy Historical Society, 1991.

Gordon, Dennis. *The Lafayette Flying Corps*. Atglen, PA: Schiffer, 2000.

Hall, James Norman, and Charles B. Nordhoff. *The Lafayette Flying Corps*. 2 vols. Boston: Houghton Mifflin, 1920.

Hall, James Norman. *My Island Home: An Autobiography*. Boston: Little, Brown, 1952.

Journal des Marches et Operations Escadrille N. 124.

Kane, John B. *The Khaki Road of Yesterday*. Million Dollar Sips LLC, 2017.

Letters of William Thaw to Mr. H. C. Hoskier, 12, 14, 18, 24, 27 March 1924.

Parsons, Edwin. *The Great Adventure*. Garden City, NY: Doubleday. Doran, 1937.

Rickenbacker, Edward Vernon. *Fighting the Flying Circus*. New York: Frederick A. Stokes, 1919.

Rockwell, Paul A. *American Fighters in the Foreign Legion*. Boston: Houghton Mifflin, 1930.

Stevenson, William York. *At the Front in a Flivver*. Cambridge, MA: Houghton Mifflin; Boston and New York: Riverside, 1917.

Thenault, Colonel Georges. *L'Escadrille Lafayette*. Paris: Librairie Hachette, 1939.

Toelle, Alan. "A White-Faced Cow and the Operational History of the Escadrille Americaine N.124 to September 1916.". Over the Front Journal 24, no. 4 (Winter 2009).

Walcott, Benjamin Stuart. *Above French Lines: Letters of Stuart Walcott-American Aviator, July 4, 1917, to December 8, 1917*. Princeton, NJ: Princeton University Press, 1918.

War Letters of Kiffin Yates Rockwell. Garden City, NY: Country Life, 1925.

Weeks, Alice S. *Greater Love Hath No Man*. Boston: Bruce Humphries, 1939.

Additional sources: Dennis Gordon personal archive, Raoul Lufbery family archive.

Index

Adamson, Lawrence Arthur 12, 13, 14, 15, 19, 20, 21, 22, 23, 24, 25
Balsley, Clyde 88
Bigelow, Stephen 101
Campbell, Andrew Courtney 156
Chapman, Victor 88, 151, 175
Cowdin, Elliot 203
Crenshaw, Lewis 208, 210
Culbert, Lt. Kenneth, USMC 110
Davis, Lt. Philip 197
Defries, Colin 5, 9, 10, 11, 12, 13, 14, 19, 21, 22, 24
DeLaage de Meux, Lt. Alfred 102, 154, 175, 181, 183
DePougy, Liane 3, 4, 177, 201, 205, 222–230
Dolan, Carl 184, 190
Fequant, Major Philippe 152, 184
Garros, Roland 142
Genet, Edmond 153, 177
Gude, Lt. Oscar 197
Hall, Bert 181
Hall, James Norman 139, 159, 184, 190, 191, 195, 196, 197
Hamilton, Edgar 205, 208
Happe, Captain Maurice 151
Haviland, Willis 101, 177
Hill, Dudley 181, 185
Hinkle, Edward 101, 114, 115, 153, 157, 165, 183, 184
Hoskier, Ronald 101, 153, 177
Houdini, Harry 20, 22, 23
Huffer, Major Jean 195, 197
Kitchener, Lord 131, 132
La Curieuse 33, 34, 44, 47, 54, 55, 56, 57, 60, 61, 66, 68, 69, 128, 129
Lafayette Escadrille 149, combat patrols 173, roster 150, squadron locations 151–156, 163, 190, 194
le taillar 131, 132
Lufbery, Anne Vesseire 120
Lufbery, Bertha 120, 201
Lufbery, Charles 97, 120, 121, 122, 123, 200, 202, 203
Lufbery, Edward 48, 120, 121, 123, 199, 201, 204, 208
Lufbery, Germaine 120, 122, 201
Lufbery, Jean-Xavier 142
Lufbery, Julien 97, 104, 120, 121, 122, 206
Lufbery, Marie-Louise 120, 122, 201
Lufbery, Raoul 47, 48, 49, 59, 62, 63, 65, 67, 69, 76, 78, 80–81, 83, 120, 130, 172, victories 174, 176
Lufbery, Yvonne 120, 122, 123, 201, 203
MacMonagle, Douglas 156, 177
McConnell, James 89, 90, 175
Masson, Didier 95
Nungesser, Lt. Charles 105
Parsons, Edwin 147, 153, 155, 156, 159, 177, 199
Pourpe, Marc 125, 126, 127, 128, 129, 130, 132, 133, 134, 135, 140, 142, 201, 204
Prince, Frederick Henry 208, 210, 211
Prince, Norman 88, 95, 96, 147, 152, 208
Rickenbacker, Captain Edward 109, 195, 196
Rockwell, Kiffin 91, 92, 151, 175
Rockwell, Paul 175
Rumsey, Laurence 182
Soda 153, 156, 183, 185
Stevenson, William York 182
Tellier aircraft 31, 32
Thaw, Willian 91, 101, 153, 164, 176, 181, 182, 183, 190, 194, 210, 211
Thenault, Georges 146, 157, 158, 163, 167, 169, 181, 183, 211
Verminck, Georges 5, 33, 35, 37, 38, 39, 40, 42, 43, 46, 126, 127, 128
Walcott, Cpl. Benjamin 148
Weeks, Alice 177
Whiskey 91, 92, 152, 153, 156, 182, 183, 184, 185, 191
Willis, Harold 153

Major Raoul Lufbery standing before his Nieuport 28 fighter aircraft in April 1918.